"This textbook is a timely, thoughtful, and comprehensiv committed to the treatment of individuals seeking care becau from the broad range of destructive and disintegrating e: Co-edited artfully by Drs. Leo Leiderman and Bonnie Buchel~, ... ~~~.. .~~p~...~~ .~ ...~~~ clinical demands in a thorough, thoughtful, effective, and accessible fashion. In addition to a state-of-the-art review of theory, new neuroscience and neurobiology contributions, the book is replete with rich clinical illustrations that demonstrate how theory shapes practice and can be applied meaningfully and effectively."

Molyn Leszcz, *MD, FRCPC, CGP, AGPA-DF, Professor of Psychiatry, University of Toronto Past-President, American Group Psychotherapy Association*

"This is a must-read book! It masterfully weaves interventions for trauma-based overactivation and/or dissociative enactments in group using critical aspects of attachment theory, multi-cultural competence, and experience-near group leadership principles. The clinical examples bring to life multiple treatment approaches adapted to both short- and long-term group treatments."

Gary M Burlingame, *PhD, Professor of Psychology, Brigham Young University; Past President, American Group Psychotherapy Association*

"This is a fascinating book providing a comprehensive update to treatment of trauma in group therapy summarizing the advances in the field in one source for practicing clinicians as well as academics. The editors have compiled chapters from leaders and innovators in the field with emphasis on culturally informed group therapy; artfully blending advances in biological imprint of trauma and the role of group therapy in healing it. This update is remarkable for the way in which subtle and complex concepts paired with clinical examples enhance learning, making the ideas accessible to everyone. In my opinion, this book is an essential read for all students and clinicians involved in the practice of group therapy."

Farooq Mohyuddin, *MD, CGP, FAPA, AGPA-F, Chair Psychiatry Training, Director Residency Training Program, Saint Elizabeths Hospital/DBH Washington DC. Past President MAGPS*

Advances in Group Therapy Trauma Treatment

Advances in Group Therapy Trauma Treatment contains compelling theoretical, clinical, and research advances in group trauma therapy by leading experts in the field. This timely book includes short-term integrated and long-term psychodynamic group therapy models from several theoretical perspectives, with informative clinical illustrations in each chapter describing how to foster co-regulation of affect, treat disturbances in attachment, and address dissociation, shame, primitive defenses, and enactments associated with PTSD, complex PTSD, and sexual abuse. Interventions to address the harm and loss of safety following mass trauma that are often mirrored in large and small psychotherapy groups are described. Unique to this volume is the role of diversity, the necessary adaptations of group therapy models to different cultures, and the relationship of trauma to structural and systemic racism, hate, and bigotry. Finally, leadership considerations such as training, ethical guidelines, supervision, pre-group preparation, and self-care for group therapists will be enumerated. Integrating well-established group theory and techniques with new practice and research findings, this book is indispensable to mental health professionals who treat traumatized individuals.

Leonardo M. Leiderman, PsyD, is President-Elect of the American Group Psychotherapy Association and a Diplomate in Clinical and Group Psychology. He has published extensively on group psychotherapy in treating trauma.

Bonnie J. Buchele, PhD, is President-Elect of the American Psychoanalytic Association and Past President of the American Group Psychotherapy Association. She has publications focused on group, psychoanalysis, and trauma.

AGPA Group Therapy Training and Practice Series
Series Editors: Les R. Greene and Rebecca MacNair-Semands

The American Group Psychotherapy Association (AGPA) is the foremost professional association dedicated to the field of group psychotherapy, operating through a tri-partite structure: AGPA, a professional and educational organization; the Group Foundation for Advancing Mental Health, its philanthropic arm; and the International Board for Certification of Group Psychotherapists, a standard setting and certifying body. This multidisciplinary association has approximately 3,000 members, including psychiatrists, psychologists, social workers, nurses, clinical mental health counselors, marriage and family therapists, pastoral counselors, occupational therapists and creative arts therapists, many of whom have been recognized as specialists through the Certified Group Psychotherapist credential. The association has 26 local and regional societies located across the country. Its members are experienced mental health professionals who lead psychotherapy groups and various non-clinical groups. Many are organizational specialists who work with businesses, not-for-profit organizations, communities and other "natural" groups to help them improve their functioning.

The goal of the AGPA Group Therapy Training and Practice Series is to produce the highest quality publications to aid the practitioner and student in updating and improving his/her knowledge, professional competence and skills with current and new developments in methods, practice, theory, and research in the group psychotherapy field. Books in this series are the only curriculum guide and resource for a variety of courses credentialed by the International Board for Certification of Group Psychotherapists. While this is the series' original and primary purpose, the texts are also useful in a variety of other settings including as a resource for students and clinicians interested in learning more about group psychotherapy, as a text in academic courses, or as part of a training curriculum in a practicum or internship training experience.

For more information about this series, please visit https://www.routledge.com/AGPA-Group-Therapy-Training-and-Practice-Series/book-series/AGPA.

Books in this Series:

Advances in Group Therapy Trauma Treatment
Edited by Leonardo M. Leiderman and Bonnie J. Buchele

Core Principles of Group Psychotherapy
An Integrated Theory, Research, and Practice Training Manual
Edited by Francis J. Kaklauskas, Les R. Greene

The Ethics of Group Psychotherapy
Principles and Practical Strategies
by Virginia Brabender and Rebecca MacNair-Semands

Advances in Group Therapy Trauma Treatment

Edited by Leonardo M. Leiderman
and Bonnie J. Buchele

Routledge
Taylor & Francis Group

NEW YORK AND LONDON

Designed cover image: © Getty Images

First published 2025
by Routledge
605 Third Avenue, New York, NY 10158

and by Routledge
4 Park Square, Milton Park, Abingdon, Oxon, OX14 4RN

Routledge is an imprint of the Taylor & Francis Group, an informa business

ISBN: 9781032901268 (hbk)
ISBN: 9781032890784 (pbk)
ISBN: 9781003546252 (ebk)

DOI: 10.4324/9781003546252

Typeset in Optima
by Apex CoVantage, LLC

To our families and friends – your love and support are forever treasured

and

To our patients who have trusted us to witness their trauma, pain, and deepest vulnerable selves, who have taught us how to contain the unspeakable wounds and to foster recovery and who have changed us, hopefully to become more compassionate and humane people.

This book is dedicated to the memory and in honor of the legacy of Robert H. Klein, PhD, ABPP, CGP, AGPA-DLF, dear friend, esteemed and beloved clinical psychologist, and icon in the trauma group psychotherapy specialty field. Bob encapsulated the highest professional and personal qualities found in an exemplary leader including being past president of the American Group Psychotherapy Association (AGPA). His contributions to AGPA spanning over 50 years are enormous and incalculable. He was an accomplished author and in the forefront of emphasizing the need for empirically based group psychotherapy research. He authored over 130 publications, coauthoring seven books.

He touched the hearts and souls of so many of us with his vibrant and caring personality, altruism, colorful spirit, wisdom, brilliance, great sense of humor, and infinite generosity to others and meaningful humanitarian causes.

May his memory be a blessing!

This Jewish blessing means: It is up to those who bear his memory to keep his goodness alive.

Contents

About the Editors

Leonardo M. Leiderman is a trilingual/tricultural Diplomate in Clinical Psychology and Group Psychology. He is in private practice and the director of Neurofeedback & Psychological Services in Purchase, New York. He is the President-Elect of the American Group Psychotherapy Association (AGPA) and is the editor of *The Group Circle* newsletter of the AGPA and the International Board for Certification of Group Psychotherapists. His interest in the group treatment of trauma began while working at community mental health centers with traumatized underserved Latinx migrant children and families in the 1980s. He was instrumental in establishing the first bilingual/bicultural mental health treatment program at Saint Vincent Catholic Medical Centers, Harrison, New York, where he served as the director. He has presented nationally and internationally and has published extensively, with special focus on interpersonal/relational group psychotherapy in treating complex PTSD and dissociation. He received the Alonso Award for Excellence in Psychodynamic Group Psychotherapy from the Group Foundation for Advancing Mental Health for *Psychodynamic group therapy with Hispanic migrants: Interpersonal, relational constructs in treating complex trauma, dissociation, and enactments.* He is a member of the editorial board of the *International Journal of Group Psychotherapy.*

Bonnie J. Buchele is a group psychotherapist and psychoanalyst in private practice in Kansas City, Missouri, having received her training at Menninger, where she eventually became the Director of the Group Psychotherapy Service. Currently, she is the President-Elect of the American Psychoanalytic Association and is a Personal and Supervising Analyst as well as a former director of the Greater Kansas City Psychoanalytic Institute. She was the President of the American Group Psychotherapy Association during the events of 9/11 and co-authored with Henry Spitz, MD, the original volume *Group Interventions for Treatment of Psychological Trauma.* Her interest in the impact and treatment of trauma arose when she began working with rape victims in the mid-1970s and broadened as she treated survivors of incest, directed an incest perpetrator diversion program, and was instrumental in the creation of an AGPA group program for survivors of 9/11. She has published about her work in all these areas, as well as leadership, receiving the Alonso Award for Excellence in Psychodynamic Group Psychotherapy in 2007 and 2019. She is also a member of the editorial board of the *International Journal of Group Psychotherapy.*

Contributors

Hanieh Abeditehrani is a PhD candidate in clinical psychology at the University of Amsterdam, Netherlands. Her PhD research is focused on comparing the effectiveness of psychodrama, cognitive behavioral group therapy, and the integration for social anxiety disorder. She does individual and group therapy in the Academic Center for Trauma and Personality (ACTP).

Carlos Canales is affiliated with Vida Psychotherapy, an outpatient psychotherapy clinic. He is a bicultural psychologist in private practice in Des Moines, Iowa. He specializes in working with affect, the body, core personality issues, and relational psychodynamics. He leads training and consultation groups and is a regular presenter emphasizing clinical applications of attachment-focused and somatic psychotherapies.

Yifei Du is from China and affiliated with George Washington University (GWU). She is a doctoral candidate in Clinical Psychology at GWU. She holds a Master of Psychology from GWU, and a Master of Expressive Arts Therapy and a Bachelor of Social Sciences from the University of Hong Kong. She has authored research review articles for the *Group Circle* and *The Group Psychologist*.

Robert Grossmark is a psychoanalyst in New York City. He teaches at the New York University Postdoctoral Program in Psychoanalysis and lectures nationally and internationally. His books include *The Unobtrusive Relational Analyst: Explorations in Psychoanalytic Companioning* and *The One and The Many: Relational Approaches to Group Psychotherapy*.

Bojun Hu is a China-based Clinical Psychologist who has a focus on sexual trauma support since 2015. In 2021, she co-founded China's first online sexual trauma support group program and continues to supervise. She takes a phenomenological stance in research and in everyday life through embodied practices, such as dancing and tai chi.

J. Joana Kyei is a licensed clinical psychologist in Ghana and the Commonwealth of Pennsylvania. She has been facilitating process and support groups for individuals with relational traumas for over 12 years and is currently the head for Counseling Services at the Ghana Institute of Management and Public Administration.

Molyn Leszcz is a Professor, Department of Psychiatry, University of Toronto. He is the Past President and a Distinguished Fellow of the American Group Psychotherapy Association. His academic and clinical work has focused on improving the integration in psychiatric care and broadening the application of the psychotherapies within psychiatry. He has worked extensively in the areas of physician wellness and leadership, along with the effects of pandemic stress on health-care providers. He co-authored the *Theory and*

Practice of Group Psychotherapy with Irvin Yalom, and the Psychotherapy Essentials to Go series *Achieving Psychotherapy Effectiveness*. He received the Alonso Award for Excellence in Psychodynamic Group Psychotherapy in 2009 and 2024.

Yi Liu is a PsyD candidate in clinical psychology at George Washington University and has provided psychotherapy in China and the United States. As a member of the APA and AGPA, she is interested in translating attachment theory and trauma research into culturally informed group therapy interventions.

Cheri L. Marmarosh is a Professor of Clinical Psychology at the George Washington University and has published over 50 articles focusing on how group and individual psychotherapies facilitate change. She is the author of *Attachment in Group Psychotherapy* and is the current editor for *The International Journal of Group Psychotherapy*.

Reginald Nettles is a psychologist in independent practice in Columbia, Maryland. An alumnus of the Group Psychotherapy Training Program and the Advanced Psychotherapy Training Program at the Washington School of Psychiatry, he served as the Director of the Counseling Center, University of Maryland, Baltimore County; as the Clinical Director of a residential substance abuse treatment; and on the staff of Howard University and American University Counseling Centers.

Victor L. Schermer is a psychologist and psychotherapist in private practice and clinic settings in Philadelphia, Pennsylvania. He is the author and co-editor of nine books and over 50 vetted journal articles, including the book co-edited with Robert H. Klein, *Group Psychotherapy for Psychological Trauma*.

Thomas Treadwell practices at the Center for Cognitive Therapy, University of Pennsylvania, United States. He serves as the editor of *The Group Psychologist*, American Psychological Association, Division 49; is a co-executive editor for the *Journal of Group Psychotherapy, Psychodrama, and Sociometry*; and serves on the editorial boards for the *International Group Psychotherapy* and *Group Psychotherapy* journals.

Ayana Watkins-Northern is a licensed psychologist in private practice in the District of Columbia. She was the Executive Director of Howard University Counseling Services; is the Director of Group Training, Faculty of the National Group Psychotherapy Institute, and a founding member of the Center for Study of Race Ethnicity and Culture, both of New Washington School of Psychiatry; and is also involved with large group work.

Haim Weinberg is a psychologist and group psychotherapist from Sacramento, California, and Israel. Co-editor of books about the social unconscious and online therapy, he is the sole author of ten books (translated in China, Japan, Romania, South Korea, the Czech Republic, and Israel), 24 book chapters, and 55 articles. He leads online training process groups for therapists around the world.

Foreword

"My past is an armor I cannot take off, no matter how many times you tell me the war is over." This statement, attributed to the ancient Greek historian Herodotus, written over 2,500 years ago following the Battle of Marathon, may be the first description of *posttraumatic stress* – and the continuing impact suffered by individuals when they are exposed to overwhelming, traumatizing experiences. These experiences may shatter one's sense of self, one's physical and psychological integrity, and the basic sense of trust and security in the world necessary for our healthy functioning. This ancient and eloquent statement reverberates with contemporary definitions of *trauma* and *posttraumatic stress* with its hallmark symptoms of intrusion and re-experiencing, avoidance and numbing, and hyperarousal and dysregulation.

This textbook is a timely, thoughtful, and comprehensive guide for group therapists committed to the treatment of individuals seeking care because of the trauma that emerges from the broad range of destructive and disintegrating experiences that surround us. These traumas include early life abuse and neglect, sexual abuse, interpersonal violence, war, natural disasters, pandemics, accidents, social trauma, and racism.

Co-edited artfully by Drs. Leo Leiderman and Bonnie J. Buchele, this book responds to these clinical demands in a thorough, thoughtful, effective, and accessible fashion. Drs. Leiderman and Buchele have compiled a stellar international crew of authors, ensuring that this textbook will represent a broad view and range of approaches and not be restricted to traditional Western perspectives alone. The contributors to this text honor the importance as well of working in culturally competent and culturally responsive fashion in addressing social trauma due to racism, discrimination, prejudice, and the psychological impacts of dehumanization of the other. The text covers focuses on brief and structured group interventions, psychodynamic and process-oriented longer-term groups, and large group perspectives that illuminate the impact of the social unconscious on the intrapsychic and the interpersonal.

Importantly, this book also honors an original editor of the text, an iconic figure in group therapy and the American Group Psychotherapy Association (AGPA), Dr. Robert H. Klein. Sadly, Dr. Klein passed away during the preparation of this text. I first met Bob Klein in 1984 at the annual conference of the AGPA. I was familiar with and admired his work and used it in my own clinical practice. I presented on my inpatient group therapy work, my first such presentation at AGPA, and Bob attended the session. He was wise, warm, welcoming, and encouraging. That meeting launched a four-decade relationship with Bob and the AGPA. Bob was a visionary in recognizing the unique role group therapy could play in the treatment of trauma – but he also knew that we had to ensure that group therapy was delivered by well-trained, well-prepared group therapists: The quality of care mattered. His vision was to integrate science and practice. In so doing, we would be able to expand the capacity of clinicians to provide effective and meaningful care. That led him to create AGPA's Science to Service Task Force in his role as AGPA President at that time. That task force continues to be highly influential in the field and the impetus for a series of well-received contemporary group therapy textbooks. This text is one of that series.

Drs. Buchele and Leiderman, outstanding group therapists, AGPA leaders, and major contributors to the literature in our field, carry Dr. Klein's vision forward in this textbook. Dr. Buchele's work has long been influenced by serving as AGPA President during 9/11. She recognized the crisis of 9/11 demanded AGPA's response, providing group therapy to those impacted by the 9/11 crisis. Dr. Leiderman has contributed significantly to the group therapy literature as well, and together they have brought their experience and expertise to co-editing this text.

As noted in this book, *trauma* can be conceptualized as a sensorimotor/affective/cognitive/behavioral response to traumatic exposures. Deepening understanding of the impacts of trauma has moved beyond singular traumatic events to encompass the lifelong exposure to trauma contributing to the diagnosis of complex PTSD (CPTSD). Our patients with CPTSD are shaped by repetitive traumatic exposures, as well as the neglect and abuse that become interwoven into the personhood of the individual. They experience the cardinal symptoms of PTSD along with emotional dysregulation and a disordered sense of self.

There is no part of the traumatized individual that is immune to the trauma impacts. Psychological trauma is the chameleon of psychological illness manifesting in a multiplicity of expressions covering a range of psychological, emotional, behavioral, personality, as well as somatic distress and bodily disturbance. Both the primary symptoms and the patients' coping behaviors are foci for care.

In addition to a state-of-the-art review of theory, of new neuroscience and neurobiology contributions, the book is replete with rich clinical illustrations that demonstrate how theory shapes practice and can be applied meaningfully and effectively. The hallmark features of effective group therapists echo throughout: Empathy, interpersonal flexibility, emotional attunement, proper pacing and tolerability in exposure to trauma, compassion, cultural humility, warmth, and technical skill are intertwined and integrated with theoretical depth (Yalom & Leszcz, 2020).

This book is so well-timed. We are confronted with trauma and its impacts every day. We feel it and see it streaming into our living rooms and on our smartphones with images of natural disasters, of war, of terrorism, of school shootings, of enduring racism, and of the widespread dehumanization of the other. The clinical demands for effective therapy are great: The world needs our expertise now more than ever.

Robust evidence supports group therapy's essential role in the treatment of trauma. I believe group interventions may also play a role in the prevention of the development of posttraumatic stress disorder through early intervention for those exposed to potentially traumatic events. In my work at Mount Sinai Hospital at the University of Toronto, we have used groups to intervene when our colleagues faced acute traumatic experiences ranging from SARS to COVID and a variety of other traumatic events, including the suicide of a colleague, unexpected deaths, and catastrophic medical outcomes.

In a related vein, I recently was asked by a pediatric dentist if I could help her and her colleagues. A nightmarish event occurred in a clinic. An arterial malformation of a young child was cut inadvertently; the child bled to death in the dental office. It was a horrific scene. I was asked to meet with the staff to try to help them process this nightmare. They were overwhelmed, and the office had shut down. A staff of around 20 presented with hallmark symptoms of an acute stress response: intrusion, avoidance, hyperarousal, nightmares, not being able to sleep, and a profound sense of guilt and shame about this catastrophic event. I met with the group, encouraged by my understanding of the power of the group to protect and heal and guided by the five principles articulated by Hobfoll et al. (2007). I aimed to restore a sense of safety, promote calming strategies, renew a sense of team and self-efficacy, promote reconnection at a time when they were withdrawing from one another, and encourage realistic hope about their capacity to recover. I provided education about the traumatic stress response and its hallmark symptoms and tried to detoxify their shame and guilt. They reported to me how those two sessions were very helpful in allowing them to recover and return to their work.

My appreciation for the impact of trauma antedates my professional life. I am the child of Holocaust survivors and grew up in a community that consisted largely of other Holocaust survivor families. There was no older grandparent generation, and the Holocaust survivors became a very close community, focused on building lives in the new world. No doubt my early roots influenced my interest as a young psychiatry resident in the then new literature emerging about intergenerational transmission of trauma and the impacts on the second generation. That interest led to an invitation for me to speak at a conference held for Holocaust survivors in Winnipeg. I naïvely agreed, not knowing what I would be encountering.

I remember that day as though it happened yesterday. I anticipated 10 or 15 people for my talk and found the room packed with 200 people – standing-room only – many of them members of the community that I knew. As I talked about some of the literature about second-generation effects, Mrs. H, a close friend of my parents, broke down, sobbing in tears. It was a massive cathartic experience, unlike anything I have seen since. Through her sobbing, Mrs. H disclosed the need to share something with us that she had never shared before in her life and that she had carried alone for the last 30 years. She recalled that she was in hiding from Nazis in Europe with her husband, baby, and some family. As enemy soldiers approached, her baby started to cry. With unbearable intensity, Mrs. H described the existential dilemma she faced. She had to either silence her baby or they would all be discovered and killed. In her efforts at silencing her baby, she suffocated her child in her own arms. She had never told that story to anybody until that massive catharsis – in a room with 200 people in a group facilitated by a naïve 23-year-old junior resident in psychiatry.

The people around her immediately moved in to hold her, caress her, soothe her, and share with her their identification with that kind of crushing dilemma. They understood fully the life-and-death choices that they made then that continued to haunt them to this day. I was initially stunned but marshalled the ability to respond. I thanked her for her courage. I expressed my hope that she could absorb the compassion from the people in the room, and that in sharing her secret, she made it possible for others to choose to do the same themselves. After that session, I found myself hyperaroused in a way that I had never encountered before. It was impossible for me to settle that day or night. It was only later, when I had learned through my parents that Mrs. H had regained her composure and expressed gratitude for the opportunity to unburden herself, that I was able to calm myself. I saw the power of the group to support, contain, universalize, create safety for catharsis, and detoxify blame and shame with even the most overwhelming events. That is the promise of group therapy. As Judith Herman describes, the cohesion of the group provides the survivor with the strongest protection against terror and despair, as well as the strongest antidote to traumatic experience (Herman, 1997).

That group experience introduced me to the impact of countertransference. I became acutely aware of the effects of doing this kind of work on the group leader. Rates of burnout in health-care providers have skyrocketed in the last number of years. Mental health professionals are particularly vulnerable in this regard because of our exposure to the traumatic experiences of our patients, our limitations in meeting their needs and being able to effect healing and change, and our own vulnerability to traumatic exposure in the current world in which we live. Group therapists working with trauma patients must attend to their own psychological care and well-being. This is difficult work to do in isolation, and I urge people who work with traumatized patients to be part of a community practice or to seek consultation and collegial support.

Thoughtful readers of this textbook will learn to use themselves more fully as therapeutic agents. They will be better able to promote the capacity of their groups to heal by promoting meaningful and authentic connections, securing attachment, and restoring relationally based emotional regulation. This outstanding textbook will promote the capacity of providers to think like group therapists and not only as individuals who deliver a group intervention. This requires tending to group dynamics, group process, group therapeutic factors that contribute to healing, and enhancing cohesion and safety in an environment where there are many pulls toward fragmentation, disconnection, and disengagement. When we do our work well, we not only assist those we see directly in our groups but also launch a positive cascade that ripples into our patients' lives well beyond our group rooms or computer screens. This text meaningfully reinforces that mission.

by Molyn Leszcz, MD, FRCPC

References

Herman, J. (1997). *Trauma and recovery*. Basic Books.

Hobfoll, S. E., Watson, P., Bell, C. C., Bryant, R. A., Brymer, M. J., Friedman, M. J., Friedman, M., Gersons, B. P., de Jong, J. T., Layne, C. M., Maguen, S., Neria, Y., Norwood, A. E., Pynoos, R. S., Reissman, D., Ruzek, J. I., Shalev, A. Y., Solomon, Z., Steinberg, A. M., & Ursano, R. J. (2007). Five essential elements of immediate and mid-term mass trauma intervention: Empirical evidence. *Psychiatry*, *70*(4), 283–369. https://doi.org/10.1521/psyc.2007.70.4.283

Yalom, I. D., & Leszcz, M. (2020). *The theory and practice of group psychotherapy*. Basic Books.

Acknowledgments

Throughout our careers, we have had a fascination with the power of group psychotherapy in treating people with unresolved trauma. Thus, group psychotherapy for the treatment of trauma became an early focus for both of us. We have worked in a wide variety of clinical settings, including community mental health centers and hospitals serving some of the most underserved populations in the USA, several of the finest clinical settings in the world, and private practices. Group therapy became our treatment modality of choice to address the long-term complexities of trauma. For many years, we have witnessed trauma survivors making significant progress while enhancing coping skills as they utilized this modality, which empowered them to verbalize and symbolize their unspeakable emotional pain and restore a sense of self and belonging. Concurrently, they acquired hope, safely worked through conflicts and ruptures with others, and enhanced their abilities to co-regulate fear-based trauma symptoms when overactivated.

There were several factors contributing to our wish to publish this book. We reviewed the literature, finding it insufficient and leading us to believe the field would benefit from a volume that incorporated the contemporary developments in the group trauma field; those developments include advances in neurophysiology, diagnosis (i.e., complex PTSD), dissociative enactments and other correlates of trauma, and previously neglected theoretical, clinical, and research in group trauma therapy for the treatment of traumatized persons by leading experts in the field. We also wanted to provide interventions to address the harm, loss of safety, and control following mass traumata that happen to entire societies and are often transported and mirrored in large and small psychotherapy groups – especially important are large group traumata, such as sociopolitical racial trauma and micro- and macroaggressions. Lastly, we wanted to incorporate much-needed non-Eurocentric trauma group approaches by authors who identify as marginalized and/or Black, Indigenous, People of Color (BIPOC).

Many have participated in assembling this volume. We want to express our appreciation to our contributing authors and to AGPA's Science to Service Task Force members Les R. Greene, Rebecca MacNair-Semands, and Angela Stephens. Most especially, we wish to thank all those who have survived trauma. Without their courage and willingness to share their experiences, accompanied by such emotional vulnerability, none of this work would have been possible.

by Leonardo M. Leiderman and Bonnie J. Buchele

1 Introduction and Overview

Creating a Container for Healing Trauma

Leonardo M. Leiderman, Bonnie J. Buchele, and Robert H. Klein

Exposure to *trauma*, most broadly defined as experiencing a threat to one's survival, has always been part of the human condition and experience. Therefore, given its ubiquity, an important question is this: What do we mean by "trauma"? It has become a much-used, perhaps overused, term in recent years (McNally, 2016). We, the editors, think of *trauma* as an experience that results when an individual is emotionally and/or physiologically overwhelmed and destabilized by a threatening external or internal event. Psychological mechanisms that normally help the person cope with extreme stimulation are insufficient, resulting in feelings of fright, helplessness, loss, being trapped, as well as feeling overactivated and unable to cope and/or regulate oneself back to a state of calm. Often, these emotional and physiological reactions to trauma are behaviorally responded to by fearful, avoidant tendencies, such as isolation, disconnectedness, and abandonment. The Oxford definition of *trauma*, on the other hand, is "a deeply distressing or disturbing experience" – not really capturing the depth of the experience, in all its complexity and ubiquity.

We now live in a time when trauma is so widely accepted as a possibility in the existence of human beings that it has decreased the stigmatization which, in prior times, typically accompanied the diagnosis. The research of Figley et al. (2017) conveys that the majority of individuals have encountered at least one or more events during their lifetime that meet the definition of trauma. Unfortunately, however, as it has become more popularized, its definition has often been used in a far less precise, sometimes indiscriminate, way than the clinical diagnosis requires, that is, its meaning has at times been watered down. The public and parts of the mental health world think less specifically about what *trauma* actually is. What is also important to note is that, nevertheless, trauma is now accepted as ubiquitous by most clinicians and the world in general.

Defining and Differentiating PTSD and Complex PTSD

Within the medical world, *trauma*, diagnostically, is most often known as posttraumatic stress disorder (PTSD). (For interested readers, North et al. (2016) and McNally (2012, 2018) provide a history of how the term evolved.) When the response is less severe, especially when it is of shorter duration, a diagnosis of acute stress disorder may be appropriate; sometimes, distinguishing between the two can be a challenge to the clinician. The International Classification of Diseases, Tenth Edition (ICD-10), defines *PTSD* as a condition in response (delayed or protracted) to a stressful event or situation that is extremely threatening or catastrophic in nature (of either brief or long duration), with a high likelihood of causing universal distress in almost anyone. The Diagnostic and Statistical Manual of Mental Disorders, Fifth Edition, Text Revision (DSM-5-TR), defines *PTSD* as intense or prolonged psychological

DOI: 10.4324/9781003546252-1

and/or physiological distress in response to exposure to internal or external cues that resemble an aspect of the traumatic event(s). The reader will notice that these definitions include no reference to the individual's actual experience of being overwhelmed.

Herman (1997) suggested that a new diagnosis, complex PTSD (CPTSD), was needed to describe the symptoms of long-term trauma. These symptoms include impulsive, self-destructive patterns; emotional dysregulation; dissociation; lack of sense of self; chaotic interpersonal relations; and somatic medical problems. *CPTSD* often denotes the long-term, interconnected impact on the brain and the central nervous system and the accompanying ingrained fearful, avoidant behaviors. The World Health Organization's ICD-11 (2018) defined *CPTSD* to encompass re-experiencing fear-provoking avoidance reactions of PTSD with additional disturbances in self-organization (DSO) – long-term problems with affect dysregulation, identity, negative self-concept, and relational capacities (Karatzias et al., 2020; Simon et al., 2019). CPTSD is associated with childhood abuse and neglect (Herman, 2015); greater functional impairment and increased risk for psychopathology (Marusak et al., 2015); comorbidity, including substance use (Roberts et al., 2015), personality disorders (Harned, 2013), and dissociation (Resick et al., 2012); and lower quality of life and trauma symptoms across the lifespan (Cloitre et al., 2020). CPTSD is identified as a significant risk factor shaping individuals' responses (e.g., Brewin et al., 2000; Courtois & Ford, 2015; Courtois et al., 2009; Ford, 2021; Howell & Itzkowitz, 2016).

Survivors of childhood abuse and neglect often present with a psychiatric diagnosis that has "functional autonomy" (Klein & Schermer, 2000, p. 16) (i.e., it is not immediately apparent that the symptomatology emanates from the trauma), which may lead to incorrect diagnoses and treatment. The recognition of trauma impact also broadened our understanding of other phenomena, for example, borderline personality disorder. Prognoses were more positive for persons previously diagnosed as borderline and other personality disorders when trauma was a part of their histories (Cloitre & Koenen, 2001; Frías & Palma, 2015; Sachsse et al., 2006).

An Overview of Trauma and Its Psychological Correlates

When did the study of trauma begin? Figley et al. (2017) convey that sometime in the 19th century, the concept of trauma transitioned from solely focusing on physical injury to including psychological and emotional impact following catastrophic events. Trauma was first focused on scientifically as a pathological response by Freud (1920) to an event or series of events such as war, that is, wartime casualties, war neurosis, and battle fatigue, during World Wars I and II (Klein & Schermer, 2000). Concurrently, a leap forward in the understanding of trauma was achieved by Sigmund Freud when he discovered that child molestation within families did occur, leading to the explication of his "seduction theory," which he later abandoned (Freud, 1953). However, he did note before abandoning the theory that children overwhelmed in this way came away with serious psychopathology. Again, the focus was on a response to an external event(s). Only much later was it observed that internal cues, such as overactivation of somatic activities, can also stimulate a traumatic experience.

The study of trauma itself, accelerated when the Vietnam conflict occurred simultaneously with the Women's Movement in the 1960s; the latter shed light on the frequency of rape and victimization in the lives of women. For example, trauma study led to the creation and acceptance of concepts such as *battered women's syndrome* (Walker, 1984).

As the study of trauma evolved, no longer was the clinical existence of trauma confined to obvious catastrophic events, such as violent victimizations that occurred during war and rape. Clinicians became aware that traumatic experiences had a long-term impact on subsequent stages of development (Frías & Palma, 2015; Ogle et al., 2015; Van der Kolk, 2015). Just as the effects of the trauma impact an individual's characterological structure and personality, the conception of self, other, and the world is also fractured (e.g., Boulanger, 2011; Herman, 1997; Klein & Schermer, 2000; Van der Kolk, 2015). Depending on the idiosyncratic makeup of each individual, the responses to the same event can differ dramatically.

In 2006, the American Psychological Association (APA) officially recognized trauma as a field of study that warrants its separate division within the APA: Division 56, the Division of Trauma Psychology. Increasing numbers of mental health professionals became interested in how to diagnose and treat trauma. Most had undergone limited or no formal training in trauma treatment. Only a limited number of graduate or residency training programs offered systematic training for working with trauma. While some members of the mental health community represented themselves as "trauma specialists," the special training required for such a designation remained unclear. Currently, there continues to be no nationally accepted credential, designation, or criteria in place. In fact, the question of what constitutes adequate training necessary to effectively diagnose and treat trauma remains a subject for debate (American Psychological Association, 2015).

As awareness and interest in diagnosing and treating trauma increased, so did concern about the immediate and longer-term impacts of this work upon those who provided the required care. Immersion in this area of clinical work can be daunting, difficult, and emotionally draining. Consequences such as "burnout," "compassion fatigue," "secondary trauma," and "vicarious trauma" (Kelly, 2020; Pearlman & Saakvitne, 1995; Thomas & Wilson, 2004) began to appear in the literature. Care for the caregivers soon was identified as crucial to ensure the well-being of clinicians. From a psychodynamic perspective, common forms of countertransference were identified (e.g., fears of feeling sad, desperate, or angry; wanting to be invulnerable, to rescue, to be omnipotent or omniscient), along with the typical defenses relied upon by both patients and therapists (e.g., avoidance, denial, dissociation) to protect them from the full emotional impact of overwhelming, frightening, and frequently fragmented experiences that characterize trauma (Klein & Phillips, 2008; Van der Kolk, 2015; Ziegler & McEvoy, 2000).

Dissociation

Dissociation has been at the core in understanding long-term effects of developmental trauma and the triggering of behavioral, neurophysiological, and other defensive reactions. The origin of dissociation is related to the individual's overexposure to terror and shock (Reik, 1936). Bromberg's (1993) overview of trauma and dissociation reaffirms Reik's distinction between shock and fear:

> Reik (1936) stated: "I hold that shock is in general characteristic of a traumatic situation, fear is one of danger. Fear is itself a signal preceding shock, it anticipates the emotion of shock in miniature, and so protects us from it and from its profound and harmful effects" (pp. 267–268).
>
> (p. 151)

Dissociation represents "a dead spot inside the self or between the person and the world" (Hegeman & Wohl, 2000, p. 64), "the escape when there is no escape" (Putnam, 1992, p. 104), "a global defense against trauma or the fear of potential trauma" (Bromberg, 1993, p. 164). "Connections among and between internal experiences (e.g., thoughts, memories, feelings, sensations, time, place, sense of self) and external experiences (e.g., relationships, surroundings) can become severed or disrupted" (Leiderman & Klein, 2021, p. 37). These disconnected, dissociated responses developed as a means of self-protection in response to perceived overwhelming threats to survival and confronting these threats alone again.

Dissociative symptoms develop as people ward off overexposure to painful feelings of loneliness, hurt, and betrayal. The anguish associated with loneliness is avoided at all costs, and proximity to re-experiencing these feelings leads to intense re-enactments. Dissociative reactions preserve original experiences as encapsulated fragments and prevent them from being symbolized, subject to examination, detoxified, and metabolized. Group psychotherapy has been used to treat persons suffering from severe dissociative disturbances for several decades (Buchele, 1995).

Parental Abuse and Neglect

Psychoanalytic and psychodynamically oriented clinical practitioners recognized that a previous history of an insecure attachment style predisposed an individual to a more severe trauma response (Bowlby, 2019; Fonagy et al., 2017; Holmes, 2014; Ogle et al., 2015). Traumatizing parents often induce guilt and shame in their children (Buchele, 2000), which is frequently accompanied by humiliation, especially when children fail in the eyes of this parent to make them the unconditional priority in their lives (Schore, 2003a, 2003b).

Bowlby (1973, 1979) and Sroufe (2005) emphasized both empirical and theoretical implications of understanding attachment, dissociative psychopathology, and the impact of neglect, abandonment, and abuse on the development of children exposed to trauma. Psychoanalytic and developmental paradigms focused on studying the effects of early childhood abandonment and betrayal traumas (e.g., Bowlby, 1988; Cassidy & Shaver, 1999; Freyd et al., 2007). Schore (1994, 2003a) found that the child up to 3 years of age who is without an optimum amount of maternal awareness, understanding, and connection, especially when stressed, can develop long-term heightened vulnerability to being unable to self-sooth and self-regulate adequately.

Bowlby (1988), Freyd (1997), and Sroufe et al. (2005) emphasized that abused children may attempt to preserve the attachment with their entrusted caregivers and therefore collude with parental denial of abuse; this collusion facilitates dissociation of the traumatic memory (Liotti, 2006). "The child would rather be bad himself than have bad objects" (Fairbairn, 1952, p. 64).

Others focused on the correlation between abuse, neglect, and lifelong patterns of self-hate and self-destructiveness. Spotnitz (1961, 1985) emphasized that the abused, neglected child defensively turned all angry, rageful feelings inward, against oneself, because it was unsafe to verbalize these feelings outwardly – towards one's parents. The neglect, symbolized by a lack of parental love, protection, and compassion, can reinforce the individual's self-hate and self-destructive behaviors, accompanied by self-hating constructs. These strategies can be used by survivors of neglect to numb painful feelings but then intensify self-hate (Rubin, 1975).

Case Illustration 1

Heather, a 61-year-old White cisgendered married female, sought treatment with the principal author to address self-deprecating ruminations, panic, diminished self-esteem, affect dysregulation, dissociative symptoms, and poor relations with others.

She was a successful lawyer. As a child, she was terrified and withdrew from the frequent volatile outbursts by her mother, including raging verbal abuse, hitting her in the face, and often punishing her "for just being a kid." She tested as gifted intellectually and excelled academically and in the arts. Her father was described as passive and unprotective, and she felt hated and scapegoated by her parents and siblings.

She was a member of a developmentally mature co-ed heterogeneous trauma group. Early in treatment, a powerful enactment occurred when another member, Kim, became verbally abusive toward her after Heather elatedly expressed pride for a professional accomplishment. Heather responded forcefully to the altercation by raging at Kim, which led to several longtime members joining with Kim and aligning against Heather. Others shared Heather was attacked unfairly by Kim. Heather subsequently withdrew, and she appeared to be dissociating.

The group leader (GL) initially intervened to re-engage Heather. In part, the GL was anticipating the possibility of her being scapegoated by the group, so the GL interacted with her compassionately. She immediately responded, saying, "That's what my mother did to me whenever I achieved anything," and expressed no remorse for "defending herself" against Kim. This led to Kim raging at the GL for "taking her" (Heather's) "side."

In subsequent sessions, the space was created for the group to process and derive the symbolic meaning of the enactment, including examination of the rupture and processing the repair. Initially, their reliance upon primitive modes of defense, especially splitting, projection, and denial, prevented them from seeing one another in the moment. They eventually recognized that their dynamics in the group paralleled what happened to both in their families. Other members related to the traumatic family dynamics that were discussed. Kim was also able to address the GL about how the enactment with him symbolized the long-term pattern of her never feeling protected, especially in her family. Her feelings, reactions, and perceptions were supported and validated by the GL.

Deciphering the symbolic meaning, understanding, repairing ruptures, and learning from dissociative enactments often require multiple sessions to process. These interactions serve as opportunities to relive overwhelmingly painful experiences under safe therapeutic conditions. Instead of going through the turmoil alone and feeling further injured, demeaned, disqualified, or neglected, the safety afforded by group can offer the opportunity for alternative perspectives to emerge because the group can collectively hold, contain, detoxify, understand, and make meaning of these episodes.

Applying Psychiatric, Neurophysiological Perspectives to Trauma

In studying traumatic processes, the psychiatric lens has focused primarily on physical survival and on posttraumatic stress disorder (PTSD) (e.g., Van der Kolk, 2015). The trend toward the medicalization and symptom remediation goals of trauma treatment has been based on our vastly increased knowledge about the underlying neurophysiology of trauma. Contemporary neuroscience has focused on the impact of trauma on cortical networks and structures (Leiderman & Smith, 2017), the neurophysiological correlates to trauma (Van der Kolk et al., 1996), and the correlates of developmental trauma with the fear-based brain (Fisher, 2014). What is happening at neurophysiological and biochemical levels to the body and the brain in the face of trauma? What are the implications for understanding and treating neurophysiological dysregulated trauma responses utilizing a group psychotherapy modality? Unfortunately, much of this knowledge has remained in the purview of neurophysiologists and researchers who do not practice group psychotherapy. Many group therapists know little about this work, much less how it can be integrated with ongoing clinical care. While the medical emphasis on the response can be useful for descriptive diagnostic purposes, it is essential that the experience itself be known to the clinician for treatment purposes, so the authors will be referring to trauma in that manner. What we believe practitioners should know to increase their effectiveness as treaters deserves further explication, is critical, and will be addressed in Chapter 2.

The Somatic Imprint of Trauma

Similarly, the mental health field has focused on how unresolved trauma leaves an enduring somatic imprint. "Somatically, recent research points increasingly towards the notion that trauma can leave a lasting physical representation" (Lanius et al., 2020). For example, new evidence-based research (Bussières et al., 2023) underscores the profound impact of childhood trauma on adult health. The study evaluating (via metanalysis) 75 years of research involving 826,452 adults revealed that physical, sexual, or emotional abuse, along with neglect during childhood, increases the risk of chronic pain and related disability in adulthood.

The psyche–soma interrelationship may have a lasting noxious impact and may contribute significantly to why so many group members with trauma avoid re-experiencing the same *neuro-emotional-physiological* discomfort associated with their recall of traumatic events, as well as narrating their trauma in groups. Understanding the psyche–soma features in traumatized group members can allow therapists to create more optimal opportunities to address, recall, narrate, understand, and make meaning of these symptoms as they arise in the group process.

Levine (1997) introduced the "bottom-up" approach called somatic experiencing. This approach focuses on the somatic, trauma-related stress response (Ogden & Minton, 2000), where treatment is focused on internal sensations, both visceral (interoception) and musculoskeletal (proprioception and kinesthesia), rather than primarily cognitive or emotional experiences. A somatic-based approach will be discussed in later chapters.

Traumatic Loss and Grief

"All trauma involves loss of some kind" (Leiderman & Klein, 2021, p. 37). Trauma theory emphasizes that the grief process of mourning the multiple losses impacted by one's unresolved familial trauma is central to recovery (Herman, 1997; Klein & Schermer, 2000; Schermer, 2005). Bromberg (1993) defined the *mourning process* as encapsulating and accepting the loss of never having, and anticipating never being able to have, loving, caring, protective parents, which is like a "quasi death." "The rebuilding of linkages, the reentry into life, involves pain not unlike that of mourning. The return to life means the recognition and facing of death" (p.154). Thus, those with trauma may experience difficulties related to termination, emotionally denying the impending loss and separation, and the reawakening of the emotional pain of the loss of another caregiver (Zorzella et al., 2015). For some, the fear of abandonment and anticipated loss of another is as overwhelming as the dread of death. These trauma-driven feelings can be reactivated at times, including the anticipated loss of a fellow group member during the termination process.

Individual Variability, Resilience, and Recovery Potential

Clinicians have also recognized that not only the personal meaning attributed to a particular event but also people's degree of vulnerability/resilience to experiencing trauma vary. After 9/11, for example, it was discovered that only a relatively small percentage of those who witnessed that event developed PTSD (about 10%), while the vast majority did not exhibit a sustained pattern of symptoms that met diagnostic criteria (Neria et al., 2011). Efforts were then made to try to identify those factors that influenced susceptibility or vulnerability to trauma and those that provided resilience against trauma. These investigations paved the way for others to follow that focused on individuals' resilience and their potential for posttraumatic growth (those who are subjected to trauma can often see positive growth afterward) (Blackie et al., 2017; Boals & Schuler, 2017; Frazier et al., 2014; Infurna & Jaya-wickreme, 2019; Levine et al., 2009; Tedeschi & Calhoun, 2004).

Clinicians noticed that internal events can stimulate trauma responses as well. Studies of anniversary reactions, for example, appeared in literature (Bruce & Matsuo, 2022; Nemeth et al., 2012). Also noted was that the presence of an available support network dramatically impacted recovery and severity of subsequent psychopathology, facilitating recovery (Sippel et al., 2015; Walsh, 2007).

Sociopolitical Factors and Systemic/Structural Racism

Practitioners have become aware of a number of socio-political factors that can lead to traumatization of individuals and/or mass traumatization of large groups and populations; they include poverty, systemic and structural racism, oppression, political incitement, the rise of global authoritarian leadership, the epidemic of mass shootings (e.g., APA, 2020; Klein, 2020; Klein et al., 2023; Klein & Schermer, 2018; Leiderman, 2023; Peterson & Densley, 2021; Phillips, 2023; Pieterse et al., 2011), and inequalities in health-care systems, with disproportionately higher hospitalizations and death rates for Black Americans (CDC, 2020; Miller, 2020; Rene, 2023). Studies now reveal that members of marginalized groups, such as Black, Hispanic, Brown, and migrant populations, have frequently undergone traumatic experiences as part of their position in society vis-à-vis the dominant culture (Buchele, 2020; Ford et al., 2015; Leiderman, 2020; O'Dowd, 2020; Thompson, 2021; Wilkerson, 2020). Sadly, this type of trauma often impacts future generations and is referred to as intergenerational trauma (Yehuda & Lehrner, 2018). The impact of slavery, the Holocaust, and genocide is felt decades later.

Currently, awareness of diversity, equity, and inclusion has also led the clinical community to realize the generalized use of Eurocentric models to understand (or fail to understand) traumatization for members of minoritized groups (e.g., Raque-Bogdan et al., 2021) can be inappropriate because of the cultural and racial mismatch. Additionally, the vast majority of research on trauma has been conducted from a Eurocentric perspective (Burl-ingame, 2022), so that White trauma survivors are over-represented, while non-Whites are under-represented. Conclusions based upon such research reflect this limitation and, therefore, must be interpreted accordingly. Most recently, adding both complexity and confusion to the situation, the subject of trauma has become part of political dialogue, moving on from strictly medical conceptualization.

History of Treating Trauma: The Use of Groups

Both the understanding of trauma and appreciation of the unique efficacy of group psychotherapy grew exponentially when WWII British psychological war casualties were sent to Northfield Hospital, staffed by a group of brilliant psychiatrists; they discovered that the treatment of trauma could be effectively facilitated when taking place in a group setting. Once successfully treated, impacted soldiers could be sent back to the front (Bion, 1969). At a clinical level, there was an implicit recognition that treating trauma in groups offered some unique advantages. A limited number of staff could offer treatment to a large number of wartime casualties. Being treated in a group provided an antidote to the isolation, shame, and stigmatization veterans often endured. Bearing witness while in the company of others with similar symptoms served to normalize individuals' responses to stress and trauma. Hope, acceptance, a sense of belonging, and a willingness to trust others could be reawakened. Group treatment provided a new forum to conceptualize and verbalize the unspeakable, often unformulated trauma combat soldiers and veterans experienced. The growth of understanding regarding the value of group psychotherapy took off from there in Europe as well as the USA. Opportunities were created for interpersonal learning and engagement, as well as for helping others, both central to rebuilding damaged self and self-esteem. These observations were later identified by Yalom (1970) and Yalom and Leszcz (2020) as critical elements in the "therapeutic factors" that underlie all forms of group psychotherapy.

In the interval between the Northfield experiment begun during World War II and the 9/11 tragedy in 2001, the use of groups in the treatment of trauma slowly expanded (Klein & Schermer, 2000). Attention was devoted to using groups as a method for dealing with mass psychological trauma following a natural or man-made disaster, for example, the Vietnam War, when providers were faced with a sudden influx of casualties in need of treatment. "Rap groups," for example, proliferated to meet the growing clinical need in the aftermath of the war. Anecdotal and clinical accounts involving the use of groups for the treatment of trauma continued to appear in the literature (e.g., Koller et al., 1992), but there were few published clinical trials at that time. Even fewer accounts were reported about the scientifically controlled use of groups for treating large-scale mass trauma outside of the wartime situation.

Research Evidence: Groups Treating Trauma

Researchers have reviewed the effectiveness of using small groups to treat trauma (Foy et al., 2001; Mahoney et al., 2019; Schwartze et al., 2019). While the findings are positive, these studies are generally limited to the use of short-term, structured groups (Greene, 2021). Others investigated short-term, cognitive behavioral approaches conducted with female White survivors of childhood or adulthood sexual abuse. These studies demonstrated improvements in group members' levels of distress at the end of treatment. Several reports involving weekly longer-term psychodynamic approaches also produced successful participant outcomes (Foy et al., 2002). As early as 1988, clinicians such as Ganzarain and Buchele (1988) were documenting similar accounts of treatment successes with traumatized persons molested in their families. In a subsequent review, Foy et al. (2009) classified cognitive behavioral group approaches into those that "uncovered" versus those that "covered" traumatic memories and reported successful outcomes with the use of each. They concluded that regardless of type, group psychotherapy was associated with favorable outcomes across a number of psychiatric symptoms.

It is important to note that these conclusions were based primarily on group treatments provided in controlled settings long after the actual trauma had occurred. Group methods were carefully defined, usually with the use of treatment manuals, as an important factor within cognitive behavioral approaches, rigorously followed and monitored. Study participants were typically White adult females who had survived sexual trauma, usually in childhood. Leaders were trained and supervised in the application of procedures and techniques. These treatments were conducted with patients in "homogeneous" groups, that is, all participants met a particular, usually narrowly defined, diagnostic criterion. This differs from the more typical clinical situation involving "heterogenous groups," wherein patients in the same group may have multiple, differing diagnoses. A patient diagnosed as a trauma survivor is likely to find themselves in a group with others who have no such specific experiences. How the clinician thinks about these differences, along with questions about the type, depth, and duration of group treatment, will be discussed in greater detail in later chapters.

The Advent of Evidence-Based Care

Roughly at the turn of the century, the entire health-care field, including mental health, was struggling to come to terms with a new standard for care, which was that for treatment to be considered adequate, it should be "evidence-based treatment" (EBT) or reflect empirically based practice. Much ambiguity, however, surrounded these terms. Were we talking about "evidence-supported treatment" as defined by the American Psychological Association (APA, 2005), in which randomized controlled trials (RCTs) were the "gold standard"? Or were we talking about following the recommendations of the American Psychiatric Association for "Practice Guidelines" (APA, 2004), a more descriptive than prescriptive set of standards? More fundamentally, what constituted legitimate evidence worthy of consideration? How were successful outcomes being defined and measured, by whom, from whose perspective, and at what points in time? Hotly contested debates raged as to what treatments could qualify as evidence-based and who should make such determinations, using what definitions and criteria (Klein & Phillips, 2008). Several of these questions have remained continuing sources of controversy. It is important to note that Measurement-Based Care (MBC) is the contemporary systematic evaluation of patient symptoms before or during an encounter to inform behavioral health treatment (Lewis et al., 2019). MBC is a clinical process consisting of intermittently collecting subjective, patient-reported outcomes throughout the course of treatment; providing feedback to the patient about their reported progress scores and trends over time; and incorporating these data via collaborative decision-making regarding treatment in the context of the course of care (MacNair-Semands & Whittingham, 2023; Oslin et al., 2019; Resnick & Hoff, 2020).

Case Illustration 2

A brief clinical example may be useful to illustrate these issues.

John is a 46-year-old depressed privileged White cisgendered male physician with a history of trauma in his relationship with his father, for which he was treated in a long-term psychodynamic group psychotherapy. When Donald Trump became President, John became increasingly concerned and agitated about the unresolved crises facing US citizens, what he considered to be the erosion of our moral values and integrity, and the rhetoric, policies, and actions of our US government.

Considerable time was devoted by the group to discussing these concerns. The group remained consistently interested and supportive. Throughout his life, however, John had been haunted by fears of not being able to do things correctly, evidenced by his feeling only marginally competent and maintaining a low-profile career compared to his peers. He tended to handle stress poorly, often attempting to avoid or to deny problems, wishing instead to retreat, as he had done in childhood, hiding under his bed. A failed marriage and what he regarded as limited professional success only added to his low level of self-esteem and diminished sense of capacity.

Examination of these concerns invariably led back to his relationship with his father, whose voice echoed in his head since childhood, abusively belittling and criticizing whatever he did. President Trump's tendency to divide, denigrate, and blame others seemed all too familiar to John. It served to reawaken many moments of early childhood trauma. Ironically, even his becoming a physician never silenced his father's admonitions that he could not do things well and was destined to fail.

He experienced enactments in group therapy with the leader and his fellow group members, characterized by his perception of being criticized, accompanied by the re-experiencing of unresolved feelings of shame, hurt, betrayal, and being misunderstood. These highly charged enactments, often without provocation, resulted in John angrily blaming and criticizing the leader and group members. Creating the emotional space following these enactments to safely understand, process, validate, metabolize, provide alternative perspectives, and create symbolic meaning when the group leader or members took on features of his father was meaningful.

Over more than ten years in treatment, that voice in his head became substantially less frequent, loud, and convincing. In the group, he became a visible and active member, much better able to examine his own and others' behavior as well as his relationships with group members. His capacity for courage and honesty was recognized and applauded. In addition, his clinical practice grew much more robust, and he was able to maintain a successful long-term relationship with a woman. During a group session in the latter stages of treatment, he proclaimed, "I feel like I was reborn five years ago. My life is so different now. . . . How I feel about myself, my relationships, and how I deal with situations and challenges in my life, is completely different."

Should we accept this as legitimate data? Or should we dismiss this as simply a testimonial provided by an inherently biased participant? These data are not based upon measurable changes using standardized scales. There are no experimental controls in place to permit rigorous assessment of the treatment. What accounted for these changes cannot be easily specified. Nevertheless, the current editors believe these are meaningful data, that the reported changes are real and corroborated, and the changes can be ascribed to the documented group treatments.

Simultaneous with the growth of knowledge about trauma, the field of psychiatry turned away from an emphasis on psychodynamic understanding to an emphasis on the use of medication and treatment of symptoms, both of which are structured and lend themselves to evidence-based research. Symptom-focused ways of working with trauma have proliferated. Practice Guidelines provided from various sources (e.g., the Department of Veteran's Affairs and Department of Defense (2017), the International Society for Traumatic Stress Studies (ISTSS) (2019), and the National Institute for Health and Care Excellence (NICE) (2018)) have focused on evidence-based methods, primarily cognitive behavioral, aimed at symptom reduction. ISTSS, for example, recommended a group cognitive behavioral approach with a trauma focus over other group therapies.

When the American Psychological Association revised its Practice Guideline (2017), symptom-focused treatments supported by evidence-based research again prevailed.

Psychodynamic treatment of trauma was not listed as recommended despite considerable research to support its use (e.g., Busch et al., 2021; Fonagy, 2015; Gaskin, 2012; Levi et al., 2017; Litwack et al., 2022; Schottenbauer et al., 2008; Weinberg et al., 2005). They strongly recommended cognitive behavioral therapy (CBT), cognitive processing therapy (CPT), cognitive therapy (CT), and prolonged exposure therapy (PE) and suggested the use of brief eclectic psychotherapy (BEP), eye movement desensitization and reprocessing (EMDR), and narrative exposure therapy (NET).

This Practice Guideline, however, met with significant criticism. Courtois and Brown (2019) and Kudler (2019) noted that it was developed in a vacuum, was focused primarily on reducing symptoms of PTSD, and failed to take into account other important factors. They argued for a more "ecologically informed" model that considered the body of research on the psychotherapy relationship, psychotherapy process, and a broader array of psychotherapy outcomes. Similarly, Norcross and Wampold (2019a) referred to the Practice Guideline as a "misguided effort" to advance a biomedical model of psychotherapy focused upon those treatment methods. They then provided an excellent review of the importance of relationships and responsiveness in the psychological treatment of trauma. In their examination of the implications of the Practice Guideline for trauma education and training, Henning and Brand (2019) concluded that students and professionals may "inadvertently overwhelm" some clients diagnosed incorrectly with complex PTSD, resulting in poor outcomes and even harm, an important ethical consideration. They also note that, with regard to training, the Guideline fails to take into consideration the client's cultural and individual needs, as well as clinician self-care, revealing additional ethical concerns. The need for ongoing innovation remains salient (Brown & Courtois, 2019).

During the past two decades, awareness of the relatively high frequency of trauma within the general population has resulted in increased accuracy in regard to patient diagnosis. Practitioners are now more alert to the signs and symptoms associated with patients' having survived trauma. Consistent with that development, the entire field of treatment of trauma has grown exponentially. An increasing number of articles and books have appeared in the literature about the treatment of trauma generally. Specialized professional associations and journals that focused exclusively upon trauma have appeared. In addition, this area of concern is given far greater consideration in graduate education and training and is regularly featured during many professional association meetings. Trauma-informed assessment interviewing has gained traction in research and clinical practice (Armstrong, 2017).

The use of group approaches during treatment has also received increased attention. Detailed presentations of specific group models have appeared, including publication of treatment manuals and guidebooks for clinicians who wish to apply cognitive behavioral models (e.g., Litwack et al., 2022; Wattenberg et al., 2021), as well as those interested in applying a psychodynamic approach (e.g., Busch et al., 2021). While substantial advances have been made in empirically supported individual treatment of trauma-related disorders (Beck & Sloan, 2021), research support for group treatment approaches has, in general, lagged behind, often due to methodologic problems inherent in conducting research with group methods (Greene, 2021; Litwack et al., 2022).

Intersection of Sociopolitical Factors and Trauma Research

Until recently, relatively limited attention had been given to the application of the recently documented knowledge about small groups and group dynamics to understand and work with systemic and structural problems that result from trauma associated with racism within organizations and, more broadly, within American society (O'Dowd, 2020;

Wilkerson, 2020). Converging developments, however, have stimulated renewed interest in exploring these potential applications. To begin with, a number of newer theories of psychotherapy bear directly upon the intersection of sociopolitical and psychotherapy considerations, including feminist theories of psychotherapy (e.g., Brown, 2010), theories of intersectionality (e.g., Crenshaw, 1989), liberation (e.g., Comas-Díaz & Rivera, 2020), and critical psychologies (e.g., Fox et al., 2009). Each of these theoretical contributions arose largely in response to issues of systemic and structural inequities centering on sexism, racism, social activism, and community involvement; all are relevant during discussions of widespread trauma. They call attention to social justice and inclusion concerns in relation to oppressed and impoverished communities and focus attention on therapists tackling oppressive and discriminatory social conditions. They encourage closer examination of systemic and structural racism, inequities, microaggressions, and macroaggressions existing within society (Pieterse et al., 2011); inequities in professional mental health organizations (Leiderman & Klein, 2021); and alternative, non-Eurocentric approaches to trauma group treatment, especially by authors who identify as Black, Hispanic, Brown, Indigenous, and/or from a marginalized group. Eurocentrically focused authors can now also incorporate these considerations into their theoretical approaches and interventions to minimize the harm and trauma caused by structural and systemic racism. Not addressing these issues risks maintaining the marginalized status of various minorities, thus likely contributing significantly to their levels of mental distress and exposure to trauma and, therefore, should become a legitimate part of therapeutic dialogue and aspirations of mental health organizations.

A Social Systems Perspective

Contributions from group analysts and British object relations theorists have drawn our attention to the concept of the "social unconscious" (e.g., Dalal, 2001; Hopper, 2003; Weinberg, 2007), and have linked their concerns with broader contemporary conceptualizations of what constitutes trauma. Volkan (2001; 2021) has systematically examined the intergenerational transmission of "chosen trauma" within national groups. Chosen traumas are central to the large-group's identity and are the result of "catastrophic loss, humiliation, and helplessness at the hands of a neighboring group. When the members of the victim group are unable to mourn such losses or reverse the humiliation, they pass on the images of their injured selves and even the object images of those who hurt them." (Volkan, 1999, p. 152). Chosen traumas revive when a large group is under threat and/ or when political leaders knowingly enflame the embodied trauma in the minds of the members of the large group; they are transmitted intergenerationally.

The impact of slavery is an example of the intergenerational transmission of trauma. Mental health organizations, like other institutions in America, have themselves begun to identify and grapple with the effects of racism within their own organizations. The American Group Psychotherapy Association, the American Psychological Association, and the American Psychoanalytic Association are cases in point.

In addition to self-scrutiny, current work in this area has taken several forms. One has focused attention on how systemic and structural racism and racial disparities influence employment practices, housing, education, health care, and the administration of social justice (e.g., Raque-Bogdan et al., 2021; Rene, 2023). Another has involved investigations of violence in America and the use of force by our police (e.g., Klein & Schermer,

2018; Peterson & Densley, 2021; Phillips, 2023; Thompson, 2021). A third strand has begun to examine how groups can be used within organizations and larger systems to provide protection against trauma (e.g., Leszcz, 2023a). Efforts using a systems lens now are underway to understand how different complex systems evolve and function, and how to use groups to educate, intervene, and change prevailing and dominant cultures toward becoming more aware and equitable. The interest here is shifting from diagnosis and treatment to prevention.

Why Groups Work

Of interest in this connection is the case which has been made to warrant the general use of groups in the treatment process. Burlingame (2022) points to the 3Es: efficacy, equivalence, and efficiency. He notes that the efficacy of group psychotherapy has been well documented (e.g., Burlingame & Strauss, 2021). It clearly works. The average member in group therapy will have a better outcome than 86% of those receiving no treatment. When it comes to PTSD, the average participant in group treatment ends therapy with improvement that exceeds 75.8% of those with no treatment (Barkowski et al., 2020; Burlingame, 2022; Schwartze et al., 2019; Sloan et al., 2013). Smaller but nevertheless substantial improvements are found when comparisons are drawn between participants in group treatment compared to those in another active treatment or "treatment as usual."

More than 40 meta-analyses comparing individual and group psychotherapy have found no differences in treatment outcome, dropout rate, and remission (Burlingame et al., 2016; Burlingame, 2022). Thus, equivalence has been established between the two modalities. Lastly, group treatment is more efficient. This is so in two respects: Fewer clinicians can serve more patients in less time, and the cost for treatment per patient is considerably less. These factors promote access to treatment (Whittingham et al., 2023).

In addition, we now have a better idea of why group therapy is effective. Solid research evidence has linked evidence-based group factors with participant improvement. Group cohesion, the analogue of the therapeutic alliance in individual treatment, accounts for roughly 25% of client improvement in interpersonal groups (Burlingame et al., 2018). Therapist factors account for an additional 5–10% improvement (Owen, 2013). Group leaders who encourage member interactions, carefully monitor the therapeutic relationship and leader–member alliance, show an ability to intervene in group process, and demonstrate cultural competence produce better outcomes among participants (Burlingame, 2022). Therapists who have multicultural competence skills tend to be perceived as more expert, trustworthy, and attractive (Tao et al., 2015). For example, Miles et al. (2021) discussed how group leaders utilize the concepts of cultural humility (willingness and comfort in addressing cultural issues) and multicultural competencies and espouse a multicultural orientation to address the ruptures caused by microaggressions. Such therapists demonstrate cultural humility by remaining curious, open, and respectful of participants' cultural identities. In turn, this allows participants to feel "seen." These matters are intrinsically linked with diversity, equity, and inclusion.

What other intersubjective qualities in the trauma group therapist and with the therapeutic relationship can be considered to enhance positive group member treatment outcomes? Increasingly, researchers have recognized the importance of the therapeutic relationship, and that certain relationships "work" and are linked with successful treatment outcome (e.g., DeAngelis, 2019; Gelso et al., 2018; Norcross & Wampold, 2019b). Perlitz (2019), an individual psychoanalyst, suggests that "implicit qualities" of the therapist are crucial to treatment success, including the ability to maintain hope and curiosity, to remain emotionally responsive, to privilege the patient's interest ahead of his/her own, to model a non-judgmental, accepting stance, to acknowledge fallibility, to tolerate ambiguity, and to feel compassion for a fellow human sufferer. Klein (2020) proposes that therapist role boundaries require re-examination to ensure that attention be devoted to sociopolitical conditions, including prevailing oppressive and discriminatory social conditions which powerfully influence the marginalized status and mental health of individual citizens. Based upon recent theoretical developments in psychodynamic/psychoanalytic thinking, he highlights the importance of maintaining more mutual, active, experience-near, emotionally responsive, and validating relationships with patients. Watson and Wiseman (2021) point to the importance of remaining emotionally responsive and attuned to clients. Leiderman (2020, 2023) and Leiderman and Klein (2021) make the case for adopting an integrated role as a systems-oriented, socially responsible, interpersonal/intersubjective therapist when working with trauma in groups where one must deal with unfolding enactments and dissociative phenomena. Maintaining such a role in the treatment process, of course, heightens the level of emotional exposure and stress the therapist must endure to create a safe, stable holding environment that enables patients to find their own voices, examine and detoxify painful dissociated inner experiences, and attempt to fashion new, more adaptive, and flexible reintegrations.

Two Different Traditions

It can be said, then, that much of the work over the past several decades on the use of groups to treat trauma can be traced to two different traditions: the psychoanalytic and the evidence-based treatment traditions (Greene, 2021; Yalch et al., 2022). The psychoanalytic tradition, originated by Freud and his acolytes, encompasses several streams of thought: the more broadly based psychodynamic models that contain several derivations (e.g., self-psychology, object relations, interpersonal/group analysis, modern analytic attachment theory), plus theory and research about group dynamic and social systems models that, beginning with Lewin (1975) and the National Training Laboratories (Schein & Bennis, 1965), sparked interest in examining various levels of process (intrapersonal, interpersonal, group-as-a-whole) within and between groups. This work was extended by the work of Bion (1969) at the Tavistock Institute and by von Bertalanffy (1968), who addressed general systems, and later by Agazarian (1997), who included the study of functional subgroups.

Trauma groups that owe their origins to this tradition have relied upon the use of an unstructured format and have been classified broadly as psychodynamic or "process" groups (Yalch et al., 2022). This format holds that, over the course of unstructured group sessions, the dynamic factors associated with participants' traumas will spontaneously emerge and be replicated among and between members and leader(s) intersubjectively so they can be safely understood and processed. The re-enactments that occur within the here and now of the group will then allow for in-the-moment reworking, detoxification, and reintegration of traumatic experiences. These groups tend to be longer in duration; pursue more broad-based treatment goals involving changes in overall levels of patient functioning and increased coping and resilience, especially with regard to self-concept and relationships with others; and often aim toward changes in enduring aspects of personality linked with initial symptom presentation. Shedler (2010), discussing psychodynamic treatment, notes that, in general, treatment goals extend beyond remission of symptoms to include increasing the capacity to have more fulfilling relationships, maintain a more realistic sense of self and self-esteem, make better use of one's talents and abilities, tolerate a broader range of affect, and face life's challenges with greater flexibility and freedom. Optimally, long-term trauma groups allow members access to loving, trusting relationships that are internalized, as well as the restoration of hope.

The second tradition, that of evidence-based treatment, has given rise to the growth and development of "structured" groups for use in the treatment of trauma (Ruzek et al., 2023; Yalch et al., 2022). These groups are based upon some variant of a cognitive behavioral approach (CBT). Some are trauma-focused (e.g., exposure-based or cognitive processing group therapy), while others are non-trauma-focused (e.g., affect regulation, interpersonal skills, or mindfulness stress reduction). These groups tend to be shorter in duration, make use of a more highly structured format, and follow a specific sequence of tailored group sessions usually based upon a treatment manual. The format is less focused on group dynamics, group process, and re-enactments and generally aims at more limited treatment goals, such as symptom reduction, cognitive restructuring, and skills acquisition, designed to promote emotional regulation and prevent relapse. Participant diagnostic selection criteria are often more tightly drawn; both leader training and behavior are more rigorously monitored. Session length, content, sequence, and leader technique are predetermined via treatment manual. Outcome criteria are more clearly specified (e.g., symptom reduction) and measurable. Such "manualized" groups, therefore, lend themselves better to the application of research controls and replicability. Despite the methodological problems inherent in doing research upon any kind of groups, these are reported upon far more frequently in the clinical research literature than process groups.

This heavy representation of cognitive behavioral approaches, in contrast to psychodynamic or process groups in the literature and in training programs that use groups to treat trauma, probably reflects several relevant factors: (1) We live in an era in which evidence-based treatment has increasingly become the standard for evaluating clinical practice; (2) cognitive behavioral group approaches are more easily researched and therefore appear to be more "scientific" and legitimized; (3) such groups have "targeted" goals, which means goals are more specific and measurable; (4) they take less time and are more affordable than process or psychodynamic treatment groups – a consideration that fits with the US predilection for speed and efficiency; and (5) conducting such groups protects practitioners from the emotional stress and exposure associated with working with trauma using less-structured psychodynamic approaches in which the role of the therapist is experience-near.

Several comprehensive resources are now available for clinicians treating trauma (e.g., Friedman et al., 2021; Ruzek et al., 2023; Schnyder & Cloitre, 2022). Friedman et al. (2021) contains a historical overview that sets the context, elucidates the scientific foundations and theoretical perspectives of this area of study, and examines clinical practice in terms of the evidence-based state of the art. Ruzek et al. (2023) and Schnyder and Cloitre (2022) provide excellent reviews of evidence-based treatment for trauma explicating basic principles of traumatic stress, stress- and trauma-related disorders, psychotherapy, short-term modalities, and comorbidity. Although comprehensive in scope, none of these volumes focuses on the special challenges involved in how to use groups during the treatment process.

Despite the enormous growth in the overall field of trauma, research investigations into the use and effectiveness of groups are still in their infancy. However, it is important to note here that some meta-analyses have endorsed the efficacy of group psychotherapy in the treatment of PTSD (Schwartze et al., 2019; Sloan et al., 2013). A number of important factors have been identified as clinical considerations when deciding whether a patient might benefit from group treatment. Among the several patient variables are the patient's interest in and motivation for participating in a group, his/her/their abilities to work within a group format, particular personality characteristics, willingness to share the stage and the therapist, the presence of comorbid issues, and ability to regulate affect. Equally important, therapist variables crucial to consider are therapist's skills, training and knowledge, personality characteristics, therapeutic model, technique., etc.

Issues of group composition, however, continue to remain more problematic. Consider, for example, the following set of questions: Should patients with different types of trauma be treated in different groups? Can patients with different traumata be treated effectively in the same group? In other words, should membership in a trauma group be determined by homogeneity regarding type of trauma (e.g., Herman et al., 2018; Jackson et al., 2019)? How important is the length of time elapsed between the trauma itself and the beginning of treatment? Are there phases of response and recovery following trauma (Mendelsohn et al., 2011)? Do certain approaches work better during certain phases (e.g., Herman et al., 2018; Yalch et al., 2022)? Should patients with chronic, recurrent, and CPTSD be treated in the same group (Courtois & Ford, 2015; Spermon et al., 2010)? How important is it to maintain a multicultural orientation during the group (APA, 2019; Comas-Díaz, 2014; Grimes & Kivlighan, 2021; Kivlighan et al., 2021)? These and related questions about group composition (and therapist orientation) require further investigation.

Several important questions remain. First, most cognitive behavioral group models were developed initially as individual treatment approaches. They were then modified for use with groups (e.g., Castillo et al., 2016; Lamp et al., 2019). As mentioned earlier, most devote limited attention to group variables *per se*. The opportunities to use and examine group dynamics, group characteristics (e.g., cohesion), group process, enactments, or dissociative episodes in the group as *tools* to promote achievement of treatment goals remain largely unspecified. Some cognitive behavioral therapists may try to take these group variables into account, while others may not. For the latter, the group itself may merely serve as the treatment *context*, not as a vital part of the treatment *process*. Further research will be required to determine whether the effectiveness of cognitive behavioral group treatment can be enhanced if therapists using these approaches learn how to incorporate and make use of these important group variables in the treatment process.

Second, much of the research on the use of groups to treat trauma has focused on the theoretical model and techniques that characterize the work. There is a danger, we believe, that we have become overly enamored with our theories and placed too much importance upon them. A large body of evidence suggests that group approaches may be effective primarily because of group variables that cut across specific theoretical frames. Variables such as cohesion, like the therapeutic relationship in individual psychotherapy, seem to carry the variance in outcome research. They seem far more important than specific theoretical framework. Might the same findings be relevant for the group treatment of trauma? Furthermore, might variables like group cohesion assume greater importance at certain phases during the treatment of responses to trauma? On the other hand, might certain theoretical approaches be particularly useful in reducing specific symptoms of trauma, but not others? Conversely, might the theoretical approach be less important when one considers the efficacy of longer-term groups for trauma treatment? We know clinically that unless one can establish a group that is cohesive and serves as a safe container in which participants can find their own voices and foster trust in others, there is little chance they will benefit. Experienced levels of personal safety, for example, may be a critical variable that influences clinical outcome. Thus, we would suggest that there is a need for further research to tease apart what portion of outcome variance can be attributed to one specific theory or model versus cross-theoretical factors inherent in all group approaches. Unfortunately, despite our wishes as a discipline to remain objective and scientific, we are aware that, often, the fate of a given theory rests not just upon the weight of the research evidence but upon the prominence, productivity, and longevity of its supporters.

At a broader level, of course, we cannot yet definitively answer whether there is any single treatment model that is more effective in treating certain kinds of trauma, as opposed to others. The answer, therefore, to the most essential but puzzling question, namely, that of "fit," continues to elude us: Which type of patient is likely to benefit from which type of group treatment, using which theory and techniques, composed along which dimensions, with which type of group characteristics, with which type of therapist, at which point in time? There is no body of research currently available to answer this question. Practitioners must rely for guidance upon some combination of knowledge of the literature, research evidence, clinical and personal experience, supervision, accumulated wisdom, and belief/ faith. Hopefully, the chapters to follow will contain some useful suggestions.

An Ethical Trauma Group Psychotherapy Practice

An ethical group therapy practice involves a therapist protecting clients by upholding the ethical standards and principles of autonomy (i.e., a client's unconditional freedom to choose their treatment course), nonmaleficence (i.e., observing a therapist's mandate to do no harm, including attempting to foresee and prevent circumstances that could inadvertently harm clients), beneficence (i.e., working for clients by finding them the best group fit, managing countertransference), justice (i.e., all clients will be treated equally without discrimination or bias), and fidelity (i.e., therapists will be loyal, faithful to clients, and fulfill all mutually agreed-upon commitments) (Kaklauskas & Olson, 2020). In addition, the practice of group therapy is unique in that the ethical standards and practice are simultaneously applied to each individual group member and to the group-as-a-whole. As Leszcz (2023b) emphasizes, "[t]he potential for ethical quandaries, missteps, and unintentional harm are therefore much greater within group psychotherapy at every turn – running the gamut from client selection, preparation, clinical treatment, training, to supervision" (p. 167).

For the group leader, following state and federal laws, as well as professional guidelines regarding documentation of group therapy sessions, and providing Informed Consent disclosure forms are fundamental to ethical practice. Recommended Informed Consent documents stipulate but are not limited to providing information about the following: (1) Health Insurance Portability and Accountability Act (HIPPA), the federal law that enforces privacy protections and patient rights with regard to the use and disclosure of Protected Health Information (PHI) used for the purpose of treatment, payment, and health-care operations; (2) fees, billing, cancellation, and scheduling practices; and (3) confidentiality practices in group therapy and its limitations. Group norms/rules meant to protect confidentiality may include using first names only in group sessions, encouraging limited or no socializing outside of sessions, and soliciting a group agreement to not disclose information about a group member outside the group; offering a brief description of the therapist's practice and areas of specialty; promoting awareness of good group therapy practice, including risks, benefits, the rights, freedom to leave treatment, and obligations of group members; incorporating appropriate, new technological platforms in the way group therapy is delivered; and incorporating an evaluation process that may take several sessions and will offer recommendations to enhance the individual's group therapy efficacy and progress.

When screening new members, leaders may consider asking themselves thus: What are the risks/harms/benefits of adding this member to the group? Will they be capable of receiving constructive feedback, alternative perspectives? What psychological defenses do they utilize that may place them or the group-as-a-whole at risk if they joined the group? Is there a better fit regarding treatment utilizing another group modality or therapist to address their presenting problem(s)? Kealy et al. (2016) recommend improving the risk–benefit analysis through early identification of high-risk members, that is, those who are likely to be destructive to the group process.

Ethical principles particularly applicable to group process should be given consideration. Trauma group leaders should be conscious of the potential for misusing their power, control, status in the group, and group member(s) vulnerabilities to re-experience shame and humiliation. The editors believe the facilitation of trauma group psychotherapy is a sub-specialty and requires advanced training and supervision. Treatment documentation, depending on the specific nature of the trauma, may require special consideration; the clinician should be aware that, in some cases, that is, domestic violence situations, records may eventually be utilized in legal proceedings and should be written giving careful thought to writing in such a way that the report minimizes potential misinterpretation that can eventually harm the person undergoing treatment. The clinician providing treatment for traumatized persons has an ethical obligation to exercise adequate self-care, as failure to do so can inadvertently harm the patient.

For a comprehensive overview of group therapy ethical guidelines, the following resources are recommended:

- AGPA and IBCGP Guidelines for Ethics. (2002). www.agpa.org/home/practice-resources/ethics-in-group-therapy
- Brabender, V., and MacNair-Semands, R. (2022). The ethics of group psychotherapy: Principles and practical strategies. Routledge.
- International Association for Group Psychotherapy and Group Process. (2009). *Ethical Guidelines and professional standards for Group Psychotherapists*. www.iagp.com/about/ethicalguidelines.htm

Overview of Volume

The idea of publishing a new volume on the group treatment of trauma at this moment makes sense, for several reasons: (1) Given the rapid growth and interest in the field, it seems timely to provide an update of previous work done under the auspices of the American Group Psychotherapy Association. (2) There have been significant advances in neuroscience and its application to understanding traumatized individuals and the implications for group therapists treating group members with CPTSD. (3) We have come to realize the need to address trauma as it relates to structural and systemic racism, microaggressions, macroaggressions, hate, and bigotry. (4) There is a need to publish non-Eurocentric approaches to trauma, especially by authors who identify as Black, Hispanic, Brown, Indigenous, and/or from a marginalized group. (5) We recognize the need for a comprehensive resource explicating how to use group psychotherapy and group intervention for working with trauma since, to our knowledge, no such resource is currently available. Our volume incorporates contemporary integrated trauma group psychodynamic approaches, including the latest advances in neuroscience, large group interventions, as well as the role of racial trauma and sexual abuse, distinguishing it from other recent books (Ruzek et al., 2023). (6) In view of the infrequent opportunities provided within most graduate and residency training programs for clinicians to acquire education/expertise/knowledge of how to create and lead trauma groups, we are in a position, based upon our experience, to make some effort to address this area of deficiency.

Our intent in this volume is to provide an up-to-date, comprehensive practical clinical guide for mental health professionals on the utilization of groups in the treatment of trauma. This volume is organized into the following seven sections: We begin with (1) the dramatic developments in the evidence-based research on the neuropsychological correlates of trauma and the efficacy of group psychotherapy, which includes a chapter on an integrated neurophysiological psychodynamic group therapy approach to treat trauma. (2) The psychological correlates of psychological trauma, which include chapters on the long-term impact of early familial neglect and abuse, trauma and attachment, and dissociation, regression, and primitive defenses in both members and leaders. (3) Preparation for beginning a trauma group, including the overall treatment planning considerations regarding when and how to make use of group approaches, short-term versus long-term group treatment, supervision, and clinical training considerations for trauma group leaders. (4) Treating trauma using short-term integrated CBT psychodrama groups. (5) Treating psychological trauma via long-term groups using interpersonal/relational and analytic approaches. This section will also include subtopics of fostering reliance and restoring hope in group members. (6) The role of trauma as it relates to structural and systemic racism, including chapters focusing on racism, race-based trauma, and their impact on attachment. (7) Specialized group models, including chapters on sexual abuse and a systems-oriented trauma large group approach. The volume will conclude with a discussion section summarizing the publications in this volume and future directions, including the topics of further research, education, training, supervision, and support.

We would like our readers to come away with increased awareness and knowledge of (1) the rationale for using groups in the treatment of trauma; (2) the ways in which different group models have been used in the treatment process; (3) the treatment effectiveness of groups; (4) the role and importance of diversity, equity, and inclusion considerations; (5) the common/essential elements that characterize successful use of groups in treating psychological trauma; and (6) what critical questions remain to be answered and what future directions require exploration.

Because this volume includes substantial material about the basics of trauma and the impact this work has upon providers, we hope it will be useful in the preparation, education, and training of all mental health professionals who may work with trauma. The first of the earlier volumes published by AGPA (Buchele & Spitz, 2005) was prepared in the aftermath of 9/11 for the provision of necessary immediate assistance. By contrast, the current volume provides a more comprehensive understanding and synthesis of contemporary knowledge about trauma and group approaches.

Clinicians considering referring patients for group treatment may find the volume useful as well. Such a comprehensive practical clinical guide about the use of groups in the treatment of psychological trauma will constitute a welcome addition to fill an existing void in the literature.

These, then, are our hopes and expectations. We aspire to assess, summarize, and integrate knowledge on the current state of thinking about using groups to treat psychological trauma. They will also help shed light on how much and what we do not yet know.

References

Agazarian, Y. (1997). *Systems-centered therapy for groups*. Karnac Books. https://www.karnacbooks. com/product/systems-centered-therapy-for-groups/18440/

American Psychiatric Association. (2004). *Practice guideline for the treatment of patients with acute stress disorder and posttraumatic stress disorder*. APA. https://psychiatryonline.org/pb/assets/raw/ sitewide/practice_guidelines/guidelines/acutestressdisorderptsd.pdf

American Psychological Association. (2005). *Policy statement on evidence-based practice in psychology*. APA. https://www.apa.org/practice/guidelines/evidence-based-statement

American Psychological Association. (2015). *Guidelines on trauma competencies for education and training*. http://www.apa.org/ed/resources/trauma-competencies-training.pdf

American Psychological Association. (2017). *Clinical practice guideline for the treatment of posttraumatic stress disorder (PTSD) in adults*. APA. https://www.apa.org/ptsd-guideline

American Psychological Association. (2019). *APA guidelines on race and ethnicity in psychology*. APA. https://www.apa.org/about/policy/guidelines-race-ethnicity.pdf

American Psychological Association. (2020). *Stress in America: 2020 a national mental health crisis*. APA. https://www.apa.org/news/press/releases/stress/2020/sia-mental-health-crisis.pdf

Armstrong, J. (2017). Incorporating trauma into an assessment interview. In S. N. Gold (Ed.), *APA handbook of trauma psychology: Trauma practice* (pp. 31–40). American Psychological Association. https://doi.org/10.1037/0000020-002

Barkowski, S., Schwartze, D., Strauss, B., Burlingame, G. M., & Rosendahl, J. (2020). Efficacy of group psychotherapy for anxiety disorders: A systematic review and meta-analysis. *Psychotherapy Research, 30*(8), 965–982. https://doi.org/10.1080/10503307.2020.1729440

Beck, J., & Sloan, D. (2021). Group treatments for PTSD. In M. Friedman, P. Schnurr, & T. Keane (Eds.), *Handbook of PTSD: Science & practice* (3rd ed., pp. 400–413). Guilford Press. https://psycnet.apa. org/record/2021-54181-022

Bion, W. R. (1969). *Experiences in groups: And other papers*. Routledge. https://www.routledge.com/ Experiences-in-Groups-and-Other-Papers/Bion/p/book/9780415040204

Blackie, L. E. R., Jayawickreme, E., Tsukayama, E., Forgeard, M. J. C., Roepke, A. M., & Fleeson, W. (2017). Post-traumatic growth as positive personality change: Developing a measure to assess within-person variability. *Journal of Research in Personality, 69*, 22–32. https://doi.org/10.1016/j. jrp.2016.04.001

Boals, A., & Schuler, K. (2017). Reducing reports of illusory posttraumatic growth: A revised version of the Stress-Related Growth Scale (SRGS-R). *Psychological Trauma: Theory, Research, Practice, and Policy, 10*(2), 190–198. https://doi.org/10.1037/tra0000267

Boulanger, G. (2011). *Wounded by reality: Understanding and treating adult onset trauma*. Routledge. https:// www.routledge.com/Wounded-By-Reality-Understanding-and-Treating-Adult-Onset-Trauma/ Boulanger/p/book/9781138005846

Bowlby, J. (1973). *Attachment and loss, vol. 2: Separation: Anxiety and anger*. Hogarth Press.

Bowlby, J. (1979). On knowing what you are not supposed to know and feeling what you are not supposed to feel. *Canadian Journal of Psychiatry, 24*, 403–408. https://psycnet.apa.org/record/ 1981-21404-001

Bowlby, J. (1988). *A secure base: Clinical applications of attachment theory*. Routledge. https://www. routledge.com/A-Secure-Base/Bowlby/p/book/9780415355278

Bowlby, J. (2019). *Trauma and loss: Key texts from the John Bowlby archive*. https://www.routledge. com/Trauma-and-Loss-Key-Texts-from-the-John-Bowlby-Archive/Duschinsky-White/p/book/ 9780367349998

Brewin, C. R., Andrews, B., & Valentine, J. F. (2000). Meta-analysis of risk factors for posttraumatic stress disorder in trauma-exposed adults. *Journal of Consulting and Clinical Psychology, 68*(5), 748–766. https://doi.org/10.1037/0022-006x.68.5.748

Bromberg, P. M. (1993). Shadow and substance: A relational perspective on clinical process. *Psychoanalytic Psychology, 10*(2), 147–168. https://doi.org/10.1037/h0079464

Brown, L., & Courtois, C. A. (2019). Trauma treatment: The need for ongoing innovation. *Practice Innovations, 4*(3), 133–138. https://doi.org/10.1037/pri0000097

Brown, L. S. (2010). *Feminist therapy*. American Psychological Association. https://www.apa.org/pubs/ books/4317192

Bruce, M. J., & Matsuo, H. (2022). "Burned into my brain:" Trauma anniversary reactions examined from a qualitative perspective. *Journal of Loss & Trauma, 27*(8), 717–730. https://doi.org/10.1080/1 5325024.2022.2079204

Buchele, B. J. (1995). Group psychotherapy for persons with multiple personality and dissociative disorders. In *Diagnosis and treatment of dissociative disorders: A multidisciplinary approach*. J. Aronson.

Buchele, B. J. (2000). Group psychotherapy for survivors of sexual and physical abuse. In R. H. Klein & V. L. Schermer (Eds.), *Group psychotherapy for psychological trauma* (pp.170–187). Guilford Press. https://psycnet.apa.org/record/2000-03901-007

Buchele, B. J. (2020). Immigration and implications for group work: Commentary on the works included in this special issue. *International Journal of Group Psychotherapy, 70*(2), 293–306. https://doi.org/10.1080/00207284.2020.1717881

Buchele, B., & Spitz, H. (Eds.). (2005). *Group interventions for psychological treatment of trauma*. American Group Psychotherapy Association.

Burlingame, G. M. (2022). The future of group therapy is bright! *International Journal of Group Psychotherapy*, 1–19. https://doi.org/10.1080/00207284.2022.2133717

Burlingame, G. M., McClendon, D. T., & Yang, C. (2018). Cohesion in group therapy: A meta-analysis. *Psychotherapy, 55*(4), 384–398. https://doi.org/10.1037/pst0000173

Burlingame, G. M., Seebeck, J. D., Janis, R. A., Whitcomb, K. E., Barkowski, S., Rosendahl, J., & Strauss, B. (2016). Outcome differences between individual and group formats when identical and nonidentical treatments, patients, and doses are compared: A 25-year meta-analytic perspective. *Psychotherapy, 53*(4), 446–461. https://doi.org/10.1037/pst0000090

Burlingame, G., & Strauss, B. (2021). Efficacy of small group treatments: Foundation for evidence-based practice. In M. Barkham, W. Lutz, & L. G. Castonguay (Eds.), *Bergin and Garfield's handbook of psychotherapy and behavior change: 50th anniversary edition* (pp. 583–624). John Wiley & Sons, Inc. https://psycnet.apa.org/record/2021-81510-017

Busch, F. N., Milrod, B., Chen, C. K., & Singer, M. B. (2021). *Trauma focused psychodynamic psychotherapy: A step-by-step treatment manual*. Oxford University Press. https://global.oup.com/academic/product/trauma-focused-psychodynamic-psychotherapy-9780197574355?cc=us&lang=en&

Bussières, A., Hancock, M. J., Elklit, A., Ferreira, M. L., Ferreira, P. H., Stone, L. S., Wideman, T. H., Boruff, J. T., Zoubi, F. A., Chaudhry, F., Tolentino, R., & Hartvigsen, J. (2023). Adverse childhood experience is associated with an increased risk of reporting chronic pain in adulthood: A stystematic review and meta-analysis. *European Journal of Psychotraumatology, 14*(2), 2284025. https://doi.org/10.1080/20008066.2023.2284025

Cassidy, J., & Shaver, P. (1999). *Handbook of attachment: Theory, research, and clinical applications*. Guilford Press. https://www.guilford.com/books/Handbook-of-Attachment/Cassidy-Shaver/9781462536641

Castillo, D. T., Chee, C. P., Nason, E. E., Keller, J. E., Baca, J. C., Qualls, C., Fallon, S., Haaland, K. Y., Miller, M. W., & Keane, T. M. (2016). Group-delivered cognitive/exposure therapy for PTSD in women veterans: A randomized controlled trial. *Psychological Trauma: Theory, Research, Practice, and Policy, 8*(3), 404–412. https://doi.org/10.1037/tra0000111

CDC. (2020). *Centers for disease control and prevention: Cases, data, and surveillance*. https://www.cdc.gov/coronavirus/2019-ncov/covid-data/investigations-discovery/hospitalization-death-by-race-ethnicity.html

Cloitre, M., Brewin, C. R., Bisson, J. I., Hyland, P., Karatzias, T., Lueger-Schuster, B., Maercker, A., Roberts, N. P., & Shevlin, M. (2020). Evidence for the coherence and integrity of the complex PTSD (CPTSD) diagnosis: Response to Achterhof et al. (2019) and Ford (2020). *European Journal of Psychotraumatology, 11*(1). https://doi.org/10.1080/20008198.2020.1739873

Cloitre, M., & Koenen, K. C. (2001). The impact of borderline personality disorder on process group outcome among women with posttraumatic stress disorder related to childhood abuse. *International Journal of Group Psychotherapy, 51*(3), 379–398. https://doi.org/10.1521/ijgp.51.3.379.49886

Comas-Díaz, L. (2014). Multicultural psychotherapy. In F. T. L. Leong, L. Comas-Díaz, G. C. Nagayama Hall, V. C. McLoyd, & J. E. Trimble (Eds.), *APA handbook of multicultural psychology, vol. 2: Applications and training* (pp. 419–441). American Psychological Association. https://doi.org/10.1037/14187-024

Comas-Díaz, L., & Rivera, E. T. (2020). *Liberation psychology: Theory, method, practice, and social justice*. https://www.apa.org/pubs/books/liberation-psychology-sample-chapter.pdf

Courtois, C. A., & Brown, L. (2019). Guideline orthodoxy and resulting limitations of the American Psychological Association's clinical practice guideline for the treatment of PTSD in adults. *Psychotherapy, 56*(3), 329–339. https://doi.org/10.1037/pst0000239

Courtois, C. A., & Ford, J. D. (2015). *Treatment of complex trauma: A sequenced, relationship-based approach*. Guilford Publications. https://www.guilford.com/books/Treatment-of-Complex-Trauma/Courtois-Ford/9781462524600

Courtois, C. A., Norton-Ford, J. D., Herman, J. L., & Van Der Kolk, B. A. (2009). *Treating complex traumatic stress disorders: An evidence-based guide.* The Guilford Press EBooks. http://ci.nii.ac.jp/ncid/BA89147024

Crenshaw, W., K. (1989). *Demarginalizing the intersection of race and sex: A Black feminist critique of antidiscrimination doctrine, feminist theory and antiracist politics* (pp. 139–167). University of Chicago Legal Forum.

Dalal, F. (2001). The social unconscious: A post-Foulksean conception. *Group Analysis, 34,* 539–554. http://www.dalal.org.uk/The%20Social%20Unconscious-%20A%20Post-Foulkesian%20Perspective.pdf

DeAngelis, T. (2019). *Better relationships with patients lead to better outcomes: A good relationship is essential to helping the client connect with, remain in and get the most from therapy.* American Psychological Association. https://www.apa.org/monitor/2019/11/ce-corner-relationships

Department of Veterans Affairs & Department of Defense. (2017). *VA/DoD clinical practice guidelines for the management of posttraumatic stress.* Washington, DC: US Government Printing Office. https://www.healthquality.va.gov/guidelines/MH/ptsd/VADoDPTSDCPGFinal012418.pdf

Fairbairn, W. R. D. (1952). *Psychoanalytic studies of the personality.* Tavistock Publications Ltd.

Figley, C. R., Ellis, A. C., Reuther, B. T., & Gold, S. N. (2017). The study of trauma: A historical overview. *American Psychological Association eBooks,* 1–11. https://doi.org/10.1037/0000019-001

Fisher, S. F. (2014). *Neurofeedback in the treatment of developmental trauma: Calming the fear-driven brain.* Norton. https://psycnet.apa.org/record/2014-11428-000

Fonagy, P. (2015). The effectiveness of psychodynamic psychotherapies: An update. *World Psychiatry, 14*(2), 137–150. https://doi.org/10.1002/wps.20235

Fonagy, P., Luyten, P., Allison, E., & Campbell, C. (2017). What we have changed our minds about: Part 1. Borderline personality disorder as a limitation of resilience. *Borderline Personality Disorder and Emotion Dysregulation, 4,* 11. https://doi.org/10.1186/s40479-017-0061-9

Ford, J. D. (2021). Progress and limitations in the treatment of complex PTSD and developmental trauma disorder. *Current Treatment Options in Psychiatry, 8*(1), 1–17. https://doi.org/10.1007/s40501-020-00236-6

Ford, J. D., Grasso, D. J., Elhai, J. D., & Courtois, C. A. (2015). Social, cultural, and other diversity issues in the traumatic stress field. *Elsevier EBooks,* 503–546. https://doi.org/10.1016/b978-0-12-801288-8.00011-x

Fox, D., Prilleltensky, I., & Austin, S. (2009). *Critical psychology: An introduction.* SAGE. https://uk.sagepub.com/en-gb/eur/critical-psychology/book232372

Foy, D., Glynn, S., Schnurr, P., Jankowski, M., Wattenberg, M., Weiss, D., & Gusman, F. (2009). Group therapy. In E. Foa, T. Keane, & M. Friedman (Eds.), *Effective treatments for PTSD: Practice guidelines from the International Society for Traumatic Stress Studies* (2nd ed., pp. 155–175). Guilford Press. https://www.guilford.com/books/Effective-Treatments-for-PTSD/Forbes-Bisson-Monson-Berliner/9781462543564

Foy, D. W., Eriksson, C. B., & Trice, G. A. (2001). Introduction to group interventions for trauma survivors. *Group Dynamics: Theory, Research, and Practice, 5*(4), 246–251. https://doi.org/10.1037/1089-2699.5.4.246

Foy, D. W., Ruzek, J. I., Glynn, S. M., Riney, S. J., & Gusman, F. D. (2002). Trauma focus group therapy for combat-related PTSD: An update. *Journal of Clinical Psychology, 58*(8), 907–918. https://doi.org/10.1002/jclp.10066

Frazier, P. A., Coyne, J. C., & Tennen, H. (2014). Post-traumatic growth: A call for less, but better, research. *European Journal of Personality, 28*(4), 337–338. https://psycnet.apa.org/record/2014-33979-009

Freud, S. (1920). Beyond the pleasure principle. In *The Standard edition of the complete psychological works of Sigmund Freud, 18 (1920–1922)* (pp. 7–64). Hogarth. https://www.sas.upenn.edu/~cavitch/pdf-library/Freud_Beyond_P_P.pdf

Freud, S. (1953). *The standard edition of the complete psychological works of Sigmund Freud.* Hogarth Press.

Freyd, J. J. (1997). *Betrayal trauma: The logic of forgetting child abuse.* Harvard University Press. https://www.hup.harvard.edu/books/9780674068063

Freyd, J. J., DePrince, A. P., & Gleaves, D. (2007). The state of betrayal trauma theory: Reply to McNally (2007) – Conceptual issues and future directions. *Memory, 15,* 295–311. https://doi.org/10.1080/09658210701256514

Frías, Á., & Palma, C. (2015). Comorbidity between post-traumatic stress disorder and borderline personality disorder: A review. *Psychopathology, 48*(1), 1–10. https://doi.org/10.1159/000363145

Friedman, M. J., Schnurr, P. P., & Keane, T. M. (2021). *Handbook of PTSD: Science and practice* (3rd ed.). Guilford Press. https://www.guilford.com/books/Handbook-of-PTSD/Friedman-Schnurr-Keane/9781462553785/new-to-edition

Ganzarain, R., & Buchele, B. (1988). *Fugitives of incest: A perspective from psychoanalysis and groups*. International Universities Press.

Gaskin, C. (2012). The effectiveness of psychodynamic psychotherapy: A systematic review of recent international and Australian research. *Psychotherapy and Counselling Journal of Australia*. https://www1.health.gov.au/internet/main/publishing.nsf/Content/phi-natural-therapies-submissions-containerpage/$file/PACFA%20Psychodynamic%20Psychotherapy%20Lit%20Review.pdf

Gelso, C. J., Kivlighan, D. M., & Markin, R. D. (2018). The real relationship and its role in psychotherapy outcome: A meta-analysis. *Psychotherapy, 55*(4), 434–444. https://doi.org/10.1037/pst0000183

Greene, L. R. (2021). The research-practice psychotherapy wars: The case of group psychotherapy in the treatment of PTSD. *International Journal of Group Psychotherapy, 71*(3), 393–423. https://doi.org/10.1080/00207284.2021.1890088

Grimes, J. S., & Kivlighan, D. M. (2021). Whose multicultural orientation matters most? Examining additive and compensatory effects of the group's and leader's multicultural orientation in group therapy. *Group Dynamics: Theory, Research, and Practice, 26*(1), 58–70. https://doi.org/10.1037/gdn0000153

Harned, M. S. (2013). Treatment of posttraumatic stress disorder and comorbid borderline personality disorder. In E. Storch & D. McKay (Eds.), *Handbook of treating variants and complications in anxiety disorders*. Springer. https://doi.org/10.1007/978-1-4614-6458-7_14

Hegeman, E., & Wohl, A. (2000). Management of trauma-related affect, defenses and dissociative states. In R. H. Klein & V. L. Schermer (Eds.), *Group psychotherapy for psychological trauma* (pp. 64–88). Guilford Press. https://psycnet.apa.org/record/2000-03901-000

Henning, J. A., & Brand, B. L. (2019). Implications of the American Psychological Association's posttraumatic stress disorder treatment guideline for trauma education and training. *Psychotherapy, 56*(3), 422–430. https://doi.org/10.1037/pst0000237

Herman, J. L. (1997, 2015). *Trauma and recovery: The aftermath of violence – From domestic abuse to political terror*. Basic Books. https://www.hachettebookgroup.com/titles/judith-lewis-herman-md/trauma-and-recovery/9780465098736/?lens=basic-books

Herman, J. L., Kallivayalil, D., & Program, A. M. O. T. V. O. V. (2018). *Group trauma treatment in early recovery: Promoting safety and self-care* (1st ed.). The Guilford Press. https://www.guilford.com/books/Group-Trauma-Treatment-in-Early-Recovery/Herman-Kallivayalil-Program/9781462537440

Holmes, J. (2014). *John Bowlby and attachment theory*. Routledge. https://www.routledge.com/John-Bowlby-and-Attachment-Theory/Holmes-Holmes/p/book/9780415629034

Hopper, E. (2003). *Traumatic experience in the unconscious life of groups: The fourth basic assumption: Incohesion: Aggregation/massification or (ba) I:A/M*. Jessica Kingsley Publishers. https://us.jkp.com/products/traumatic-experience-in-the-unconscious-life-of-groups

Howell, E. F., & Itzkowitz, S. (2016). *The dissociative mind in psychoanalysis: Understanding and working with trauma*. Routledge. https://www.routledge.com/The-Dissociative-Mind-in-Psychoanalysis-Understanding-and-Working-With-Trauma/Howell-Itzkowitz/p/book/9780415736015

Infurna, F. J., & Jayawickreme, E. (2019). Fixing the growth illusion: New directions for research in resilience and posttraumatic growth. *Current Directions in Psychological Science, 28*(2), 152–158. https://doi.org/10.1177/0963721419827017

International Society for Traumatic Stress Studies (ISTSS). (2019). *International practice guidelines*. https://istss.org/clinical-resources/treating-trauma/international-practice-guidelines-for-post-trauma

Jackson, C., Weiss, B., & Cloitre, M. (2019). STAIR group treatment for veterans with PTSD: Efficacy and impact of gender on outcome. *Military Medicine, 184*(1–2), e143–e147. https://doi.org/10.1093/milmed/usy164

Kaklauskas, F. J., & Olson, E. A. (2020). The ethical group psychotherapist. In F. J. Kaklauskas & L. R. Greene (Eds.), *Core principles of group psychotherapy: An integrated theory, research, and practice training manual*. Routledge. https://www.taylorfrancis.com/books/edit/10.4324/9780429260803/core-principles-group-psychotherapy-francis-kaklauskas-les-greene-marsha-block-angela-stephens

Karatzias, T., Shevlin, M., Fyvie, C., Grandison, G., Garozi, M., Latham, E., Sinclair, M., Wing Ka Ho, G., McAnee, G., Ford, J. D., & Hyland, P. (2020). Adverse and benevolent childhood experiences in Posttraumatic Stress Disorder (PTSD) and Complex PTSD (CPTSD): Implications for trauma-focused therapies. *European Journal of Psychotraumatology, 11*(1). https://doi.org/10.1080/20008198.2020.1793599

Kealy, D., Ogrodniczuk, J. S., Piper, W. E., & Sierra-Hernandez, C. A. (2016). When it is not a good fit: Clinical errors in patient selection and group composition in group psychotherapy. *Psychotherapy, 53*(3), 308–313. https://doi.org/10.1037/pst0000069

Kelly, L. A. (2020). Burnout, compassion fatigue, and secondary trauma in nurses. *Critical Care Nursing Quarterly, 43*(1), 73–80. https://doi.org/10.1097/cnq.0000000000000293

Kivlighan, D. M., Swancy, A. G., Smith, E., & Brennaman, C. (2021). Examining racial microaggressions in group therapy and the buffering role of members' perceptions of their group's multicultural orientation. *Journal of Counseling Psychology, 68*(5), 621–628. https://doi.org/10.1037/cou0000531

Klein, R. (2020). Introduction to the special issue on migration problems in the US and their implications for group work. *International Journal of Group Psychotherapy, 70*(2), 141–161. https://doi.org/10.1080/00207284.2020.1718503

Klein, R., Leiderman, L., Phillips, S., & Rene, R. (2023). *Violence, systemic racism and trauma in America: The impact on groups and communities.* AGPA Connect 2023.

Klein, R., & Phillips, S. (Eds.). (2008). *Public mental health service delivery protocols: Group interventions for disaster preparedness and response.* American Group Psychotherapy Association.

Klein, R., & Schermer, V. L. (2000). *Group psychotherapy for psychological trauma.* Guilford Press. https://psycnet.apa.org/record/2000-03901-000

Klein, R. H., & Schermer, V. L. (2018). *Violence in America: Group therapists reflect on causes and solutions.* Routledge. https://www.routledge.com/Violence-in-America-Group-therapists-reflect-on-causes-and-solutions/Klein-Schermer/p/book/9780367077037

Koller, P., Marmar, C. R., & Kanas, N. (1992). Psychodynamic group treatment of posttraumatic stress disorder in Vietnam veterans. *International Journal of Group Psychotherapy, 42*(2), 225–246. https://doi.org/10.1080/00207284.1992.11490687

Kudler, H. (2019). Clinical practice guidelines for posttraumatic stress disorder: Are they still clinical? *Psychotherapy, 56*(3), 383–390. https://doi.org/10.1037/pst0000236

Lamp, K., Avallone, K. M., Maieritsch, K. P., Buchholz, K. R., & Rauch, S. A. (2019). Individual and group cognitive processing therapy: Effectiveness across two Veterans Affairs posttraumatic stress disorder treatment clinics. *Psychological Trauma: Theory, Research, Practice, and Policy, 11*(2), 197–206. https://doi.org/10.1037/tra0000370

Lanius, R. A., Terpou, B. A., & McKinnon, M. C. (2020). The sense of self in the aftermath of trauma: Lessons from the default mode network in posttraumatic stress disorder. *European Journal of Psychotraumatology, 11*(1). https://doi.org/10.1080/20008198.2020.1807703

Leiderman, L. (2020). Psychodynamic group therapy with hispanic migrants: Interpersonal, relational constructs in treating complex trauma, dissociation, and enactments. *International Journal of Group Psychotherapy, 70*(2), 162–182. Taylor & Francis. https://doi.org/10.1080/00207284.2019.1686704

Leiderman, L. (2023). *An integrative system-oriented interpersonal/relational group therapy approach in understanding and addressing mass trauma, dissociation and enactments in small psychotherapy groups.* AGPA Connect 2023.

Leiderman, L., & Klein, R. (2021). An integrative systems-oriented interpersonal/relational group approach to understanding and treating mass trauma, dissociation and enactments during the COVID-19 pandemic. *International Journal of Group Psychotherapy,* 1–30. https://doi.org/10.1080/00207284.2021.1991234

Leiderman, L. M., & Smith, M. L. (2017). Neuroimaging measures to assess the effectiveness of a two-day marathon group of individuals with early developmental trauma: A pilot study. *International Journal of Group Psychotherapy, 67*(1), 91–107. https://doi.org/10.1080/00207284.2016.1203568

Leszcz, M. (2023a). *Promoting our colleagues' well-being: Group work during the pandemic with healthcare providers.* AGPA Connect 2023.

Leszcz, M. (2023b). The ethics of group psychotherapy: Principles and practical strategies. *International Journal of Group Psychotherapy, 73*(2), 166–173. https://doi.org/10.1080/00207284.2022.2155001

Levi, O., Shoval-Zuckerman, Y., Fruchter, E., Bibi, A., Bar-Haim, Y., & Wald, I. (2017). Benefits of a psychodynamic group therapy (PGT) model for treating veterans with PTSD. *Journal of Clinical Psychology, 73*(10), 1247–1258. https://doi.org/10.1002/jclp.22443

Levine, P. A. (1997). *Waking the tiger: Healing trauma. The innate capacity to transform overwhelming experiences.* North Atlantic Books. https://www.northatlanticbooks.com/shop/waking-the-tiger-healing-trauma/

Levine, S. Z., Laufer, A., Stein, E., Hamama-Raz, Y., & Solomon, Z. (2009). Examining the relationship between resilience and posttraumatic growth. *Journal of Traumatic Stress, 22*(4), 282–286. https://doi.org/10.1002/jts.20409

Lewin, K. (1975). *Field theory in social science: Selected theoretical papers.* Greenwood Publishing Group.

Lewis, C. C., Boyd, M., Puspitasari, A., Navarro, E., Howard, J., Kassab, H., Hoffman, M., Scott, K., Lyon, A., Douglas, S., Simon, G., & Kroenke, K. (2019). Implementing measurement-based care in behavioral health: A review. *JAMA Psychiatry, 76*(3), 324–335. https://doi.org/10.1001/jamapsychiatry.2018.3329

Liotti, G. (2006). A model of dissociation based on attachment theory and research. *Journal of Trauma & Dissociation, 7*(4), 55–73. https://doi.org/10.1300/J229v07n04_04

Litwack, S. D., Beck, J. G., & Sloan, D. M. (2022). Group treatment for trauma-related psychological disorders. In *Evidence based treatments for trauma-related psychological disorders* (pp. 499–516). https://doi.org/10.1007/978-3-030-97802-0_24

MacNair-Semands, R., & Whittingham, M. (2023). *Group psychotherapy assessment and practice: A measurement-based care approach*. Routledge. https://doi.org/10.4324/9781003255482

Mahoney, A., Karatzias, T., & Hutton, P. (2019). A systematic review and meta-analysis of group treatments for adults with symptoms associated with complex post-traumatic stress disorder. *Journal of Affective Disorders, 243*, 305–321. https://doi.org/10.1016/j.jad.2018.09.059

Marusak, H. A., Etkin, A., & Thomason, M. E. (2015). Disrupted insula-based neural circuit organization and conflict interference in trauma-exposed youth. *NeuroImage: Clinical, 8*, 516–525. https://doi.org/10.1016/j.nicl.2015.04.007

McNally, R. J. (2012). The ontology of posttraumatic stress disorder: Natural kind, social construction, or causal system? *Clinical Psychology: Science and Practice, 19*(3), 220–228. https://doi.org/10.1111/cpsp.12001

McNally, R. J. (2016). The expanding empire of psychopathology: The case of PTSD. *Psychological Inquiry, 27*(1), 46–49. https://doi.org/10.1080/1047840X.2016.1108168

McNally, R. J. (2018). Posttraumatic stress disorder as a growth industry: Comment on Asmundson and Asmundson (2018). *Journal of Anxiety Disorders, 56*, 14–16. https://doi.org/10.1016/j.janxdis.2018.03.008

Mendelsohn, M., Herman, J. L., Schatzow, E., Coco, M., Kallivayalil, D., & Levitan, J. (2011). *The trauma recovery group: A guide for practitioners* (1st ed.). The Guilford Press. https://www.guilford.com/books/The-Trauma-Recovery-Group/Mendelsohn-Herman-Schatzow-Coco/9781609180577

Miles, J. R., Anders, C., Kivlighan, D. M., III, & Belcher Platt, A. A. (2021). Cultural ruptures: Addressing microaggressions in group therapy. *Group Dynamics: Theory, Research, and Practice, 25*(1), 74–88. https://doi.org/10.1037/gdn0000149

Miller, E. D. (2020). The COVID-19 pandemic crisis: The loss and trauma event of our time. *Journal of Loss & Trauma, 25*(6–7), 560–572. https://doi.org/10.1080/15325024.2020.1759217

National Institute for Health and Care Excellence (NICE). (2018). *Guideline for post-traumatic stress disorder*. National Institute for Health and Clincial Practice. https://www.nice.org.uk/guidance/ng116

Nemeth, D. G., Kuriansky, J., Reeder, K., Lewis, A., Marceaux, K., Whittington, T., Olivier, T. W., May, N. E., & Safier, J. A. (2012). Addressing anniversary reactions of trauma through group process: The Hurricane Katrina anniversary wellness workshops. *International Journal of Group Psychotherapy, 62*(1), 129–142. https://doi.org/10.1521/ijgp.2012.62.1.129

Neria, Y., DiGrande, L., & Adams, B. (2011). Posttraumatic stress disorder following the September 11, 2001, terrorist attacks: A review of the literature among highly exposed populations. *American Psychologist, 66*(6), 429–446. https://doi.org/10.1037/a0024791

Norcross, J. C., & Wampold, B. E. (2019a). *Psychotherapy relationships that work: Volume 2: Evidence-based therapist responsiveness* (Vol. 2). Oxford University Press. https://global.oup.com/academic/product/psychotherapy-relationships-that-work-9780190843960?cc=us&lang=en&

Norcross, J. C., & Wampold, B. E. (2019b). Relationships and responsiveness in the psychological treatment of trauma: The tragedy of the APA Clinical Practice Guideline. *Psychotherapy, 56*(3), 391–399. https://doi.org/10.1037/pst0000228

North, C. S., Surís, A. M., Smith, R. P., & King, R. V. (2016). The evolution of PTSD criteria across editions of DSM. *Annals of Clinical Psychiatry, 28*, 197–208. https://pubmed.ncbi.nlm.nih.gov/27490836/

O'Dowd, M. F. (2020). Explainer: What is systemic racism and institutional racism? *The Conversation*. https://theconversation.com/explainer-what-is-systemic-racism-and-institutional-racism-131152

Ogden, P., & Minton, K. (2000). Sensorimotor psychotherapy: One method for processing traumatic memory. *Traumatology, 6*(3), 149–173. https://doi.org/10.1177/153476560000600302

Ogle, C. M., Rubin, D. T., & Siegler, I. C. (2015). The relation between insecure attachment and posttraumatic stress: Early life versus adulthood traumas. *Psychological Trauma: Theory, Research, Practice, and Policy, 7*(4), 324–332. https://doi.org/10.1037/tra0000015

Oslin, D. W., Hoff, R., Mignogna, J., & Resnick, S. G. (2019). Provider attitudes and experience with measurement-based mental health care in the VA implementation project. *Psychiatric Services, 70*(2), 135–138. https://doi.org/10.1176/appi.ps.201800228

Owen, J. (2013). Early career perspectives on psychotherapy research and practice: Psychotherapist effects, multicultural orientation, and couple interventions. *Psychotherapy, 50*(4), 496–502. https://doi.org/10.1037/a0034617

Pearlman, L. A., & Saakvitne, K. W. (1995). *Trauma and the therapist: Countertransference and vicarious traumatization in psychotherapy with incest survivors*. W W Norton & Company Incorporated. https://www.tandfonline.com/doi/abs/10.1080/00029157.1996.10403354

Perlitz, D. (2019). The implicit analyst: Qualities of salience. *Psychoanalysis, Self and Context, 14*, 428–444. https://doi.org/10.1080/24720038.2019.1596272

Peterson, J., & Densley, J. (2021). *The violence project: How to stop a mass shooting epidemic*. Abrams Press. https://www.theviolenceproject.org/about-us/our-book/

Phillips, S. (2023). *The trajectory of the school shooter: From exclusion to humiliate ion to gun violence*. AGPA Connect 2023.

Pieterse, A., Todd, N., Neville, H., & Carter, R. (2011). Perceived racism and mental health among black American adults a meta-analytic review. *Journal of Counseling Psychology, 59*, 1–9. https://psycnet.apa.org/record/2011-25743-001

Putnam, F. W. (1992). Discussion: Are alter personalities fragments or figments? *Psychoanalytic Inquiry, 12*, 95–111. https://www.taylorfrancis.com/chapters/edit/10.4324/9781315803234-5/discussion-frank-putnam

Raque-Bogdan, T. L., Mitchell, A., Coleman, M. N., Coleman, J. T. H., & Owen, J. (2021). Addressing racial equity in health psychology research: An application of the multicultural orientation framework. *American Psychologist, 76*(8), 1266–1279. https://doi.org/10.1037/amp0000888

Reik, T. (1936). *Surprise and the psycho-analyst*. Kegan Paul. https://psycnet.apa.org/record/1937-02275-000

Rene, R. (2023). *When healthcare becomes traumatic: A closer look at addressing healthcare inequities*. AGPA Connect 2023.

Resick, P. A., Suvak, M. K., Johnides, B. D., Mitchell, K. S., & Iverson, K. M. (2012). The impact of dissociation on PTSD treatment with cognitive processing therapy. *Depression & Anxiety, 29*, 718–730. https://doi.org/10.1002/da.21938

Resnick, S. G., & Hoff, R. A. (2020). Observations from the national implementation of measurement based care in Mental Health in the Department of Veterans Affairs. *Psychological Services, 17*(3), 238–246. https://doi.org/10.1037/ser0000351

Roberts, N. P., Roberts, P. A., Jones, N., & Bisson, J. I. (2015). Psychological interventions for post-traumatic stress disorder and comorbid substance use disorder: A systematic review and meta-analysis. *Clinical Psychology Review, 38*, 25–38. https://doi.org/10.1016/j.cpr.2015.02.007

Rubin, T. I. (1975). *Compassion and self-hate*. Simon and Schuster. https://www.simonandschuster.com/books/Compassion-and-Self-Hate/Theodore-I-Rubin/9780684841991

Ruzek, J. I., Yalch, M. M., & Burkman, K. M. (2023). *Group approaches to treating traumatic stress: A clinical handbook*. Guilford Press. https://www.guilford.com/books/Group-Approaches-to-Treating-Traumatic-Stress/Ruzek-Yalch-Burkman/9781462553297

Sachsse, U., Vogel, C., & Leichsenring, F. (2006). Results of psychodynamically oriented trauma-focused inpatient treatment for women with complex posttraumatic stress disorder (PTSD) and borderline personality disorder (BPD). *Bulletin of the Menninger Clinic, 70*(2), 125–144. https://doi.org/10.1521/bumc.2006.70.2.125

Schein, E. H., & Bennis, W. G. (1965). *Personal and organizational change through group methods: The laboratory approach*. Wiley.

Schermer, V. L. (2005). Identification and management of masked trauma reactions in groups. In B. Buchele & H. Spitz (Eds.), *Group interventions for treatment of psychological trauma* (pp. 250–286). American Group Psychotherapy Association.

Schnyder, U., & Cloitre, M. (2022). *Evidence based treatments for trauma-related psychological disorders: A practical guide for clinicians* (2nd ed.). Springer. https://link.springer.com/book/10.1007/978-3-030-97802-0

Schore, A. (2003a [1994]). *Affect dysregulation and disorders of the self*. Norton. https://wwnorton.com/books/9780393704068

Schore, A. N. (2003b). Early relational trauma, disorganized attachment, and the development of a predisposition to violence. In M. F. Solomon & D. J. Siegel (Eds.), *Healing trauma attachment, mind, body, and brain* (pp. 107–167). W.W. Norton & Company. https://wwnorton.com/books/9780393703962

Schottenbauer, M. A., Glass, C. R., Arnkoff, D. B., & Gray, S. H. (2008). Contributions of psychodynamic approaches to treatment of PTSD and trauma: A review of the empirical treatment and psychopathology literature. *Psychiatry: Interpersonal and Biological Processes, 71*(1), 13–34. https://doi.org/10.1521/psyc.2008.71.1.13

Schwartze, D., Barkowski, S., Strauss, B., Knaevelsrud, C., & Rosendahl, J. (2019). Efficacy of group psychotherapy for posttraumatic stress disorder: Systematic review and meta-analysis of randomized controlled trials. *Psychotherapy Research*, *29*(4), 415–431. https://doi.org/10.1080/10503307.2017.1405168

Shedler, J. (2010). The efficacy of psychodynamic psychotherapy. *American Psychologist*, *65*(2), 98–109. https://doi.org/10.1037/a0018378

Simon, N., Roberts, N. P., Lewis, C. E., Gelderen, M. J. V., & Bisson, J. I. (2019). Associations between perceived social support, posttraumatic stress disorder (PTSD) and complex PTSD (CPTSD): Implications for treatment. *European Journal of Psychotraumatology*, *10*(1). https://doi.org/10.1080/20008198.2019.1573129

Sippel, L. M., Pietrzak, R. H., Charney, D. S., Mayes, L. C., & Southwick, S. M. (2015). How does social support enhance resilience in the trauma-exposed individual? *Ecology and Society*, *20*(4). https://doi.org/10.5751/es-07832-200410

Sloan, D. M., Feinstein, B. A., Gallagher, M. W., Beck, J. G., & Keane, T. M. (2013). Efficacy of group treatment for posttraumatic stress disorder symptoms: A meta-analysis. *Psychological Trauma: Theory, Research, Practice, and Policy*, *5*(2), 176–183. https://doi.org/10.1037/a0026291

Spermon, D., Darlington, Y., & Gibney, P. (2010). Psychodynamic psychotherapy for complex trauma: Targets, focus, applications, and outcomes. *Psychology Research and Behavior Management*, 119. https://doi.org/10.2147/prbm.s10215

Spotnitz, H. (1961). The narcissistic defense in schizophrenia. *Psychoanalysis and the Psychoanalytic Review*, *48*(4), 24–42.

Spotnitz, H. (1985). Discovering new truths: How to channel destructivity. *Modern Psychoanalysis*, *10*(1), 5–12. https://psycnet.apa.org/record/1986-22435-001

Sroufe, L. A. (2005). Attachment and development: A prospective, longitudinal study from birth to adulthood. *Attachment & Human Development*, *7*(4), 349–367. https://pubmed.ncbi.nlm.nih.gov/16332580/

Sroufe, L. A., Egeland, B., Carlson, E., Collins, W. A., Grossmann, K. E., Grossmann, K., & Waters, E. (2005). Placing early attachment experiences in developmental context. In *Attachment from infancy to adulthood: The major longitudinal studies* (pp. 48–70). Guilford Publications. https://psycnet.apa.org/record/2005-08055-003

Tao, K. W., Owen, J., Pace, B. P., & Imel, Z. E. (2015). A meta-analysis of multicultural competencies and psychotherapy process and outcome. *Journal of Counseling Psychology*, *62*(3), 337–350. https://doi.org/10.1037/cou0000086

Tedeschi, R. G., & Calhoun, L. (2004). Posttraumatic growth: A new perspective on psychotraumatology. *Psychiatric Times*, *21*(4). https://www.psychiatrictimes.com/view/posttraumatic-growth-new-perspective-psychotraumatology

Thomas, R. B., & Wilson, J. (2004). Issues and controversies in the understanding and diagnosis of compassion fatigue, vicarious traumatization, and secondary traumatic stress disorder. *International Journal of Emergency Mental Health*, *6*(2), 81–92. https://pubmed.ncbi.nlm.nih.gov/15298079/

Thompson, C. W. (2021, January 25). *Fatal police shootings of unarmed black people reveal troubling patterns*. NPR. https://www.npr.org/2021/01/25/956177021/fatal-police-shootings-of-unarmed-black-people-reveal-troubling-patterns

Van Der Kolk, B., McFarlane, A., & Weisaeth, L. (1996). *Traumatic stress*. Guilford. https://www.guilford.com/books/Traumatic-Stress/Kolk-McFarlane-Weisaeth/9781572304574

Van Der Kolk, B. A. (2015). *The body keeps the score: Brain, mind, and body in the healing of trauma*. Penguin Books. https://www.penguinrandomhouse.com/books/313183/the-body-keeps-the-score-by-bessel-van-der-kolk-md/

Volkan, V. (1999). The tree model: A comprehensive psychopolitical approach to unofficial diplomacy and the reduction of ethnic tension. *Mind and Human Interaction*, *10*, 142–206.

Volkan, V. D. (2001). Transgenerational transmissions and chosen traumas: An aspect of large-group identity. *Group Analysis*, *34*(1), 79–97. https://doi.org/10.1177/05333160122077730

Volkan, V. D. (2021). Trauma, prejudice, large-group identity and psychoanalysis. *American Journal of Psychoanalysis*, *81*(2), 137–154. https://doi.org/10.1057/s11231-021-09285-z

von Bertalanffy, L. (1968). *General system theory: Foundations, development, applications*. Braziller.

Walker, L. E. (1984). *The battered woman syndrome*. Springer Publishing Company. https://www.springerpub.com/the-battered-woman-syndrome-9780826170989.html

Walsh, F. (2007). Traumatic loss and major disasters: Strengthening family and community resilience. *Family Process, 46*(2), 207–227. https://doi.org/10.1111/j.1545-5300.2007.00205.x

Watson, J. C., & Wiseman, H. (2021). *The responsive psychotherapist: Attuning to clients in the moment.* American Psychological Association. https://www.apa.org/pubs/books/the-responsive-psychotherapist

Wattenberg, M. S., Gross, D. L., & Niles, B. L. (2021). *Present-centered group therapy for PTSD: Embracing today.* Routledge. https://www.routledge.com/Present-Centered-Group-Therapy-for-PTSD-Embracing-Today/Wattenberg-Gross-Niles-Unger-Shea/p/book/9780367338831

Weinberg, H. (2007). So what is this social unconscious anyway? *Group Analysis, 40*(3), 307–322. https://doi.org/10.1177/0533316407076114

Weinberg, H., Nuttman-Shwartz, O., & Gilmore, M. (2005). Trauma groups: An overview. *Group Analysis, 38*(2), 187–202. https://doi.org/10.1177/0533316405052378

Whittingham, M., Marmarosh, C. L., Mallow, P., & Scherer, M. (2023). Mental health care equity and access: A group therapy solution. *American Psychologist, 78*(2), 119–133. https://doi.org/10.1037/amp0001078

Wilkerson, I. (2020). *Caste: The origins of our discontents.* Random House.

World Health Organization. (2018). *International statistical classification of diseases and related health problems* (11th revision). https://icd.who.int/browsw11/l-m/en

Yalch, M. M., Moreland, M. L., & Burkman, K. M. (2022). Integrating process and structure in group therapy for survivors of trauma. *European Journal of Trauma & Dissociation, 6*(3). https://doi.org/10.1016/j.ejtd.2022.100272

Yalom, I. D. (1970). *The theory and practice of group psychotherapy.* Basic Books. https://psycnet.apa.org/record/1970-12728-000

Yalom, I. D., & Leszcz, M. (2020). *The theory and practice of group psychotherapy.* Hachette UK. https://www.hachettebookgroup.com/titles/irvin-d-yalom/the-theory-and-practice-of-group-psychotherapy/9781541617568/?lens=basic-books

Yehuda, R., & Lehrner, A. (2018). Intergenerational transmission of trauma effects: Putative role of epigenetic mechanisms. *World Psychiatry, 17*(3), 243–257. https://doi.org/10.1002/wps.20568

Ziegler, M., & McEvoy, M. (2000). Hazardous terrain: Countertransference reactions in trauma groups. In R. H. Klein & V. L. Schermer (Eds.), *Group psychotherapy for psychological trauma* (pp. 116–140). Guilford Press. https://psycnet.apa.org/record/2000-03901-000

Zorzella, K. P., Muller, R. T., & Classen, C. C. (2015). Trauma group therapy: The role of attachment and therapeutic alliance. *International Journal of Group Psychotherapy, 64*(1), 24–47. https://doi.org/10.1521/ijgp.2014.64.1.24

Section I

The Neurophysiological Correlates of Trauma

2 The Fear-Driven Brain

An Integrated Interpersonal/Relational
Neurophysiological Model to Foster
Co-regulation and Synchrony in Trauma
Psychotherapy Groups

Leonardo M. Leiderman

Fear, possibly the most common feature found in group members with a history of trauma, encompasses the fear of being shamed, being abandoned, being humiliated, being harmed, and/or re-experiencing painful feelings. The original trauma occurred under unsafe, fear-inducing conditions and is often associated with being alone and not adequately shielded from harm. The cumulative impact of repeated chaotic, harmful parenting, overwhelming the brain's fear networks (to be discussed later in this chapter), while being alone, leads to ingrained, lifelong difficulties autoregulating and co-regulating trauma symptoms. As Kearney and Lanius point out, "an inability to seek co-regulation from another or engage neural circuitry related to self-regulatory mechanisms due to a history of insecure attachment and somatic sensory disintegration results in persisting trauma-related symptoms" (2022).

Fear can also contribute to long-term patterns of avoidance, isolation, difficulties trusting others, and lack of intersubjective relatedness. The symptoms of posttraumatic stress disorder (PTSD) and complex posttraumatic stress disorder (CPTSD) are responses to the fearful perceptions of threat (real or otherwise) causing the brain to react with physiological arousal, dysregulation, impulsivity, a diminished sense of agency, an altered sense of time, and social difficulties or isolation (American Psychiatric Association [APA], 2013; Cox et al., 2014), and feelings of terror and/or a threat to one's life, flashbacks or dissociative re-experiencing, hypervigilance, increased startle responses, behavioral avoidance of potential triggers, and pervasive negative cognitions (American Psychiatric Association [APA], 2013).

Utilization of neuroscientific findings to understand the fear-driven brain can broaden group psychotherapy trauma theory and provide additional empirically driven research on the efficacy of group psychotherapy in the treatment of trauma. A neurophysiologically informed treatment can ultimately offer group therapists more tools to effectively address the multiple fear-driven *neuro-emotional-physiological* trauma-associated challenges that frequently emerge in psychotherapy groups, as well as co-regulating interventions to promote the emotional, motivational learning needed for change to occur.

In this chapter, I will provide a basic understanding of attachment trauma and dissociation, a neurophysiological understanding of trauma symptoms often displayed by group members with PTSD and CPTSD, and the brain structures and networks impacted by trauma. I will then propose an integrated, interpersonal/relational neurophysiological trauma group psychotherapy model to foster co-regulation, coupling synchrony, and intersubjective relating. This model can also address group members' fear-based trauma symptoms, especially during dissociative enactments, incorporating advances in neuropsychoanalysis and interpersonal neuroscience, by utilizing the intersubjective "relational unconscious" of the right hemisphere among and between group members and leader to safely process emotionally painful feelings. The model emphasizes the "experience-near" leader, necessary to enhance safety and connectedness, restore hope, promote interpersonal learning, and encourage potential growth.

DOI: 10.4324/9781003546252-3

Attachment Trauma and Dissociation

Bowlby (1973) proposed that humans are born with a neurological system geared toward seeking proximity to a nurturing, emotionally attuned, and safe caretaker (Mikulincer et al., 2015; Schore, 2003). Ideally, this infant–maternal bond fosters soothing sensory input, co-regulation with the mother, and the development of autoregulation in the young child (Ciaunica et al., 2021). Positive attachment experiences between the infant and mother play a critical role in the establishment and maintenance of the limbic system (which is vital for the management of affective behaviors) (Ziabreva et al., 2003), cortical areas of the developing right cerebral hemisphere (which is responsible for emotional regulation, as well as intersubjective, intuitive, empathic, and creative abilities) (Henry, 1993; Schore, 1994, 2005; Siegel, 1999), healthy brain stem–level development (facilitating optimal mood, motivation, and motor activity), and multisensory integration, leading to optimal somatic sensory functioning – embodiment, motor planning, agency, abstract thought, and emotional regulation (Kearney & Lanius, 2022).

Bowlby (1969) and Trevarthen (1993) proposed that attachment patterns are fortified by facial, vocal, and posturing-attuned nonverbal communications with the mother, which enhance positive feelings and security in the infant. Wass et al. (2019) noted that nurturing parents mirror and foster the infant's autonomic activities through affective state matching. "Secure attachment is the primary defense against trauma- induced psychopathology" (Schore, 2009b, p. 110).

The primary caretaker is not always attuned to the emotional and physiological needs of the infant. A major construct of attachment theory is the importance of the *intersubjective repair*, carried out by the caretaker in a timely, sensitive, and attuned manner. This repair by the caretaker leads to the infant internalizing self-regulation after being exposed to a nega-tively charged emotional arousal state and intersubjective exchange (Schore, 1994/2016, 2022). In this manner, the infant feels soothed, emotionally seen, and cared for in the adap-tive repair after a temporary severing in infant–primary caretaker attachment.

Disorganized and insecure attachment, neglect, and abuse are linked to the risk for psychiatric disorders and trauma-related disorders (Besser & Neria, 2012; Main, 1996; Mikulincer et al., 2015; Ogle et al., 2015; Roche et al., 1999; Woodhouse et al., 2015) and have been specifically implicated in the etiology of dissociation (Chefetz, 2004; Liotti, 2004; Schore, 1997) and dissociative symptoms in adulthood (Lyons-Ruth et al., 2006; Ogawa et al., 1997; Schore, 2003). Emotional abuse or neglect by a caretaker is most predictive of dissociation (Sar et al., 2009).

The most significant consequence of disorganized, insecure attachment and early rela-tional trauma with the caregiver is the child's subsequent inability to develop the capacity for emotional self-regulation (Toth & Cicchetti, 1998); the child (and eventual adult) can-not adequately regulate affective intensity and duration (Van der Kolk & Fisler, 1994). Early trauma alters the cortex's physiological and emotional development, stunting its trajectory and creating a predisposition for later psychopathology and chronic dissociation.

What is important to note here is that Schore (2022) recently conveyed how modern attachment theory emphasizes the maternal–infant intersubjective role in the development of the early unconscious, preverbal right hemisphere, thus explicating primitive emotional attachment dynamics.

Overactivated, Underactivated Fear Responses

Hyperarousal is the infant's primary response to heightened stress (Schore, 2009b). Perry et al. (1995) found that chronic stress stimulates the sympathetic nervous system to secrete corticotropin-releasing factor (the brain's major stress hormone) and leads to infant *fear-terror* reactions. Adrenaline, noradrenaline, and dopamine levels dramatically elevate in the developing brain, causing long-lasting patterns of hyperarousal when the infant perceives its environment to be unsafe.

Both hyper- and hypo-arousal are common phenomena in traumatized individuals (Kearney & Lanius, 2022). Trauma has long been correlated with sensory modulation difficulties, manifested as either overactivated/hyperarousal/hyper-responsivity or underactivated/hypoarousal/hypo-responsivity to sensory input (Devine et al., 2020; Engel-Yeger et al., 2013; Joseph et al., 2021; Schore, 2009a; Yochman & Pat-Horenczyk, 2020).

Trauma group therapists can encounter group members with hyperarousal who demonstrate pressured, rambling speech, heightened sensory and emotional reactivity, hypervigilance, and talking at others rather than to others in groups. During hyperarousal, trauma-inducing sympathetic nervous system responses can be overwhelmingly felt in the body, leading to psychosomatic symptoms, a common indicator of trauma (Lanius, 2015). Hypo-aroused group members can present with blunted, flat, constricted affect as well as rigid and concrete ways of relating, including withdrawal patterns from the group. Traumatized individuals can also present with a blend of intermittent hyper- and hypoarousal, indicative of broadly disrupted arousal modulation patterns (Kearney & Lanius, 2022).

People suffering from hyper- and hypoarousal trauma symptoms demonstrate profound cognitive, emotional, and somatic disturbances in their perceived sense of self because it has become linked with their traumatic experiences (Lanius et al., 2020). During fear-based hyperarousal, group members may re-experience a loss of sense of self and can demonstrate regressed behaviors. As a group member experiencing this phenomenon once shared in a group I was facilitating, "it's like navigating in an ocean without a rudder."

They may also experience significant difficulties perceiving their own emotions as well as the emotional states of others and how others are perceiving them. At a cortical level, they have become dysregulated (not functioning optimally). Visual, prosocial, and relational networks in the cortex are disrupted (Martin et al., 2020). They often lose eye contact when undergoing hyper- and hypoaroused states.

Traumatized group members who are experiencing emotional dysregulation, evidenced by hyper- and hypoarousal, will benefit from interventions aimed at co-regulation and restoration (regulation of the areas of the brain dysregulated during dissociation). This can occur in a group via intersubjective emotional connection with others.

Both hyperarousal and hypoarousal are fear-driven responses and ingrained behavioral patterns. Where do they originate in the brain? What brain structures and networks are involved?

The Psyche-Soma Connection: A Neurophysiological Perspective

Critical to understanding the impact of trauma and dissociation with group members is the psyche-soma interrelationship, that is, where trauma symptoms are stored in the body. Dum et al. (2016, 2019) focused on the mind–body connection and the adrenal medulla (which is impacted by trauma) in identifying the neural circuits linked to psychosomatic illness. They identified the frontal lobe, the supplementary motor areas, and the cingulate motor areas in top-down control of the adrenal medulla; these cortical areas are involved in aspects of cognition and affect. The authors believe psychosomatic disease "may be fundamental to conditions like posttraumatic stress disorder" (Dum et al., 2016, p. 4).

Hypervigilance

Hypervigilance is a symptom of trauma mediated by neural networks in the amygdala, sympathetic nervous system, and the hypothalamic-pituitary-adrenal axis, leading to neurophysiological hyperarousal (Kleshchova et al., 2019). When group members re-experience emotionally overwhelming traumatic events, they can dissociate. This often manifests in hypervigilance, increased threat detection, and limited facial recognition (Leiderman & Smith, 2017), leading to distortions about self and others.

Brain Structures, Networks Impacted by Trauma

Limbic Lobe, Amygdala, the Default Mode Network, and the Salience Network

What, then, can be said about underlying brain functioning during trauma? Neuroscience has focused on trauma since the phenomena at the core of causing traumatic symptoms manifest from specific overwhelming environmental influences (e.g., early familial trauma) that often appear to be separate and independent from neurochemical factors (Cloitre et al., 2020). Neuroscience has also been interested in identifying the long-term brain-based ramifications of trauma that impact the central nervous system.

Contemporary neuroscience research highlights a paradigm shift with interpersonal neurobiology; the empirically based evidence is provided by neuroimaging that has enhanced the understanding of the impact of trauma on brain functioning intersubjectively (Schore, 2019a, 2019b). Interbrain neuroimaging (among and between individuals) is highly relevant since groups involve intersubjective relating and trauma symptoms often re-emerge within this interpersonal context. This lens highlights how trauma symptoms will resurface within the context of others. This shift provides opportunities for trauma-based group theorists to formulate models involving co-regulation and interbrain coupling when one or more group members experience hyper- and/or hypo-arousal and dissociative symptoms.

Trauma-related symptomology manifests from brainstem–level somatic sensory processing dysfunction and its influences on dysregulating physiological arousal modulation, affect regulation, and higher-order capacities (Kearney & Lanius, 2022; Schore, 2022). Core limbic regions of the brain are highly correlated with fear reactions, emotional expression, motivation, memory, and emotional learning. The amygdala plays a central role within the limbic system in fear learning (Liberzon & Abelson, 2016). It interacts with other regions, such as the hypothalamus, the thalamic circuits, the frontal and prefrontal lobes, and the hippocampus (the librarian of the brain, where long-term memories are stored). These structures are also central to learning. When impacted by trauma, amygdala function is characterized by a reduction in memory and executive functioning, thereby leading to "brain fog." When trauma is reenacted in groups via dissociative reactions, the amygdala triggers a sympathetic autonomic response.

Recent studies have investigated the relationships between the limbic lobe and various brain networks. Self-related thoughts and experiences are represented neurobiologically by the Default Mode Network (DMN). Thus, the Limbic lobe, together with the DMN, mediates self-consciousness, self-awareness, and interoceptive experience. Together they play a key role in the learning that occurs in group psychotherapy (Lanius et al., 2020). The salience network (SN) identifies important stimuli, whether emotional, cognitive, or homeostatic. The SN functions as a brain switch between the DMN and the executive network, promoting appropriate behavioral responses (Marusak et al., 2015). Hyper-reactivity or over-connectedness in the nodes of the SN contributes to hypervigilance and increased danger detection and physiological overpreparedness (Liberzon & Abelson, 2016). Over-connectedness between DMN and SN following unresolved childhood trauma leads to lifelong risk of cognitive problems (Marusak et al., 2015), impeding memory as well as cognitive and executive functioning (Liberzon & Abelson, 2016).

Since the areas of the brain involving executive functioning are highly impacted by PTSD and CPTSD, children and adults with these diagnoses will have difficulties with attention, focus, concentration, and ability to learn. This can lead to misdiagnoses and the prescribing of inappropriate treatments. For example, highly anxious, hyperaroused children who are negative-attention-seeking and have lowered executive functioning while being raised by traumatizing parents may be misdiagnosed as having Attention Deficit Hyperactivity Disorder (ADHD) (Fisher, 2014).

The Brain's FEAR Network

The brain contains a FEAR network, found in the periaqueductal gray (PAG), a region of gray matter surrounding the midbrain which relays information to the insula (the brain's main structure answering the crucial question of "What am I feeling now?") and the SN, contributing to interoceptive and emotional awareness (Craig, 2003, 2009; Critchley et al., 2004). When group members experience hyper- or hypoaroused fear states, these areas of the brain do not function optimally, thereby predisposing these individuals to experiencing a disconnection from their feelings. Panksepp (2000) defined the brain's FEAR system as consisting of the amygdala, which is receptive to the conditioned fear that descends into the amygdala-hypothalamus-PAG circuit. The hypothalamus has vital functions, including hormone release, appetite control, and body temperature regulation. Interestingly, the top-down influences from the hypothalamus may also be involved in the conditioning of positive emotional experiences, such as nurturance (Panksepp & Trevarthen, 2009; Yu et al., 2022).

An understanding of the brain's FEAR network may provide understanding and interventions that address the inability to emotionally process positive emotional experiences, like being praised, receiving affection, and having fun, joy, and pleasure in group members with CPTSD. The unconscious trauma-based fear *overpowers* their capacity to consciously experience positive feelings.

Case Illustration 1

John, who identifies as a gay Black man in his 50s, attended a weekly co-ed trauma group with this writer for several years. He had a history of emotional neglect by both parents. He described feeling unsafe growing up, with a highly volatile father whose raging, according to John, "often appeared out of nowhere. [John] was always walking on eggshells, not knowing when [his father] would explode." He also recalled several dissociative episodes in childhood when he was shamed and humiliated by his intoxicated father. There were poor boundaries marked by his being aware, since childhood, of his father's frequent affairs, as well as his "feeling manipulated" by his mother, who, he believed, used him for her emotional comfort. He was referred to a group to address his trauma symptoms, including negative ruminating thoughts, lack of sense of self, dissociative symptoms, and limited interpersonal/intimate relations. He was an active and admired group member who could be intuitive, understanding, and emotionally supportive of others. Despite these gains, he often voiced hopelessness, as related to his inability to "feel good," feel relief, and/or make progress in group therapy. He repeatedly unemotionally stated that he was uncomfortable when others praised him or were affectionate toward him.

Robin *(directing her feelings toward John after an exchange in which she felt his understanding and support):*	I am so grateful to have you in my life. I feel such care, warmth, and love for you and admire how in tune you are with me.
Ken *(sounding frustrated after John is nonverbal for an extended period):*	What are you feeling, John?
John:	Uncomfortable. I have a hard time with compliments. I don't like them.
Group Leader (GL):	I am wondering if you have other feelings other than uncomfortable?
John:	I don't know. I can feel my body tensing up and getting hot again. It happens every time anyone tries to get close to me – my body starts to burn up.
GL *(addressing the group-as-a-whole):*	What feeling(s) may John be experiencing beyond his discomfort?
Robin:	Fear. *(Other group members agree and echo Robin's observation.)*
John *(eyes slowly welling up while the group is silent, and then tears rolling down his face):*	Yes. I can't recall being told I was loved growing up. It is so hard for me to believe it, even today. I have lost out on so many relationships. *(Cries uncontrollably and with grief as he recalls painful childhood experiences of abandonment, hurt, and rejection.)*

Several aspects of this exchange warrant further discussion. The inability to access positive feelings, such as love, admiration, affection, joy, pleasure, and hope, is common for group members with CPTSD. This may be related to the brain's FEAR network. Interestingly, this disconnection is unconscious, thereby preverbal and beyond the ability to be consciously accessed and emotionally expressed. Fear may also encompass other feelings. When the disconnected fear is brought into John's consciousness, deeper feelings of grief, sadness, and loss begin to emerge. The physiological response ("getting hot again") by John also highlights the frequent primitive, preverbal way trauma is stored in the body (Van der Kolk, 2014). The GL discerned the disconnection from his fearful feelings and intervened by asking others what emotions John might be having that were being experienced physiologically, via the physical discomfort he described in the increase of his body temperature. When the space was created in the group for him to identify feeling(s) from which he was disconnected, he was able to access fear of trusting praise/intimacy since he correlated these positive feelings with early traumatic familial memories of hurt and abandonment. He also acknowledged that this pattern occurred throughout his life whenever he grew close to another. As he emotionally accessed the fear and verbalized it, he was then able to access the emotional pain associated with loss and grief of being alone.

Lack of Intersubjective Relatedness

Those who are subjected to abuse and neglect often suffer from inconsistent nurturing and a dearth of protective parenting. Their parents typically lack intersubjective relatedness, as evidenced by limited capacities to demonstrate empathy and compassion for their children when they were emotionally vulnerable. Since trauma survivors were not adequately emotionally seen by their caregivers, they often enter group psychotherapy with minimal capacities for intersubjective relatedness; in other words, they lack the ability to emotionally see others (Leiderman, 2020). The goal of most trauma group psychotherapy models is to foster intersubjective relatedness; therefore, understanding its neurophysiological foundations may aid in the utilization of reparative interventions.

A Neurophysiological Understanding of Intersubjective Relatedness

In the 1990s, neuroscientists discovered mirror neurons, which are activated in one individual while observing behaviors of interest in another (Di Pellegrino et al., 1992). Mirror neurons focus on the facial gestures of others (Ferrari et al., 2003), thereby enhancing empathy between individuals. Similarly, brain coupling (Hasson & Frith, 2016) occurs when the brain of a listener fires in synchrony with the brain of a communicator, denoting intersubjective relating. Koole and Tschacher (2016) provided their compelling interpersonal synchrony model of psychotherapy based on the coupling of neural activity between the brains of the patient and the therapist.

Polyvagal theory (Porges, 2011) proposes that, visually, we scan through "neuroception" whether we are safe or unsafe in the company of other(s). When feeling unsafe, the physiological cortical networks intermediated by the unmyelinated vagal pathways shift toward dissociation. Connection with others is severed. Safety is restored through contact with one another via reciprocal, bidirectional, empathic communication, that is, mutual attunement, engaged facial expressivity, gestures, and vocalizations. The polyvagal theory suggests that safety or danger is detected by cortical areas and physiological states that are communicated interpersonally from movements of the upper part of the face, eye contact, rhythm of speech, and body posture.

The Complementary Right and Left Hemispheres

Researchers have emphasized we have complementary cortical–subcortical hemispheres: A rational, detail-oriented, cognitive, analytically data-driven, conscious brain in the left hemisphere complemented by the emotionally driven, intersubjective, intuitive, empathic, creative, nonverbal, regressively activated, unconscious right hemisphere (Dumas et al., 2010; Schore, 2020, 2022). The left hemisphere represents the *conceptual self*, while the right hemisphere represents the *integrated self* (the integration of the corporeal and unconscious aspects of self) (Kuhl et al., 2015).

The right hemisphere stores intense, emotionally positive, and negative affect; painful, trauma-related feelings; and preconscious regulated and dysregulated affective states monitored by the right orbitofrontal system (Schore, 2019a, 2020, 2022). The left hemisphere's intellectualized, rational, cognitive properties block out emotionally painful, trauma-driven experiences/enactments in the group therapy process. The left hemisphere allows us to control our interpersonal interactions. It is also responsible for avoiding emotional vulnerability with others. Defensively, the left hemisphere has an important role in "trip wiring" and protecting us from experiencing/re-experiencing the more painful, unconsciously driven *neuro-emotional-physiological* trauma-associated feelings of shame, humiliation, guilt, rage, and hatred both within and outside of groups.

Schore (2019a, 2019b, 2020, 2022) denotes that therapeutic change occurs via the unconscious, emotionally driven regressions of the right hemisphere to dilute the repressive defensive dominance of the left hemisphere. This may be significantly relevant to the importance of working through dissociative enactments in trauma groups, which will be covered later in this chapter.

The Right Hemisphere's Temporo-Parietal- Occipital Junction (rTPO)

Individuals with unresolved trauma are often harmed by abusive parents with narcissistic traits (Shaw, 2021, 2014). Understanding where egocentrism and narcissism arise from in the brain is imperative since it is found in those who are abusive or neglectful and also found in group members with CPTSD (Leiderman, 2020). Neuroimaging research on narcissism and egocentrism has focused on the right hemisphere's temporo-parietal-occipital junction (rTPO). Interestingly, when this region is optimally functioning, it promotes prosocial behavior, such as empathic understanding, compassion, social generosity, altruism, taking other people's interests into account, overcoming self-centeredness, egocentrism, and narcissism (Mars et al., 2011, 2013; Soutschek et al., 2016; Strombach et al., 2015). Mars et al. (2013) reported that the most advanced interpersonal-relating structures in the rTPO are the last to develop during right hemisphere brain maturity. They found these regions of the brain seem to develop only between 9 years and adulthood. As emphasized earlier in this chapter, parental abuse and neglect stunt the neurological development of the right hemisphere. The rTPO also integrates cognitive, emotional, and somatic awareness, maintaining a sense of one's body and emotional/physiological processing (Leiderman & Smith, 2017). Additionally, the rTPO junction plays an important role in unconscious attentional functions (Chelazzi et al., 2018) and is dominant in the process of co-regulation, empathy, and emotionally seeing others following regressive dissociative enactments (Schore, 2019a).

Dumas et al. (2010) found empirical evidence of an interpersonal neurobiological model and interbrain synchronization in the rTPO between two individuals during spontaneous, nonverbal, empathic communications. This right-brain-to-right-brain co-regulation of one another highlights how emotional communication (Schore, 2019a), that is, interbrain coupling that allows access to another's internal emotional state (Koole & Tschacher, 2016), can be nonverbal.

An Interpersonal/Relational Neurophysiological Model to Foster Co-Regulation and Coupling Synchrony in Trauma Psychotherapy Groups

Neuroscience can provide the foundation for an interpersonal/relational trauma group psychotherapy model that integrates recent advances in evidence-based interpersonal neurobiology. This model incorporates the affect-regulating properties of the right hemisphere (Schore, 2020, 2019a) and the coupling of the neural activity of the brains of group members and the leader (Koole & Tschacher, 2016) to enhance co-regulation and synchrony among group members and leader(s). Group psychotherapy provides multiple fields among and between group members and leader and/or the group-as-a-whole to foster co-regulation and coupling synchrony opportunities. This model also contains the following: (1) an *experience-near* group leadership (Leiderman & Klein, 2022), (2) an interpersonal/relational approach when working through dissociative enactments (Grossmark, 2017, 2018) approach, and (3) a group process that advances emotional vulnerability and processes unmetabolized, trauma-based regressions and painful feelings unconsciously stored in the right hemisphere.

The Experience-Near Group Therapist

Utilizing an *experience-near* interpersonal relational approach to group leadership includes personality traits of trustworthiness, self-awareness of personal psychological trauma, emotional transparency, and clinical abilities to facilitate an emotionally attuned and enriching group process.

Effective group leadership personality traits that enhance safety and trustworthiness include being compassionate, curious, consistent, measured, flexible, non-judgmental, accepting, and emotionally responsive; inspiring hope and optimism; and having a unidirectional focus on the patient's emotional wants, needs, and feelings (Leiderman & Klein, 2022). This type of leader is interactive, is interpersonally authentic, and models acceptance and accountability of imperfections and regressions. With the appropriate supervision, training, and psychotherapy, the group leader can address personal regressive participation in dissociative enactments with the group-as-a-whole. In other words, the group therapist needs to be aware of their capacity for primitivity. Additionally, this leader creates opportunities for group members to safely confront them (without retaliation), understanding this as central to the restoration of a sense of self in traumatized group members.

An Integrated Neurophysiological Interpersonal/Relational Approach

Emotional dysregulation is common in trauma group members and leader(s) during the group process. In general, it is most pronounced during dissociative enactments. In the *beginning stages, prior to the emotional peak of the dissociative enactment*, the group members and leader(s) often undergo emotional and physiological dysregulation caused by overactivation of neural networks and structures. Contemporary research on dissociation (Shaw et al., 2023) emphasizes that the hyperconnectivity among brain networks of those with CPTSD impacts their sensory and motor-related regions; during dissociation, the SN is overactivated, causing hypervigilance and hyperarousal, and the DMN is also overactivated, causing disturbances in attention and sense of self-related processing. In the *working-through process of the dissociative enactment*, the leader and group members co-create a safe space within the group context to utilize right-brain-to-right-brain communications, thereby enhancing rTPO-to-rTPO interhemispheric coupling synchrony among and between group members and leader to restore prosocial capabilities, empathy, compassion, and the capacity to *emotionally see others* as well as *be seen by others*. It is believed the right-brain-to-right-brain communications among and between group members and leader activate the parasympathetic nervous system (the calming part of the nervous system, involved in resting states and digestion), thereby relaxing overactive structures of the brain. We often witness the parasympathetic properties when breathing patterns become synchronized in psychotherapy (Koole & Tschacher, 2016; McFarland, 2001). The DMN and SN are also believed to become less activated when working through dissociative enactments in a group (Leiderman & Smith, 2017). This may result in increasingly optimal and adaptive levels of autonomic arousal, associated with an enhanced sense of self, with greater awareness of what one is feeling in the moment and with more acceptance of change. Research has emphasized that when the DMN is regulated, this increases self-related, prosocial-cognitive functions, allowing a gain in insight and learning from the inferences derived from the emotional and physical self-experiences while simultaneously understanding those conditions in others (Lanius et al., 2020). Neuroimaging research has discovered that the deactivation of the DMN utilizing hallucinatory drugs has led to increased awareness of self and interoception or internal observation (Carhart-Harris et al., 2014; Mithoefer et al., 2016, 2018). In groups, this is carried out non-invasively. It is likely that these areas of the brain are utilized extensively to register, focus upon, capture, and learn during the group process when focusing on dissociative enactments among and between group members and leader. This group process also enhances the eventual development of the sense of self with the repeated working-through of dissociative enactments. The repetition of co-regulation from multiple fields, including group-as-a-whole, other members, and the leader, may also lead to the development of autoregulation, since autoregulation is fostered by the repeated emotionally attuned mother when infants are dysregulated (Schore, 2022).

The regulation of an individual's *neuro-emotional-physiological* PTSD and CPTSD symptoms occurs via the intersubjective "relational unconscious" of the right hemisphere, when individuals are emotionally connecting, relating, and empathically attuned to one another (Dumas et al., 2010; Schore, 2019a, 2020, 2022). This simultaneous process fosters coupling synchronization, cohesion with another's relational unconscious, and mutual access to each other's right hemispheres via emotionally supportive words as well as by engaging bodily and through facial gestures (Porges, 2011). This is highly relevant for psychodynamic, interpersonal/relational trauma group therapy models. "Right brain interpersonal neurobiology continues to be directly relevant to the relational trend in psychodynamic models" (Schore, 2019a, p. 192).

Group members with unresolved developmental trauma often enter group psychotherapy with underdeveloped right hemispheres and overactivated left hemispheres (thereby causing trauma-correlated symptoms of stress, panic, depression, anger, dysregulation of affect, disorganized sense of self, etc.). In addition, lifelong fearful, avoidant defenses often manifest from the left hemisphere. Conversely, those who present with blunted, flat, and disconnected, unemotional reliant defenses have underactivated and underdeveloped right hemispheres. An interpersonal/relational neurophysiological model can potentially enhance the development of group members' right hemispheres, thereby enhancing their capabilities for autoregulation of trauma symptoms, verbalization of their body-based feelings, intersubjective relating, and reduction in their reliance on fear-driven left hemispheric defenses, thus fostering the development of self. Utilizing this approach will also enhance group-as-a-whole development, capabilities for co-regulation between group members and leader, and interhemispheric coupling synchrony between members and leader.

To address these multifaceted goals, the group leader and members co-create group norms of (1) right-hemisphere-to-right-hemisphere emotional communications, thereby enhancing the development of their right hemispheres. The emphasis here is minimizing talking about one's feelings in an intellectualized manner (left hemisphere) but expressing what one feels from a bottom-up, bodily manner, by locating what one unconsciously feels in one's body in the group process (originating from the brain stem, limbic system, and right hemisphere). (2) Facilitating a process that is non-interpretive, non-critical of left hemisphere defenses (such as feeling entitled, intellectualizations, rationalization, self-deprecation, splitting, projecting, and being hypercritical) and enhances a group process that flexibly shifts into right hemisphere, intersubjective relating in which members feel emotionally seen, held, and empathized with. (3) Creating the space to access, express, and understand painful feelings (described later). (4) Creating the therapeutic space to process, metabolize, and make symbolic meaning of spontaneous, unsymbolized, unconscious right hemispheric–driven regressions and dissociative enactments in members, the leader, and/or the group-as-a-whole.

Containing and Processing Painful Feelings

As humans, we fear and avoid physiological and emotional pain. The group member and leader may avoid re-experiencing the feelings of shame, humiliation, abandonment, traumatic loss, and grief which are stored, unmetabolized (unconscious), in the right hemisphere. Trauma groups serve as an effective modality to intersubjectively co-regulate the unconscious, dissociated, painful affects so they can be safely contained, metabolized, processed, and understood via the right brain subjective self (Schore, 2019a, 2020) in psychotherapy groups. Importantly, the empirically based neuroscience emphasizes that therapeutic growth, the restoration of the right hemisphere, and advances in intersubjective learning are fostered by processing and working through (via containment and understanding) emotionally painful feelings. The phrase "no pain, no gain" is no longer exclusively related to workouts but now can also be applied to psychotherapy. There is also research emphasizing the intercorrelation of the most painful feelings of shame and dissociation (Dorahy et al., 2017a, 2017b) correlated with the shame/rage interrelationship (Schore, 2020), thereby highlighting a complex process of navigating so as to access, understand, and work through these feelings. This process is highlighted with the following case examples.

Case Illustration 2

Gary, who identifies as a cisgendered married White privileged man in his 50s, attended a weekly co-ed trauma group with the writer. He had a history of being subjected to verbal abuse, rage, and emotional neglect by both parents. He was referred to group psychotherapy to address encapsulated, dissociative raging (especially toward wife), emotional dysregulation, lack of sense of self, self-deprecating ruminations, and limited interpersonal relationships. His history also included food addiction and polysubstance abuse, although he had been sober for over 20 years. He was successful occupationally, an executive in a thriving hedge fund company.

Gary (*addressing the group-as-a-whole with pressured, rambling speech*): I need help. I can't stop feeling hatred towards myself, even though objectively I have nothing to complain about. I am doing really well on the job, have a nice house, wife, and kids. But the hateful thoughts don't stop. All I keep on feeling is that I am a fat piece of sh*t, I am ugly, I hate what I look like. *(Continues to share similar obsessive, self-deprecating ideations for a few minutes.)*

Group Leader (GL): *(GL understands these self-deprecating ruminations, overly detailed descriptions, and pressured speech to be manifesting from the left hemisphere. Similarly, it also appears that Gary is talking at members and talking about feelings rather than feeling and expressing his feelings. Group members appear to be following the details of what Gary is conveying to them yet appear emotionally disconnected from him. As the process continues, his peers ask Gary questions about what he is conveying, which lead to more detail-oriented, unemotional descriptions by him. GL believes the group process is dominated by left-hemisphere-to-left-hemisphere communications, so GT intervenes with the goal of accessing more emotionally driven, right-hemisphere-to-right-hemisphere communications.)* You looked like you were feeling something significant, powerful, Gary, when you told us you "are a fat piece of sh*t?" (*Before GL can continue, Gary impulsively interrupts GL.*)

Gary *(responding in an intellectualized, agitated, defensive manner):* That I feel hatred at myself. I feel fat. (*Continuing to exclusively utilize his left hemisphere.*)

GL: What is the feeling you feel in your body (*gently touching his chest, heart area*) when you call yourself fat?

Gary: (*The stress and agitation slowly dissipate from his face. For the first time, there is a pause, a slowing down in this interaction. He appears to be introspective in terms of what he is feeling in his body and seems to be accessing the feelings stored in his brain stem, limbic system, and right hemisphere. His response is sad and subdued.*) Shame.

GL: If you feel comfortable, can you also share with us the earliest memory you have related to the shame and your body?

Gary: (*In a highly emotional manner, Gary shares the pain stored in his right hemisphere. Gary recalls a highly distressing period of several years during adolescence in which he felt neglected by his parents, despite his acting out in several ways. During that time, he became obese, disheveled, and unkempt, withdrew significantly from his peers and family, and spent the majority of his time alone in his room. "It was as if I didn't exist," according to Gary. He described "soothing and numbing" himself by compulsively eating junk food and masturbating several times a day. He acknowledged being consumed by unresolved shame, grief, and loss while recalling these memories and feelings. The emotional pain and expressions of grief were highly visible on Gary's face. Group members were silent but appeared emotionally engaged. A group space was created for the right hemisphere painful feelings to be contained, processed, and therapeutically metabolized. As he finished, several members initiated compassionate, caring, and emotionally attuned exchanges – rTPO-to-rTPO juncture interhemispheric coupling synchrony communications among and between group members. This led to other group members expressing similar feelings and memories.*)

When a group member can effectively process right hemisphere, unconscious, painful, unresolved trauma-based feelings, this can lead to group-as-a-whole coupling synchrony (members and group leader are collectively holding the emotional pain of a member or members while mirroring back the emotionally attuned empathy and compassion needed for right-hemisphere-to-right-hemisphere therapeutic recovery). The mirroring and coupling among and between group members and leader, as well as the emotional attunement that led to the synchrony of the group-as-a-whole, in this case example highlight the *neuro-emotional-physiological* reparative process in working through the feelings of neglect in trauma psychotherapy groups. The right hemisphere–based emotional vulnerability of a member or members also *empowers* the group-as-a-whole, resulting in a successful outcome when a vulnerable member can trust and safely rely on others who are genuinely caring toward them.

Case Illustration 3

Joan identifies as a single cisgender White woman in her 40s with a history of trauma, including physical abuse, neglect, and abandonment by both her parents. She reports that at the age of 3 years, she was kicked by her father down a flight of stairs. Both parents abused alcohol. She recalls being left alone as a child when her parents would go out drinking. She was referred to a group to address her history of unresolved trauma, limited interpersonal relations, suspiciousness, and encapsulated, dissociated raging with intimate partners. Professionally, she was an accomplished actress. She was engaged in the combination of individual and group psychotherapy with the group leader.

Joan begins the session describing a terrifying altercation with a drunk subway rider who became verbally abusive and threatening toward her. Her tone is panicked, pressured, agitated, and she does not make eye contact with anyone. The incident touched off an emotionally dysregulated state for days, one marked by dissociation, uncontrolled fear, isolation, trembling, and crying spells, resulting in her being unable to work. The group was initially emotionally engaged, but the combination of the intensity of her recall in excessive detail and as well as the flood of topics eventuated in what appeared to be members feeling overwhelmed, losing interest, and lacking the capacity to understand her. After several minutes, Jose interrupted her, saying he was lost in what she was sharing. Aaliyah agreed with him and stated she was interested in hearing more about Joan's feelings related to the altercation.

Joan *(clearly injured by the feedback, manifesting from left hemisphere defensive properties):*	This happens every time I open my mouth in here. I haven't slept in days, my mind is spinning out of control, and I have not been able to calm down. I probably should stay quiet since I suck at this.
George:	That frustrates me. I want to help you, but I don't know how.
Joan *(beginning to sob quietly, with tears rolling down her cheeks, then expressing herself angrily):*	That makes two of us! *(George and other group members appear afraid.)*
Aaliyah *(addressing Joan after a few moments of tense silence):*	When you relate this way, I feel rejected. I just want to be there for you.
Jose *(demonstrating empathy):*	It is hard to relate to you, although I'd like to.

Joan *(apparently not hearing the attempts of Aaliyah and Jose to emotionally engage her, directing her rage at Jose, a response originating from regressive, dissociative features of right hemisphere):*	That's why I hate you, and I have never trusted you! I should leave the group.
Jose *(now appearing frustrated and hurt):*	I just tried to support you.
Joan *(in a self-deprecating tone):*	When I am like this, I can't hear anyone. I think I need to leave, because this is too much for me. I can't tolerate this.
Joe:	I feel like leaving too.
Susan:	Me too. (*Group members withdraw into prolonged silence.*)
Group Leader (GL) *(waiting to intervene until the dissociative enactment has reached its peak):*	I believe we, as a group, can understand, hold, and demonstrate compassion towards the terrifying experience of one of our members, outside the group, that is being re-experienced, mirrored, and transported inside the group. Can we, knowing Joan's history, emotionally relate to what is being recreated during her interaction on the subway, here with us? With her family? What is being recreated for others? Can we safely discuss this, make meaning of what symbolically is occurring, without the abandonment or loss of any of our group members?

Prior to addressing the group, the GL observes that several members appear dysregulated with overactivation in their left hemispheres, DMN, and SNs (with limited abilities to access prosocial rTPO junctures to empathize with each other); others are dissociated and/or regressing (right hemisphere) due to the intensity of the angry exchanges or the threats of abandonment. The GL attempts to engage the group in order to begin the process of addressing the dissociative enactment. He hopes to promote curiosity about the dissociative enactment within the context of a non-judgmental, non-interpretive, uncritical process that will facilitate acceptance of each other's feelings, regressions, reactions, perceptions, and differences. The goal is to enhance mutual understanding, acceptance, and interpersonal learning by restoring right-hemisphere-to-right-hemisphere communications.

In this case example, the GL was interactive during the working through of the dissociative enactment, reframing (non-interpretively) left hemispheric defensiveness into right hemispheric empathic exchanges among and between group members. This process advances the working through of dissociative enactments and allows a paradigm shift in the group process that can safely contain the primitive, unsymbolized trauma that has been transported into the group.

The GL also observed that Joan did not make eye contact initially when sharing her experience on the subway. It was only during the working through of the dissociative enactment that she made eye contact with group members and the leader, thereby restoring access to rTPO-to-rTPO, emotionally attuned nonverbal and verbal communications; she could then see and be seen by others.

The process of making symbolic meaning of dissociative enactments also involves the analytical functions of the left hemisphere. Traumatic memories and recounting of traumatic experiences are unformulated (unconsciously stored in the right hemisphere) and can activate primitive reactions between members and/or with the leader. In this case example, an additional important element in the re-enactment within the group was the group's denial of Joan's re-experiencing of trauma at the hands of an intoxicated and threatening subway rider, similar to the familial denial of the harmful threats she was subjected to by her intoxicated parents as a child. This became meaningfully symbolized and validated in the working-through process (left-hemisphere-to-left-hemisphere therapeutic interpretations to enhance learning). The group also addressed Joan's threat of abandonment (leaving the group), which triggered dissociative reactions and regressions in some group members, since this threat reawakened past familial experiences of abandonment. It was also important to note that no one left the group, and all was safely contained within the group process. The group was able to contain, hold, and work through the volatile conflict between members, thereby creating a restorative experience wherein conflict and difference could be managed without long-term harm via group-as-a-whole co-regulation and synchrony.

Discussion

In this chapter, the writer proposes an integrated neurophysiological, interpersonal/relational trauma group psychotherapy model formulated from contemporary advances in evidence-based neuroscience. It incorporates the affect-regulating properties of the right hemisphere, as well as the coupling of the neural activity of the brains of group members and leader, to foster co-regulation and synchrony among the group-as-a-whole and leaders(s) when addressing overactivated, underactivated trauma symptoms in group members, including dissociative reactions. Utilizing appropriately timed right hemisphere nonverbal gestures (i.e., warm facial gestures captured by eye-to-eye contact) and/or emotionally compassionate, caring right hemisphere verbal communications with dysregulated group members restores the affect-regulating properties of the right hemisphere. Emoting and receiving nonverbal empathic gestures and verbal communications from another promote co-regulation (Schore, 2019a, 2020) and the coupling of the neural activity of the brains of group members and leader (Koole & Tschacher, 2016) that can be transmitted to multiple fields, resulting in group-as-a-whole optimal neural synchrony. Group members with unresolved CPTSD enter group treatment with underdeveloped right hemispheres and limited abilities to access, understand, and emotionally process painful feelings. Utilizing this approach may lead to neuroplasticity in the right hemisphere (Schore, 2022).

Importantly, one of the long-term goals for members of a trauma group is to enhance their capabilities for autoregulation. This is achieved via the repeated exposure to group member and/or leader co-regulation during experiences of fear-based *neuro-emotional-physiological* overactivation and/or dissociative enactments in group. Ideally, the ability to autoregulate, once learned and internalized, can be utilized outside of the group context.

This model also applies an emotionally attuned, unidirectionally focused, *experience-near* group leadership (Leiderman & Klein, 2022) to develop the safety within the group context needed for emotional vulnerability and to treat unconscious, trauma-based painful feelings stored in the right hemisphere. This leader models emotional vulnerability, especially by being accountable for mis-attunements, mistakes, regressions, and imperfections.

Dissociative reactions frequently occur along a spectrum (mild to severe) in trauma groups; they are fear-based trauma responses that are expressed as unconscious, unformulated enactments containing the re-experiencing of elements of the early, unprotected, familial danger that group members were subjected to as children. A member's dissociative reactions represent the unique, preverbal, brain-based, *neuro-emotional-physiological* imprint left from the family of origin in the form of anticipated harm, rejection, and being misunderstood or neglected that are dynamically transported into trauma psychotherapy groups.

In psychodynamic-focused trauma groups, there are at least two group-as-a-whole process patterns that can trigger member(s), leader, or group-as-a-whole dissociative enactments. The first originates from the left hemisphere, when a member, members, or a leader *talks at others* (overutilizing their left hemisphere) without "seeing" others and/or by responding defensively to constructive feedback from others utilizing denial, projection, splitting, anger, rationalization, and/or intellectualization. The speaker, therefore, takes on features of the traumatizing parent(s) or family members. The second group process pattern originates from the right hemisphere, when one or more members or the leader unconsciously regresses or has a dissociative enactment. The regression or dissociative enactment within a group context replicates unsafe, chaotic, harmful family dynamics, thereby triggering the same fear-based, dissociative reactions with member(s) and/or group leader(s).

The neurophysiological process of working through dissociative enactments is complex. It involves the group process restoring optimal functioning of cortical networks and structures, including the DMN, SN, and rTPO, and restoring right and left hemisphere intra- and interhemispheric functioning. Clinically, the process also includes creating the safe space within the group context to enhance nonverbal and verbal right-hemisphere-to-right-hemisphere coupling synchrony among and between group members, combined with left-hemisphere-to-left-hemisphere group-as-a-whole communications, in order to make symbolic meaning of the dissociative enactment. The working through of dissociative enactments often involves going from a stressful, at times chaotic, situation to the *calming after the storm* that is created when the group-as-a-whole holds and contains the dissociative enactments. This process activates the parasympathetic nervous system, thereby relaxing overactive structures of the brain, resulting in their becoming less active. This occurs in a top-down manner, manifesting from the right hemisphere to the limbic system (enhancing the DMN and SN) and brain stem to relax the body, and then back up to the right and left hemispheres. We can visibly witness the bodies of overactivated group members relax as they emit *sighs of relief* and report being emotionally seen, understood, and held by the group. The work may result in more adaptive levels of autonomic arousal associated with optimal learning and an enhanced sense of self accompanied by greater awareness of feelings in the moment and an ability to embrace change.

Chronic physiological tension, coupled with an inability to experience *neuro-emotional-physiological* relief, is common for those with unresolved CPTSD. This symptomatology may be stimulated by the brain's FEAR network. To address this issue, a group leader can ask a group member, "What are you feeling?" after the group leader observes the transition from a state of significant physiological tension to physiological relief following the working through of a dissociative enactment and/or processing painful traumatic feelings. These individuals are often unable to consciously (left hemisphere) feel the relief, despite demonstrating facial and bodily relaxation. Inquiring facilitates growth of the ability to unconsciously (via the right hemisphere, limbic system, DMN, SN, brain stem) access what is felt within the body (top-down) facilitating verbalization (via the left hemisphere) of relief.

Future Evidence-Based Neurophysiological Group Therapy Research Is Needed

The interpersonal neuroscience which provides understanding of the brain structures and networks that benefit from psychotherapy by utilizing empirically based and valid intersubjective, interbrain neuroimaging is in its infancy. Ideally, future research could utilize empirical age and gender-matched and controlled, databased, interbrain neuroimaging among and between group members and leader to provide the empirical validation needed to promote the efficacy and efficiency of group psychotherapy. Future neurophysiological interbrain-to-interbrain group-as-a-whole research can be conducted with new and advanced multiple portable EEG devices that can be worn by group members and leader(s) simultaneously to measure their intersubjective, interbrain neuroimaging as they interpersonally relate to one another during the group process. Neuroimaging might become the gold standard in evidence-based practices, since it could empirically measure PTSD and CPTSD symptoms before, during, and after trauma groups, demonstrating which group therapy interventions are effective and efficient. There are at least two obstacles, however, that may minimize the opportunities for such research. The first obstacle is that there are few clinicians who are both group therapists and neurophysiologists (trained in conducting QEEG neuroimaging brain mapping). A second problem is that intersubjective, interbrain neuroimaging can be costly and time-consuming and requires modern neuroimaging technology. However, ideally, this methodology could accurately measure the neuroplasticity in group members from trauma psychotherapy groups and replicate the recent scientific and clinical advances of interbrain neuroimaging of the rTPO junctures between two emotionally attuned individuals (Schore, 2019a).

References

American Psychiatric Association. (2013). *Diagnostic and statistical manual of mental disorders* (5th ed.). American Psychiatric Publishing. https://doi.org/10.1176/appi.books.9780890425596

Besser, A., & Neria, Y. (2012). When home isn't a safe haven: Insecure attachment orientations, perceived social support, and PTSD symptoms among Israeli evacuees under missile threat. *Psychological Trauma: Theory, Research, Practice, and Policy, 4*, 34–46. https://doi.org/10.1037/a0017835

Bowlby, J. (1969). *Attachment and loss: Attachment* (Vol. 1). Basic Books.

Bowlby, J. (1973). *Attachment and loss: Volume II: Separation, anxiety and anger.* Basic Books.

Carhart-Harris, R. L., Wall, M. B., Erritzoe, D., Kaelen, M., Ferguson, B., De Meer, I., & Nutt, D. J. (2014). The effect of acutely administered MDMA on subjective and BOLD-fMRI responses to favorite and worst autobiographical memories. *International Journal of Neuropsychopharmacology, 17*(4), 527–540. https://doi.org/10.1017/S1461145713001405

Chefetz, R. A. (2004). The paradox of "detachment disorders": Binding-disruptions of dissociative process. *Psychiatry, 67*, 246–255. https://doi.org/10.1521/psyc.67.3.246.48980

Chelazzi, L., Bisley, J. W., & Bartolomeo, P. (2018). The unconscious guidance of attention [Editorial]. *Cortex: A Journal Devoted to the Study of the Nervous System and Behavior, 102*, 1–5. https://doi.org/10.1016/j.cortex.2018.02.002

Ciaunica, A., Constant, A., Preissl, H., & Fotopoulou, K. (2021). The first prior: From co-embodiment to co-homeostasis in early life. *Consciousness and Cognition, 91*, 103117. https://doi.org/10.1016/J.CONCOG.2021.103117

Cloitre, M., Brewin, C. R., Bisson, J. I., Hyland, P., Karatzias, T., Lueger-Schuster, B., Maercker, A., Roberts, N. P., & Shevlin, M. (2020). Evidence for the coherence and integrity of the complex PTSD (CPTSD) diagnosis: Response to Achterhof et al., (2019) and Ford (2020). *European Journal of Psychotraumatology*, *11*(1). https://doi.org/10.1080/20008198.2020.1739873

Cox, K. S., Resnick, H. S., & Kilpatrick, D. G. (2014). Prevalence and correlates of posttraumautic distorted beliefs: Evaluating DSM-5 PTSD expanded cognitive symptoms in a national sample. *Journal of Traumatic Stress*, *27*, 299–306. https://doi.org/10.1002/jts.21925

Craig, A. D. (2003). Interoception: The sense of the physiological condition of the body. *Current Opinion in Neurobiology*, *13*, 500–505. https://doi.org/10.1016/s0959-4388(03)00090-4

Craig, A. D. (2009). Emotional moments across time: A possible neural basis for time perception in the anterior insula. *Philosophical Transactions of the Royal Society B*, *364*, 1933–1942. https://doi.org/10.1098/rstb.2009.0008

Critchley, H. D., Wiens, S., Rotshtein, P., Öhman, A., & Dolan, R. J. (2004). Neural systems supporting interoceptive awareness. *Nature Neuroscience*, *7*, 189–195. https://doi.org/10.1038/nn1176

Devine, S. L., Walker, S. C., Makdani, A., Stockton, E. R., McFarquhar, M. J., McGlone, F. P., & Trotter, P. D. (2020). Childhood adversity and affective touch perception: A comparison of United Kingdom care leavers and non-care leavers. *Frontiers in Psychology*, *11*, 557171. https://doi.org/10.3389/fpsyg.2020.557171

di Pellegrino, G., Fadiga, L., Fogassi, L., Gallese, V., & Rizzolatti, G. (1992). Understanding motor events: A neurophysiological study. *Experimental Brain Research*, *91*(1), 176–180. https://doi.org/10.1007/BF00230027

Dorahy, M. J., Corry, M., Black, R., Matheson, L., Coles, H., Curran, D., Seager, L., Middleton, W., & Dyer, K. F. (2017b). Shame, dissociation, and complex PTSD symptoms in traumatized psychiatric and control groups: Direct and indirect associations with relationship distress. *Journal of Clinical Psychology*, *73*(4), 439–448. https://doi.org/10.1002/jclp.22339

Dorahy, M. J., McKendry, H., Scott, A., Yogeeswaran, K., Martens, A., & Hanna, D. (2017a). Reactive dissociative experiences in response to acute increases in shame feelings. *Behaviour Research and Therapy*, *89*, 75–85. https://doi.org/10.1016/j.brat.2016.11.007

Dum, R. P., Levinthal, D. J., & Strick, P. L. (2016). Motor, cognitive, and affective areas of the cerebral cortex influence the adrenal medulla. *Proceedings of the National Academy of Sciences*, *113*, 9922–9927. https://doi.org/10.1073/pnas.1605044113

Dum, R. P., Levinthal, D. J., & Strick, P. L. (2019). The mind–body problem: Circuits that link the cerebral cortex to the adrenal medulla. *PNAS*, *52*, 26321–26328. https://doi.org/10.1073/pnas.1902297116

Dumas, G., Nadel, J., Soussignan, R., Martinerie, J., & Garnero, L. (2010). Inter-brain synchronization during social interaction. *PLoS One*, *5*(8), e12166. https://doi.org/10.1371/journal.pone.0012166

Engel-Yeger, B., Palgy-Levin, D., & Lev-Wiesel, R. (2013). The sensory profile of people with post-traumatic stress symptoms. *Occupational Therapy for Mental Health*, *29*, 266–278. https://doi.org/10.1080/0164212X.2013.819466

Ferrari, P. F., Gallese, V., Rizzolatti, G., & Fogassi, L. (2003). Mirror neurons responding to the observation of ingestive and communicative mouth actions in the monkey ventral premotor cortex. *The European Journal of Neuroscience*, *17*(8), 1703–1714. https://doi.org/10.1046/j.1460-9568.2003.02601.x

Fisher, S. F. (2014). *Neurofeedback in the treatment of developmental trauma: Calming the fear- driven brain*. Norton. https://wwnorton.com/books/9780393707861

Grossmark, R. (2017). Narrating the unsayable: Enactment, repair, and creative multiplicity in group psychotherapy. *International Journal of Group Psychotherapy*, *67*(1), 27–46. https://doi.org/10.1080/00207284.2016.1202680

Grossmark, R. (2018). *The unobtrusive relational analyst: Explorations in psychoanalytic companioning*. Routledge. https://www.routledge.com/The-Unobtrusive-Relational-Analyst-Explorations-in-Psychoanalytic-Companioning/Grossmark/p/book/9781138899063

Hasson, U., & Frith, C. D. (2016). Mirroring and beyond: Coupled dynamics as a generalized framework for modelling social interactions. *Philosophical Transactions of the Royal Society of London: Series B, Biological Sciences*, *371*. https://doi.org/10.1098/rstb.2015.0366

Henry, J. P. (1993). Psychological and physiological responses to stress: The right hemisphere and the hypothalamo-pituitary-adrenal axis, an inquiry into problems of human bonding. *Integrative Physiological and Behavioral Science*, *28*, 369–387. https://doi.org/10.1007/BF02690935

Joseph, R. Y., Casteleijn, D., van der Linde, J., & Franzsen, D. (2021). Sensory modulation dysfunction in child victims of trauma: A scoping review. *Journal of Child & Adolescent Trauma*, *14*, 455–470. https://doi.org/10.1007/s40653-020-00333-x

Kearney, B. E., & Lanius, R. A. (2022). The brain-body disconnect: A somatic sensory basis for trauma-related disorders. *Frontiers in Neuroscience, 16*, 1015749. https://doi.org/10.3389/fnins.2022.1015749

Kleshchova, O., Rieder, J. K., Grinband, J., & Weierich, M. R. (2019). Resting amygdala connectivity and basal sympathetic tone as markers of chronic hypervigilance. *Psychoneuroendocrinology, 102*, 68–78. https://doi.org/10.1016/j.psyneuen.2018.11.036

Koole, S. L., & Tschacher, W. (2016). Synchrony in psychotherapy: A review and an integrative framework for the therapeutic alliance. *Frontiers in Psychology, 7*, Article 862.

Kuhl, J., Quirin, M., & Koole, S. L. (2015). Being someone: The integrated self as a neuropsychological system. *Social and Personality Psychology Compass, 9*, 115–132. https://doi.org/10.1111/spc3.12162

Lanius, R. A. (2015). Trauma-related dissociation and altered states of consciousness: A call for clinical, treatment, and neuroscience research. *European Journal of Psychotraumatology, 6*(1). https://doi.org/10.3402/ejpt.v6.27905

Lanius, R. A., Terpou, B. A., & McKinnon, M. C. (2020). The sense of self in the aftermath of trauma: Lessons from the default mode network in posttraumatic stress disorder. *European Journal of Psychotraumatology, 11*(1). https://doi.org/10.1080/20008198.2020.1807703

Leiderman, L. (2020). Psychodynamic group therapy with hispanic migrants: Interpersonal, relational constructs in treating complex trauma, dissociation, and enactments. *International Journal of Group Psychotherapy, 70*(2), 162–182. Taylor & Francis. https://doi.org/10.1080/00207284.2019.1686704

Leiderman, L. M., & Klein, R. H. (2022). An integrative systems-oriented interpersonal, relational group approach to understanding and treating mass trauma, dissociation, and enactments during the COVID-19 pandemic. *International Journal of Group Psychotherapy, 72*(1), 34–63. https://doi.org/10.1080/00207284.2021.1991234

Leiderman, L. M., & Smith, M. L. (2017). Neuroimaging measures to assess the effectiveness of a two-day marathon group of individuals with early developmental trauma: A pilot study. *International Journal of Group Psychotherapy, 67*(1), 91–107. https://doi.org/10.1080/00207284.2016.1203568

Liberzon, I., & Abelson, J. L. (2016). Context processing and the neurobiology of post-traumatic stress disorder. *Neuron, 92*, 14–30. https://doi.org/10.1016/j.neuron.2016.09.039

Liotti, G. (2004). Trauma, dissociation, and disorganized attachment: Three strands of a single braid. *Psychotherapy: Theory, Research, Training, 41*, 472–486. https://doi.org/10.1037/0033-3204.41.4.472

Lyons-Ruth, K., Dutra, L., Schuder, M. R., & Bianchi, I. (2006). From infant attachment disorganization to adult dissociation: Relational adaptations or traumatic experiences? *Psychiatric Clinics of North America, 29*, 63–86. https://doi.org/10.1016/j.psc.2005.10.011

Main, M. (1996). Introduction to the special section on attachment and psychopathology: 2. Overview of the field of attachment. *Journal of Consulting and Clinical Psychology, 64*, 237–243. https://psycnet.apa.org/buy/1996-00433-001

Mars, R. B., Jbabdi, S., Sallet, J., O'Reilly, J. X., Croxson, P. L., Olivier, E., Noonan, M. P., Bergmann, C., Mitchell, A. S., Baxter, M. G., Behrens, T. E. J., Johansen-Berg, H., Tomassini, V., Miller, K. L., & Rushworth, M. F. S. (2011). Diffusion-weighted imaging tractography-based parcellation of the human parietal cortex and comparison with human and macaque resting-state functional connectivity. *Journal of Neuroscience, 31*(11), 4087–4100.

Mars, R. B., Sallet, J., Neubert, F.-X., & Rushworth, M. F. S. (2013). Connectivity profiles reveal the relationship between brain areas for social cognition in human and monkey temporoparietal cortex. *Proceedings of the National Academy of Sciences of the United States of America, 110*, 10806–10811.

Martin, A. K., Kessler, K., Cooke, S., Huang, J., & Meinzer, M. (2020). The right temporoparietal junction is causally associated with embodied perspective-taking. *Journal of Neuroscience, 40*(15), 3089–3095. https://doi.org/https://doi.org/10.1523/JNEUROSCI.2637-19.2020

Marusak, H. A., Etkin, A., & Thomason, M. E. (2015). Disrupted insula-based neural circuit organization and conflict interference in trauma-exposed youth. *NeuroImage: Clinical, 8*, 516–525. https://doi.org/10.1016/j.nicl.2015.04.007

McFarland, D. H. (2001). Respiratory markers of conversational interaction. *Journal of Speech, Language, and Hearing Research, 44*(1), 128–143. https://doi.org/10.1044/1092-4388(2001/012)

Mikulincer, M., Shaver, P. R., & Solomon, Z. (2015). An attachment perspective on traumatic and posttraumatic reactions. In M. Safir, H. Wallach, & A. Rizzo (Eds.), *Future directions in post-traumatic stress disorder: Prevention, diagnosis, and treatment* (pp. 79–96). Springer. https://doi.org/10.1007/978-1-4899-7522-5_4

Mithoefer, M. C., Grob, C. S., & Brewerton, T. D. (2016). Novel psychopharmacological therapies for psychiatric disorders: Psilocybin and MDMA. *The Lancet Psychiatry, 3*(5), 481–488. https://doi.org/10.1016/S2215–0366(15)00576–3

Mithoefer, M. C., Mithoefer, A. T., Feduccia, A. A., Jerome, L., Wagner, M., Wymer, J., & Doblin, R. (2018). 3,4-Methylenedioxymethamphetamine (MDMA)-assisted psychotherapy for post-traumatic stress disorder in military veterans, firefighters, and police officers: A randomised, double-blind, dose-response, phase 2 clinical trial. *The Lancet Psychiatry, 5*(6), 486–497. https://doi.org/10.1016/S2215-0366(18)30135-4

Ogawa, J. R., Sroufe, L. A., Weinfield, N. S., Carlson, E. A., & Egeland, B. (1997). Development and the fragmented self: Longitudinal study of dissociative symptomatology in a nonclinical sample. *Development and Psychopathology, 9*, 855–879. https://doi.org/10.1017/s0954579497001478

Ogle, C. M., Rubin, D. C., & Siegler, I. C. (2015). The relation between insecure attachment and post-traumatic stress: Early life versus adulthood traumas. *Psychological Trauma, 7*, 324–332. https://doi.org/10.1037/tra0000015

Panksepp, J. (2000). Fear and anxiety mechanisms of the brain: Clinical implications. In E. E. Bittar & N. Bittar (Eds.), *Principles of medical biology* (Vol. 14, Issue C, pp. 155–177). JAI Press. https://doi.org/10.1016/S1569-2582(00)80010-0

Panksepp, J., & Trevarthen, C. (2009). The neuroscience of emotion in music. In S. Malloch & C. Trevarthen (Eds.), *Communicative musicality: Exploring the basis of human companionship* (pp. 105–146). Oxford: Oxford University Press. https://psycnet.apa.org/record/2008-14595-007

Perry, B. D., Pollard, R. A., Blakley, T. L., Baker, W. L., & Vigilante, D. (1995). Childhood trauma, the neurobiology of adaptation, and 'use-dependent' development of the brain: How states become traits. *Infant Mental Health Journal, 16*, 271–291. https://doi.org/10.1002/1097-0355(199524)16:4<271::AID-IMHJ2280160404>3.0.CO;2-B

Porges, S. W. (2011). *The polyvagal theory: Neurophysiological foundations of emotions, attachment, communication, self-regulation.* Norton & Company. https://wwnorton.com/books/The-Polyvagal-Theory/

Roche, D. N., Runtz, M. G., & Hunter, M. A. (1999). Adult attachment: A mediator between child sexual abuse and later psychological adjustment. *The Journal of Interpersonal Violence, 14*, 187–207. https://doi.org/10.1177/088626099014002006

Sar, V., Islam, S., & Öztürk, E. (2009). Childhood emotional abuse and dissociation in patients with conversion symptoms. *Psychiatry and Clinical Neurosciences, 63*, 670–677. https://doi.org/10.1111/j.1440-1819.2009.02012.x

Schore, A. N. (1994 [2016]). *Affect regulation the origin of the self: The neurobiology of emotional development.* Routledge. https://www.routledge.com/Affect-Regulation-and-the-Origin-of-the-Self-The-Neurobiology-of-Emotional-Development/Schore/p/book/9781138917071

Schore, A. N. (1994). *Affect regulation and the origin of the self: The neurobiology of emotional development.* Erlbaum. https://psycnet.apa.org/record/1994-97604-000

Schore, A. N. (1997). Early organization of the nonlinear right brain and development of a predisposition to psychiatric disorders. *Development and Psychopathology, 9*, 595–631.

Schore, A. N. (2003). Effects of a secure attachment relationship on right brain development, affect regulation, and infant mental health. *Infant Mental Health Journal, 22*, 7–66. https://doi.org/10.1002/1097-0355(200101/04)22:1<7::AID-IMHJ2<3.0.CO;2-N

Schore, A. N. (2005). Attachment, affect regulation and the developing right brain: Linking developmental neuroscience to pediatrics. *Pediatrics in Review, 26*, 204–211. https://doi.org/10.1542/pir.26-6-204

Schore, A. N. (2009a). *The science of the of art of psychotherapy.* Norton. https://wwnorton.com/books/9780393706642

Schore, A. N. (2009b). Attachment trauma and the developing right brain: Origins of pathological dissociation. In P. F. Dell & J. A. O'Neil (Eds.), *Dissociation and the dissociative disorders: DSM-V and beyond* (pp. 107–141). Routledge/Taylor & Francis Group. https://www.taylorfrancis.com/books/edit/10.4324/9780203893920/dissociation-dissociative-disorders-paul-dell-john-neil

Schore, A. N. (2019a). *Right brain psychotherapy.* Norton. https://wwnorton.com/books/9780393712858

Schore, A. N. (2019b). *The development of the unconscious mind.* Norton. https://wwnorton.com/books/9780393712919

Schore, A. N. (2020). Forging connections in group psychotherapy through right brain-to-right brain emotional communications. Part 1: Theoretical models of right brain therapeutic action. Part 2: Clinical case analyses of group right brain regressive enactments. *International Journal of Group Psychotherapy, 70*(1), 29–88. https://doi.org/10.1080/00207284.2019.1682460

Schore, A. N. (2022). Right brain-to-right brain psychotherapy: Recent scientific and clinical advances. *Annals of General Psychiatry*, *21*, 46. https://doi.org/10.1186/s12991-022-00420-3

Shaw, D. (2014). *Traumatic narcissism: Relational systems of subjugation*. Routledge. https://www.routledge.com/Traumatic-Narcissism-Relational-Systems-of-Subjugation/Shaw/p/book/9780415510257

Shaw, D. (2021). *Traumatic narcissism and recovery: Leaving the prison of shame and fear*. Routledge. https://www.routledge.com/Traumatic-Narcissism-and-Recovery-Leaving-the-Prison-of-Shame-and-Fear/Shaw/p/book/9780367775322

Shaw, S. B., Terpou, B. A., Densmore, M., Theberge, J., Frewen, P., McKinnon, M. C., & Lanius, R. A. (2023). Large-scale functional hyperconnectivity patterns in trauma-related dissociation: An rs-fMRI study of PTSD and its dissociative subtype. *Nature Mental Health*. https://doi.org/10.1038/s44220-023-00115-y

Siegel, D. J. (1999). *The developing mind: Toward a neurobiology of interpersonal experience*. Guilford Press. https://www.guilford.com/books/The-Developing-Mind/Daniel-Siegel/9781462542758

Soutschek, A., Ruff, C. C., Strombach, T., Kalenscher, T., & Tobler, P. N. (2016). Brain stimulation reveals crucial role of overcoming self-centeredness in self-control. *Science Advances*, *2*(10). https://doi.org/10.1126/sciadv.1600992

Strombach, T., Weber, B., Hangebrauk, Z., Kenning, P., Karipidis, I., Tobler, P. N., & Kalenscher, T. (2015). Social discounting involves modulation of neural value signals by temporoparietal junction. *Proceedings of the National Academy of Sciences of the United States of America*, *112*, 1619–1624. https://doi.org/10.1073/pnas.1414715112

Toth, S. C., & Cicchetti, D. (1998). Remembering, forgetting, and the effects of trauma on memory: A developmental psychopathologic perspective. *Developmental and Psychopathology*, *10*, 580–605. https://doi.org/10.1017/s0954579498001771

Trevarthen, C. (1993). The self born in intersubjectivity: The psychology of an infant communicating. In U. Neisser (Ed.), *The perceived self: Ecological and interpersonal sources of self- knowledge*. Cambridge University Press. 9780521415095ws.pdf

Van der Kolk, B. (2014). *The body keeps the score: Brain, mind, and body in the healing of trauma*. Penguin Random House. https://www.penguinrandomhouse.com/books/313183/the-body-keeps-the-score-by-bessel-van-der-kolk-md/

Van der Kolk, B. A., & Fisler, R. E. (1994). Childhood abuse and neglect and loss of self-regulation. *Bulletin of the Menninger Clinic*, *58*, 145–168. https://psycnet.apa.org/record/1994-37692-001

Wass, S. V., Smith, C. G., Clackson, K., Gibb, C., Eitzenberger, J., & Mirza, F. U. (2019). Parents mimic and influence their infant's autonomic state through dynamic affective state matching. *Current Biology*, *29*, 2415–2422. https://doi.org/10.1016/j.cub.2019.06.016

Woodhouse, S., Ayers, S., & Field, A. P. (2015). The relationship between adult attachment style and post-traumatic stress symptoms: A meta-analysis. *Journal of Anxiety Disorders*, *35*, 103–117. https://doi.org/10.1016/j.janxdis.2015.07.002

Yochman, A., & Pat-Horenczyk, R. (2020). Sensory modulation in children exposed to continuous traumatic stress. *Journal of Child & Adolescent Trauma*, *13*, 93–102. https://doi.org/10.1007/s40653-019-00254-4

Yu, H., Miao, W., Ji, E., Huang, S., Jin, S., Zhu, X., Liu, M. Z., Sun, Y. G., Xu, F., & Yu, X. (2022). Social touch-like tactile stimulation activates a tachykinin 1-oxytocin pathway to promote social interactions. *Neuron*, *110*, 1051–1067. https://doi.org/10.1016/j.neuron.2021.12.022

Ziabreva, I., Poeggel, G., Schnabel, R., & Braun, K. (2003). Separation-induced receptor changes in the hippocampus and amygdala of *Octodon degus*: Influence of maternal vocalizations. *Journal of Neuroscience*, *23*, 5329–5336. https://doi.org/10.1523/JNEUROSCI.23-12-05329.2003

Section II

The Psychological Correlates of Individual Trauma and Attachment

3 Attachment and Trauma in Group Psychotherapy

Theory, Intervention, and Fostering Change

Cheri L. Marmarosh, Yi Liu, and Yifei Du

Trauma and attachment insecurity go hand in hand (Mikulincer & Shaver, 2023). We know that child maltreatment hinders the development of a secure attachment during infancy (Bowlby, 1988), and later-life trauma erodes adult secure attachments (Mikulincer et al., 2015). In addition to attachment trauma, intergenerational trauma is transmitted from prior generations to the current generation, sometimes contained within systems, such as the case with racism, and can lead to disorganized attachment and mistrust of people (Davis, 2007; Stern et al., 2022). Secure attachment, on the other hand, can act as a safeguard when individuals encounter traumatic life events that include abuse, oppression, and war (Mikulincer & Shaver, 2022). Adults can obtain secure attachments, including those with therapists, caregivers, friends, and partners, which can reduce insecure attachment issues, thereby helping people cope with adversity (Sroufe et al., 2005). In essence, trauma can erode secure attachment, but secure attachments can reduce trauma. Therefore, understanding this bidirectional relationship is an important part of any psychological treatment, including group psychotherapy, that aims to help those who experience trauma.

Group psychotherapy has been shown to improve insecure attachment in adults (Keating et al., 2014) and offers opportunities for important interventions for group members struggling with trauma (Marmarosh et al., 2013). This chapter will integrate attachment theory into the treatment of group members who experience trauma, both outside the group, that is, victims of abuse and rape, and within the group, that is, microaggressions and verbal attacks. The authors will include the impact of group psychotherapy in the treatment of those suffering from intergenerational trauma (i.e., genocide, Holocaust) and systemic traumas that are part of the social environment, that is, racism, antisemitism, homophobia. The chapter begins with a review of attachment theory and explicates how trauma applies to attachment theory. The chapter contains a review of the empirical link between attachment and trauma. Attachment theory interventions will be utilized with group therapy case vignettes. The chapter will conclude with implications for diverse group members, group leader training, and research.

Attachment Theory: A Brief Review

According to Bowlby (1969, 1988), infants instinctively initiate attachment behaviors, like clinging and crying, to seek and maintain proximity, especially during stressful times, because this raises the likelihood of surviving from an evolutionary perspective. Ainsworth expanded upon Bowlby's attachment theory and suggested that a mother's sensitivity to the proximity-seeking signals of her infant is a crucial factor in determining attachment quality as secure or insecure (Bretherton, 1992; Keller, 2013). If caregivers function as a secure base

DOI: 10.4324/9781003546252-5

for infants to explore their surroundings, the child develops self-reliance, self-efficacy, and self-esteem, while also building trust in others (Bowlby, 1969; Bretherton, 1992; Bryant, 2023).

Attachment in Childhood: Three Attachment Styles and the Impact on Adults

Ainsworth et al. (1978) categorized three attachment styles: Secure, insecure-avoidant, and insecure-resistant – based on her observations of infants in the *Strange Situation*, where the mother and a stranger alternately entered and left a playroom (Keller, 2013). The infants demonstrated stress when their caregivers left the room. Infant attachment behaviors were assessed under the conditions of a strange environment, separation from the caregiver, and then reuniting with the caregiver (Van Rosmalen et al., 2015). Securely attached infants presented as distressed when their mothers left, but they were comforted and resumed exploration when the caregiver returned. Infants who were insecure-avoidant exhibited little to no discomfort when their mothers left or returned. They focused on exploration and play to regulate their distress. Infants with an insecure-resistant attachment style showed intense distress when separated from caregivers, but they were not easily soothed by the caregiver when returning and struggled to resume exploration (Bryant, 2023).

Attachment Theory and Trauma: The Disorganized Attachment

Building upon Ainsworth and her colleagues' three-category attachment system, Main and Solomon (1986, 1990) identified a fourth category of attachment pattern, namely, the disorganized/disoriented (D) attachment orientation. In their observation, infants classified as Type D exhibited odd, disorganized, seemingly inexplicable, and conflicting behavioral patterns in their parent's presence in the strange situation (Main & Solomon, 1986, 1990). Main and Solomon (1986) hypothesized that the caregiving environment of the D infants is usually bizarre, threatening, unpredictable, violent, or frightening. In observing the interaction between D infants and their caregivers, Main and Hesse (1990, 1992) found that, due to the caregivers' own unsolved trauma, those infants exhibited frightened and dissociative facial expression and behaviors toward their caregivers. When the infant failed to match the parent's unconscious expectation or the parent's attachment style, the parent became aggressive and frightening to the infant (Liotti, 1992).

More importantly, when D infants faced an acute dilemma in the stressful circumstances, instead of being comforted and protected by their caregivers, their caregivers became the primary source of fear, but also the sought source of protection (Main & Solomon, 1986, 1990). As a result, these infants were unable to internalize a coherent strategy for ensuring protective access to their caregivers and remained in a state of "fright without solution" (Hesse & Main, 2000, p. 1,106). To be more specific, in the *Strange Situation*, D infants developed features of an agnostic system, compelling them to move away from their caregivers (Liotti, 1992). The inherent incompatibility of these innate behavioral systems between caregiver and infant contributes to detachment – an early type of dissociative defense (Barach, 1991). Over time, D infants develop multiple, incompatible representations of self and the attachment figure, resulting in dissociative dynamics within their memory and consciousness (Liotti, 1992). Trauma and attachment, thus, are transmitted intergenerationally.

As Bowlby (1973) asserted that early attachment experiences lay a foundation for the course and quality of future relationships, disorganized attachment formed in infancy typically persists into childhood and adulthood and predicts individuals' future attachment patterns with caregivers, peers, and romantic partners (Sroufe et al., 2005). For instance, Main and Cassidy (1988) observed that D infants develop a consistent controlling strategy toward their caregivers by age 6, taking the form of either a punitive or caregiving approach. Sroufe et al. (1999) summarized D children's difficulties in peer relationships, which included tendencies (1) to perceive peers as potential threats and (2) to lack a strong motivational foundation for peer interaction. Moreover, due to their accustomed helpless/controlling relationships with caregivers, D children lack social skills for reciprocal communication, because power within peer interaction precludes the equality required for reciprocity. Meanwhile, their emotional limitations cause D children to oscillate between extreme social withdrawal and defensively aggressive behaviors within peer interactions (Sroufe et al., 1999). Research suggests that young D adults have the greatest difficulties in intimate relationships and that disorganized attachment in infants is a strong predictor for unresolved conflict and intimacy issues in couple interactions two decades later (Sroufe et al., 2005). In addition, disorganized attachment is associated with later psychopathology (Mikulincer & Shaver, 2016). For example, infant and child disorganized attachment style is associated with the development of externalizing disorders, such as aggression, and oppositional defiant disorder (see Fearon et al., 2010, for a review).

Trauma, Attachment Security/Insecurity, and Coping

Traumatic experiences, particularly person-made trauma, disrupt a person's psychological stability; shatter one's positive views of self, others, and the world; and result in a range of intrusive and avoidant posttraumatic symptoms. Individual differences in their adjustment and recovery from traumatic events vary based on their risk and protective factors stemming from their earlier experience, their current circumstances, as well as their ongoing immediate or contextual support (Carlson et al., 2009).

An individual's prior attachment security can be a potential risk or a protective factor contributing to one's trauma reaction and recovery. Mikulincer and Shaver (2022) reviewed how individuals develop their affect regulation, impulse control, arousal modulation, sense of self, beliefs of others and the world, interpersonal strategies, and distress management styles differently according to their varying attachment styles. As a result, when individuals with secure attachment orientation are exposed to trauma, their attachment system is activated, prompting them to search for external or internalized attachment figures for protection (Mikulincer et al., 2015). This capacity to mobilize internal and external resources in response to trauma enhances an individual's ability to restore emotional balance.

However, individuals with insecure attachment orientations tend to hyperactivate or deactivate their attachment systems to cope with trauma (Cassidy & Kobak, 1988). For instance, individuals with an anxious attachment orientation are inclined to rely on hyperactivating strategies, including exaggerating threats, intensifying distress, and ruminating on distress-eliciting thoughts to exact care and support from their attachment figures (Davis et al., 2003; Shaver & Mikulincer, 2002). These hyperactivating features amplify the overwhelming shock and intense feelings of panic, vulnerability, helplessness, and exhaustion provoked by the trauma, further exacerbating intrusive trauma symptoms (Horowitz, 1982).

In contrast, individuals with an avoidant attachment orientation tend to keep their attachment systems deactivated by staying away from threats, distress, vulnerabilities, and weaknesses to suppress their need to seek support and closeness with others (Mikulincer et al., 2015). These deactivating strategies encourage posttraumatic avoidant responses of psychic numbing, denial of significance and consequences of the traumatic event, and behavioral inhibition (Horowitz, 1982).

In addition, individuals falling into the category of fearful avoidance are the most suscep-tible to trauma. Similar to infants with disorganized attachment, fearful avoidant adults (high on both attachment anxiety and attachment avoidance) tend to have difficulty in choosing between the hyperactive and deactivate strategies and end up reacting in a haphazard, con-fused, and chaotic manner or becoming completely paralyzed by distress and withdrawal (Bartholomew, 1990; Simpson & Rholes, 2002).

Research supports the association between attachment insecurity and trauma symptoms with victims of childhood sexual or physical abuse, civilians living under life-endangering conditions, prisoners of war, war veterans, Holocaust survivors, survivors of the 9/11 terror attacks, security workers, and victims of interpersonal violence (see Mikulincer et al., 2015, for a review). Moreover, in a meta-analysis of 46 studies, Woodhouse et al. (2015) found that secure attachment is associated with lower levels of posttraumatic stress disorder (PTSD) symptoms following trauma, while insecure attachment is associated with higher levels of PTSD symptoms. For example, Fraley et al. (2006) found that both attachment anxiety and avoidance, as assessed 7 months after the 9/11 terror attacks, predicted more severe PTSD symptoms 11 months later.

On the other hand, constant exposure to trauma and posttraumatic symptoms can erode attachment security. As mentioned earlier, trauma, particularly human-made trauma, shat-ters one's positive views of self, others, and the world, leading to trauma survivors feeling isolated, helpless, and dehumanized. Meanwhile, prolonged and pervasive posttraumatic symptoms disrupt regulatory functions of the attachment system (Mikulincer et al., 2015). In most circumstances, when detecting danger or feeling distress, one's attachment system can be activated, and turning to one's internalized and/or external attachment figures can engender feelings of security which allow for a restoration of baseline functioning. However, with prolonged and pervasive posttraumatic symptoms, activation of the attachment system fails to induce a positive mood or reduce trauma-related thoughts, leaving trauma survivors stuck in a state of frustration, despair, and helplessness (Mikulincer et al., 2015).

Mikulincer and colleagues conducted extensive research (see reviews 2020) and iden-tified the reciprocal, recursive, amplifying cycle of attachment insecurities and trauma (Mikulincer et al., 2014, 2015). For example, Mikulincer et al. (2014) followed Israeli ex-prisoners of war for 17 years, investigating attachment-related consequences of war cap-tivity and trajectories of PTSD. Their findings revealed that persistent PTSD is associated with a disruption of the regulatory and healing benefits of attachment security. Moreover, they found that ex-prisoners of war with a stable PTSD trajectory still automatically activate their attachment systems in response to threat. However, the activation of these representa-tions does not result in adequate comfort or relief, leaving trauma survivors trapped in a self-amplifying cycle of frustration, despair, and helplessness.

In the same line of research, psychologists also noticed the links among maltreatment and trauma, attachment insecurity, and psychopathology. For example, in a longitudinal study, significant links were found between borderline personality symptoms in adulthood (dis-turbances of interpersonal relations, self-image, and affect regulation) and environmental history in early childhood (attachment disorganization, maltreatment, maternal hostility and boundary dissolution, family disruption related to father presence, and family life stress) and disturbance across domains of child functioning (attention, emotion, behavior, relationship, and self-representation) (Carlson et al., 2009).

Implications for Treatment

Due to the nature of attachment insecurity, trauma survivors usually respond worse than other psychiatric conditions to conventional therapies because of their mistrust in relationships

(Farina et al., 2019). Psychologists have identified several important, attachment-related tasks for therapists to work on in sessions. For example, Bowlby (1988) considered the development of a therapeutic alliance as a prerequisite for therapy. The therapist's main task is to create a warm and comforting alliance to which the patient can safely feel distress or confusion and then delve deep into memories and distorted wishes and feelings in order to expand self-understanding (Bowlby, 1988). Applying these concepts, the therapist supports and encourages the patient to explore (1) how their working models of self and others influence the way they think, feel, and act in relationships; (2) how their current thoughts, feelings, and behaviors may have originated from childhood experiences with parents or other caregivers; (3) in what ways their historically influenced modes of thinking and behaving are poorly adapted to their current lives; and (4) alternative and healthier ways of coping and interacting. A relational therapeutic approach is utilized with trauma survivors.

The Features of the Attachment-Oriented Therapist

Therapists are recommended to "share formulation of therapeutic goals and tasks, share and respect the mutual therapeutic roles, safeguard setting rules, and adopt a generally open, frank, honest, welcoming, calm, kind, and respectful attitude of sincere interest and empathic attunement to the client's need" (Farina et al., 2019, p. 11). Moreover, therapists need to have the ability to ground dissociative patients in the concrete internal and external reality, orienting them to the here and now, to be attuned to, validate, and stabilize their intense emotions and somatoform symptoms; to recognize and predict maladaptive interpersonal dynamics; and to manage empathetic failures and repair recurrent ruptures in the therapeutic alliance (Farina et al., 2019). Through such therapeutic processes, trauma survivors will enhance their capacity to mentalize and understand themselves, improve their emotion regulation, and develop more reality-attuned working models (Mikulincer & Shaver, 2023).

Many individual psychotherapy models treating trauma incorporate attachment theory (Ford & Courtois, 2020; Fosha, 2000; Schore, 2022). These theories share a prioritization of the therapeutic relationship (Bowlby, 1988), emotional regulation in sessions (Fosha, 2000; Schore, 2022), integration of the body in therapy (Ford & Courtois, 2020), and reduction of the fight-or-flight response (Porges, 2021; Schore, 2022). More contemporary theories have also integrated attachment theory when coping with therapeutic ruptures caused by micro-aggressions, unintentional comments, or reactions that are devaluing to people with diverse or marginalized identities (Mikulincer & Shaver, 2022; Stern et al., 2022). Attachment theory can help guide interventions for people who have been victims of systemic oppression, discrimination, and racism (Mikulincer & Shaver, 2020).

Attachment and Group Psychotherapy

Group psychotherapy has been shown to be an effective treatment for trauma (Classen et al., 2021; Foy et al., 2001), with meta-analyses demonstrating that therapy groups reduce post-traumatic symptoms for people with trauma disorders (Schwartze et al., 2019; Sloan et al., 2013). Schwartze et al. (2019) reviewed 20 randomized control trials with 2,244 patients. They found no differences in efficacy between group psychotherapy and the other treatments studied, and they argue that group therapy is an important treatment for people who have experienced diverse traumas. This research is supported by many scholars who describe how group therapy can help migrants surviving complex PTSD (Leiderman, 2020), individuals who survived traumatic interpersonal relationships (Chouliara et al., 2020), native populations suffering from intergenerational trauma (Brave Heart et al., 2020), and people who are reintegrating into the community after traumatic experiences (Mendelsohn et al., 2007).

Attachment theory concepts and constructs contribute to the efficacy of group therapy in the treatment of trauma survivors (Marmarosh, 2014). Group therapy, unlike other forms of treatment intervention, unites people who often feel lonely, isolated, and traumatized (Marmarosh, 2017). The group offers members a secure attachment to a leader/co-leader, fellow members, and the group-as-a-whole (Marmarosh et al., 2013). Similar to individual therapy, where an individual can explore traumatic experience with a therapist who has become a secure base, group members also gain a group identity which includes an attachment to the group that can buffer them from stress and re-traumatization (Marmarosh, 2014, 2022; Marmarosh & Tasca, 2013).

The secure attachments within the group (from leaders, members, and group) create a safe environment for members who can (1) share their fears and negative internal representations of others and (2) take risks to have here-and-now interactions that challenge past internal representations (Marmarosh et al., 2013). Over time, the repeated experience of positive relationship experiences becomes more automatic and replaces the automatic fight-or-flight trauma response (Marmarosh & Tasca, 2013). In groups addressing trauma, the group also empowers members to develop supportive relationships with group members that are affirming and that challenge internal representations of the self as a "victim or bad" and others as "dangerous or abusive." Group therapists have described how group therapy can help victims of trauma by developing attachment security within the group (Mendelsohn et al., 2007; Zorzella et al., 2014).

The Features of the Attachment-Oriented Group Therapist

Marmarosh et al. (2013) argue that attachment-oriented group leaders, as secure bases, are critical to fostering safety within a therapy group. Mikulincer and Shaver (2017) describe how leader responsiveness fosters the secure base, thus facilitating the open expression of painful feelings, enhancing insight and awareness of personal and interpersonal needs, and creating the optimal therapeutic environment for revising internal working models of self and others derived from trauma. The leader creates an environment where group members can openly share painful, traumatic experiences with one another and then explore the internal representations that follow. The interactions among members and leaders create new experiences (i.e., compassion, care, empathy, etc.), new internal representations of self and others (i.e., "I am not bad," "I am not alone," "I am not a victim," "Others are caring," "Others can be trusted," etc.), and new scripts for relationships (i.e., "When I am distressed, I can turn to people and receive compassion and love").

Case Illustration 1: The Group-as-a-Whole and Trauma

The following clinical vignette is an interpersonal process group in a community mental health clinic where five women with different racial and ethnic identities have been meeting to address relationship struggles. The women were in the group for many months. All had histories of emotional abandonment, intergenerational trauma, and trauma with early caregivers. Members also struggled with current traumas of repeated pregnancy loss, systemic racial trauma, and partner abuse. The actual details of the group and members have been altered to protect patient confidentiality.

During one session, the group members retreated into silence after a member described a painful experience at work. The leaders, both women of Color, imagined the silence was based on the members' feelings about the topic of racism and fears of exploring more deeply. Throughout the history of the group, sharing anger, setting limits, or being assertive in the context of their emotional needs was difficult. During this session, the leaders drew attention to the silence and wondered what had precipitated the members' need to protect themselves by pulling away and withdrawing. The members remained quiet. Many had fearful attachment styles wherein they alternated between being flooded with feelings and withdrawing into silence. They worried about being rejected by the other members (hyperactivation) and coped with their shame and guilt by pulling away and withdrawing into silence (deactivation). *Marmarosh (2022)* describes how groups can take on a group attachment based on the attachment styles of the members, which can explain the fight-or-flight response often seen in groups (*Bion, 1950*).

The leaders remained patient and compassionate with the members, realizing the trauma that they had endured and the need for emotional regulation. They focused on empathizing with the need to pull back when painful traumas, such as experiences involving racism, were raised, utilizing empathy to lessen the pressure to talk if members felt it was "too" difficult. Gradually, members took more risks and talked about the trauma related to racism.

In a subsequent session, a member shared the discomfort she felt at work when she was being treated differently as a woman of Color. Another member described the painful experience of being the recipient of a microaggression at work. The group members were slowly relating to one another about their experiences of racism. The leaders noticed the descriptions were often void of feelings, and asked what feelings came up when sharing. Initially, the feelings were of fear, grief, and then relief. The leaders slowly suggested the possibility of their also feeling anger and rage. Members denied these feelings at first; it took months for members to access angry feelings, due to fears of being racially stereotyped as "angry Black women."

With the support of the leaders, the members explored these internalized schemas related to the trauma of racism and systemic oppression. Initially, members struggled to identify what they had internalized. Over time, they realized that the painful experiences in different White spaces had become internalized as something negative about themselves. They needed to prove they were "not angry," were "worthy," and were "just as competent." The secure base of the group, initiated by the alliance with the leaders, allowed the members to hear a different perspective of who they truly were, listening to other members say they were not "only angry" but were also "strong, talented, and valuable." As *Bryant-Davis et al. (2021)* describe, the women felt more empowered in the group, enabling them to see what was likely internalized based on White supremacy and the intergenerational trauma of racism. Over time, other traumatic experiences were explored in the group, including multiple pregnancy losses, early childhood neglect and abuse, and domestic violence.

In this case example, we see how the group-as-a-whole was a secure base for the members, who were then able to rely on members to begin sharing intergenerational and current trauma. The leaders facilitated the creation of a safe space to regulate their distress, but the group members were the ones who provided shared experiences of trauma and allowed for the here-and-now experience of compassion, empathy, and support. Group members shared their personal experiences of racial microaggressions and the intergenerational trauma of being a person of Color (*Davis, 2007*), thereby challenging the internal representations that included representations based on racism and White supremacy. The group provided the opportunity to have new experiences of self and others within multiple attachment relationships (with leaders and members).

Utilizing an attachment theory focus, instead of being alone, the members begin to support one another. The leaders later link how the trauma impacts their internal voices regarding who they are in the world. Members can then begin to question their feelings of guilt and shame. They also begin to feel more empowered, angry, and frustrated, and that fosters more self-compassion (*Bryant-Davis et al., 2021*).

In the next example, an insecurely attached group member does not feel safe enough in the group to share her traumatic experience, and the individual therapist, functioning as a secure base, collaborates with the group leaders to undo the result of complex trauma.

Case Illustration 2: Disorganized Attachment and Combined Group and Individual Therapy

MG identifies as a 38-year-old cisgender White woman. She was self-referred to therapy, seeking support as she struggled to conceive a child. Her history of anorexia had included a hospitalization during high school. She described being an independent child, focused on getting straight As and wanting to be perfect. Her anorexia started after being sexually abused by a relative. Her abuse was a family secret. MG described deactivating strategies (i.e., withdrawing and disengaging when overwhelmed and escaping into work). She also engaged in hyperactivating strategies (taking care of others to prevent them from leaving). Her disorganized attachment style included oscillating among taking care of others, avoiding her own needs, and dissociating from painful feelings.

MG was a parentified child and had been praised for being a "good little girl." The anorexia was a way to express her angry feelings and to have control over her body after the sexual abuse. MG began therapy to address her anorexia and repeated pregnancy losses. The traumas of the multiple losses were overwhelming, and the stress was taking a toll on her marriage. The individual therapist referred MG to group therapy to increase her support.

MG came to the group but found it difficult to disclose anything that left her feeling vulnerable. She did not tell the group about her eating disorder or sexual abuse. She often focused on listening to others in the group and avoiding her own needs. She believed her anorexia was the cause of her infertility, despite physicians telling her the contrary.

During one individual session, the therapist asked MG what she thought would happen if she shared more of herself in the group. MG feared she would be blamed or that members would pity her. The internal script of "feeling shamed and humiliated and then worse if she sought out emotional support" became a focus in the individual therapy. The individual therapist, with MG's consent, contacted the group leaders to collaborate on treatment goals.

During an ensuing group session, MG took a risk. She disclosed her history of anorexia and her belief that it may have impacted her pregnancy losses. The members were very supportive. One member shared a similar eating issue that she had been too afraid to verbalize; another member talked about how her self-blame was something she often struggled with. MG talked more about her self-blame for the pregnancy losses. The leaders and members were able to contain the shame and tearful sadness as she revealed more vulnerable parts of herself. Members told her "she was not bad," which was unexpected. She stated that she had not relied on her parents as a child and did not cry in front of anyone, including her husband; the experience in the group was a new one.

In the individual therapy, MG described her group experiences. She could not believe the therapeutic effects, which included feeling lighter and less alone. She conveyed the progress in the group stemmed from the trust in the individual therapist. In essence, the individual therapist was a secure base from which MG could take risks in the group, culminating in a more secure attachment to the group.

This case example highlights how the group leaders collaborated with the individual therapist to foster the safety and emotion regulation needed to start processing the trauma in the group. It was the group that created the possibility for new relational experiences leading to the development of a new script for what happens when one seeks out intersubjective relatedness. The group members' openness with regards to their own traumas, their own pain, and their own struggles created an environment where MG was able to address her perfectionism, defensive self-sufficiency, and avoidance of feelings. The group afforded the safety MG needed, as others were also vulnerable, facilitating disclosure of her own suffering. Gradually, MG grew more connected and empowered in the group, decreasing her attachment avoidance and defensive deactivation when experiencing pain and personal needs.

Discussion and Implications

These clinical examples highlight how attachment dimensions influence group members' difficulties with closeness, self-worth, interpersonal connections, and feeling comfortable in group psychotherapy (Marmarosh et al., 2024). Individuals with trauma histories can have greater attachment anxiety and a more intense struggle to self-disclose and avoid the expression of anger due to their overwhelming anxiety over real or imagined rejection (Chen & Mallinckrodt, 2002; Shechtman & Dvir, 2006). Similarly, group members who have experienced trauma may also have more attachment avoidance and dissociative/deactivating behaviors in group sessions (Hammond & Marmarosh, 2011) than others. These members often disengage from the groups and may require the secure attachment of the individual therapist to tolerate and benefit from the group (Hammond & Marmarosh, 2011; Shechtman & Dvir, 2006).

Limitations

Although there are more recent papers addressing trauma and group therapy (Chouliara et al., 2020; Classen et al., 2021), addressing intergenerational trauma and group work (Bryant-Davis et al., 2021; Brave Heart et al., 2020), or with a focus on different cultures, values, and systemic forces that influence attachment (Stern et al., 2022), there have been fewer publications bridging attachment theory group interventions that address intergenerational/systemic traumas. Given the incredible need to provide mental health care to people who are suffering from poverty, war, oppression, and trauma, group therapy models that integrate attachment-based principles with the presence of these social experiences could provide enormous relief to many.

Why Group Therapy Is a Recommended Intervention in the Treatment of Trauma

Applying attachment theory and group therapy to trauma work has been supported in theory and research, but available training that includes this combination is insufficient. Many patients in inpatient settings are receiving group therapy intervention as the primary treatment modality, but outpatient treatment in diverse settings that include community mental health clinics, college counseling centers, and private practice still prioritizes individual treatment approaches (Whittingham et al., 2023). The future of trauma work requires utilization of therapy groups to foster improved emotion regulation, facilitate insight from observing others, and challenge internal models of themselves and others in here-and-now relationship experiences. No treatment has the power to activate the attachment system, foster a secure base, and encourage repair as much as group psychotherapy does. It may be the ideal treatment for healing the damage of trauma.

References

Ainsworth, M. D. S., Blehar, M. C., Waters, E., & Wall, S. (1978). *Patterns of attachment: A psychological study of the strange situation*. Lawrence Erlbaum. https://psycnet.apa.org/record/1980-50809-000

Barach, P. (1991). Multiple personality disorder as an attachment disorder. *Dissociation, IV*(3), 117–123. http://hdl.handle.net/1794/1448

Bartholomew, K. (1990). Avoidance of intimacy: An attachment perspective. *Journal of Social and Personal Relationships, 7*, 147–178. https://doi.org/10.1177/0265407590072001

Bion, W. R. (1950). Experiences in groups: V. *Human Relations, 3*(1), 3–14. https://doi.org/10.1177/001872675000300101

Bowlby, J. (1969). *Attachment and loss, volume 1. Attachment*. Basic Books. https://www.hachette-bookgroup.com/titles/john-bowlby/attachment/9780465005437/

Bowlby, J. (1973). *Attachment and loss, vol. 2: Separation*. Basic Books. https://www.hachettebookgroup.com/titles/john-bowlby/separation/9780465097166/

Bowlby, J. (1988). *A secure base*. Basic Books. https://www.hachettebookgroup.com/titles/john- bowlby/a-secure-base/9780465075973/?lens=basic-books

Brave Heart, M. Y. H., Chase, J., Myers, O., Elkins, J., Skipper, B., Schmitt, C., & Waldorf, V. (2020). Iwankapiya American Indian pilot clinical trial: Historical trauma and group interpersonal psychotherapy. *Psychotherapy, 57*(2), 184–191. https://doi.org/10.1037/pst0000267

Bretherton, I. (1992). The origins of attachment theory: John Bowlby and Mary Ainsworth. *Developmental Psychology, 28*(5), 759–775. https://doi.org/10.1037/0012-1649.28.5.759

Bryant, R. A. (2023). Attachment processes in posttraumatic stress disorder: A review of mechanisms to advance theories and treatments. *Clinical Psychology Review, 99*, 102228. https://doi.org/10.1016/j.cpr.2022.102228

Bryant-Davis, T., Fasalojo, B., Arounian, A., Jackson, K. L., & Leithman, E. (2021). Resist and rise: A trauma-informed womanist model for group therapy. *Women & Therapy, 47*(1), 34–57. https://doi.org/10.1080/02703149.2021.1943114

Carlson, E., Egeland, B., & Sroufe, L. A. (2009). A prospective investigation of the development of borderline personality symptoms. *Development and Psychopathology, 21*, 1311–1334. https://doi.org/10.1017/S0954579409990174

Cassidy, J., & Kobak, R. R. (1988). Avoidance and its relationship with other defensive processes. In J. Belsky & T. Nezworski (Eds.), *Clinical implications of attachment* (pp. 300–323). Erlbaum.

Chen, E. C., & Mallinckrodt, B. (2002). Attachment, group attraction and self-other agreement in interpersonal circumplex problems and perceptions of group members. *Group Dynamics: Theory, Research, and Practice, 6*(4), 311–324. https://doi.org/10.1037/1089-2699.6.4.311

Chouliara, Z., Karatzias, T., Gullone, A., Ferguson, S., Cosgrove, K., & Burke Draucker, C. (2020). Therapeutic change in group therapy for interpersonal trauma: A relational framework for research and clinical practice. *Journal of Interpersonal Violence, 35*(15–16), 2897–2916. https://doi.org/10.1177/0886260517696860

Classen, C. C., Hughes, L., Clark, C., Hill Mohammed, B., Woods, P., & Beckett, B. (2021). A pilot RCT of a body-oriented group therapy for complex trauma survivors: An adaptation of sensorimotor psychotherapy. *Journal of Trauma & Dissociation, 22*(1), 52–68. https://doi.org/10.1080/15299732.2020.1760173

Davis, D., Shaver, P. R., & Vernon, M. L. (2003). Physical, emotional, and behavioral reactions to breaking up: The roles of gender, age, emotional involvement, and attachment style. *Personality and Social Psychology Bulletin, 29*, 871–884. https://doi.org/10.1177/0146167203029007006

Davis, S. (2007). Racism as trauma: Some reflections on psychotherapeutic work with clients from the African-Caribbean Diaspora from an attachment-based perspective. *Attachment, 1*(2), 179–199. https://terapia.co.uk/wp-content/uploads/2020/05/racism-as-trauma.pdf

Farina, B., Liotti, M., & Imperatori, C. (2019). The role of attachment trauma and disintegrative pathogenic processes in the traumatic-dissociative dimension. *Frontiers in Psychology, 10*, 933–933. https://doi.org/10.3389/fpsyg.2019.00933

Fearon, R. P., Bakermans-Kranenburg, M. J., Van IJzendoorn, M. H., Lapsley, A.-M., & Roisman, G. I. (2010). The significance of insecure attachment and disorganization in the development of children's externalizing behavior: A meta-analytic study. *Child Development, 81*(2), 435–456. https://doi.org/10.1111/j.1467-8624.2009.01405.x

Ford, J. D., & Courtois, C. A. (Eds.). (2020). *Treating complex traumatic stress disorders in adults: Scientific foundations and therapeutic models* (2nd ed.). Guilford Publications. https://www.guilford.com/books/Treating-Complex-Traumatic-Stress-Disorders-in-Adults/Ford-Courtois/9781462543625

Fosha, D. (2000). *The transforming power of affect: A model for accelerated change.* Basic Books. https://www.hachettebookgroup.com/titles/diana-fosha/the-transforming-power-of-affect/9780465095674/

Foy, D. W., Eriksson, C. B., & Trice, G. A. (2001). Introduction to group interventions for trauma survivors. *Group Dynamics: Theory, Research, and Practice, 5*(4), 246. https://doi.org/10.1037/1089-2699.5.4.246

Fraley, R. C., Fazzari, D. A., Bonanno, G. A., & Dekel, S. (2006). Attachment and psychological adaptation in high exposure survivors of the September 11th attack on the World Trade Center. *Personality and Social Psychology Bulletin, 32*, 538–551. https://doi.org/10.1177/0146167205282741

Hammond, E. S., & Marmarosh, C. L. (2011). The influence of individual attachment styles on group members' experience of therapist transitions. *International Journal of Group Psychotherapy, 61*(4), 596–620. https://doi.org/10.1521/ijgp.2011.61.4.596

Hesse, E., & Main, M. (2000). Disorganized infant, child, and adult attachment: Collapse in behavioral and attentional strategies. *Journal of the American Psychoanalytic Association, 48*, 1097–1127. https://doi.org/10.1177/00030651000480041101

Horowitz, M. J. (1982). Psychological processes induced by illness, injury, and loss. In T. Millon, C. Green, & R. Meagher (Eds.), *Handbook of clinical health psychology* (pp. 53–68). Plenum Press. https://doi.org/10.1007/978-1-4613-3412-5_3

Keating, L., Tasca, G. A., Gick, M., Ritchie, K., Balfour, L., & Bissada, H. (2014). Change in attachment to the therapy group generalizes to change in individual attachment among women with binge eating disorder. *Psychotherapy, 51*(1), 78–87. https://doi.org/10.1037/a0031099

Keller, H. (2013). Attachment and culture. *Journal of Cross-Cultural Psychology, 44*(2), 175–194. https://doi.org/10.1177/0022022112472253

Leiderman, L. (2020). Psychodynamic group therapy with hispanic migrants: Interpersonal, relational constructs in treating complex trauma, dissociation, and enactments. *International Journal of Group Psychotherapy, 70*(2), 162–182. https://doi.org/10.1080/00207284.2019.1686704

Liotti, G. (1992). Disorganized/disoriented attachment in the etiology of the dissociative disorders. *Dissociation: Progress in the Dissociative Disorders, 5*, 196–204. https://www.apc.it/wp-content/uploads/2018/08/1992-Liotti-DAttachment_Dissociativedisorders1992.pdf

Main, M., & Cassidy, J. (1988). Categories of response to reunion with the parent at age six: Predictable from infant attachment classifications and stable over a 1-month period. *Developmental Psychology, 24*, 415–426. https://doi.org/10.1037/0012-1649.24.3.415

Main, M., & Hesse, E. (1990). Parent's unresolved traumatic experiences are related to infant disorganized/disoriented attachment status: Is frightened and/or frightening parental behavior the linking mechanism? In M. T. Greenberg, D. Cicchetti, & E. M. Cummings (Eds.), *Attachment in the preschool years: Theory, research, and intervention* (pp. 161–182). University of Chicago Press. https://press.uchicago.edu/ucp/books/book/chicago/A/bo3774473.html

Main, M., & Hesse, E. (1992). Disorganized/disoriented infant behavior in the Strange Situation, lapses in the monitoring of reasoning and discourse during the parent's Adult Attachment Interview, and dissociative states. In M. Ammaniti & D. Stern (Eds.), *Attaccamento e psicoanalisi (Attachment and psychoanalysis)* (pp. 86–140). Laterza.

Main, M., & Solomon, J. (1986). Discovery of a new, insecure-disorganized/disoriented attachment pattern. In T. B. Brazelton & M. Yogman (Eds.), *Affective development in infancy* (pp. 95–124). Ablex.

Main, M., & Solomon, J. (1990). Procedures for identifying infants as disorganized/disoriented during the Ainsworth Strange Situation. In M. T. Greenberg, D. Cicchetti, & E. M. Cummings (Eds.), *Attachment in the preschool years: Theory, research, and intervention* (pp. 121–160). University of Chicago Press. https://press.uchicago.edu/ucp/books/book/chicago/A/bo3774473.html

Marmarosh, C., Markin, R., & Spiegle, E. (2013). *Attachment in group psychotherapy*. American Psychological Association. https://doi.org/10.1037/14186-000

Marmarosh, C. L. (2014). Empirical research on attachment in group psychotherapy: Moving the field forward. *Psychotherapy, 51*(1), 88–92. https://doi.org/10.1037/a0032523

Marmarosh, C. L. (2017). Attachment in group psychotherapy: Bridging theories, research, and clinical techniques. *International Journal of Group Psychotherapy, 67*(2), 157–160. https://doi.org/10.1080/00207284.2016.1267573

Marmarosh, C. L. (2022). Attachments, trauma, and COVID-19: Implications for leaders, groups, and social justice. *Group Dynamics: Theory, Research, and Practice, 26*(2), 85–91. https://doi.org/10.1037/gdn0000187

Marmarosh, C. L., Solorio, A., Koroma, M. B. Z., Xing, F., & Robelo, A. (2024). Attachment theory and the transition to online group therapy during COVID-19: A preliminary investigation. *Group Dynamics: Theory, Research, and Practice, 28*(1), 17–27. https://doi.org/10.1037/gdn0000209

Marmarosh, C. L., & Tasca, G. A. (2013). Adult attachment anxiety: Using group therapy to promote change. *Journal of Clinical Psychology, 69*(11), 1172–1182. https://doi.org/10.1002/jclp.22044

Mendelsohn, M., Zachary, R. S., & Harney, P. A. (2007). Group therapy as an ecological bridge to new community for trauma survivors. *Journal of Aggression, Maltreatment & Trauma, 14*(1–2), 227–243. https://doi.org/10.1300/J146v14n01_12

Mikulincer, M., & Shaver, P. R. (2016). *Attachment in adulthood: Structure, dynamics, and change* (2nd ed.). Guilford Press. https://www.guilford.com/books/Attachment-in-Adulthood/Mikulincer-Shaver/9781462533817

Mikulincer, M., & Shaver, P. R. (2017). Augmenting the sense of attachment security in group contexts: The effects of a responsive leader and a cohesive group. *International Journal of Group Psychotherapy, 67*(2), 161–175. https://doi.org/10.1080/00207284.2016.1260462

Mikulincer, M., & Shaver, P. R. (2020). Enhancing the "broaden and build" cycle of attachment security in adulthood: From the laboratory to relational contexts and societal systems. *International Journal of Environmental Research and Public Health, 17*(6), 2054. https://doi.org/10.3390/ijerph17062054

Mikulincer, M., & Shaver, P. R. (2022). Enhancing the "broaden-and-build" cycle of attachment security as a means of overcoming prejudice, discrimination, and racism. *Attachment & Human Development, 24*(3), 260–273. https://doi.org/10.1080/14616734.2021.1976921

Mikulincer, M., & Shaver, P. R. (2023). *Attachment theory applied: Fostering personal growth through healthy relationships.* The Guilford Press. https://www.guilford.com/books/Attachment-Theory-Applied/Mikulincer-Shaver/9781462552337

Mikulincer, M., Shaver, P. R., & Solomon, Z. (2015). An attachment perspective on traumatic and post-traumatic reactions. In M. P. Safir, H. S. Wallach, & S. Rizzo (Eds.), *Future directions in post-traumatic stress disorder: Prevention, diagnosis, and treatment* (pp. 79–96). Springer Press. https://doi.org/10.1007/978-1-4899-7522-5_4

Mikulincer, M., Shaver, P. R., Solomon, Z., & Ein-Dor, T. (2014). Attachment-related consequences of war captivity and trajectories of posttraumatic stress disorder: A 17-year longitudinal study. *Journal of Social and Clinical Psychology, 33*, 207–228. https://doi.org/10.1521/jscp.2014.33.3.207

Porges, S. W. (2021). *Polyvagal safety: Attachment, communication, self-regulation (IPNB)*. WW Norton & Company. https://doi.org/10.1111/jmft.12585

Schore, A. (2022). Right brain-to-right brain psychotherapy: Recent scientific and clinical advances. *Annals of General Psychiatry, 21*(1), 46. https://doi.org/10.1186/s12991-022-00420-3

Schwartze, D., Barkowski, S., Strauss, B., Knaevelsrud, C., & Rosendahl, J. (2019). Efficacy of group psychotherapy for posttraumatic stress disorder: Systematic review and meta-analysis of randomized controlled trials. *Psychotherapy Research, 29*(4), 415–431. https://doi.org/10.1080/10503307.2017.1405168

Shaver, P. R., & Mikulincer, M. (2002). Attachment-related psychodynamics. *Attachment and Human Development, 4*, 133–161. https://doi.org/10.1080/14616730210154171

Shechtman, Z., & Dvir, V. (2006). Attachment style as a predictor of behavior in group counseling with preadolescents. *Group Dynamics: Theory, Research, and Practice, 10*(1), 29–42. https://doi.org/10.1037/1089-2699.10.1.29

Simpson, J. A., & Rholes, W. S. (2002). Fearful-avoidance, disorganization, and multiple working models: Some directions for future theory and research. *Attachment & Human Development, 4*(2), 223–229. https://doi.org/10.1080/14616730210154207

Sloan, D. M., Feinstein, B. A., Gallagher, M. W., Beck, J. G., & Keane, T. M. (2013). Efficacy of group treatment for posttraumatic stress disorder symptoms: A meta-analysis. *Psychological Trauma: Theory, Research, Practice, and Policy, 5*(2), 176–183. https://doi.org/10.1037/a0026291

Sroufe, L. A., Egeland, B., & Carlson, E. (1999). One social world: The integrated development of parent-child and peer relationships. In W. A. Collins & B. Laursen (Eds.), *Relationships as developmental contexts: The 30th Minnesota symposium on child psychology.* Erlbaum. https://doi.org/10.4324/9781410601902-19

Sroufe, L. A., Egeland, B., Carlson, E. A., & Collins, W. A. (2005). *The development of the person: The Minnesota study of risk and adaptation from birth to adulthood.* Guilford Publications. https://www.guilford.com/books/The-Development-of-the-Person/Sroufe-Egeland-Carlson-Collins/97816 06232491

Stern, J. A., Barbarin, O., & Cassidy, J. (2022). Attachment perspectives on race, prejudice, and anti-racism: Introduction to the special issue. *Attachment & Human Development, 24*(3), 253–259. https://doi.org/10.1080/14616734.2021.1976920

Van Rosmalen, L., Van der Veer, R., & Van der Horst, F. (2015). Ainsworth's strange situation procedure: The origin of an instrument. *Journal of the History of the Behavioral Sciences, 51*(3), 261–284. https://doi.org/10.1002/jhbs.21729

Whittingham, M., Marmarosh, C. L., Mallow, P., & Scherer, M. (2023). Mental health care equity and access: A group therapy solution. *American Psychologist, 78*(2), 119–133. https://doi.org/10.1037/amp0001078

Woodhouse, S., Ayers, S., & Field, A. P. (2015). The relationship between adult attachment style and post-traumatic stress symptoms: A meta-analysis. *Journal of Anxiety Disorders, 35*, 103–117. https://doi.org/10.1016/j.janxdis.2015.07.002

Zorzella, K. P., Muller, R. T., & Classen, C. C. (2014). Trauma group therapy: The role of attachment and therapeutic alliance. *International Journal of Group Psychotherapy, 64*(1), 24–47. https://doi.org/10.1521/ijgp.2014.64.1.24

4 Deconstructing the Wall of Dissociation, Regression, and Primitive Defenses in Both Group Members and Therapists

A Holistic, Systems Perspective

Victor L. Schermer

In the last four decades, trauma theory and research have made significant contributions to advancing personality theory and developmental psychology. Conversely, as a plethora of newer perspectives and interventions have been applied to trauma itself, the practitioner requires new ways to incorporate these theories and perspectives into practice. The purpose of this chapter is to explore one aspect of theory and practice, specifically the treatment of traumatic defense mechanisms and coping strategies in group psychotherapy. I contrast opposing and sometimes divisive perspectives of trauma group theory to proposing a holistic and systems view in which diverse constructs and perspectives are seen to be intertwined ways to view the group rather than regarded as detached "things-in-themselves" which are assumed to be "real" but are actually constructs grasped through a particular theoretical frame or ideology. Hopefully, such a holistic understanding will help the group therapist utilize diverse theories while remaining open to the process experience as it occurs, staying creative in response to what happens, and being engaged, authentic, and vulnerable while maintaining sufficient objectivity and boundaries to be effective and ethical in the therapist's role. My contention is that such a holistic viewpoint promotes the kind of "resilience" (Burton et al., 2015) that allows the therapist to help the victims of trauma relate in the group with a feeling of safety and trust while exploring new experiences and behaviors that facilitate healing and propel forward movement in their lives.

Two Historically Dominant Perspectives on Trauma

When people are traumatized emotionally, it becomes apparent over time that their minds and bodies (psyche and soma) change in ways that reflect a wound damaging to mental functioning. Thus, we see in response to the trauma various cognitive, emotional, and interpersonal efforts to repair the harm and restore a sense of safety and self-protection. One way that the mind/body protects itself is to use "defense mechanisms," specific sensorimotor/affective/cognitive/behavioral strategies for restoring psychological equilibrium. When trauma first came to the attention of psychiatrists in the latter part of the 19th century, two defense mechanisms or coping strategies were proposed by different practitioners. For Freud (Boag, 2012), the primary defense was *repression*, the motivated forgetting of the painful experiences. For Janet (van der Hart & Horst, 1989), one of the pioneering trauma researchers and practitioners using hypnosis, the primary defense was *dissociation*, the keeping apart of elements of experience that were previously interconnected.

Other defense mechanisms, such as reaction formation, denial, intellectualization, and projection, as well as symptoms, such as numbness, paralysis, withdrawal, and avoidance, emerge as ways in which the mind wards off an overwhelming emotional encounter with

DOI: 10.4324/9781003546252-6

traumatic memories. Janet did not use the term "defense mechanism" per se, ultimately rejecting Freud's whole theory as "metaphysical" rather than based on scientific method. But he described several adaptations and symptoms of patients who suffered from hysteria that serve the function of defense mechanisms.

The point for the current discussion is that the subject matter of this chapter, namely, the psychological and specifically defensive responses to trauma that have been observed and discussed over the course of more than a century, has mostly been conceptualized and discussed from (at least) these two broad perspectives: (1) a theory of consciousness (Janet's) emphasizing changes in experience and behavior resulting from trauma, and (2) a dynamic theory of unconscious "forces" (Freud) which determine what enters or does not enter consciousness, wherein consciousness is but the smallest fraction of psychological functioning. The ramifications of such paradigmatic differences in theorizing have been part of psychological theory and practice since the medical and academic disciplines of psychiatry and psychology were born (Ellenberger, 1981).

Other Conceptual Splits or Divisions That Call for Integration

There are other dichotomies as well which are valid in their own terms but force us into a procrustean bed when we are providing group psychotherapy *in vivo*. In addition to the split between "conscious" (some might prefer to use the term "phenomenological") psychology and the "dynamic" psychology of unconscious forces, there are several other splits in perspective which lead to a confusion of tongues when it comes to making sense out of the phenomena that must be addressed by the therapist in groups that treat psychological trauma. For example, there are traditional divisions between individual and group psychology, and between patients (regarded as pathologized disease entities) and therapist (regarded as a detached observer) that appear arbitrary when working in the cauldron of the group matrix (Foulkes, 1973).

As we learn more and more about the prevalence of trauma in both the general and mental health populations (van der Kolk, 2015), and as we discover how trauma induces neurophysiological changes, lifelong attachment issues, developmental difficulties, undiagnosed disorders, feelings of abandonment, and narcissistic injuries (Canales, 2025; Grossmark, 2025; Hu & Kyei, 2025; Leiderman, 2025; Leiderman & Buchele, 2025; Marmarosh et al., 2025), we come to know how trauma is much more contributory to a wide variety of psychopathology and diagnoses than we thought. Moreover, we are more than ever aware of "collective trauma," or mass trauma events that traumatize a large number of individuals, large groups and populations (Leiderman & Klein, 2022; Weinberg, 2025). The 9/11 terrorist attacks stand as a powerful reminder of such events. Thus, the dynamics of groups and the impact of trauma appear more and more intertwined. Volkan (2001) addressed "chosen trauma," those large-scale societal and ethnic "wounds" that are transmitted throughout a culture over many generations, and Hopper (1997) proposed a "fourth basic assumption" that results from the emergence of traumatic memories, ideation, and affect in the "social unconscious." Traumatic events and experiences can be part and parcel of group-as-a-whole dynamics as much as they occur within individuals.

For such reasons, the author will here consider dissociation, regression, and primitive defenses in groups from *three holistic group systems vantage points*: (1) "The Group-as-a-Whole: Regression, the fourth Basic Assumption, Chosen Trauma, and Enactments"; (2) "The Traumatized Individual in the Group: The Dissociative Matrix"; and (3) "The Role and Vulnerability of the Therapist: Detachment, Empathy, and Authenticity."

The initial focus on the group-as-a-whole is not to suggest that the group process should be the primary focus of interventions, which it is for some schools of thought (Bion, 1961; Colman & Bexton, 1975), but rather that applying this perspective provides a link between the personal trauma and the system. It is the author's belief that defense mechanisms, dissociation, and other forms of adaptation and development are more than expressions of the individual: They are inter-systemic in nature, appearing at the individual, interpersonal, and group levels. Finally, the author will articulate the position that group therapists are not detached observers; they are vulnerable and sometimes traumatized human beings assigned a specific role as leaders. They have their own training, responsibilities, and boundary conditions, but like the group members, they have their own trauma, vulnerabilities, and defenses which must be addressed.

The Group-as-a-Whole: Regression, the Fourth Basic Assumption, Chosen Trauma, and Enactments

Looking back in time to the origins of both trauma theory and analytically oriented group psychotherapy, it is striking that, although collective trauma stared them in the face, Freud, in his essay "Group psychology and the analysis of the ego" (1921), and Bion, in *Experiences in Groups* (1961), both wrote as if the group members under study were "normative" human beings, that is, as if the group dynamics were unrelated to individual pathology or trauma.

Freud was writing shortly after the wave of war trauma from World War I and had just published "Beyond the Pleasure Principle" (1920), in which he attempted to expand psychoanalysis to include the impact of aggression and trauma on the personality, emphasizing the trauma-based repetition compulsion. Even so, when he advanced his main hypothesis that group members project their ego ideal onto the leader (Freud, 1921), a form of collective projective identification (Turquet, 1975) which can result in authoritarianism (Adorno et al., 1993 [1950]), he did not connect this group defense to trauma. Bion (1961) was working as a psychiatrist in a hospital in England in the so-called *Northfield Experiment* (Coombe, 2019), where he and others were "experimenting" with the use of group therapy for soldiers, many of whom suffered from posttraumatic stress disorder, then known as shell shock. When he wrote about the "basic assumptions," that is, the group formations of dependency, fight-or-flight, and pairing, he assumed that these forms of *group regression* were simply the result of bringing people together in groups. He made little mention of trauma, even though many of the members of his experimental groups were traumatized! Both Freud and Bion assumed that group regression was a universal human experience rather than a trauma-based set of phenomena. More than that, neither realized that group regression varied in diverse cultures and might reflect racism, ethnic conflicts, and other social conflicts.

As psychological trauma (Herman & van der Kolk, 1987; van der Kolk, 1987) and cultural diversity (Eason, 2009) came to merit greater interest and research, some group practitioners and theorists began to highlight their importance in group-as-a-whole dynamics. Hopper (1997), partly from his work treating Holocaust survivors in group therapy, and partly from his own background in sociology, hypothesized a fourth basic assumption which he called I:A/M (Incohesion: Aggregation/Massification). He defined it as a state of disorganization of the individuals in the group matrix into isolated personae, for which he used the vivid metaphor "crustaceans" living in isolated hard shells or, its opposite, "amoebae" merging with others in fusion or lack of boundaries. He held that such disorganized boundary changes were defenses against primitive "annihilation anxiety," the severe loss of self (Hurvich, 2003), a psychotic-like state resulting from the trauma and dehumanization of, for example, the

Shoah and the concentration camps which Hopper's patients had experienced. Shengold (1991), with respect to child abuse and neglect, proposed a similar deterioration of the self which he called "soul murder," the psychotic loss of selfhood resulting from severe trauma.

However useful Hopper's idea of a fourth basic assumption may be, a holistic, systemic view of group dynamics would suggest that *all* the basic assumptions are fueled or evoked by implicit or "masked trauma" (Schermer, 2004), provoked within the context of the coming together of people in small and large unstructured groups. Bennis and Shepard (1956), in a group developmental alternative to basic assumptions, suggested that the group evolves from "dependence" to "counter-dependence" and then, by displacing the leader and internalizing the leadership role, achieves a more functional state of "interdependence." The shifting power differential between "dependents" (people who rely on others) and "counter-dependents" (people who oppose or control others) incorporates the importance of personality types and power differentials in group formation. Some, though certainly not all, of this power differential might be an expression of the dominance–submission factor (victim–victimizer) of trauma.

An additional way of theorizing about the appearance of trauma in group dynamics at a societal and historical level was proposed by Volkan (1988) in his efforts to explain the recurrent appearance of hostility, marginalization, and war between members of different ethnic groups even when their important interests would benefit from cooperation, thus creating a win–win situation for both sides. Volkan (2001) provided significant evidence that members of ethnic groups, nationalities, and majority/minority groups pass on collective trauma from generation to generation by remembering and giving symbolic long-term importance to a particular catastrophic event, which he called a *chosen trauma*. This *chosen trauma* begins with a mourning process but, given the collective nature of the hurt or wound, perpetuates the polarization, prejudice, and animosity between groups, often over generations. An example of such a chosen trauma consists of the recollections of Palestinians and Israelis of hurts inflicted centuries ago by one on the other and then repeated throughout repetition compulsion at the societal "large group" level.

The expression of chosen trauma in small therapy groups appears when there arise conflicts between men and women, Blacks and Whites, gays and straights, and other populations. The collective memories and dominance–submission power struggles have crossed many generations through stories, symbols, and attitudes. They are not simply stereotypes of conflicting groups who marginalize one another; they have a long socioeconomic and political history. One way to resolve such conflicts based on chosen trauma, according to Volkan (2001), is to reinitiate the mourning process that had been suppressed for many generations. The generations-old grief is a shared emotion on both sides and helps each experience their common humanity.

Like Volkan, Rando (1993) held that traumatic experiences always involve loss and grief. The following is an example of how uncovering and addressing the grief underlying the anger and defenses of an intergroup conflict led to reconciliation between the two subgroups in a workshop situation.

Case Illustration 1: Partial Resolution of Chosen Trauma Through a Mourning Process

An urban community mental health center that suffered from Black–White segregation and racism which persisted decades after the beginning of the Civil

Rights Movement held a one-day gathering of political leaders, community organizers, and citizens to discuss possible solutions to the ongoing systemic racism. The attendees participated in small groups to address the problems. In one group, the leader used some of the aforementioned principles to resolve conflicts emanating from racism, expressed via micro- and macroaggressions that were re-enacted. There were 12 group members, roughly half of whom were Black, and the other half were White and Latinx.

The group began with a very abstruse, detached discussion of ideas. The leader pointed out the lack of emotion in the conversation and wondered if members could share more personal experiences about their problems. Two Black women reflected upon the hurt and emotional harm from years of racism, discrimination, and personal trauma they had experienced. Other Black participants shared similar experiences. The White and Latinx attendees, while responding, were not empathic but talked about the faults and even criminal activity of Blacks in their neighborhoods. They were seemingly unaware of their lack of empathy as well as its accompanying injurious impact experienced as micro- and macroaggressions by Black women. The two Black women were hurt, withdrew, and dissociated. The leader intervened by tending to the injuries and asked the group, "Can we, as a group, safely contain, process, discuss, be accountable to, and address the systemic racism inside our group that parallels what many in the Black community experience in isolation outside the group?" This enabled the women who were harmed and other Black members who identified with what transpired in the group to express their hurt and disappointment in the others. The group members who made the hurtful remarks shared their remorse and apologized for the harm they had committed. As the awareness emerged in the group that the group could serve as a safe container to hold and process the unresolved, systemic racism occurring in their communities at large and what was re-enacted in their group, a Black woman began to weep, sharing the emotional pain she feels when shamed, as well as her experiences of racism both within and outside of the group, and a White woman hugged her and expressed her empathy and sorrow. There was then an expression of grief and reconciliation among all the members of the group. The leader explained how sharing the "chosen trauma" and its wounds and shame brought out the grief, which facilitated human understanding. There was a "wall" of defenses and coping strategies that led to protracted conflict and unresolved racism. The leader chose to intervene with the suggestion that the conflicting parties share the grief and emotional pain caused by racism, thus partially deconstructing the "wall" of defenses and coping strategies.

The Traumatized Individual in the Group: The Dissociative Matrix

Basic assumptions and chosen trauma are hidden ways in which trauma can appear in therapy groups. In groups consisting of identified trauma patients convened for the purpose of witnessing and working through trauma, the traumas are identified by sharing and processing the specific experiences of each member of the group. Witnessing, sharing, and processing specific traumatic experiences are a crucial beginning to healing the effects of trauma (Herman, 1992).

But as these groups continue over time, the trauma will become increasingly manifest at the group-as-a-whole level. This can be thought of in terms of Agazarian's *living systems theory*: the expression of a given phenomenon in all levels of the system. As Agazarian (2012) pointed out, the various levels of living systems have certain parallels, called *isomorphisms*. For example, a living cell processes and metabolizes nutrients just the way the whole body does. In the therapy group, the individual system, the subgroup systems, and the group-as-a-whole have common properties or isomorphisms. One could add that the large group, institutional, and/or societal systems as containing and isomorphic to the others.

Agazarian's theory provides some of the reasoning and concepts through which the group therapist can begin to understand and interpret intragroup experiences and events from a multi-systems perspective, which can help interventions to be healing holistically rather than just "fixing" a particular component of the individual's problem.

Case Illustration 2: A Group Enactment

In a heterogeneous, long-term trauma therapy group for people with a variety of traumas as well as other diagnoses, the group seemed to be evolving well, with members sharing some of their trauma histories, beginning to bond with each other, and forming a cohesive group. The therapist was working with Arnie (pseudonym), a gay Latinx man in his 50s, who had been abused physically and emotionally by beatings, harsh criticism, shaming, and isolation throughout his childhood and early adolescence at the hands of his father, a former military officer who had experienced untreated war trauma. Arnie was sharing his memories of abuse in some detail, but without emotion. The group members, however, were listening intently. Suddenly, he went into a trancelike state that looked a little like the beginning of a seizure. He burst into a tirade, shouting epithets at the leader, accusing him of being a "wimp" and an "asshole." "Why don't you take more control of this f***ing group, so we can get some real work done in here?" He got up, grabbed his coat, and started to leave, but the therapist and the group were able to re-establish rapport with him, and relieved, he regained his composure and sat down, saying, "I'm sorry. I don't know what happened that I got that way."

This sudden, seemingly irrational, emotion-laden incident was interpreted by the therapist as an enactment or replay of his traumatic experiences with his father, in which Arnie became both his rageful father and the hurt, angry, and protesting child. The therapist, thinking holistically and systemically, realized that Arnie was also expressing the suppressed hostility of the whole group. The therapist suggested to the group that everyone in the group had put the angry parts of themselves into Arnie for containment, that is, projective identification. Now, the therapist was able to help each member verbalize their anger more constructively, examine its sources, and become more assertive. The therapist could use the experience, which was frightening to everyone in the room, to provide help to the whole group rather than just one person.

Over time, however, the incident resurfaced, with members becoming restless and expressing a strong need for help from the therapist. They joined with Arnie, demanding in a critical and hostile tone that the therapist be more actively helpful to them. The therapist, rather than interpreting the request as transference of feelings of abandonment by parent figures or abusers, decided to engage interpersonally, saying, "How do you think I feel when you gang up on me like that?" When he stepped out of the consultant role, showing more vulnerability, the group members empathized and engaged more fully with the therapist.

The members voiced a variety of hurts and unresolved traumatic memories with one another. Soon their narratives brought in a whole cast of characters: the teacher who doled out physical punishments, the parents' contentious divorce, the boss who sexually seduced, the peer group who bullied, etc. It appeared that everyone in the group was containing not only a personal trauma but also those of the other group members as well. Dissociated aspects of trauma were projectively identified into one another for containment.

Ever since Janet and his cohorts connected the two ideas of trauma and dissociation, the word *dissociation* has become part of the vocabulary of trauma studies. This connection is partially because many of the victims report that at the moment of the traumatic event, they experienced feelings of numbness and/or leaving their bodies and/or engaging in a neutral activity like smoking or reading a newspaper and/or blacking out into a state of amnesia. To cope with the overwhelming fear, they dissociated or separated one part of themselves from another. This process of dissociation continued in the months, or even years, after the trauma as a generalized coping mechanism. An extreme outcome of dissociation is dissociative identity disorder (ICD-10 F44. 81, World Health Organization, 1994)), or "multiple personality." Kluft's (1984) extensive work on such disorders has advanced our understanding from a curious phenomenon with a few astonishing case studies and biographies to a thoroughgoing scientific endeavor which also illuminates the nature of complex posttraumatic stress disorder (CPTSD) and dissociation within the context of other disorders.

Group therapy provides a special opportunity to illuminate the dissociative process for patients and to help reintegrate the dissociated aspects of self into the central core of their personalities. Over time, the members projectively identify the dissociated images, memories, and repetition enactments into other members, the therapist, and the group-as-a-whole. The recipients become "containers" of the projective identifications, and eventually can be helped to "return" them in an empathic way which facilitates reintegration of the self.

What can be called the *dissociative matrix* (Schermer, 2004) is a useful construct for this mutual containment of dissociative elements in trauma groups by the group members. As the various traumatic experiences break through the traumatic walls of defenses, a kind of "crazy quilt" of containment emerges, such that the component aspects of trauma of the group members reappear and/or are re-enacted in other individuals, interpersonal interactions, and the group-as-a-whole. This eventuality can become difficult for the therapist to manage, but it also can become a useful therapeutic tool if the members can hold and contain the projective identifications in a non-interpretive, compassionate, healthier form so that they can be re-owned.

Such a process has, for a long time, been productively utilized in psychodrama (Moreno, 2020), where the group members take on the roles of important personae and aspects of self of the identified patient. More recently, Schwartz's Internalized Family Systems (IFS) approach (Schwartz & Sweezy, 2019/1995) provides a particular road map to the sub-selves seen as parents, siblings, extended family members, and others. IFS helps the therapist utilize concepts from family therapy to bring about internal change.

From neuroscience and other disciplines, there is now increasing interest in "multiplicity," the existence of multiple roles, multiple selves, and even multiple consciousness, as a normal aspect of brain functioning (Dulberg et al., 2023). From such a perspective, we can begin to see that dissociation is an extreme instance of a normal division of the self into components, roles, and problem-solving elements. These multiple selves can be transformed and utilized by groups to form productive elements of the work group (Bion, 1961), that is, the constructive projects and tasks the group sets itself to do.

Case Illustration 3: A Mini-Instance of Containment and Resolution of Dissociated Affect and Memories in the Group

This example illustrates how the therapist's unconscious regression and re-enactment can become a useful therapeutic tool. An inpatient group of eight substance abusers met daily for several days without productivity. The members sat in silence, complained about the facility, or made cynical comments about each other and the leader. A new member, Marston, a cisgendered privileged White man, joined the group. He was a big man who could easily pass for a defensive guard on an NFL football team. He wore a business suit in an environment where casual clothes were the norm. Marston looked angry, and when asked what brought him into treatment, he scowled and said, "I got into a brawl. They arrested me, and the judge gave me a choice between jail and this. I don't need any of this treatment bulls**t."

The therapist, feeling scared and without thinking, put the teddy bear sitting on his desk in Marston's lap and then froze, fearing Marston might respond with a tirade or even physical assault. The group therapist, addressing his regression in group, admitted his fear of Marston, saying it reminded him of others who had bullied him growing up. He added that, just as he did as a child, he knew he was trying to placate "the bully."

There was dead silence while Marston held the teddy bear in his hands and stared at it for a few minutes. Suddenly, to everyone's surprise and relief, he broke down and sobbed. The group and therapist remained silent, allowing him to shed all his tears. Then he lifted his head, looked around the room at everyone, and said, "When I was a kid, I had a great big teddy bear. When my mother wasn't around, or when my father got angry with me, I would go to my room and hug it. My parents quarreled a lot and eventually divorced. For a period of time, I think that the teddy bear helped me survive all the tension and abandonments." And then he added that his father told him he should never cry but be a "macho" male and bite the bullet.

The therapist praised him for being able to show his vulnerability and suggested that maybe his drinking was a way to anesthetize himself from all the suppressed anger and hurt. Then, virtually every member of the group disclosed traumatic or hurtful events in their lives. The therapist pointed out how all that hurt and victimization had previously led to a dissociative wall of silence in the group.

The shame the members had carried for many years was temporarily dissolved by what happened. The next day, they referred to themselves as "the A-team" and told other patients in the larger community how well they were doing. Thus, the shame and guilt that had kept them silent and dissociated through a wall of defenses were partially resolved, at least for the moment, and led to productive therapy work and a collective improvement in self-esteem.

> For the group, Marston was like a gift from the outside world who contained and expressed the dissociated thoughts and affects that each member had carried on his own for many years. The concept of the dissociative matrix suggests that all the various dissociated experiences are brought into the group, seeking containers that can receive them and, hopefully, as Marston did, return them to the members in a more integrated, holistic way. This is a systems viewpoint, very different from the idea that traumatic defenses and affects are housed in individual minds and should be treated in individual therapy or in groups that emphasize individual treatment in groups.

The Role and Vulnerability of the Therapist From a Holistic, Systems Perspective: Detachment, Empathy, and Authenticity

Consistent with a systems/holistic process, and in accordance with developments in interpersonal psychiatry (Sullivan, 1955) and relational psychoanalysis (Mitchell, 1988), a specific psychotherapist has emerged in which they are not so much a detached and neutral observer but holistically skilled and knowledgeable while nevertheless being engaged, often flawed, and in various degrees, a traumatized individual, given a specific role as caregiver, with specific boundary conditions that help maintain the caregiving role. Wolf (2002), for example, pointed out that the inevitable failures of the therapist to understand the patient's narcissistic vulnerability and hurts can be used productively in the treatment by the therapist admitting to the patient their failure to perceive and acknowledge the patient's feelings and to help the latter sort out emotional reactions and developmental history related to such "narcissistic injuries." Langs (1978) stated that the mutual projective identifications of patient and analyst can be recognized in order to clear the interpersonal field of transference/countertransference distortions facilitating the patient's gaining insight into maladaptive relationship patterns rather than achieving a so-called "transference cure," in which patient and therapist collude to produce an illusion of change.

Mitchell (1988) initiated a rich field of "relational psychoanalysis" in which the "distortions" of transference and countertransference become part of an interactive process with many realistic and adaptive components as well. With respect to group therapy, Billow (2003) used the ideas from relational psychoanalysis to point out the therapist's use of self, including conflicts and defenses, as a tool in therapy groups rather than an obstacle to treatment.

Into this mix, a massive literature on child development and the mother–infant dyad (Schechter et al., 2021) has led to studies of attachment (Wallin, 2007) and affect regulation (Hill & Schore, 2015), demonstrating that a systemic, interactive view can facilitate caregiver–child relationships as well as psychotherapies and can result in positive changes that are unresponsive to interpretations of individual dynamics.

Such paradigm shifts in the understanding of psychotherapy and human interaction have changed our understanding of trauma and the "defensive wall" as well as dissociative processes that emerge. Most generally, we now can use perspectives that regard trauma, defenses, and treatment as mutual relational processes among all participants: patients, therapists, family members, and social institutions. Rather than saying, for example, that the group member has "repressed" or "dissociated" the traumatic memories and emotions, we can look for some aspect of the therapist's stance and relationship that prevents those memories and emotions from surfacing in the group process. We may find elements in the current culture of the group or society that stimulate censoring or disguising these traumatic experiences. Group psycho-therapy can become a repetition of the dominance–submission aspect of trauma, an accusation that the member is "sick." By being open to the possibility that trauma symptoms are sometimes subtly maintained as well as successfully treated by the therapist and/or the group and context, we may be able to redirect our intentions and strategies to create more compassionate and productive healing environments for victims of trauma.

As part of the search for improvement, it may be helpful to specifically apply this new, holistic perspective on trauma and defense to the group therapist and the therapist role.

The Role and Vulnerability of the Group Therapist: Non-Attachment, Empathy, and Authenticity

One can conceptualize the group therapist's role as one of a *participant*/observer (Sullivan, 1955). "Participant" is highlighted because it is too often neglected in depicting therapist involvement, especially in group therapy; the relational paradigm entirely deconstructs the idea of the therapist as a neutral, clinically detached observer. Furthermore, since traumas are re-experienced, vicariously experienced, and re-enacted in trauma groups, attempting to be neutral and detached can place the group therapist in the role of the "bystander," that is, someone who knows about or sees the trauma happening but, in the presence of others, does nothing to help the victim (Cramer et al., 1988).

The therapist must be fully engaged and empathically attuned to the group and its members, but going to the other extreme from neutrality and detachment to a state of over-involvement in the process can lead to a loss of boundaries, in which the therapist is placed in the role of either a victim or a perpetrator. Agazarian (Simon & Agazarian, 2000) conveys the role as follows: Good therapeutic boundaries are *semipermeable*, that is, they are selective about what is going in and out of the self-boundaries of the therapist and group members. For example, therapist self-disclosure can sometimes be very helpful in treatment, and without it, the therapist may come across as a robot. But the disclosures must be selective for the purpose of therapeutic gain, and the therapist should know how to follow up on the sharing of self.

The Buddhist idea of *mindfulness* has become popular in Western psychotherapy circles for some time now, providing another potential model of how a group therapist can participate in the trauma group (Tempone-Wiltshire, 2024). The key components of therapeutic mindfulness for trauma are *presence* and *compassion*. The therapist should be present in the group in the moment and with a clear mind. At the same time, the therapist must be empathically attuned with care. The Buddhists use the word *compassion* for this. The most important therapeutic stance that can be conveyed to a traumatized individual is compassion, that is, that the patient knows that the therapist is attuned and empathic with the suffering, as well as non-judgmental. To make compassion known to the patient (and group), the therapist must also be *available*: alert, accessible, and ready to respond in a helpful way. Curiously, the term *availability* is rarely used in therapy or spiritual/religious jargon. But almost everyone appreciates it when a parent, a mentor, a friend "makes themselves available." The late psychoanalyst Abraham (1980) used to emphasize "making a space" for the patient. He meant that the therapist should free themselves of distractions and be emotionally available to respond with meaningful understanding. This is similar to what Leiderman and Klein (2022) conceptualized as *experience-near* leadership when facilitating trauma groups. This kind of emotional availability and responsiveness is what the traumatized patient requires, whether shortly after the trauma or many years later.

Discussion: Feeling Safe Being Vulnerable

Utilizing the concepts and constructs by the author proposed in this chapter, the question arises as to what the goal of group therapy for traumatized individuals is. There are, of course, many goals: alleviation of symptoms, resuming one's life and/or changing it for the better, renewed optimism, and a hopeful sense of a future. Today, with the technology that is available, goals might also include looking for more alpha rhythms in an electroencephalogram, changes in brain physiology seen in various types of scans, hormonal changes, and others.

But there is one change that fits with the holistic/systemic framework and which transcends and facilitates them all: that change is when a patient senses and shows that he/she/they "feel safe being vulnerable." It is not clear who originated this phrase, but in the group therapy field, it was Livingston (2001) who brought the idea to the attention of clinicians. He elaborated this concept when discussing the role of shame, which is one of the most potent negative affects generated by traumatic experiences. As shame and other consequences of trauma heal, the patients do not become "all better." Rather, they become capable of being vulnerable with resilience and liveliness in response to their vulnerability. That may be what Hemingway meant when he said that "[t]he world breaks everyone, and afterward, some are strong at the broken places."

Such strength in living is not like a fortress or a wall, a wall of defenses, or life strategies that prevent pain and suffering; rather, it is a renewed openness to experience, both painful and joyful, positive and negative, belonging and being different. The defenses do not disappear; they become reorganized in a semipermeable way to allow selective vulnerability to a wider breadth of life experiences and emotions.

Clinical Example 4: Feeling Safe Being Vulnerable

Adrienne, a married transgender Black woman in her 50s, came to group after several decades of intermittent alcohol and drug abuse, as well as a history of sexual and physical abuse in both childhood and adulthood. Despite these traumatic and sometimes debilitating experiences, Adrienne had been a very successful advertising consultant with her own thriving business. At first, she could not find anything useful in the group, saying that it might not be right for her. Being in public relations, she could immediately intuit what to say that would make a positive impression on the others, but she didn't see how that would help her change. After a few weeks, the group members sensed how she was manipulating them rather than being authentic and spontaneous. They conveyed they "did not emotionally feel" her when she spoke, and that there was a "lack of sense of self." After a few sessions, she came in and said excitedly, "Hey, now I see how this is going to be a great group for me! I realized that I've been confusing my professional identity to cover up my real feelings and who I am inside!"

Adrienne had always functioned as a very bright individual who could successfully manipulate situations to her advantage. Suddenly, she realized that there was a whole other self within her that she had dissociated from and was barely aware of. It was the side of herself that endured many wounds of abuse with Spartan-like self-discipline. It was the shamed, hurt, and wounded "child" that she buried in a "vault" deep within to protect it from further harm. The group helped her "feel safe being vulnerable." Over time, she reclaimed deep and hidden parts of herself by hearing the other group members share their feelings. She was able to recoup these parts of herself from their projective identification into the dissociative matrix of the group.

The problem was that the "wall" of her hardened defenses was an asset in her very successful career and all the positive feedback she received from others. The breakdown of that defensive wall led to difficulties earning a living and the loss of many acquaintances. The gradual recovery of the various parts of herself that were hidden from her view became more valuable to her than her worldly success. She learned that, with support from the members of the group, she could even feel safe with failure and rejection. The group-as-a-whole provided a place where she felt accepted and valued as a whole person rather than someone who appeared totally calm and solely showed parts of herself that generated approval.

Discussion

The treatment of psychological trauma in groups holds great promise and also poses many problems of management and technique. This chapter proposes a holistic/systems model for addressing some of the complexities that emerge as a result of the multiple systems – individual, interpersonal, and group-as-a-whole – which are present in the small group therapy process. It is suggested that, as a result, traumatic experiences and defenses can be projected into any of these systems, contributing to the impact trauma has on the interpersonal, familial, and social realms as well as the specific individual. The proposed model, rooted in relational psychoanalysis and systems-centered group theory as integrating frameworks while incorporating theories of group development, basic assumptions, and chosen trauma, provides ways to explicate changes in therapy groups where trauma is a significant factor.

Although the details of theory and practice presented here are of great importance and certainly can be subject to disagreement and controversy among theorists and practitioners, a broader implication is implied: Each person's trauma is also a trauma for the broader communities, which must contain it and, therefore, have a responsibility for addressing it. It is hoped that a major takeaway from this chapter, and perhaps this entire volume, is the awareness that trauma affects us all and needs to be addressed on multiple levels of individual, group, and societal awareness. As John Donne wrote, "[n]o man is an island; each is part of the whole" (Baldwin, 2020). This chapter suggests that this is not merely a sentimental thought, but that each of us carries the wounds of our brothers and sisters in the groups to which we belong.

References

Abraham, G. (1980). *Unpublished class lecture at the institute for psychoanalytic psychotherapies.* Bryn Mawr, PA.

Adorno, T., Frenkel-Brunswik, E., Levinson, D., & Sanford, N. (1993 [1950]). *The authoritarian personality.* Studies in Prejudice Series (Vol. 1). Harper & Row. https://ia601506.us.archive.org/28/items/THEAU-THORITARIANPERSONALITY.Adorno/THE%20AUTHORITARIAN%20PERSONALITY.%20-Adorno.pdf

Agazarian, Y. M. (2012). Systems-centered group psychotherapy: A theory of living human systems and its systems-centered practice. *Group, 36*(1), 19–36. https://www.jstor.org/stable/41719343

Baldwin, E. (2020, May 14). For whom the bell tolls/no man is an island by John Donne. *Poem Analysis.* https://poemanalysis.com/john-donne/for-whom-the-bell-tolls/

Bennis, W. G., & Shepard, H. A. (1956). A theory of group development. *Human Relations, 9,* 415–437. https://doi.org/10.1177/0018726756009004

Billow, R. (2003). *Relational group psychotherapy: From basic assumptions to passion.* International Library of Group Analysis Book 26. Jessica Kingsley Publishers. https://us.jkp.com/products/relational-group-psychotherapy

Bion, W. R. (1961). *Experiences in groups and other papers.* Tavistock. https://doi.org/10.4324/9780203359075

Boag, S. (2012). *Freudian repression, the unconscious, and the dynamics of inhibition.* Karnac. https://www.taylorfrancis.com/books/mono/10.4324/9780429475023/freudian-repression-unconscious-dynamics-inhibition-simon-boag

Burton, M. S., Cooper, A. A., Feeny, N. C., & Zoellner, L. A. (2015). The enhancement of natural resilience in trauma interventions. *Contemporary Psychotherapy, 45*(4), 193–204. https://doi.org/10.1007/s10879-015-9302-7

Canales, C. (2025). Attachment-focused therapy and racial inequalities, who speaks and who listens. In L. M. Leiderman & B. J. Buchele (Eds.), *Advances in group therapy trauma treatment* (1st ed.) (pp. 129–141). Taylor & Francis/Routledge. ISBN 9781032890784 https://www.routledge.com/Advances-in-Group-Therapy-Trauma-Treatment/Leiderman-Buchele/p/book/9781032890784?srsltid=AfmBOoobDwivSES4RksUdtPC5XoSBQCol87art52OAKapyarNdb_W5lf

Colman, A. D., & Bexton, W. H. (Eds.). (1975). *Group relations reader.* A. K. Rice Institute. https://auaspace3.wrlc.org/public/repositories/3/archival_objects/12438

Coombe, T. (2019). The Northfield experiments: A reappraisal 70 years on. *Group Analysis, 73*(2), 162–176. https://doi.org/10.1177/0533316419870127

Cramer, R. E., McMaster, M. R., Bartell, P. A., & Dragna, M. (1988). Subject competence and minimization of the bystander effect. *Journal of Applied Social Psychology, 18*(13), 1133–1148. https://doi.org/10.1111/j.1559-1816.1988.tb01198

Dulberg, Z., Dubey, R., Berwian, I. M., & Cohen, J. D. (2023). Having multiple selves helps learning agents explore & adapt in complex changing worlds. *Proceedings of the National Academy of Sciences, 120*(28), e22210120. https://doi.org/10.1073/pnas.2221180120

Eason, E. A. (2009). Diversity and group theory, practice, & research. *International Journal of Group Psychotherapy, 59*(4), 563–574. https://doi.org/10.1521/ijgp.2009.59.4.563

Ellenberger, H. (1981). *The discovery of the unconscious: The history and evolution of dynamic psychiatry.* Basic Books. https://www.hachettebookgroup.com/titles/henri-f-ellenberger/the-discovery-of-the-unconscious/9780465016730/?lens=basic-books

Foulkes, S. H. (1973). The group as matrix of the individual's mental life. In L. R. Wolberg & E. K. Schwartz (Eds.), *Group therapy: An overview.* Intercontinental Medical Books. https://psycnet.apa.org/record/2011-14204-013

Freud, S. (1920). Beyond the pleasure principle. In *The Standard edition of the complete psychological works of Sigmund Freud, 18* (1920–1922), 7–64. Hogarth. https://www.sas.upenn.edu/~cavitch/pdf-library/Freud_Beyond_P_P.pdf

Freud, S. (1921). Group psychology and the analysis of the ego. In *The standard edition of the complete psychological works of Sigmund Freud, 18* (1920–1922), 65–144. Hogarth. https://ia802907.us.archive.org/17/items/SigmundFreud/Sigmund%20Freud%20%5B1921%5D%20Group%20Psychology%20and%20the%20Analysis%20of%20the%20Ego%20%28James%20Strachey%20translation%2C%201949%29.pdf

Grossmark, R. (2025). Trauma and enactments in group psychotherapy. In L. M. Leiderman & B. J. Buchele (Eds.), *Advances in group therapy trauma treatment* (1st ed.) (pp. 103–116). Taylor & Francis/Routledge. ISBN 9781032890784 https://www.routledge.com/Advances-in-Group-Therapy-Trauma-Treatment/Leiderman-Buchele/p/book/9781032890784?srsltid=AfmBOoobDwivSES4RksUdtPC5XoSBQCol87art52OAKapyarNdb_W5lf

Herman, J. (1992). *Trauma and recovery.* Basic Books. https://www.hachettebookgroup.com/titles/judith-lewis-herman-md/trauma-and-recovery/9780465098736/?lens=basic-books

Herman, J., & van der Kolk, B. (1987). Traumatic antecedents of borderline personality disorder. In B. Van der Kolk (Ed.), *Psychological trauma* (pp. 11–126). American Psychiatric Press.

Hill, D., & Schore, A. N. (2015). *Affect regulation theory: A clinical model.* Norton Series on Interpersonal Neurobiology. W.W. Norton. https://wwnorton.com/books/Affect-Regulation-Theory/

Hopper, E. (1997). Traumatic experience in the unconscious life of groups: A fourth basic assumption. *Group Analysis, 34*(1), 439–470. https://doi.org/10.1177/0533316497304002

Hu, B., & Kyei, J. J. (2025). An integrative experiential group therapy approach to treat the trauma of sexual abuse. In L. M. Leiderman & B. J. Buchele (Eds.), *Advances in group therapy trauma treatment* (1st ed.) (pp. 158–169). Taylor & Francis/Routledge. ISBN 9781032890784 https://www.routledge.com/Advances-in-Group-Therapy-Trauma-Treatment/Leiderman-Buchele/p/book/9781032890784?srsltid=AfmBOoobDwivSES4RksUdtPC5XoSBQCol87art52OAKapyarNdb_W5lf

Hurvich, M. (2003). The place of annihilation anxieties in psychoanalytic theory. *Journal of the American Psychoanalytic Association, 51*(2), 579–616. https://doi.org/10.1177/00030651030510020801

Kluft, R. P. (1984). Aspects of treatment of multiple personality disorder. *Psychiatric Annals, 14*, 51–55. https://doi.org/10.3928/0048-5713-19840101-09

Langs, R. (1978). *The interpersonal field.* Jason Aronson.

Leiderman, L. M. (2025). The fear-driven brain: An integrated interpersonal/relational neuro-physiological model to foster co-regulation and synchrony in trauma psychotherapy groups. In L. M. Leiderman & B. J. Buchele (Eds.), *Advances in group therapy trauma treatment* (1st ed.) (pp. 31–51). Taylor & Francis/Routledge. ISBN 9781032890784 https://www.routledge.com/Advances-in-Group-Therapy-Trauma-Treatment/Leiderman-Buchele/p/book/9781032890784?srsltid=AfmBOoobDwivSES4RksUdtPC5XoSBQCol87art52OAKapyarNdb_W5lf

Leiderman, L. M., & Buchele, B. J. (2025). Discussion: Why group in the treatment of trauma. In L. M. Leiderman & B. J. Buchele (Eds.), *Advances in group therapy trauma treatment* (1st ed.) (pp. 170–186). Taylor & Francis/Routledge. ISBN 9781032890784 https://www.routledge.com/Advances-in-Group-Therapy-Trauma-Treatment/Leiderman-Buchele/p/book/9781032890784?srsltid=AfmBOoobDwivSES4RksUdtPC5XoSBQCol87art52OAKapyarNdb_W5lf

Leiderman, L. M., & Klein, R. H. (2022). An integrative systems-oriented interpersonal, relational group approach to understanding and treating mass trauma, dissociation, and enactments during the COVID-19 pandemic. *International Journal of Group Psychotherapy, 72*(1), 34–63. https://doi.org/10.1080/00207284.2021.1991234

Livingston, M. S. (2001). *Vulnerable moments: Deepening the therapeutic process.* Jason Aronson. https://www.abebooks.com/9780765703101/Vulnerable-Moments-Deepening-Therapeutic-Process-0765703106/plp

Marmarosh, C. L., Liu, Y., & Yifei Du, Y. (2025). Attachment and trauma in group psychotherapy: Theory, intervention, and fostering change. In L. M. Leiderman & B. J. Buchele (Eds.), *Advances in group therapy trauma treatment* (1st ed.) (pp. 55–67). Taylor & Francis/Routledge. ISBN 9781032890784 https://www.routledge.com/Advances-in-Group-Therapy-Trauma-Treatment/Leiderman-Buchele/p/book/9781032890784?srsltid=AfmBOoobDwivSES4RksUdtPC5XoSBQCol87art52OAKapyarNdb_W5lf

Mitchell, S. (1988). *Relational concepts in psychoanalysis: An integration.* Harvard University Press. https://www.hup.harvard.edu/books/9780674754119

Moreno, J. (2020). *Psychodrama: Volume I.* Psychodrama Press. https://www.abebooks.com/PSYCHODRAMA-VOLUME-Moreno-Jacob-Levy-Press/31413262809/bd

Rando, T. (1993). *Treatment of complicated mourning.* Research Press. https://www.researchpress.com/product/treatment-complicated-mourning/

Schechter, D., Tronick, E., Beebe, B., Trevarthen, C., Lyons-Ruth, K., Leo, G., & Nahum, J. (2021). *Infant research and psychoanalysis.* Frenis Zero Press.

Schermer, V. L. (2004). Module 9: Identification & management of masked trauma reactions in groups. In *Group interventions for treatment of psychological trauma* (pp. 250–283). American Group Psychotherapy Association.

Schwartz. R. C., & Sweezy, M. (2019/1995). *Internal family systems therapy.* Guilford. https://www.guilford.com/books/Internal-Family-Systems-Therapy/Schwartz-Sweezy/9781462541461

Shengold, L. (1991). *Soul murder: The effects of childhood abuse and deprivation.* Random House. https://www.penguinrandomhouse.com/books/165629/soul-murder-by-leonard-shengold/

Simon, A., & Agazarian, Y. (2000). The system for analyzing verbal interaction. In A. P. Beck & C. M. Lewis (Eds.), *The process of group psychotherapy: Systems for analyzing change* (pp. 357–380). American Psychological Association. https://doi.org/10.1037/10378-013

Sullivan. H. S. (1955). *The interpersonal theory of psychiatry.* Tavistock; Routledge. https://www.routledge.com/The-Interpersonal-Theory-of-Psychiatry/Sullivan/p/book/9780415510943

Tempone-Wiltshire, J. (2024). The role of mindfulness and embodiment in group-based trauma treatment. *Psychotherapy and Counselling Journal of Australia, 12*(1). https://doi.org/10.59158/001c.94979

Turquet, P. M. (1975). Threats to identity in the large group. In L. Kreeger (Ed.), *The large group: Therapy and dynamics* (pp. 87–144). Constable. https://www.taylorfrancis.com/chapters/edit/10.4324/9780429482267-5/threats-identity-large-group-pierre-turquet

Van der Hart, O., & Horst, R. (1989). The dissociation theory of Pierre Janet. *Journal of Traumatic Stress, 8*(4), 1–11. https://www.onnovdhart.nl/articles/dissociationtheory.pdf

Van der Kolk, B. (1987). *Psychological trauma.* American Psychiatric Press. https://archive.org/details/psychologicaltra0000unse_j3z8

Van der Kolk, B. (2015). *The body keeps the score: Brain, mind, and body in the healing of trauma.* Penguin. https://www.penguinrandomhouse.com/books/313183/the-body-keeps-the-score-by-bessel-van-der-kolk-md/

Volkan, V. (2001). Transgenerational transmissions and chosen traumas: An aspect of large- group identity. *Group Analysis, 34*(1), 79–97. https://doi.org/10.1177/05333160122077730

Volkan, V. D. (1988). *The need to have enemies and allies: From clinical practice to international relationships*. Jason Aronson. https://psycnet.apa.org/record/1988-97314-000

Wallin, D. J. (2007). *Attachment in psychotherapy* (Reprint ed.). Guilford. https://www.guilford.com/books/Attachment-in-Psychotherapy/David-Wallin/9781462522712/reviews

Weinberg, H. (2025). Social trauma and the social unconscious-using the large group for healing. In L. M. Leiderman & B. J. Buchele (Eds.), *Advances in group therapy trauma treatment* (1st ed.) (pp. 145–157). Taylor & Francis/Routledge. ISBN 9781032890784 and https://www.routledge.com/Advances-in-Group-Therapy-Trauma-Treatment/Leiderman-Buchele/p/book/9781032890784?gad_source=1&gclid=CjwKCAiAmMC6BhA6EiwAdN5iLbR5-bSqZ7BjZhKfdtyMEvAVcVQKZkvS2lw-87NI6e33XGTuj6JGoRoCyKMQAvD_BwE

Wolf, E. S. (2002). *Treating the self* (Revised ed.). Guilford. https://www.guilford.com/books/Treating-the-Self/Ernest-Wolf/9781572308428

World Health Organization. (1994). *ICD-10 international classification of diseases version 10*. World Health Organization.

Section III

Treating Psychological Trauma Using Short-Term Groups

5 Integrating Cognitive Behavioral Therapy With Psychodrama Theory and Practice

A Blended Group Model for Trauma

Thomas Treadwell and Hanieh Abeditehrani

Cognitive Behavioral Psychodrama Group Therapy (CBPGT) incorporates cognitive behavioral and psychodrama interventions, allowing group members to identify and modify negative thinking, behavior, and interpersonal patterns while increasing engagement in positive and success-based experiences (Abeditehrani et al., 2020, 2024; Baim, 2007; Boury et al., 2001; Fisher, 2007; Hamamci, 2002, 2006; Treadwell et al., 2004, 2011; Wilson, 2009). The Cognitive Behavioral Therapy (CBT) model is sometimes criticized for being overly structured and intellectually oriented (Woolfolk, 2000; Young & Klosko, 1994). As a result, some group directors today use an *eclectic* approach (Kellerman, 1992) based upon CBT that typically employs techniques coming from cognitive behavioral therapy and its related research. CBT is a robust, proven, and very effective treatment approach for many mental disorders, including posttraumatic stress disorder (PTSD), depression, and anxiety (Bieling et al., 2006, 2022). "Process occurs in CBT groups, it has been undervalued in the CBT group literature, and supporting and enhancing good group process leads to better outcomes" (Bieling et al., 2022, p. 393).

CBT is increasingly incorporating more experiential/process approaches from other psychotherapy modalities, such as the integrated model presented in this chapter. A possible improvement for treatments of trauma could come from Psychodrama (PD), an experiential group therapy developed by Moreno (1946). PD is an *eclectic tool* to enhance cognitive and behavioral change. In PD, patients' emotions and thoughts are evoked via taking action to express their psychological problems instead of talking about them (Blatner, 2000; Orkibi et al., 2017). PD engages patients in action with the other group members, enhancing the potency of therapeutic alliance and therapeutic bond between group members (Orkibi et al., 2017).

Thimm and Antonsen (2014) point out that, often, CBT group content is manual-driven. According to Free (2007), the groups tend to focus on content rather than process, with some leaders actively discouraging extensive discussion of emotional experiences, so that the focus is on acquisition of technical skills. White and Freeman (2000) reference the broad range of clinical populations being treated using group CBT methods and assert that the two defining variables of cognitive behavioral group therapy are cohesiveness and task focus. Subsequently, Bieling et al. (2006, 2022) and Wenzel et al. (2012) concentrated on integrating CBT strategies with the understanding and enhancement of group process to aid in learning and grasping cognitive and behavioral strategies. They concluded that the therapeutic alliance and interpersonal factors are critical elements in cognitive behavioral group therapy. The CBPGT model addresses this important matter by integrating the experiential component of psychodrama with the intellectual components provided by CBT. Incorporating experiential therapy allows patients to participate in the emotional expressions of fellow

DOI: 10.4324/9781003546252-8

group members, which, in turn, strengthens the therapeutic alliance, fostering deeper bonds among the individuals within the group.

The CBPGT environment creates a safe and supportive climate where clients can observe their emotions and thoughts during psychodrama. Group members then practice new thinking and behaviors by using experiential learning while sharing their concerns freely with group members; in this way, ample opportunities are provided for behavioral rehearsal, behavioral experiments, and in vivo exposure to situations that have been avoided (Treadwell et al., 2004); this approach is shared by Bieling et al. (2006, 2022), Wenzel et al. (2012), and Burlingame et al. (2013). This way of working is consistent with what Beck suggests is the aim of including behavioral tasks in cognitive behavioral therapy: "to produce change in negative attitudes" (Beck et al. 1979, p. 119). Furthermore, CBPGT affords the opportunity for catharsis during emotional enactment[1] (Yalom & Leszcz, 2005), in contrast to the limited discussion of emotional experiences often found in most traditional CBT groups (Free, 2007). CBPGT applies psychodramatic role-playing and cognitive behavioral techniques, for example, cognitive restructuring, to express traumatic feelings and thoughts to challenge the negative behavior(s).

The Cognitive and Behavioral Features of Posttraumatic Stress Disorder (PTSD)

Boyd and McCabe (2022) review the cognitive appraisals of a traumatic event, such as self-blaming, which can strengthen the individual's belief that they are incompetent and useless, as well as thoughts that the world is a dangerous place. This formulation is supported by the cognitive theory of Ehlers and Clark (2000), which suggests perceptions related to impending traumatic threats are fundamental in the development of PTSD. Avoidance behaviors are reliably associated with the development of PTSD following a traumatic exposure and are instrumental in limiting access to helpful learning and cognitive norms or traditions that embrace beliefs of safety, trust, intimacy, power, or control (Foa & Kozak, 1986; Resick et al., 2017). There is evidence-based data supporting cognitive behavioral approaches to PTSD, such as trauma-focused CBT, cognitive processing therapy (CPT) (Resick et al., 2017), and prolonged exposure (PE) (Foa et al., 2007), all of which integrate cognitive and behavioral methods. Trauma-focused CBT aims to challenge maladaptive beliefs by utilizing various cognitive and behavioral techniques (Ehlers, 2013). Emotional processing theory or prolonged exposure (PE) uses behavioral interventions which can include imaginal and in vivo exposures to traumatic incidents (Foa et al., 2007). Cognitive processing therapy utilizes both cognitive and behavioral interventions to identify negative thoughts and interpretations (known as *stuck points*) that are strong beliefs impeding recovery from PTSD (Resick et al., 2017). The therapy incorporates narrative writing about traumatic events and integrates in vivo behavioral strategies concentrating on safety, trust, power, control, esteem, and intimacy to assist in symptom reduction. Applying the principles of Socratic dialogue, coupled with behavioral interventions, is the cornerstone of both CPT and PE. The administration and content of CPT, particularly narrative writing exercises, can be customized to fit the specific needs and circumstances of each client. This flexibility allows therapists to adapt the therapy to maximize its effectiveness for different individuals. According to LoSavio et al. (2024), PTSD symptom reduction experienced during CPT is not just temporary but is sustained over a longer period time. However, long-term follow-up data (i.e., data extending two or more years post-therapy) are limited, representing an area that would benefit from increased research attention, particularly assessment of quality-of-life and functioning outcomes.

The Cognitive Behavioral Group Psychodramatic Therapy Model for Trauma

In CBPGT groups, all members are initially assessed by the director(s) (a term used for *group facilitator* but also called *director* in psychodrama) via the use of psychological instruments, such as the Posttraumatic stress disorder (PTSD) Checklist for DSM-5 (PCL-5; Weathers et al., 2013), the Beck Depression Inventory II (BDI), the Beck Anxiety Inventory (BAI), the Beck Hopelessness Scales (BHS) (Beck, 1988; Beck & Steer, 1993; Beck et al., 1996), and the Liebowitz Social Anxiety Scale (LSAS; clinician-administered version). The first one or two sessions are devoted to establishing group norms, explaining CBPGT cognitive behavior therapy (CBT) and schemas, and describing the session format. Participants are informed about the nature of the structured activities so they can have realistic expectations about how the trauma group will run. Each group member signs informed consent and audiovisual recording consent forms. The audiovisual recordings create an ongoing record of group activities and serve as a source for feedback to group members when needed.

The facilitator emphasizes the importance of completing each scale on a weekly basis. These instruments are administered at the beginning of each session and are stored in personal folders to serve as an ongoing gauge of participants' progress within the group (Treadwell et al., 2004).

Each group session in CBPGT is divided into three sections, a procedure borrowed from psychodrama: *warm-up*, *action*, and *sharing* (Moreno, 1934). CBT techniques (Beck, 2011) are utilized in the warm-up, including identifying upsetting situations, automatic negative thoughts, and triggered emotions; writing balanced thoughts to counter negative automatic thoughts; and recognizing distortions in thinking and imprecise interpretations of traumatic situations.

Following the initial warm-up phase, an individual is designated as the central character, often referred to as protagonist. This individual plays a pivotal role during the action stage, with the session centering on the protagonist's specific traumatic experience. Various methods for choosing the protagonist are available, as outlined by Kumar and Treadwell (1986). One approach is for the director to ask for volunteers; another involves the director selecting the protagonist, based on observations in the warm-up phase or information gained from a previous session. Each group member assumes the role of the protagonist at least once during the course of treatment.

Moving into the action phase, psychodramatic techniques, namely, role-playing, role reversal, doubling, and mirroring, are employed; they facilitate the examination of conflictual situations experienced within the group context (see Abeditehrani et al., 2020, for a more detailed description of the techniques and the intervention). The designated situation is acted out through role-playing directed by the protagonist. The therapy room is rearranged for the psychodrama, typically into a semicircular arrangement of chairs, simulating a stage, which allows the protagonist to perform in front of an audience comprised of the other group members. Within the integrated CBT and psychodramatic approach, client roles needed for the scenario(s) are typically portrayed by group members rather than a director. The protagonist chooses a group member(s) to take on the role of auxiliary ego(s), that is, someone who plays a significant part in the given situation. The protagonist and auxiliary ego(s) then act out the scenario. Throughout the action phase, the director applies various psychodrama techniques involving others in the enactment of the protagonist's experience. The choice of which psychodrama techniques to use is dependent on the specific trauma-provoking situation; this selection is made collaboratively between the director and the protagonist. This exercise helps group members better understand the nature of the negative thoughts and emotions triggered by traumatic situations. The last part of each session is sharing or closure. This is a time for patients to elaborate on the enactment and share their feelings and thoughts with the group.

The CBPGT Structure

Cognitive Behavioral Psychodrama Group Therapy (CBPGT) includes 12 weekly sessions. The first, second, and last sessions are based on Heimberg and Becker's CBGT protocol (Heimberg & Becker, 2002), and sessions 3 to 11 are based on Treadwell's (2016, 2021) cognitive experiential group therapy (CEGT) model. Each session lasts 2.5 hours and is guided by two clinical therapists. Ideal group size is 6–8 patients/clients diagnosed with social anxiety disorder and posttraumatic stress disorder (PTSD).

Session Content

Prior to the first session, each patient completes an individual treatment orientation interview to establish rapport with one of the group directors, prepare for group, and complete the individualized fear hierarchy (Heimberg & Becker, 2002).

In the first session, the directors explain the group's rules and clients share their individual problems and goals. At the end of the first session, the directors assign homework: completion of an Automatic Thought Record (ATR) for the following week.

During the second session, the homework is reviewed, and the directors use the completed ATR to identify thinking errors in addition to the fear structure.

Sessions 3 through 12 are divided into the previously described three stages: (1) warm-up, (2) action, and (3) sharing. The focus is on role-playing feared social situations in real-life settings.

Warm-Up Stage

Keeping in mind that the goal of the method is to challenge the maladaptive trauma beliefs via in vivo exposures, thus fostering behavioral and emotional change (Ehlers, 2013), the director selects the protagonist. Selection is based on the preparation in the warming-up stage using the ATR as well as information revealed during the sharing phase of the previous session; group member volunteers may also be used (Kumar & Treadwell, 1986). A step-by-step warm-up description of **Lisa's** ATR follows to illustrate the warm-up protocol, which includes implementation of the ATR (Greenberger & Padesky, 1995, 2015).

Case Illustration

Lisa, who was selected as the protagonist, identifies as a cisgender White woman in her 20s with a history of physical and verbal abuse by both parents, who had high expectations of their daughter. She remembered feeling unsupported emotionally growing up. As a young adolescent, she struggled to fit in at her new school and neighborhood.

Other members of the group serve as auxiliaries and the audience. The group members are described thus: (1) **Lucy** (27), a highly educated bisexual woman who grew up in a traditional family, feeling detached with a sense of not belonging in her family and community. She has traumatic memories of being punished by her mother for her feelings of attraction to girls at school, as well as being excluded by school peers. (2) **Dak** (27), a cisgender White man whose parents divorced when he was 11, leading to

---

the loss of his childhood house and his private school, resulting from a sudden move to a small apartment and a public school. These changes were necessary because of unpaid tuition at the private school, which was not initially disclosed to him; however, eventually, he had to explain to his peers and was bullied at the new school. His "poverty trauma" left him feeling shocked and ashamed. (3) **Jenny** (29), a cisgender woman who failed classes at school due to chronic parental fighting, which resulted in her propensity to cry easily. She was punished for crying and told if she cried more, she would get hit harder. She reports that, as an adult, she feels sadness in her throat but never cries in front of people. She finds it difficult to express emotions or establish relationships of all kinds. (4) **Lauren** (22), a transgender woman with no close friends. She reports being bullied, that is, mocked for preferring the company of girls, leading to her isolating herself. She left school and currently avoids public and social places. She fears being judged negatively by people for being transgender. (5) **Bobby** (26), a cisgender man who works as a personal trainer. He lives with a mother with a bipolar disorder and has had to take care of her since he was a child. He was sexually abused at the age of 10, and having free access to chocolate, he was bullied at school for being overweight.

Session 3: Warming Up

Lisa placed her thought record (see Table 5.1) on the whiteboard, where she reported a situation of a childhood traumatic incident wherein she was asked to speak in front of the classroom in primary school and thought, "Everyone noticed my anxiety." She selected this childhood traumatic situation because it was an example of a social situation stimulating fear of being watched and judged by others, which she avoids. This avoidant behavior has troubled her for years.

Lisa's schemas, social isolation, abandonment, and failure, coupled with her core belief of helplessness, emerged as she completed her ATR.

The director then asks the protagonist, "What would you like to further explore?" The director gives the protagonist the option of selecting which area of conflict to address first. It is essential the protagonist be given the option of making the decision.

The protagonist explains each column of the ATR (situation, emotions, automatic thoughts, evidence that supports the automatic thoughts, evidence that does not support the automatic thoughts, an alternative thought(s), and re-rate of emotions). Then the director reviews the automatic thoughts that reveal schemas or core beliefs and completes a genogram of the protagonist's family of origin to provide background information about schema/core beliefs, thus helping the protagonist and other group members prepare for action. See Table 5.1 for Lisa's thought record and completed ATR.

Facilitating Automatic Thought Record Interventions

Column 2: Emphasize Expression of Emotions/Feelings
• List emotions, such as thus:

  • Angry
  • Sad
  • Afraid

Table 5.1 Thought Record and Completed ATR by Treadwell and Abeditehrani Automatic Thought Record

1 Situation	2 Emotions	3 Immediate thoughts about yourself	4 Experiences throughout your life that support your negative self-thought	5 Experiences throughout your life that **do not** support your negative self-thought	6 Use an experience from #4 and an experience from #5 to create a "balanced thought"	7 Re-rate emotions
Childhood trauma Primary School						
Standing in front of others in the classroom	**Anxious (10) Lonely (9) Sad (8) Angry (7)**	**I always do something stupid. When you do something stupid, what does it say about you? Others laugh at me; it says I am always anxious. Being anxious says what about me? I am weak – I can't stand for myself. Being weak says what about you? I am weird. Being weird says what about me? Everybody leaves me. I am not good enough.**	**I never understood what I should do. My hands shake in front of others. I always blushed when standing in front of classmates.** Helpless core belief Failure belief Abandonment/social isolation schemas Hot thoughts	I was able to talk in front of my friends in kindergarten. During spelling bee, I was able to spell a word correctly and was praised by my teacher. I won a swim meet when I was 7.	**Even though I was anxious, during spelling bee, I was able to spell a complicated word and received praises. (7)** **Even though one person leaves me, it does not mean I will be alone forever. (7)** **Even though I do not always understand everything the teacher is explaining, I ask the teacher to clarify for me. (8)** **Even though I feel anxious, it does not mean I look anxious to everyone. (7)**	**Anxious (8) Lonely (7) Sad (6) Angry (6)**

- Depressed
- Anxious
- Empty

Effective Thought Records

- **Be succinct.** Clearly identify and distinguish emotions following a traumatic event.
- **Use a cheat sheet.** Having a list of emotions can help in accurately naming emotions.
- **Rate each emotion.** Use a 10-point scale, where 1 = low intensity and 10 = highly charged.

Director(s) Instructions

1. *Volunteer selection.* Ask for a volunteer to share their situation on the whiteboard or Zoom board.
2. *Guide through the thought record.* Assist the protagonist/patient/client in filling out their thought record step-by-step.

Identifying Automatic Thoughts (ATs)

- *Automatic thoughts.* Recognize that humans have thousands of automatic thoughts daily, but not all are linked to negative feelings.
- *Focus on hot thoughts.* Use Socratic questioning to identify "hot thoughts," which are highly charged and closely linked to negative emotions.

Examples of Hot Thoughts

- Someone not liking me might lead to the thought "I am unlovable."
- Not getting a job might lead to the thought "I am a failure."

Case Example

- Lisa's Case

    - **Failure schema:** Lisa's belief in her own failure is diminishing her self-confidence.
    - **Helpless core belief:** This belief exacerbates her negative feelings and thoughts.

Director(s)s

1. **Ask Socratic questions.** Encourage clients to explore the meaning behind their negative thoughts.
2. **Identify hot thoughts.** Help them pinpoint the thoughts that trigger intense negative emotions.
3. **Address core beliefs.** Work on challenging and reframing these beliefs to improve self-confidence and emotional regulation.

When the ATR warm-up is complete, the next step is implementing action structure and techniques of the cognitive behavioral psychodramatic blended model to address Lisa's traumatic incident.

Psychodramatic Structure and Action Techniques

Action Phase

In the action phase, the director and the protagonist focus on the problem, thus providing the director with guidance in how to set the stage for action. The director then asks the protagonist, "What would you like to further explore?" The director gives the protagonist the option of selecting which area of conflict to address first. It is essential the protagonist be given the option of making the decision. The protagonist explains each column of the ATR (situation, emotions, automatic thoughts, evidence that supports the automatic thoughts, evidence that does not support the automatic thought, an alternative thought, and related moods). Then, the director reviews the automatic thoughts that reveal schemas or core beliefs and completes a genogram of the protagonist's family of origin to provide background information about schema/core beliefs, thus helping the protagonist and other group members prepare for action.

Action Phase of Lisa's Group

The protagonist selects a "double" from the group, whose task is to echo thoughts and feelings that the protagonist is thinking and feeling but not expressing. The protagonist also selects other players (i.e., "auxiliary egos") for the anxiety-provoking situation. These auxiliary egos are people that play important roles in the protagonist's trauma-provoking situation, that is, parents, classmates, or romantic interests. The interview technique of role reversal is utilized to gain information about additional significant people by placing the protagonist in the role of a significant other. Specifically, the director interviews the protagonist about the role of auxiliary ego to achieve data as to how this person perceives the protagonist. Once all players are introduced to their roles, the director facilitates the action and encourages the doubles to help the protagonist challenge automatic thoughts. The director utilizes various psychodramatic techniques during the action stage, addressing conflictual issues that the protagonist has agreed to address. For example, the empty chair technique (the protagonist can talk to an imaginary person that is represented by an empty chair) and the soliloquy technique (a monologue in which the patients can freely express feelings and thoughts) are suitable traumatic techniques to help express suppressed emotions.

Sharing Stage

Sharing, or closure, is a time for patients to discuss and process the impact of the experience of acting the scene on them and to share their feelings and thoughts with the group. The protagonist and other clients, in the roles of auxiliary ego, doubles, or the audience, share their feelings about the action and their alternative thoughts and behaviors. Advice-giving is avoided, as it is viewed as counter-productive to the protagonist. The sharing of ideas can help the protagonist gain insight into the situation addressed; for example, a new role or an unexplored role may be conceptualized. An additional component of this stage, processing, follows the sharing portion. During processing, members comment on the action and investigate why certain techniques were applied. At the end of the sharing stage, the director assigns homework to the protagonist to provide continuity to working on the new role explored during the session.

Session 12, the last CBPGT session, is divided into two parts. During the first half, the directors do additional role-playing and cognitive restructuring as necessary. During the second half, the directors review each patient's development during treatment and work on situations that may still be problematic. The directors ask patients to set a specific goal that they will attempt to accomplish within the next month. The directors assist clients with setting goals for the future to ensure repeated exposure to trauma-provoking situations, affording opportunities to practice using rational cognitive and emotional responses.

Group Members and Their Roles

Roles are established as the psychodrama transpires; they are voluntarily taken as they develop during the psychodrama, not assigned by the director. The protagonist requests group members to take on specific roles during the action.

- Lisa – protagonist
- Lucy – auxiliary role, double
- Bobbie – auxiliary role as teacher
- Jenny – auxiliary role as Lisa
- Dak – Lisa's confident role
- Lauren – auxiliary role, Lisa's mother

Case Illustration (Continued)

After Lisa shared her ATR on the whiteboard, the director reviewed core beliefs, schemas, and group warm-up techniques with the group during session 3. The director asked Lisa, the protagonist, "What would you like to address to reduce feelings of shame and fear of being judged?" Lisa recalled and described an anxiety-provoking childhood experience on her first day of primary school. Her mother escorted her to school, where she was placed in the middle of a line. Her mother did not like this and moved her to the front of the line. Then, the teacher called on Lisa to say something in front of others. Lisa reported feeling extremely anxious: She could think of nothing to say; she averted eye contact to avoid being noticed by others, while experiencing sweaty hands, heart palpitations, and shortness of breath. She could feel herself blush, and the teacher noticed this. The teacher said in front of others, "It is not necessary to be anxious."

This is enough information to begin the psychodrama, as the director was given sufficient clinical data to set the stage for action.

The director initiated the enacting of the situation by using an interview in role-reversal technique, that is, placing Lisa in the role of her mother, to gather information about her mother. Once Lauren learned more about Lisa's mother, she was able to take on the mother role. The double (Lucy) echoed Lisa's unexpressed thoughts and feelings.

The director set the scene by asking Lauren to take on the role of Lisa's mother, who was upset when Lisa was placed at the middle of the line by the teacher. The action begins here.

The director, asking Bobbie, in the role of the teacher, told Lisa to move to the middle of the line, saying, "Lisa, go to the middle of the line." Lisa's mother was not pleased and moved Lisa to the front of the line. The director asked Lauren to play Lisa's mother, moving her daughter to the front of the line. Lauren, in the role of her mother, moved Lisa to the front of the line. Then, Bobbie, as the teacher, called on Lisa to say something in front of her classmates. Lisa responded to this situation, saying, "I was anxious, terrified, and I cried."

At this point, the director used the role-reversal technique to gain additional information about her behavior. He once again asked Lisa to take on the role of her mother, to learn what her mom was like, giving additional information about her behavior for when Lisa would assume the mother role. Additionally, the director asked Lisa, "What group member could take on your role?" Lisa selected Jenny to take on her role. This situation, the fear of being observed and judged, was placed into action with Socratic questioning.

The assembled characters are the following: the protagonist (Lisa), her double (Lucy), and her auxiliary ego (Lauren, as Lisa's mother); Bobbie as Lisa's teacher; and Jenny to take on Lisa's role.

Protagonist *(Lisa):*	I am afraid to stand and talk in front of others. I am afraid of doing or saying something stupid. It would be embarrassing.
Director:	Doing something stupid means what to you?
Double *(Lucy):*	I'm not sure. They think I am weird.
Director:	Being weird means what to you?
Double *(Lucy):*	They would not want to be friends with me.
Jenny *(in Lisa's role):*	I never want to be observed by others. I usually select positions in the back to hide.
Director:	And what will it mean?
Protagonist *(Lisa):*	Everybody will reject me, and I'm bound to be alone.
	(This short interaction provides the director and group members with data about Lisa's negative self-image and fear of being rejected, activating her core belief that she is helpless and a failure. The director needs more information about her mother and asks Lisa to take on the role of her mother.)
Director *(to Protagonist, Lisa, in role reversal as mother):*	Tell me about your relationship with Lisa.
Lisa *(as mother, in role reversal):*	We have a stunning and close relationship. Lisa is quiet but relies on me for help. I am always there for Lisa.
Protagonist *(Lisa, talking to her mother, Lauren):*	I must let you know that you ignored me for most of my childhood and you were always busy with your job. I missed out on having a mom to help me when my friends were teasing me.
Lisa's Mother *(Lauren, responding to Protagonist, Lisa):*	You could always come to me, Lisa. I was around, and you never let me know about being teased. I was always isolated as a child and felt lonely. I tried to help you to be the center of attention in groups and find friends.

	(The director has additional data validating how Lisa was not supported by her mother or teacher. Thus, the director applies Socratic questioning to uncover a potential silent positive role that has been dormant.)
Director:	Lisa, my hunch is that there is a role within yourself that has not been explored. Might you know what that role is?
Protagonist *(Lisa):*	Well, no. I never thought of any other role. I do have a strong self-role that is not visible – I talk to it when I am alone or sleeping.
Director:	What can we call that confident role?
Protagonist *(Lisa):*	I am not sure.
Double *(Lucy):*	I call it my confident role.
Director:	Your double feels it is your confident role – do you agree?
Protagonist *(Lisa):*	That will work – I like that.
	(The director speculates that Lisa learned the fear role from her mom, who had experienced isolation in her young years. With the assistance of the double and auxiliary ego, the group learns about the protagonist's negative automatic thoughts, behavior, and emotions, as well as alternative thoughts and behavioral strategies based on her notion of feeling "left out" and thinking she is "always going to be alone." This is an example of how Lisa asks for help, gets turned down, and withdraws. The next step is to test out the new role the protagonist identified: the "confident role." The director asked Lisa to select a person from the group to portray this confident role, and Lisa selected Dak. The purpose is for Dak to model how this confident role works, and Lisa will observe.)
Protagonist:	I am afraid to stand and say something in front of others. I am afraid of doing or saying something stupid.
Confident Role *(Dak):*	Do you know for certain that you will do something stupid?
Protagonist *(Lisa):*	No, I am not sure, but it is probable.
Confident Role *(Dak):*	Have you been in any embarrassing situations before?
Protagonist:	Of course, yes.
Confident Role *(Dak):*	How many times?
Protagonist:	Many times.

Confident Role *(Dak):*	And did you say or do something stupid in those situations?
Protagonist:	I do not remember. Maybe one or two times.
Confident Role *(Dak):*	When you use these numbers, the chance that you will do or say something stupid is very low. This is not completely impossible, but what happens if it really occurs?
Protagonist *(Lisa):*	What do you mean?
Confident Role *(Dak):*	My point is that even if you say or do something stupid, even if everyone notices, it will not be a ca-tastrophe. You will be embarrassed, just like others have been embarrassed. If you stand in front of oth-ers and make eye contact, you can see not all of them are focused on you, because everyone is busy with their work.
Protagonist *(Lisa):*	I can try it this time without withdrawing and make the most of my "confident role."
Director:	Lisa, how strong do you feel this confident role is? Rate it on a scale of 1, low, to 10, high.
Protagonist *(Lisa):*	Well, right now, I can rate it as a 5, because of Dak's support.
Director:	That seems much better than before. We can create homework situations for you to challenge negative thinking and enhance your confident role. Are you open to this idea?
Protagonist *(Lisa):*	I am willing to give it my "all."
Director:	Very well! I like your courage and perseverance. I am closing the action portion to focus on home-work. First, let's de-role your auxiliaries that assisted you in your psychodrama.

De-Roling

Once the psychodrama has been concluded, the protagonist and other role players (auxiliaries) are de-roled by asking, "What did you experience in the role?" De-roling is essential so that group members can disengage from the role(s) they played.

The sharing stage is the final component of the psychodrama.

Sharing Phase

The sharing stage is the final component of the psychodrama. Lisa talked about her feelings and thoughts, revealing how anxious she felt during her psychodrama. During this stage, auxiliaries and other group members shared their empathy and experiences of failure and isolation with the protagonist, focusing on feelings of being left out and rejected. Lisa was awed by being in her mother's role and could grasp what her mom was thinking. In her words: "When I played my mother's role, I understood that she wanted to help me overcome my anxiety. She did not want to bother me. When I was in her place, I realized I was only doing these things to help my child." Group members expressed their feelings of isolation and despair, as well as the conviction of feeling different, not good enough, and a failure.

The purpose of the preceding psychodrama was to employ exposure exercises and utilize cognitive restructuring before, during, and after exposure, to foster Lisa's confident role; this was accomplished by using situations with group members where she could practice talking to others to enforce her newly adopted confident role.

Homework

It is the job of the director and the group members participating in the psychodrama to address the protagonist's core beliefs and schemas with a behavioral strategy that takes the form of homework. Homework (Beck, 2011) is a key component of CBPGT because it encourages members to practice learned strategies in their own environment.

In Lisa's case, it was crucial that she practice the new confident role. Lisa, the group, and the director collaboratively design situations where she can rehearse this new role in her everyday life. For example, situations are designed to focus on developing a schedule to practice fears related to social interactions. In doing so, patients are exposing themselves to their fears in a safe environment, thereby reducing the worry around negative judgment. The director suggested that Lisa contact a group member and invite the person to spend time in a bookstore. Additionally, she was to ask the salesperson about the social anxiety and trauma section to reduce the fear of negative judgment. To encourage Lisa in her endeavor, the director(s) asks members of the group to provide their support until the next session. Lauren and Dak both volunteer to check in with her throughout the week and to be available if she needs them. The protagonist and the group members who volunteer to check in with group members typically exchange telephone numbers and arrange to either text or call each other during the week (Bieling et al., 2006, 2022; Wenzel et al., 2012).

Discussion

Etiology and Treatment of Trauma

CBPGT is beneficial for the treatment of patients with childhood traumatic experiences because they can re-enact a negative social interaction from the past and re-enact the situation in a different way than it originally occurred. The psychodrama of this past traumatic event in a safe setting assists in changing feelings, beliefs, and attitudes related to the traumatizing situations (Treadwell & Kumar, 2002). In this chapter's case example, a situational psychodrama was completed and presented as a vehicle for change. Utilizing principles of CBT and psychodrama that are integrated created a powerful and effective group process, enabling participants to address problematic situations with the support of group members. Clients find CBT helpful because it cultivates awareness of habitual dysfunctional thought patterns and belief systems that play an important role in emotional regulation. The action component of the psychodrama allows participants to see and feel the dysfunction. Focusing on schemas or core beliefs (Young & Klosko, 1994) presents an opportunity for a deeper level of insight and merges well with the psychodramatic framework. Schemas are unwanted behaviors or patterns (beliefs) in one's life – for example, "I am not worthy" or "People are not trustable." Schemas and core beliefs provide a window into the etiology of the patient's presenting problem and form the basis for treatment planning. Case conceptualization, which was presented in Lisa's case, is applied as an ongoing therapeutic tool. After three or four sessions, the director takes on a psychoeducational role, explaining central ideas behind the technique and asking group members to complete thought records on an ongoing basis as the group progresses. Group members take turns discussing their completed forms with the group. Thought records may help group members reflect on their various rules, conditional assumptions, beliefs, and means of coping (Beck, 2011). For example, applying in vivo exposure(s), clients perform activities where they gradually approach trauma-related memories, feelings, and situations that are typically avoided. Often, role-playing and role reversal are techniques used prior to the in vivo exposures. The director and client develop a hierarchy of avoided activities or situations that the patient then practices through in vivo exposure between sessions. Typically, the patient's characterization or view of self is distorted so that case formulation can be useful in challenging the patient's view of self, the world, and the future (Beck, 2011).

Multicultural Considerations

In our experience, multicultural issues can be addressed in the CBPGT model. During the warm-up, the protagonist can expand on what is important in their genogram (McGol-drick & Gerson, 2008) to understand the family and cultural relationships. The genogram, combined with the automatic thought record, allows the group to become educated and gain insight into the protagonist's values and beliefs. The psychodrama takes place within the cultural context the protagonist defines. This ensures that the psychodrama accurately depicts the environment and cultural realities (Nien-Hwa & Hsin-Hao, 2014; Remer & Remer, 2003).

Conclusion

One of the most important elements of CBPGT is that it is data-based (Beck, 2011; Treadwell et al., 2011). Group members keep track of their trauma-related symptoms, dysfunctional thoughts, and depression, anxiety, and hopelessness scores from week to week. They can easily see changes resulting from group therapy that make the therapeutic process a worthwhile one. The use of CBT techniques allied with psychodrama provides a balance between an exploration of emotionally laden situations and a more concrete, data-based, problem-solving process. CBPGT adds a new dimension to both the fields of cognitive behavioral and group therapy and is built on a proven, efficacious model. The integration of these methods may be beneficial for individuals who have not responded to more traditional approaches.

Note

1 *Enactment* in the context of this chapter means the conscious and unconscious use of action and feeling during CBPGT.

References

Abeditehrani, H., Dijk, C., Neyshabouri, M. D., & Arntz, A. (2024). Effectiveness of cognitive behavioral group therapy, psychodrama, and their integration for treatment of social anxiety disorder: A randomized controlled trial. *Journal of Behavior: Therapy and Experimental Psychiatry*, 101908. https://doi.org/10.1016/j.jbtep.2023.101908

Abeditehrani, H., Dijk, C., Toghchi, S. M., & Arntz, A. (2020). Integrating cognitive behavioral group therapy and psychodrama for social anxiety disorder: A pilot study. *Clinical Psychology in Europe*. https://doi.org/10.1016/j.jbtep.2023.101908

Baim, C. (2007). Are you a cognitive psychodramatist? *British Journal of Psychodrama and Sociodrama*, *22*(2), 23–31.

Beck, A. T. (1988). *Beck hopelessness scale*. The Psychological Corporation. https://doi.org/10.1037/t00966-000

Beck, A. T., Rush, A. J., Shaw, B. F., & Emery, G. (1979). *Cognitive therapy of depression*. The Guilford Press. https://doi.org/10.1046/j.1440-1614.2002.t01-4-01015.x

Beck, A. T., & Steer, R. A. (1993). *BAI: Beck anxiety inventory manual*. The Psychological Corporation. https://doi.org/10.1002/(sici)1097-4679(199701)53:1<7::aid-jclp2>3.0.co;2-s

Beck, A. T., Steer, R. A., & Brown, G. K. (1996). *Beck depression inventory-II manual*. The Psychological Corporation. https://doi.org/10.1037/t00742-000

Beck, J. S. (2011). *Cognitive behavioral therapy: Basics and beyond* (2nd ed.). The Guilford Press. https://www.guilford.com/books/Cognitive-Behavior-Therapy/Judith-Beck/9781462544196

Bieling, P., McCabe, R., & Martin, A. (2006). *Cognitive-behavioral therapy in groups*. The Guilford Press.

Bieling, P., McCabe, R., & Martin, A. (2022). *Cognitive-behavioral therapy in groups* (2nd ed.). The Guilford Press. https://www.guilford.com/books/Cognitive-Behavioral-Therapy-in-Groups/Bieling-McCabe-Antony/9781462549849

Blatner, A. (2000). *Foundations of psychodrama: History, theory, and practice*. Springer Publishing Co. http://psycnet.apa.org/record/2000-07509-000

Boury, M., Treadwell, T., & Kumar, V. K. (2001). Integrating psychodrama and cognitive therapy: An exploratory study. *International Journal of Action Methods: Psychodrama, Skill Training, and Role Playing*, *54*(1), 13–25. https://searchworks.stanford.edu/articles/aph__7230951

Boyd, J., & McCabe, R. (2022). Trauma and stressor related disorders. In P. J. Bieling, R. E. McCabe, & M. M. Anthony (Eds.), *Cognitive-behavioral therapy in groups* (2nd ed.). The Guilford Press.

Burlingame, G., Strauss, B., & Joyce, A. (2013). Change mechanisms and effectiveness of small group treatments. In M. J. Lambert (Ed.), *Bergin & Garfield's handbook of psychotherapy and behavior change* (6th ed., pp. 640–689). Wiley & Sons. https://doi.org/10.1080/10503301003596551

Ehlers, A. (2013). The trauma-focused cognitive behavior therapy for posttraumatic stress disorder and acute distress disorder. In G. Simos & S. G. Hoffman (Eds.), *CBT for anxiety disorders: A practitioner book* (pp. 161–189). Wiley Blackwell. https://doi.org/10.1002/9781118330043.ch7

Ehlers, A., & Clark, D. M. (2000). A cognitive model of posttraumatic stress disorder: Theory and therapy. *Behavior Research and Therapy*, *38*, 319–345. https://doi.org/10.1016/s0005-7967(99)00123-0

Fisher, J. (2007). Congenial alliance: Synergies in cognitive and psychodramatic therapies. *Psychology of Aesthetics, Creativity, and the Arts*, *1*(4), 237–242. https://doi.org/10.1037/1931-3896.1.4.237

Foa, E. B., Hembree, E. A., & Rothbaum, B. O. (2007). *Prolonged exposure therapy for PTSD: Emotional processing of traumatic experiences: Therapist guide*. Oxford University Press. https://doi.org/10.1093/med:psych/9780195308501.001.0001

Foa, E. B., & Kozak, M. J. (1986). Emotional processing of fear: Exposure to corrective information. *Psychological Bulletin*, *99*(1), 20–35. https://doi.org/10.1037/0033-2909.99.1.20

Free, M. L. (2007). *Cognitive therapy in groups: Guidelines and resources for practice*. John Wiley and Sons Ltd. https://www.wiley.com/en-us/Cognitive+Therapy+in+Groups%3A+Guidelines+and+Resources+for+Practice%2C+2nd+Edition-p-9780470024485

Greenberger, D., & Padesky, C. (2015). *Mind over mood: Change how you feel by changing the way you think* (2nd ed.). The Guilford Press. https://www.mindovermood.com/

Greenberger, H., & Padesky, C. (1995). *Mind over mood: Change how you feel by changing the way you think*. The Guilford Press. https://www.mindovermood.com/

Hamamci, Z. (2002). The effect of integrating psychodrama and cognitive behaviour therapy on reducing cognitive distortions in interpersonal relationships. *Journal of Group Psychotherapy, Psychodrama & Sociometry, Spring*, 3–14. https://psycnet.apa.org/doi/10.3200/JGPP.55.1.3-14

Hamamci, Z. (2006). Integrating psychodrama and cognitive behavioral therapy to treat moderate depression. *The Arts in Psychotherapy, 33*, 199–207. https://doi.org/10.1016/j.aip.2006.02.001

Heimberg, R. G., & Becker, R. E. (2002). *Cognitive-behavioral group therapy for social phobia: Basic mechanisms and clinical strategies.* Guilford Press. https://doi.org/10.1176/appi.ajp.161.1.183

Kellerman, P. (1992). *Focus on psychodrama: The therapeutic aspects of psychodrama.* Jessica Kingsley Publishers Ltd. https://us.jkp.com/products/focus-on-psychodrama

Kumar, V. K., & Treadwell, T. W. (1986). Identifying a protagonist: Techniques and factors. *Journal of Group Psychotherapy, Psychodrama & Sociometry.* https://psycnet.apa.org/record/1987-35271-001

LoSavio, S., Holder, N., Wells, S., & Resick, P. (2024). Clinician concerns about cognitive processing therapy: A review of the evidence. *Cognitive and Behavioral Practice, 31*(2), 152–175. https://doi.org/10.1016/j.cbpra.2022.08.005

McGoldrick, M., & Gerson, R. (2008). *Genograms: Assessment and intervention* (3rd ed.). W. W. Norton Publishing Co. https://wwnorton.com/books/9780393714043

Moreno, J. L. (1934). *Who shall survive? A new approach to the problem of human interrelations.* Nervous & Mental Disease Publishing Co.

Moreno, J. L. (1946). Psychodrama and group psychotherapy. *Sociometry, 9*(2–3), 249–253. https://doi.org/10.2307/2785011

Nien-Hwa, L., & Hsin-Hao, T. (2014). Practicing psychodrama in Chinese culture. *The Arts in Psychotherapy, 41*(4), 386–390. https://doi.org/10.1016/j.aip.2014.06.005

Orkibi, H., Azoulay, B., Regev, D., & Snir, S. (2017). Adolescents' dramatic engagement predicts their in-session productive behaviors: A psychodrama change process study. *The Arts in Psychotherapy, 55*, 46–53. https://doi.org/10.1016/j.aip.2017.04.001

Remer, P., & Remer, R. (2003). *Theoretical foundations for diversity training: Psychodrama, chaos, feminist, and self-persuasion.* Paper presented at the Sixth Pacific Rim Congress of Group Psychotherapy, Singapore.

Resick, P. A., Monson, C. M., & Chard, K. M. (2017). *Cognitive processing therapy for PTSD: A comprehensive manual.* The Guilford Press. https://www.guilford.com/books/Cognitive-Processing-Therapy-for-PTSD/Resick-Monson-Chard/9781462554270

Thimm, J. C., & Antonsen, L. (2014). Effectiveness of cognitive behavioral group therapy for depression in routine practice. *BMC Psychiatry, 14*, 292. https://doi.org/10.1186/s12888-014-0292-x

Treadwell, T., Dartnell, D., & Travaglini, A. H. (2021). *Integrating CBT with experiential theory and practice: A group therapy workbook.* Taylor & Francis/Routledge. https://doi.org/10.4324/9781003014379

Treadwell, T., Dartnell, D., Travaglini, L., Staats, M., & Devinney, K. (2016). *Group therapy workbook: Integrating cognitive behavioral therapy with psychodramatic theory and practice.* Outskirts Press Publishing. https://doi.org/10.12926/18-00013.1

Treadwell, T., Kumar, V. K., & Wright, J. (2004). Enriching psychodrama via the use of cognitive behavioral therapy techniques. *Journal of Group Psychotherapy, Psychodrama, & Sociometry, 55*, 55–65. https://doi.org/10.3200/JGPP.55.2.55-65

Treadwell, T., Travaglini, L., Reisch, E., & Kumar, V. K. (2011). The effectiveness of collaborative story building and telling in facilitating group cohesion in a college classroom setting. *International Journal of Group Psychotherapy, 61*(4), 502–517. https://doi.org/10.1521/ijgp.2011.61.4.502

Treadwell, T. W., & Kumar, V. K. (2002). Introduction to the special issue on cognitive behavioral therapy and psychodrama. *Journal of Group Psychotherapy Psychodrama and Soiometry, 55*(2–3), 51–54. https://doi.org/10.3200/JGPP.55.2.51-53

Weathers, F. W., Litz, B. T., Keane, T. M., Palmieri, P. A., Marx, B. P., & Schnurr, P. P. (2013). *The PTSD checklist for DSM-5 (PCL-5). Scale available from the National Center for PTSD at www.ptsd.va.gov.* https://doi.org/10.1037/pas0000260

Wenzel, A., Liese, B., Beck, A., & Friedman-Wheeler, D. (2012). *Group cognitive therapy for addictions.* The Guilford Press. https://www.guilford.com/books/Group-Cognitive-Therapy-for-Addictions/Wenzel-Liese-Beck-Friedman-Wheeler/9781462505494

White, J. R., & Freeman, A. S. (Eds.). (2000). *Cognitive-behavioral group therapy: For specific problems and populations.* American Psychological Association. https://doi.org/10.1037/10352-000

Wilson, J. (2009). An introduction to psychodrama for CBT practitioners. *Journal of the New Zealand College of Clinical Psychologists, 19*, 4–7. https://www.nzccp.co.nz/assets/Uploads/An-Introduction-to-Psychodrama-for-CBT-Practitioners-Jenny-Wilson.pdf

Woolfolk, R. (2000). Cognition and emotion in counseling and psychotherapy. *Practical Philosophy, 3*(3), 19–27.

Yalom, I. D., & Leszcz, M. (2005). *The theory and practice of group psychotherapy* (5th ed.). Basic Books. https://doi.org/10.1176/appi.psychotherapy.20210007

Young, J. E., & Klosko, J. S. (1994). *Reinventing your life.* Plume. https://archive.org/details/jeffrey-e.-young-janet-s.-klosko-reinventing-your-life-the-breakthough-program-t

Section IV

Treating Psychological Trauma Using Long-Term Groups

6 Trauma and Enactments in Group Psychotherapy

Robert Grossmark

In this chapter, I will address enactment as the primary language of trauma, and thus a force for narrative, generative movement, and healing in group treatment. I will describe some of the many renditions of the concept of enactment and will examine the progression of different views of nonverbal communication and action in the field of group therapy. I will address the development of the concept from the pejorative view of "acting out" as a resistance and avoidance of the work of group therapy to the contemporary view that enactments not only are ubiquitous and mutual, involving all group members, the therapist, and the group-as-a-whole, but can also be regarded as the very fulcrum of therapeutic transformation of trauma in group therapy. Indeed, I will argue that, far from being a problem to be resolved, enactment can be viewed as the core curative factor in the healing of trauma in group psychotherapy. I will address the complex relation between time, trauma, and enactment and will suggest that the mutual living-through of enactments in group therapy fertilizes the instantiation of time and the past and thus offers an opportunity for trauma processing and mourning.

We have come a long distance in a short time. In Klein and Schermer's groundbreaking first volume *Group psychotherapy for psychological trauma* (2000), there is no reference to *enactment* in the index. However, there are inferences that point to what we might now think of as enactments. For instance, they refer to group members re-experiencing traumatic occurrences in the group (p.6), and when describing roles in group (Redl, 1963), they describe how "the therapist and members at various times can be cast in the roles of the victim, perpetrator, rescuer, and bystander" (p. 8). But they do caution that configurations such as victim–victimizer be "defused" by the therapist. As in the chapters that comprise the rest of their volume, these ideas illustrate the power of the group setting for capturing in a real, vital, and alive way the actuality of trauma and the substantial demand that such processes require from the therapist and the group members. I write this chapter with immense respect for all the therapists who venture into the world of trauma and for all the group members who find the courage to try to heal their suffering. Group treatment offers a unique address for the healing and transformation of trauma, and I will argue that enactment, the living out of traumatic experiences and relationships in the crucible of a group, is the very heart of that healing.

Trauma, Dissociation, and What Cannot Be Thought

As every reader knows, the whole world of mental health treatment has been transformed in recent years by the acknowledgment of and engagement with trauma and its sequelae. Whether it is the trauma of specific unbearable and unthinkable events, such as incest,

DOI: 10.4324/9781003546252-10

rape, or other violations of the mind and body, the ongoing developmental trauma of non-recognition, mis- attunement, and neglect, or the pervasive and all-encompassing traumas of prejudice, racial or gender hatred, or economic and social oppression and violence, we now situate the human subject in a real world that can engender overwhelming suffering and trauma. Our challenge is to engage with the specific person and their unique psychology and lived experiences while maintaining a wide lens that accommodates recognition of our embeddedness in social and historical contexts. Trauma comes in many forms, and we are wise to maintain a respect for its complexity.

There are countless definitions of *trauma* in the literature, none of which can claim to be the final word. Indeed, Klein and Schermer struggled with a definition of *trauma* and ultimately settled on an accommodating operational definition referring to a "situation-specific, severe, and stressful violation or disruption that has serious psychiatric consequences for the individual either soon or long after the event itself" (2000, p. 5). One can see the challenge. By referring to a specific event, they exclude, for instance, ongoing and cumulative, developmental, or relational trauma (Bromberg, 2006) and social and "caste"-related trauma (Wilkerson, 2020). They do, however, point to an aspect of trauma that I find orienting and grounding – the serious consequences "for the individual" – thus turning our attention to the person. *Trauma* is not to be defined by the external incident, event, or circumstance but rather by the internal psychological responses and emotional and structural sediments that linger and cause suffering, psychological constraint, limit, and repetition.

I would also consider environmental response. Bach (2008) offers concise and helpful thoughts here, suggesting that we can define *early trauma* as a "situation in which some new internal or external experience of the baby cannot be adequately held or contained by the environment and in which this disruption is not repaired" (p. 786). I find the orientation to both internal and external experiences helpful, along with crucial consideration of the lack of sufficient containment and holding that helps a human manage difficult and painful experiences. We do not expect a life without adversity, pain, and suffering; it is the development of capacities to metabolize, to think about and manage overwhelming pain, that is crucial, and it is these capacities that we so often find lacking or underdeveloped in our patients.

Indeed, the lack of containment is itself at the core of what is traumatic for many people but is rarely something acknowledged or articulated. These are areas of trauma that are often unknown and invisible to the patient themselves. Our task, paradoxically, is to help our patients suffer what they have yet to experience (Bion, 1967).

Likewise with dissociation. Many have placed dissociation at the center of the understanding of trauma, and like the absence of an internalized containing function, it is not visible to the patient. When faced with overwhelming stimulation or non-recognition, the child hypnotically sequesters not simply the experience but that very self-state, thus creating a dissociative structure where different aspects of self are kept apart (Bromberg, 2006). While this process is adaptive, ensuring an ongoing sense of continuity and safety, the overstimulation is massive and poses a threat to the evolving sense of self. For instance, in the situation of sexual violation, a protective dissociative structure takes hold. Self-states are imperatively fractured, and where there should be flexibility of thought, affect, and relatedness, there can be rigidity and absence. The person's capacities for thought and relatedness are constrained, and a constant unconscious state of vigilance to protect from a recurrence of the trauma is instantiated. Attachment patterns, relatedness, thought, and experience itself evolve and are shaped accordingly. Here we enter the challenge of trauma that announces itself by what is not known, remembered, or experienced. And this is where the concept of enactment takes center stage.

Enactment

How do we find which trauma is being confined to non-awareness? Whether by ongoing failures of containment, holding, and recognition or by the desperate instantiation of a dissociative structure, we are seeking to therapeutically address that which is not known or available to the patient, therapist, or group. How, in the words of D. B. Stern (2004), does the eye see itself?

In fact, it is not quite correct to say that we are seeking that which is not known. Trauma, we might say, is "known," but that knowledge is not available to cognitive, symbolic, or verbal processes. We find trauma and its enduring presence in the realms of bodily and psychic symptomatology, in repetitive relational patterns, and in the dimension of enactment. In the group, enactment speaks and manifests trauma, dissociated self-states, and the imprint of what has never had form. Enactment speaks what cannot have words; it narrates the unsayable (Grossmark, 2017).

Action, Acting Out, and Enactment: "The Shape of Action"

As with all psychoanalytic and psychodynamic concepts, there are virtually as many meanings as there are writers and uses of the term. But all would agree that "enactment" refers to what is expressed in the realm of action and its effects rather than in words (Bohleber et al., 2013). Psychoanalysis was always oriented to action as a powerful form of communication. The patients who populated Breuer's and Freud's early papers (1895) manifested many psychosomatic and "theatrical" (Bohleber et al., 2013) behaviors that were redolent with unconscious meaning. But it was in his discussion of his treatment of Dora that Freud first talked of "agieren," referring to actions and the way that the patient "acted out" aspects of her memories and conflicts rather than talking about them (Freud, 1905). Valuing verbal communication over "agieren," Freud felt that such acts did not further the treatment and thus initiated a century of psychoanalytic and psychotherapeutic skepticism regarding the value of action and what cannot be put into words. That thread exists today in the world of group psychotherapy with the almost-universal invitation to, or even insistence on, putting feelings into words, not actions (Ormont, 2016; Yalom & Leszcz, 2020). But things were not quite so straightforward. When examining repetition, Freud (1914) not only saw repetitions, and thus actions, as blocks to remembering, remarking that "the patient repeats instead of remembering" (p. 151), but also observed that "[a]s long as the patient is in the treatment he cannot escape from this compulsion to repeat; and in the end *we understand that this is his way of remembering*" (Freud, 1914, p. 150). Here is psychoanalytic complexity: Repeating and action, rather than remembering and speaking, can be the negative of remembering and the work of therapy, and at the same time, actions and repeating can be a form of remembering and thus processing nonverbally. Such thoughts presciently foretell the interest in enactment that was to come.

Ferenczi (1931) also valued the role of action in the treatment and even used the word "enactment" to describe the phenomenon (p. 135). He vividly described a man curling up on his lap and talking to him in a child's voice as if Ferenczi were his grandfather. Rather than tell the patient to behave appropriately or to interpret this behavior to the patient, he responded as if he were the grandfather himself and "re-enacted" the scene with the patient (p. 473), a remarkable example of joining the experiential world of the patient. The point here is that he valued the role of enactment, saying:

> Freud is right when he teaches us that it is a triumph for analysis when it succeeds in substituting recollection for enactment. But I think it is also valuable to secure important material in the *shape of action* which can then be transformed into recollection.
>
> (1931, p. 473, my italics)

Here in 1931, we find recognition of the importance of "the shape of action" as a valuable register or dimension of therapeutic communication and action.

Leaping forward in psychoanalytic time, we find Sandler describing the therapist's "role responsiveness" (Sandler, 1976) and Jacobs's (1986) description of "countertransference enactments," generally regarded as the first introduction of the term in contemporary psychoanalysis (Bohleber et al., 2013). It is noteworthy that the focus here is on enactment as a phenomenon of countertransference, and while Sandler argued for the analyst's responsiveness, Jacobs warned of the counter-therapeutic dangers of allowing enactments to proceed unchecked. Generally, in psychoanalysis, and in many psychotherapeutic modalities, including group therapy, enactments have been regarded as a manifestation of the analyst's or therapist's loss of control or balance in response to pressure from the patient. Nevertheless, there has been a shift from regarding enactments as a threat to the treatment to the valuing of enactments as an opportunity for understanding and preverbal communication (Bohleber et al., 2013). Notably, Ellman and Moscowitz (1998) regarded enactments as inevitable and bidirectional, opening the analyst's inner experience to the patient for understanding (Chused, 1991).

Enactment, Dissociation, and Mutual Process

Relational psychoanalysis has placed dissociation and enactment at the very center of psychotherapeutic healing. Treatment is the place where dissociated experience presents itself in the dimension of enactment (Aron, 2003; Atlas & Aron, 2018; Bass, 2003; Benjamin, 1998, 2018; Black, 2003; Davies, 1996, 1997; Davies & Frawley, 1994). According to Bromberg (1998, 2006, 2011), dissociation is regarded as the principal activity of the mind. Rather than simply a defense, dissociation is regarded as a hypnoid capacity of the mind that facilitates adaptation to the intensities of human life, to regulate the self in the face of external and internal pressures. We are all composed of multiple self-states that help us adapt and live with presence and vitality and to experience continuity of self. The key is the flexibility of self-states and the capacity to move between them according to context and levels of arousal, as well as an optimal amount of integration. When trauma overwhelms and self-continuity is threatened, the normal process of dissociation is magnified, and rather than fluid and adaptive self-states, we find a "Balkanization" (Bromberg, 2006, p. 5) of the self into a dissociative structure where the mind is organized around self-preservation, and the anticipation of a recurrence of trauma that overwhelms the mind. Trauma is thus frozen and not allowed access to the rest of the mind, residing in non-symbolized, "sub-symbolic" (Bucci, 1997), emotional, and somatic "memories" and states. These dissociated self-states do not disappear but emerge in treatment as enactments, and they engage the dissociated states of the analyst, therapist, group therapist, or other group members. The patient experiences them as "really real" (Bromberg, 2006, p. 93), and the therapist and other group members will share in this heightened and often challenging experience, frequently provoking their own dissociated traumas and self-states. Members play out their dissociated self-states and thus engage all those around them in a mutual form of traumatic repetition. Thus, "enactment is the interpersonalization of dissociation: the conflict that cannot be experienced within one mind is experienced *between* or *across* two minds" (Stern, 2010, p. 86), or within and between other group members and the group therapist.

From this perspective, enactment is never an individual phenomenon but always a mutual and dynamic process – not simply a countertransference problem to be resolved by the analyst's or therapist's self-reflection or in supervision or further analysis, as per Jacobs (1986). It is the very thing itself, the center of a necessary and inevitable process, where the dissociated trauma can finally find a place and a context and an *other* who can engage with it and do the hard work of creating thought and connection where there has been unseen repetition. At the center of this difficult work is the analyst's or therapist's struggle to be aware of and work with their own complementary dissociation and regressive process.

The analyst's or therapist's self-revelation is thus "not just permissible, but necessary" (Bromberg, 2006, p. 128). In the therapeutic setting, the fear of traumatic repetition is evoked, and the resulting dissociations activated. The patient fears unbearable and unmanageable affective arousal and intensifies the dissociative structure, thus engaging the therapist's own dissociations and often creating ruptures and storms in the treatment. When the therapist can name and face these moments together with the patient and use their own regulatory capacities to clarify and openly process the experience, affect and states that were previously only threatening and menacing become regulatable, manageable, and thinkable. Even if this is challenging for both parties, the therapist's capacity to own their part in the enactment and find words that give shape and thought to the experience foster regulation and relatedness in the place of disconnection and despair. Rather than a focus on the accuracy of interpretation, the emphasis here is on the process itself, the "implicit relational knowing" (Lyons-Ruth et al., 2001) that arises between therapist and patient, and what is unmanageable and unthinkable becomes regulated and metabolized. The relevance of this process to the mutuality and dynamism of group therapy speaks for itself. We can now conceptualize group process as primarily organized around the living out of mutual enactments involving all group members, the group-as-a-whole, and the group therapist. The primary agent of change in group therapy from this perspective is exactly that: the working through of mutually lived enactments of trauma in the group.

Generative Enactment and the Flow of Enactive Engagement

Atlas and Aron (2018) place the vivid living-through of mutual enactments at the very heart of psychotherapy. The emergence of the patient's and the analyst's many self-states on the stage of the treatment allows for the creation of transitional space rather like a theater, where the emergence of self-states, trauma, and the unconscious present themselves in "dramatic dialogue." This process brings to dramatic and vivid life the internal world of the patient, their family and personal and intergenerational trauma. We invite the patient to the dance of therapy. They argue that psychotherapeutic healing accrues in the living-through of these dramas rather than via interpretation and explanation. From this perspective, far from being a countertransference that must be extinguished via further analysis or supervision, mutual enactments themselves are generative and constructive and crucial to the creation of our evolving selves.

With a somewhat similar sensibility, I suggest that rather than foreclose and evade enactments, there is tremendous opportunity when the therapist can be unobtrusive to the "flow of enactive engagement" (Grossmark, 2012a, 2012b, 2018a). Trauma, neglect, and their residue speak in the language of the unformulated, unrepresented, and unsymbolized: the register of the body and, most profoundly, the register of enactment. In his attempt to make space for the unconscious, Freud asked his patients to free-associate, to say whatever came to their mind, and the analyst would follow the flow of these associations with an evenly hovering attention. In our attempt to make space for trauma and neglect to speak in their own register of the unsymbolized and enactment, we can thus allow enactments to flow – just as Freud allowed free associations to flow – so that the unconscious, unprocessed, and unmetabolized trauma can speak. Violation, abuse, and trauma are encoded in the language of the body with accompanying sensations; thereby, our work is to work in that very realm. That is the register in which the trauma happened, and that is the register in which we must work. When allowed to flow unimpeded, enactments tell the story of pain, suffering, and violation. The patient and the therapist – and of course, the group – find themselves living the narrative that has never had words and form, and in so doing, patients can be known in their pain, damage, and even psychic death. From this perspective, enactments are the very core of treatment, being the only way that trauma and neglect can truly speak. The traumatized individual, haunted by the pain and overwhelm that, by their very nature, are unspeakable, seeks the *Other* with whom the silent scream inside can finally take shape and form. Psychotherapy and group therapy are that very place where the story is finally told, and rather than the familiar repetition of pain, meaninglessness, and dysfunction, the therapist and the group can hold the pain – not simply retaliate, repeat, and re-traumatize – thus finding the terrified, overwhelmed, or despairing child.

Enactments provide a witnessing. Until there is a witness, it is as if nothing has happened. When engaged in enactments, the therapist, patients, and group members give witness to the trauma. Not only by emotional responses to verbal testimonies but also by living through the trauma together. This is witnessing from the inside, a mutual knowing and survival.

We have come a long way from an approach that views enactments as disruptive to the forward motion and work of therapy and thus in need of eradication. Here, enactment takes center stage as the very core of the healing of trauma.

Enactment in Group Psychotherapy

As I mentioned earlier, enactment is not featured in Klein and Schermer's original volume *Group psychotherapy for psychological trauma*. But in recent years, a growing literature has addressed trauma and enactment in group therapy. While the view of enactments as countertransference problems or group resistances to be resolved and eliminated has lingered (Rosenthal, 2006), there has been a palpable shift toward viewing enactments as central and essential to the process of group psychotherapy, particularly in the realm of early non-symbolized and non-represented trauma and early attachment dysfunction and damage. Price (2018) described his work with enactments of early, non-symbolized trauma and emphasized the therapist's capacity to sink into regressed and diffuse states as the group enacted preverbal relational and attachment confusion and turmoil. Sagi Berg (2019) described compelling group work with difficult and highly challenging patients where the working within, and through, enactments of their dissociation and fragmentation, their "hall of broken mirrors," was the principal mode of group expression and afforded the key to their integration as a group and as people. Leiderman (2020) described group enactments of complex trauma, dislocation, and multiple losses in Hispanic migrants and demonstrated how enactments powerfully convey insecure/disorganized attachment in lived experience in the group. Integrating interpersonal neurobiology and neuropsychoanalysis, Schore (2020) highlighted the right brain mechanisms involved in regressive, preverbal group enactments caused by attachment trauma and disruption, again demonstrating how enactments are the principal mode of communication and therapeutic action when we are engaging with early and non-symbolized trauma. In an issue of *Group* in 2005, three articles (Eig, 2005; Gotta, 2005; Stern, 2005), and the discussion by Wright (2005), placed enactment as the principal focus of the group process. Additionally, Dobrich (2020) movingly described how a group of women who had lost their mothers at an early age enacted the multiple ways that the trauma of early loss shaped and distorted their memory and emotional presence and found their way together to alive and meaningful grief.

I placed enactment at the center of group psychotherapy theory and as the primary "curative factor" in group experience (Grossmark, 2007, 2017, 2018b). Viewing enactments from a hermeneutic perspective, I foregrounded the generative, meaning-making, and narrative properties that emerge in group enactments. As contrasted to an approach that would view enactments in group as resistances to be resolved (Rosenthal, 2006), this approach centrally construes the group as always doing and creating, as seeking the expression of what has never had voice, and most centrally, as narrating what has never had form. There are words in the group, but the attention tilts to what has never been symbolized and is outside the realm of language. We are in the realm where "thoughts arrive as actions" (Bollas, 2011). Picking up Bollas's perspective that humans have a drive to represent themselves (2011), and Gadamer's hermeneutic philosophy, the group and the members are regarded as striving to realize and to represent and repair early trauma and neglect. The group therapist unobtrusively companions the group in the flow of enactive engagement and in the narratives of trauma and altered states that arise and manifest in the group process.

The group is regarded as always narrating, manifesting unsymbolized and dissociated trauma in the language and register of enactment. Regarding enactment as narrative and manifestation of that which has never been symbolized, rather than resistance, I described (Grossmark, 2017) how, even when a member was late for a group session, the focus was on what was emerging in the group. And indeed, in that very lateness, the group found the presence of an absence of parental recognition instantiated within the patient that had ruled and constrained his functioning and capacities.

The group therapist is not neutral or outside the process and utilizes his/her/their experience from within the shared enactment: unobtrusive but deeply engaged. Following Foulkes's adaptation of Freud's free association as "free-floating discussion" in the group (Foulkes, 1964), the group therapist both participates in and is unobtrusive to the flow of enactment and arising narratives in the register of enactment. The group field or group-as-a-whole captures and gives shape to these emerging narratives of personal trauma and neglect, along with the echoes and ghosts of intergenerational trauma (Davoine & Gaudilliere, 2004; Grand & Salberg, 2017; Harris et al., 2016a, 2016b), and in doing so becomes the transitional space (Winnicott, 1971) and transformational object (Bollas, 1987) that fosters the witnessing and living-through of trauma that now becomes real, alive, and available to be mourned and transformed, rather than endlessly and mindlessly repeated.

Enactment and Time in Group Psychotherapy

Group therapists – and therapists in general – typically utilize immediacy, that is, being in the here and now (Rutan & Stone, 2001; Yalom & Leszcz, 2020). But the consideration of enactment of trauma in group therapy asks us to reconsider this commonly held view. When the human infant, child, or adult is subject to experiences of too-muchness – whether in terms of internal conflict, overwhelming trauma, neglect, and inner psychic pain that cannot be processed and integrated into the self – thinking and experience are miscarried, and the subject becomes, in some ways, frozen in time. In fact, the disruption in the synchrony and ongoingness of time is one of the signatures of massive and ongoing trauma. Self-states, subjectivity, memory, and the capacity for mental flexibility and relatedness become ossified and congealed. Hence the terrible legacy and burden of repetition and lifelessness that haunt the traumatized person. When enactments take hold, the group lives in many realities and many times, often giving voice and shape to what has been sequestered in the unthought zone of what has never been experienced and never had shape. Einstein famously said, "[T]he only reason for time is so that everything doesn't happen at once" (Oz & Oz-Salzberger, 2012, p. 108), and in the register of enactment we can truly say that "everything happens at once" (Grossmark, 2018a), and we must be open to the emergence of different temporalities in the flow of the group.

Written from within a psychoanalytic framework, Scarfone's concept of the "unpast" (2015) compellingly deconstructs the past-present-future axis and outlines different kinds of "now." Scarfone reassesses the commonly held belief that Freud's proposal was that there is no time in the unconscious or that the unconscious is "timeless." Paying careful attention to the text, he notes that Freud wrote of the *"unalterability* by time of the repressed" (Scarfone, 2015, p. vii, italics added), meaning, that what is repressed is not simply "timeless" but is better understood as untouched by time. This seems to open a fruitful, new perspective on the phenomenon and suggests that what is repressed exists, as it were, but in a different and special zone of time, one that Freud referred to as "actual." Here the word "actual" does not mean that which is real, as in English usage, but adheres to the Latinate meaning of the term, which refers to that which is happening now. Thus, he suggests, what is repressed – or dissociated, I would add – has the texture of reality and that "its time is always 'now'" (p.44): it is atemporal.

Thus, we can say that there is an "actuality" to repetition and enactment, meaning, that what is repeated or enacted can best be construed as that which "has not yet been given a time tag, so to speak, what has not yet been inserted into chronology or belongs to 'actual time'" (Scarfone, 2015, p. 44.) Hence, rather than see repetition and enactment as the recurrence of something from the past, we can understand repetition and enactment as actually "bringing in something *not yet belonging to the past*, because it was not marked with time" (Scarfone, p. 45, italics in original) but occurs in the "atemporal present" of the actual (p. 134). It only seems to be in the present but is actually in a different zone of temporality. Similarly, Bromberg (2006), speaking from the dissociation point of view, suggests that through the "joint cognitive processing of enactments" – played out in group or between patient and therapist – "the patient's sequestered self-states come alive as a 'remembered present' (Edelman, 1989)" (p. 6), a different temporal zone.

Scarfone refers to this different atemporal present as the "unpast," being neither past nor present, and a time that does not pass and manifests in repetitive enactments. Thus, we can now consider that what manifests in group as members interact and enactments emerge is the atemporal present, the unpast. These enactments are the manifestation of what has yet to be located in the past, because for so many of these patients who live in the atemporal present of repetitive enactments, the past has yet to truly exist. Thus, I have conceptualized group enactments as an "untelling" of an unpast (Grossmark, 2024). The focus is not only on the emergence of inchoate suffering and trauma (Grossmark, 2017, 2018a) but also on the manifestation in the group of the "atemporal present" and the different times and different forms of present that encapsulate and entomb trauma such that it is continually repeated. Thus, the work of the group is not only the connection to the experiences hitherto dissociated or repressed but also the very construction of the past itself (Scarfone, 2015). For until there is a past – rather than the atemporal present of the unpast – the only option is repetition and enactment, endless untelling. In other words, the group can become the place where the different experiences of time and subjectivity can emerge and where the past can finally take hold such that trauma and suffering can now be "marked by time" (Scarfone, 2015, p. 45) and the untelling can be transformed into a telling – a piece of experience that is owned and can be reflected upon – and the unpast can be transformed into a past, something that belongs to a time before and can be mourned. Once again, this perspective suggests that healing and transformation can best accrue when enactments are allowed to speak and unfold in the group process.

Case Illustration 1: Healing Through Mutual Enactment in Group

Sheila tells the group that she cannot talk about how her father tortured and terrified her with his volatile rage and attacks on her and her siblings. She tells the group that she just doesn't feel safe enough yet. She has been in this weekly psychotherapy group for about three years. She tells the group she worries about how they will respond. Some of the other group members respond empathically and try to reassure her that, of course, this is a safe place and we, the group, will be supportive and kind. Karen looks uncomfortable. I ask her what is going on. She says that this is not easy for her. The group is familiar with her long struggle to be assertive and find her voice, having grown up beaten and threatened regularly by an emotionally unstable mother. Karen takes a breath and says that she can appreciate Sheila's fears about how the group will respond. "But you simply can't control our reactions to you. We'll try our best, but you can't control how we will feel."

Karen is picking up and, with great difficulty, trying to address the way that Sheila has continuously turned people against her in the group. Like so many people who have suffered developmental trauma and abuse from a parent, there is the excruciating anguish of not only the fear of recurrence but also the complexity of identification with the very person who has perpetrated the abuse. Sheila herself was capable of quite abusive behavior, often wrapped in a need to control others, and we have witnessed this in the group. Both the terrified and dissociated child and the dysregulated and abusive parent have stepped onto the group stage. So Karen continues, saying that she is only able to say this to Sheila because she herself has worked so hard on boundaries and separateness. She is very sensitive to anyone seeking to control her mind.

Sheila says that somehow that is helpful to her, and she begins to talk about memories of her father's domination and sadism. It seems to me that the group is very engaged.

Douglas tells Sheila that he deeply resonates with what she is saying. It evokes memories of his own father's violent rages. And as he talks, I see that he is entering an altered state of consciousness. He freezes and seems to be visually seeing his father in front of him. His eyes flicker, and he begins to shake. I ask him to speak about what is happening in his body right now, and another member, Miriam, who also grew up with a violent and invasive father, says that she totally gets where Douglas is at this moment and reaches out to touch Douglas on the arm. Douglas calms and says, "It's OK," and adds that he is familiar with these moments. They pass quickly. He breathes, thanks Miriam and Sheila, and says how helpful it is to have a moment like this with people who get him. I can feel the bond between Douglas and Miriam, but I can see that Sheila is struggling.

Sheila explodes with rage. "This is why I can't talk about my father in this group!" she yells, and I perceive fear, along with some group members; it feels like a punch! Miriam and Douglas blink with shock. Sheila rages, "I will just leave the group. There is no place for me here. It is just too painful. No one cares about me!"

I can see that rather than take nurturance from the resonance that Douglas and Miriam were expressing, she experienced the repetition of the thing itself, a violent disruption. As the others momentarily bonded, it evoked a feeling of exclusion, violation, and terror. Her experience was stolen and degraded, leaving her empty and wounded.

The enacted dimension is fully in the foreground. The original dynamics of abuse and erasure are present, with different group members finding themselves playing the parts. In their resonance, Miriam and Douglas had momentarily excluded Sheila, and we find ourselves in an atemporal zone where everything happens at once. Everyone's unmetabolized trauma is activated: Douglas falling into a zone of perceptual hallucinosis, where he is transported to his childhood home; Sheila finding violation and erasure; Karen drawing on learned inner resources to set boundaries and still finding herself on the receiving end of an emotional and traumatic punch; and Miriam running headlong into the manipulation of her family, where her caring was regarded as selfishness.

As is always the case with the enacted traumatic dimension in group, everyone in the room is involved in their own and the collective ways. So now another member, Trisha, speaks with upset and anger. "Now I feel that you, Sheila, are punishing the group. And that's not fair!" Again, my intervention is simply oriented to keep the flow going. I ask Trisha to say more. "I feel blamed and punished," she says, then describing with deep upset how, in her chaotic household, her mother would bully the children into doing tasks for her, causing fear and confusion in the children, and then once the tasks were complete, the mother would simply say, "Oh, never mind," or, worse, would question, "Why on earth would you do that?" Trisha continues, saying that she never knew where she stood in her home and that the only truth she could hold on to was all the bad feelings swirling around and the thought that what had transpired was entirely her fault and she would sooner or later be punished. She believed that Sheila was punishing her because the group wasn't giving her, Sheila, what she wanted. And indeed, Sheila was angry with the whole group, and this included anger with Trisha. Still brimming with rage, Sheila accuses Trisha and the whole group that they are all so unable to help, to "just take her in."

Miriam, who spent many years protecting a younger sister from an abusive and psychotic older brother, engages with Sheila. She says, "We always have the same experience with you, Sheila. You often end up so hurt. Can't you, for once, just think about what is happening and your part in it and not simply react?"

Everything is happening at once, in a zone that is far more complex than the "here and now." People are experiencing these moments in an unpast, that is, neither "now" nor "then." This untelling of the unpast in enactment contains presences from unfinished trauma – most vividly in Douglas's hallucinosis, but clearly activated in everyone – that are repeating in the flow of this group enactment. Pain that has yet to be suffered is now present. And like all enactments, the germs of generative elements are fertilized as the group shares these painful moments and they are held and metabolized in the group field and in the group therapist's mind.

I name the pain. Not to extinguish it, but to make a space for it. I say to the group that Sheila is clearly in terrible pain inside and is terrified that it will break her apart. And I say that she is expressing something that everyone is in touch with: pain that will not cease in its grip.

Miriam thanks me for slowing her down. Yes, she was furious with Sheila only moments ago, but she can totally feel it. She says she can see that Sheila feels literally ripped apart by the group. She goes on to say it is like a pack of dogs. If one slips and shows their belly, the other will attack, because a weak member of the pack creates an increased threat for all of them. "You, Sheila, must feel totally raw with us." And Sheila mimes with her hands and torso the act of being ripped apart physically. "Yes," she says, "it is no joke." When she says she fears talking about the violence of her father, her very being is on the line. Everyone in the group hears her. And Douglas nods assent. That was what he felt when she began to talk and he had his flashback. And now Sheila says that she can appreciate that she was, in fact, impacting people, not being erased. When she is terrified, she can only feel threat and can lose her sense of reality. Sheila continues, "It is like I cannot get beyond this. It keeps happening. That is how I have lost so many relationships. But when you, Miriam, tell me you understand, and you, Douglas, tell me that you are affected by what I am doing, it is better for me. I feel better now." And indeed, she seems more regulated and connected. Douglas resonates and says that we all learned to protect ourselves and our teachers were our abusive families. So of course, we do to others what was done to us. He, too, feels an incredible rage inside him and just wants to tell people to get away from him.

In moments like this, the dynamics and the narratives are thick. Each member was living through aspects of their trauma. The group was untelling the unpast, narrating their traumas, with no intention or awareness, in an atemporal present. They have varying degrees of awareness of the connection between these moments and their past trauma, but the healing and generative aspects of group enactments such as this lie in the emotional reality of what is transpiring within and between people. When they find their way to each other's pain and rage, the present and the future begin to come online as there is some sense that this is different now. Sheila is aware that something in the connection between the group members helped her, and she is calmer and connected. And she did not leave the group as she had threatened to do. Her trauma and rage have not destroyed her or the group.

As described earlier, the group becomes the transitional space, in which things are real and not real at the same time, and the transformational object, where sequestered pain and trauma are transformed from silent and private scream to shared, real, and vital experience.

In time, Sheila does tell more about her experiences with her violent father, and the group is empathic and emotionally resourceful for her. But the witnessing of the trauma happens in the shared mutual enactment where they all witness from within a lived experience, rather than from hearing a verbal narrative. Trauma will continue to speak in its own vernacular of enactment and repetition. When held and contained in a group such as this, where what is unthinkable and unmetabolizable is engaged with, respected, and known in its own register, then thought, reflection, regulation, and differentiation develop, and a time that allows for things to be located in the past, and thus frees up a potential future, gradually takes hold.

Discussion

Enactment: The Primary Curative Factor in Group

In this chapter I reviewed the history of action and enactment in psychoanalysis and psychotherapy and endorsed the contemporary understanding of enactment as the primary language of trauma and thus a force for narrative, generative movement, and healing. I hope I have illustrated how working in the register of enactment is profitably construed as the primary therapeutic potential of group therapy that transforms endless repetitions of traumatic engagements and experiences into lived and manageable experience. Empty repetition in an endless unpast is transformed into a mutual untelling, where time comes back online and the past is instantiated. Only when the past is accessible can the work of mourning and repair that is so central to the healing of trauma take place. Trauma now has an address, and the person can look to a future and a freedom that beckons.

References

Aron, L. (2003). The paradoxical place of enactment in psychoanalysis: Introduction. *Psychoanalytic Dialogues, 13*, 623–631. https://doi.org/10.1080/10481881309348760

Atlas, G., & Aron, L. (2018). *Dramatic dialogue: Contemporary clinical practice*. Routledge. https://www.routledge.com/Dramatic-Dialogue-Contemporary-Clinical-Practice/Atlas-Aron/p/book/9781138555488

Bach, S. (2008). On digital consciousness and psychic death. *Psychoanalytic Dialogues, 18*, 784–794. https://doi.org/10.1080/10481880802473290

Bass, A. (2003). "E" enactments in psychoanalysis: Another medium, another message. *Psychoanalytic Dialogues, 13*, 657–675. https://doi.org/10.1080/10481881309348762

Benjamin, J. (1998). *The bonds of love*. Pantheon. https://www.penguinrandomhouse.com/books/11358/the-bonds-of-love-by-jessica-benjamin/

Benjamin, J. (2018). *Beyond doer and done to: Recognition theory, intersubjectivity and the third*. Routledge. https://www.routledge.com/Beyond-Doer-and-Done-to-Recognition-Theory-Intersubjectivity-and-the-Third/Benjamin/p/book/9781138218420

Bion, W. R. (1967). Attacks on linking. In W. R. Bion (Ed.), *Second thoughts: Selected papers on psycho-analysis*. Jason Aronson. https://www.taylorfrancis.com/books/mono/10.4324/9780429479809/second-thoughts-wilfred-bion

Black, M. (2003). Enactment: Analytic musings on energy, language and personal growth. *Psychoanalytic Dialogues, 13*, 633–655. https://doi.org/10.1080/10481881309348761

Bohleber, W., Fonagy, P., Jimenez, J., Scarfone, D., Varvin, S., & Zysman, S. (2013). Toward a better use of psychoanalytic concepts: A model illustrated using the concept of enactment. *International Journal of Psychoanalysis, 94*(3), 501–530. https://doi.org/10.1111/1745-8315.12075

Bollas, C. (1987). The transformational object. In C. Bollas (Ed.), *The shadow of the object: Psychoanalysis of the unthought known* (pp. 13–29). Free Association Books. https://cup.columbia.edu/book/the-shadow-of-the-object/9780231185073

Bollas, C. (2011). Character and interformality. In C. Bollas (Ed.), *The Christopher Bollas reader* (pp. 238–248). Routledge. https://www.routledge.com/The-Christopher-Bollas-Reader/Bollas/p/book/9780415664615

Breuer, J., & Freud, S. (1895). *Studies on hysteria. The standard edition of the complete psychological works of Sigmund Freud, volume II, 1893–1895*. https://pep-web.org/browse/document/se.002.0000a?page=PR0004

Bromberg, P. M. (1998). *Standing in the spaces: Essays on clinical process, trauma and dissociation*. The Analytic Press. https://www.routledge.com/Standing-in-the-Spaces-Essays-on-Clinical-Process-Trauma-and-Dissociation/Bromberg/p/book/9780881633566

Bromberg, P. M. (2006). *Awakening the dreamer: Clinical journeys*. The Analytic Press. https://www.routledge.com/Awakening-the-Dreamer-Clinical-Journeys/Bromberg/p/book/9780415888080

Bromberg, P. M. (2011). *The shadow of the tsunami and the growth of the relational mind*. Routledge. https://www.routledge.com/The-Shadow-of-the-Tsunami-and-the-Growth-of-the-Relational-Mind/Bromberg/p/book/9780367606220

Bucci, W. (1997). *Psychoanalysis and cognitive science: A multiple code theory.* Guilford Press. https://www.guilford.com/books/Psychoanalysis-and-Cognitive-Science/Wilma-Bucci/9781572302136

Chused, J. (1991). The evocative power of enactments. *Journal of the American Psychoanalytic Association, 39,* 615–639. https://doi.org/10.1177/000306519103900302

Davies, J. M. (1996). Linking the pre-analytic with the post-classical: Integration, dissociation and the multiplicity of unconscious processes. *Contemporary Psychoanalysis, 32,* 553–576. https://doi.org/10.1177/0003065120967741

Davies, J. M. (1997). Dissociation, therapeutic enactment, and transference-countertransference processes: A discussion of papers on childhood sexual abuse by S. Grand and J. Sarnat. *Gender and Psychoanalysis, 2,* 241–257. https://doi.org/10.1177/0003065120967741

Davies, J. M., & Frawley, M. G. (1994). *Treating the adult survivor of childhood sexual abuse.* Basic Books. https://www.hachettebookgroup.com/titles/jody-messler-davies/treating-the-adult-survivor-of-childhood-sexual-abuse/9780465066339/

Davoine, F., & Gaudilliere, J. (2004). *History beyond trauma.* Other Press. https://otherpress.com/product/history-beyond-trauma-9781590511114/

Dobrich, J. (2020). An elegy for motherless daughters: Dissociation, multiplicity and mourning. *Psychoanalytic Perspectives, 17*(3), 366–385. https://doi.org/10.1080/1551806X.2020.1801053

Edelman, G. M. (1989). *The remembered present: A biological theory of consciousness.* Basic Books. https://www.hachettebookgroup.com/titles/gerald-m-edelman/remembered-present/9780465069101/?lens=basic-books

Eig, A. M. (2005). The group analyst gets married: A relational perspective on working in the transference and countertransference. *Group, 29*(4), 407–419.

Ellman, S., & Moscowitz, M. (Eds.). (1998). *Enactment: Toward a new approach to the therapeutic relationship.* Jason Aronson. https://rowman.com/ISBN/9781461628286/Enactment-Toward-a-New-Approach-to-the-Therapeutic-Relationship

Ferenczi, S. (1931). Child analysis in the analysis of adults. In M. Balint (Ed.), *Final contributions to the problems and methods of psycho-analysis by Sandor Ferenczi.* Basic Books Inc.

Foulkes, S. H. (1964). *Therapeutic group analysis.* Karnak Books. https://www.karnacbooks.com/product/therapeutic-group-analysis/2704/

Freud, S. (1905). Fragment of an analysis of a case of hysteria. In James Strachey (Ed.), *The standard edition of the complete psychological works of sigmund Freud, VII* (pp. 7–122). The Hogarth Press.

Freud, S. (1914). Remembering, repeating and working-through. *Standard Edition, XII,* 145–156. https://pep-web.org/browse/document/se.002.0000a?page=PR0004

Gotta, H. W. (2005). The group wants top party. *Group, 29*(4), 435–445.

Grand, S., & Salberg, J. (Eds.). (2017). *Trans-generational trauma and the other: Dialogues across history and difference.* Routledge. https://www.routledge.com/Trans-generational-Trauma-and-the-Other-Dialogues-across-history-and-difference/Grand-Salberg/p/book/9781138205826

Grossmark, R. (2007). The edge of chaos: Enactment, disruption and emergence in group psychotherapy. *Psychoanalytic Dialogues, 17*(4), 479–500. https://doi.org/10.1080/10481880701487193

Grossmark, R. (2012a). The unobtrusive relational analyst. *Psychoanalytic Dialogues, 22,* 629–646. https://doi.org/10.1080/10481885.2012.737693

Grossmark, (2012b). The flow of enactive engagement. *Contemporary Psychoanalysis, 48*(3), 287–300. https://doi.org/10.1080/00107530.2012.10746505

Grossmark, R. (2017). Narrating the unsayable. *International Journal of Group Psychotherapy, 67,* 27–46. https://doi.org/10.1080/00207284.2016.1202680

Grossmark, R. (2018a). *The unobtrusive relational analyst: Explorations in psychoanalytic companioning.* Routledge. https://www.routledge.com/The-Unobtrusive-Relational-Analyst-Explorations-in-Psychoanalytic-Companioning/Grossmark/p/book/9781138899063

Grossmark, R. (2018b). The unobtrusive relational group analyst and the work of the narrative. *Psychoanalytic Inquiry, 38*(4), 246–255. https://doi.org/10.1080/07351690.2018.1444842

Grossmark, R. (2024). The untelling. *Psychoanalytic Dialogues, 34*(1), 3–19. https://doi.org/10.1080/10481885.2023.2290276

Harris, A., Kalb, M., & Klebanoff, S. (Eds.). (2016a). *Ghosts in the consulting room: Echoes of trauma in psychoanalysis.* Routledge. https://www.routledge.com/Ghosts-in-the-Consulting-Room-Echoes-of-Trauma-in-Psychoanalysis/Harris-Kalb-Klebanoff/p/book/9780415728676

Harris, A., Kalb, M., & Klebanoff, S. (Eds.). (2016b). *Demons in the consulting room: Echoes of genocide, slavery and extreme trauma in psychoanalytic practice.* Routledge. https://www.routledge.com/Demons-in-the-Consulting-Room-Echoes-of-Genocide-Slavery-and-Extreme-Trauma-in-Psychoanalytic-Practice/Harris-Kalb-Klebanoff/p/book/9781138943490

Jacobs, T. (1986). On countertransference enactments. *Journal of the American Psychoanalytic Association*, *34*, 289–307. https://doi.org/10.1177/000306518603400203

Klein, R. H., & Schermer, V. L. (Eds.). (2000). *Group psychotherapy for psychological trauma*. Guilford Press. https://psycnet.apa.org/record/2000-03901-000

Leiderman, L. (2020). Psychodynamic group therapy with Hispanic migrants: Interpersonal, relational constructs in treating complex trauma, dissociation and enactments. *International Journal of Group Psychotherapy*, *70*(2), 162–182. https://doi.org/10.1080/00207284.2019.1686704

Lyons-Ruth, K., & Boston Change Process Study Group. (2001). The emergence of new experiences: Relational improvisation, recognition process and non-linear change in psychoanalytic therapy. *Psychologist/Psychoanalyst*, *21*, 13–17. https://doi.org/10.1177/0003065113496636

Ormont, L. (2016). *The technique of group treatment: The collected papers of Louis Ormont, Ph.D.* Edited by L. Furgeri. Createspace. https://www.karnacbooks.com/product/the-technique-of-group-treatment-the-collected-papers-of-louis-r-ormont-phd/17195/

Oz, A., & Oz-Salzberger, F. (2012). *Jews and words*. Yale University Press. https://yalebooks.yale.edu/book/9780300205848/jews-and-words/

Price, J. (2018). Into the wild: Working with preverbal experiences in group. *International Journal of Group Psychotherapy*, *68*(1), 1–16. https://www.tandfonline.com/doi/full/10.1080/00207284.2017.1338522

Redl, F. (1963). Psychoanalysis and group psychotherapy: A developmental point of view. *The American Journal of Orthopsychiatry*, *33*, 135–147.

Rosenthal, L. (2006). The re-enactment of familial roles as resistance in group psychotherapy. *Group*, *30*, 3. https://www.jstor.org/stable/41719125

Rutan, J. S., & Stone, W. N. (2001). *Psychodynamic group psychotherapy*. Guilford Press. https://www.guilford.com/books/Psychodynamic-Group-Psychotherapy/Rutan-Stone-Shay/9781462516506

Sagi Berg, S. (2019). "Hall of broken mirrors" – Enactment in an analytic group of "difficult patients". *International Journal of Group Psychotherapy*, *69*(1), 1–29. https://doi.org/10.1080/00207284.2018.1455054

Sandler, J. (1976). Countertransference and role responsiveness. *International Review of Psychoanalysis*, *3*, 43–47.

Scarfone, D. (2015). *The unpast: The actual unconscious*. The Unconscious in Translation. https://www.uitbooks.com/shop/the-unpast

Schore, A. N. (2020). Forging connections in group psychotherapy through right brain-to-right brain emotional communications. Part 1: Theoretical models of right brain therapeutic action. Part 2: Clinical case analyses of group right brain regressive enactments. *International Journal of Group Psychotherapy*, *70*(1), 29–88. https://doi.org/10.1080/00207284.2019.1682460

Stern, D. B. (2004). The eye sees itself: Dissociation, enactment and the achievement of conflict. *Contemporary Psychoanalysis*, *40*, 197–237. https://doi.org/10.1080/00107530.2004.10745828

Stern, D. B. (2010). *Partners in thought: Working with unformulated experience, dissociation, and enactment*. Routledge.

Stern, L. (2005). Co-creation of group process: A member sets of the therapist's abandonment feelings. *Group*, *29*(4), 421–433.

Wilkerson, I. (2020). *Caste: The origins of our discontents*. Random House. https://www.penguinrandomhouse.com/books/653196/caste-by-isabel-wilkerson/

Winnicott, D. W. (1971). *Playing and reality*. Tavistock Publications. https://www.routledge.com/Playing-and-Reality/Winnicott/p/book/9780415345460

Wright, F. (2005). Valuing enactments in group psychotherapy: Discussion of three case studies. *Group*, *29*(4), 399–406.

Yalom, I., & Leszcz, M. (2020). *The theory and practice of group therapy* (6th ed.). Basic Books. https://www.hachettebookgroup.com/titles/irvin-d-yalom/the-theory-and-practice-of-group-psychotherapy/9781541617568/?lens=basic-books

Section V

Treating Racial Trauma Using Psychotherapy Groups

7 Group-as-a-Whole and Psychodynamic Group Psychotherapy in Treating Trauma With the African American Population at Howard University Counseling Service

Ayana Watkins-Northern and Reginald Nettles

When we first accepted the invitation to write this chapter, we were delighted and pleased to contribute to the understanding of trauma, particularly as it relates to people of African descent. What we did not know, nor expect, was to encounter our own traumas, respectively. Thinking and writing about the topic led us to recalling and sharing some of our own experiences. These are just two of many stories:

RN (Second Author)

As a 5-year-old Black boy, I said it best, after getting up to go to the bathroom before my second day of kindergarten: "Daddy, Daddy, Daddy, I can't stand up!"

Daddy came running, picked me up, and put me back to bed. Mother called the family doctor, who came to the house, as was the custom during the early 1950s.

Dr. Reyman came, examined me, and pronounced: "Margie, polio in the calf!"

Unbeknownst to me at that time, Mother cried. My parents drove me together to Grasslands Hospital in Valhalla, New York, where I stayed until returning home the day after school let out for the summer.

All this followed my brother, 4 years older, being hit by a car on his way to school in second grade. Both legs broken, he remained in dual plaster casts from his ankles to his waist for several months, visited regularly by his homebound teacher.

AW-N (First Author)

It was very important to my grandmother that all her children and grandchildren be told this story, passed down from her mother.

The story was about my great-great-grandmother Esther, who was a house slave. She did the sewing for the plantation owner's wife and the family. It was said that the wife frequently complained to Esther about very little things and spoke to her harshly as well. On a day when the wife was again enraged, she complained about Esther's husband, as she was known to do. She frequently asked Esther why she didn't have a husband that looked like all the other slave women's husbands. He was described as having very black straight hair. In a fit of rage, she took the sewing shears and stabbed Esther in the neck, severing her jugular vein. She would not allow any of the other slaves to come to Esther's aid. Esther bled out, and she died there on the floor. My great-grandmother Mary witnessed the murder of her mother. Her father was allowed to take her to his people to be raised. According to my grandmother, Esther spent a significant part of her life with the people who were/are indigenous to this country.

This is a very painful story for our family, and it continues to be. This is trauma passed on from generation to generation.

DOI: 10.4324/9781003546252-12

Trauma, Slavery, Health-Care Inequities, and African Cultural Implications

This chapter will discuss the traumatic experience of African Americans in the context of a White-dominant culture, whether acute, chronic, or complex, occurring both within present time and historically.

Historical Impact of Slavery

The history of people of African descent is replete with traumatic experiences, from the removal of individuals en masse from their homelands to their implanting as slaves in foreign lands.

While much can be said about slavery and the many ways in which its impact remains, by definition, *slavery* clearly meets the criteria for both chronic and complex trauma. Repeated witnessing, as well as experiencing, of actual life-threatening events that include prolonged abuse and cruelty, death, rape, and violence, has left indelible scars, leading to the creation of intergenerational trauma.

African Americans experience both cumulative traumata stemming from structural racism (Hankerson et al., 2022) and the historical trauma of slavery, denoting the intergenerational trauma they experience as a systemically oppressed population for generations (Ehlers et al., 2013). Historical trauma encapsulates the psychological and emotional consequences of mass traumatic experiences of slavery which have been transmitted to subsequent generations through physiological, environmental, and social pathways (Ehlers et al., 2013; Sotero, 2006).

Following the Civil War and subsequent events such as Reconstruction and the growth of the "Jim Crow South," long periods of racially motivated crimes, including lynchings of slaves and runaway slaves, ushered in a culture of racially motivated hate crimes and continued violence against African Americans. Continuing recently, the resurgence of police shootings of African Americans is too reminiscent of the post–Civil War past.

Medical Segregation

Racial segregation served as a challenge based on the race to acquiring adequate health care and medical treatment during the polio epidemics which besieged and encumbered the United States during the early 1900s. The Roosevelt Warm Springs Institute for Rehabilitation Center was created for treatment of polio and founded by Franklin Roosevelt in the 1920s before he became president, but after contracting polio. The center maintained a Whites-only policy of admission, mirroring the racial segregation in medical treatment of the times. This policy was also sustained by a persuasive scientific argument about polio itself: that Blacks were not susceptible to this disease (Rogers, 2007).

After a decade of civil rights activism, the notion of polio as a White disease was challenged. Black health professionals, reflecting a new integrationist epidemiology, demanded that in polio, as in American medicine at large, health care should be provided regardless of racial differences.

In 1939, the director of the National Foundation for Infantile Paralysis announced that it would provide its largest single grant to build and staff a polio center at the Tuskegee Institute in Alabama, its purposes being to treat Black polio patients and to train Black physicians and other medical staff to provide treatment.

The orthopedic care at the Tuskegee Center was touted as helping hundreds of children who may have otherwise been doomed to a lifetime of crippling. Yet from the outset, the center, with 36 beds, could only help a fraction of the patients who sought care.

Through a calculated convergence of politics, civil rights activism, and philanthropy, minority polio survivors were first made visible. It was then affirmed that they, too, deserved specialized care. Finally, as the notion of polio as a White disease became disreputable, Blacks were seen as appropriate subjects of research and recipients of advances in medical services. The new politics of polio made Black and White bodies analogous and forced a new epidemiology. Clinical visibility informed social awareness of neglect, which in turn empowered larger claims for social justice and medical equity.

Mental Health

Noteworthy health and mental health inequities in the United States are reflected in differences in average length of life, quality of life, rates of disability, severity of illness, and access to treatment (Coombs et al., 2021).

Mental health research indicates significant disparities among Black, Latinx, and White children and adults. Black youth are less likely than White youth to receive treatment for their depression (Hankerson et al., 2022). Over 25% of Black youth exposed to violence are at high risk for posttraumatic stress disorder (PTSD). Bridge et al. (2018) found that the suicide rate of Black children aged 5 to 12 was nearly twice that of White children of the same age. Among adults, similar racial disparities have been correlated, with Blacks having higher suicide rates.

Individuals identifying as biracial, being of two or more races (24.9%), are more likely to report having a mental disorder within the past year than any other race or ethnic group, followed by the Indigenous people of America/Alaska Natives (22.7%), Whites (19%), and Blacks (16.8%) (American Psychiatric Association, 2017). Black American adults are 20% more likely to experience serious mental problems, such as major depressive disorder or generalized anxiety disorder. Although rates of depression are lower in Blacks (24.6%) and Hispanics (19.6%) than in Whites (34.7%), depression in Blacks and Hispanics is likely to be more disabling and persistent. American Indians/Alaskan Natives report higher PTSD and alcohol dependence rates than any other ethnic or racial group. According to Sibrava et al. (2019), African Americans have the highest lifetime prevalence of PTSD (8.7%), compared to their White (7.4%), Latino (7%), and Asian (4%) counterparts. Further data is provided on racial disparities in homelessness and housing, employment and education, incarceration and mental health, racism, mistrust, as well as barriers in access to care (Hankerson et al., 2022).

The African Concept of Ubuntu

The cultural history of group life, by description/definition, goes as far back as 4500 BC, in African history, and perhaps farther. Williams (1987), in his book *The Destruction of Black Civilization*, describes the perception of the collective (the whole) as central to ancient African philosophy and culture.

The concept of *Ubuntu* (Brown, 2005) is an ancient African concept and word that represents this view. It is the philosophical and cultural practice of identification of oneself as an essential component of the other, and the other an essential component of the person or the self. Although Ubuntu is a word from Zulu, the language of the Zulu people of South Africa, the concept of Ubuntu was intricately woven into the cultures and philosophies of African people, existing throughout the continent of Africa: Angola, Botswana, Burundi, Cameroon, Republic of the Congo, Democratic Republic of Congo, Kenya, Malawi, Mozambique, Namibia, Rwanda, South Africa, and Ghana. Each country has a word in its language for the concept of Ubuntu. This concept prioritizes group or communal existence over individualism, prioritized by the Western world. In Battle's book (1997), Archbishop Benjamin Tutu is quoted as saying, "I am what I am because of who we all are," a rephrasing of this ancient African saying, illustrating the basic principle of Ubuntu.

Group Psychotherapy in Treating Trauma With African Americans

The Concept of the Group in North America With African and Indigenous Cultures

Many traumatic experiences are present in the histories of the peoples of North America, and they have similarities to those experiences of Black Africans violently seized from Africa. So too is their cultural history of group life. For example, the Indigenous people of North America utilized groups as a part of their societal structure. They identified themselves based on specific tribes, each having its own social structure, language, and cultural practices. The community was prioritized over the individual, and they governed themselves by way of consensus (Savio, 2022). Groups identified specific sectors of the community: elders, governing entities, women, and youth preparing for adulthood, as examples. These subgroups could also be identified based on their memberships, purpose, and tasks. Common interests, such as safety and trade, were motivating factors for the formation of confederacies (Mann, 2005). Then, larger communities were developed, but they consisted of sub-communities or tribes, each maintaining its own societal structure.

Following the arrival of Europeans and the advent of slavery, the dismantling of these groups became one of the essential systemic strategies in the establishment of slavery. The Indigenous people faced genocide, were displaced, died of disease, and were killed through slavery, rape, and war, declining their population by 90–95% after the arrival of the Europeans (McKenna & Pratt, 2015). The Europeans engaged in the enslavement of both African and Indigenous cultures; therefore, cultural identity and group cohesion posed a threat to their acquisition of power and control over the enslaved population. Consequently, names, familial kinship, language, and African traditional practices were forbidden. The power inherent in the group posed a threat to the subjugation of both peoples. We speculate that the intergenerational transmission of cultural identity plays a role in the ideal nature of the suitability of group for these populations.

History of the Howard University Counseling Service (HUCS)

Shortly after the end of the Civil War, members of the First Congregational Society of Washington considered establishing a theological seminary for the education of African American clergymen. Within a few weeks, they established Howard University, which is one of the oldest historically Black universities in the United States. It was established by an act of Congress in 1867 and named for Oliver Otis Howard, a Union general in the Civil War and a director of the Freedmen's Bureau.

Founded in 1948, the Howard University Counseling Service (HUCS) began fulfilling its mission to provide psychological care and support, career counseling, and guidance, as well as administration of standardized tests. The first director of HUCS was Dr. Frederick Watts. A member of the Department of Psychology faculty, Dr. Watts played a key role in the establishment of HUCS. Perhaps his presence influenced the staffing of HUCS, in that from the beginning, it was staffed by doctoral-level clinical psychologists.

Following the tenure of Dr. Watts, Dr. Carolyn R. Payton became the director of HUCS, having returned to the university after serving as director for the eastern Caribbean region of the United States Peace Corps within the Carter administration. Laying the foundation for clinical training and scholarship, she was the major architect of HUCS and its continued evolution of services and advancement in clinical training.

The early literature on group psychotherapy emphasized that African Americans, as well as a broad sweep of Asian populations, were unsuitable for group therapies (Fenster, 1996). The explanation for this misconception was that groups were for intelligent and articulate individuals. Consequently, this assumption ruled out African Americans. The rationale for exclusion of people of Asian descent was based on misperceptions about the influence of their cultural beliefs and practices. Their deference to authority was assumed to be an obstacle preventing people of Asian cultures from speaking in groups in the presence of perceived authority. In general, it was thought that the characteristics of both populations, referenced earlier, would render them deficient in verbal communication and, therefore, incapable of utilizing the modality (Fenster, 1996).

These alleged findings from the late 1940s through the early 1960s were disturbing to Dr. Payton and the staff. She therefore addressed the false stereotypes and prejudices that African Americans and Asians could not benefit from group therapy by establishing in HUCS an exceptionally viable group training and treatment program in the early 1970s. A variety of groups was developed, including ongoing long-term psychotherapy groups, short-term psychotherapy groups, short-term counseling groups, psychoeducational groups, supervision groups, and eventually, exposure to work with the large group. Coincident with the formation of these diverse groups, clinical staff were expected to matriculate through a group training program, initially established by the Psychiatric Institute Foundation of Washington, DC. The staff was trained in both group psychotherapy and group counseling. The thinking was that a group model would best enable the staff to fulfill part of the mission of HUCS, specifically supporting entering freshman students in establishing solid and firm foundations as they transitioned to university life.

Case Illustration 1

The main author facilitated a group for freshman students at HUCS early in the program's inception, when trauma was typically unnamed in many clinical and societal settings. This was a co-ed, short-term group (12-week duration) focusing on issues concerning academic success. In the beginning stages of the group, members began to discuss traumatic experiences they had been subjected to during younger years. These traumas ranged from the experience of domestic violence, substance abuse, and being subjected to angry and aggressive ridicule by family members. Group members became aware of the power of words, which can be profoundly traumatic, leaving many of the students with internalized self-ridicule, challenging their abilities to academically succeed. They experienced a level of support that enabled them to look with deeper curiosity at how they shared struggles despite coming from such different environments.

This is an illustration of how the group and the perception of the group as a collective provided a successful pathway to taming the pernicious impact of trauma on attaining academic success. The students discovered together that, indeed, these experiences had been traumatic and were shared, thus validating the emotional pain and impact of these events. Many found their first group therapy experience to be empowering and rewarding; therefore, they decided, during the termination process, to join long-term psychodynamic groups that were provided at HUCS.

Advanced clinical training was the expectation of all HUCS staff. This, in turn, laid the foundation for the provision of advanced clinical training for graduate students in psychology programs at the university and the evolution of a formal training program that, in 1983, received full accreditation from the American Psychological Association (APA). The key characteristics of the program were training in group work and, though out of awareness at that time, provided the mechanism for the actual integration of diversity into every aspect of the program. Emphasis on these features was seen as paramount for learning and training, as well as for acquiring competency in treating diverse populations. The model of infusing group treatments into the clinical services and the training program proved to be a natural fit for HUCS. Application of group modalities was most effective for teaching and training clinicians about diversity. Since the staff, clients, and trainees were also from diverse backgrounds, the use of group provided real-time illustration of theory through experiential learning.

Early in the development of HUCS and its conceptualizations of the presenting problems of students of African descent, the role of trauma could typically be identified as a central aspect of their presenting problems. HUCS staff also incorporated the concept of spirituality when facilitating trauma groups. Spirituality is primary within African cultures, providing a source of hope in the midst of collective trauma.

An important aspect in the evolution of HUCS is our discovery that the group model is a good cultural fit for a historically Black college and university (HBCU). Our tradition as people of African descent includes the concept of the whole being of particular importance rather than prioritizing the individual: "The sum of the whole is greater than its parts."

Psychodynamic group psychotherapy, in particular, has been very effective as a treatment approach for trauma-related psychopathology with the African American student population at HUCS. Psychodynamic theory, with its focus on the unconscious residing within the unseen part of the self, is a conceptualization that runs parallel to traditional African cultures. Often, the feelings, memories, and painful thoughts caused by traumatic events are located in the unconscious. The techniques used in psychodynamic group psychotherapy allow for a very careful and slow process of uncovering the traumatic events through articulation of the experiences of trauma among other group members. The group can hold and support one another through members' respective journeys.

As past HUCS faculty (including principal author being the past executive director of the Howard University Counseling Services), we witnessed the efficacy of group treatment in facilitating the growth of many group members, which was quite encouraging. It was an effective way of providing treatment and greater understanding of trauma and its relationship to what they were experiencing.

Group treatment became a common area of interest for HUCS clinical staff members. Consequently, some continued to pursue advanced training in group work. One of the results of pursuing additional training was staff exposure to large group experiences, including those provided by A. K. Rice and Tavistock models. Central to this training is the systemic emphasis on the group-as-a-whole and the potential for one or two individuals to be voicing unconscious group dynamics shared by many in the group-as-a-whole. While the large group had not typically been used to address problems within the student population at HUCS or in other student settings, the large group turned out to be an approach of interest, eventually embraced by the university and used as a means of addressing systemic issues within the larger institution.

Case Illustration 2

During a particularly tumultuous time at Howard University, the first author participated in a large group experience. Emerging from the group process was the agitation
of the students regarding them being treated dismissively and unfairly by members of
the administration who were present. The administrators were dismayed that they were
perceived this way and were able to share this with the students non-defensively while
listening to the pain of being unimportant expressed by the students.

The group conductors created the space for a transformative dialogue to take place.
The process evolved as many students emotionally shared they had never before been
allowed to challenge authority figures.

The group conductors emphasized that in many Black families, there is an elevation
of authority and a culturally conditioned fear of challenging authority. A group attend-
ee tearfully recounted being told by her mother continuously throughout childhood,
"I brought you into the world, and I can take you out." Others related to the verbally
violent and threatening story.

The large group served as a safe container to examine the origins of this transferential view of authority as simultaneously frightening and dismissive. Repair occurred
because they were able to verbalize their protest and safely verbalize their feeling of
being insignificant without retaliation from those in power and authority.

Psychodynamic Group Work

Psychodynamic therapy utilizes the understanding and appreciation for the power of the
impact of the unseen on the seen or the intangible on the tangible. This premise also exists
at the very core of traditional and historical African thinking, specifically the value that is
placed upon knowledge regarding the experiences of one's ancestors. For example, the term
"whipping" often used in current times to describe the administration of corporal punish-
ment by parents of children in some African American populations has its origins in slavery,
where slaves were whipped by their masters. Typically, this origin is unconscious but transmitted via intergenerational trauma and takes the form of identification with the aggressor.
Likewise, a major tenet of psychodynamic theory is that negative early influences, mostly
unconscious, play a central role in human suffering.

One of the basic, essential tenets in group work is beginning with a theoretical frame,
through which the group facilitator understands the group. For reasons previously mentioned, psychodynamic theory was, and continues to be, the lens through which the clinicians of HUCS conceptualize groups. It is the cultural connection around the concept of the
unconscious that makes it such a good fit to the African culture.

Psychodynamic theory is based on the concept of an existing unconscious that typically
affects human behavior in significant ways. The unconscious is understood to be the part of
the person that never sleeps. It is always at work and functions as a determinant of human
behavior, including the process of thought.

The confluence between what has been usually thought of as a concept developed by
Europeans and Western civilization, psychodynamic theory, and the very ancient perceptions

of the psyche in people of African descent is typically not considered by either group. Another example of how we all have much more in common than not.

The combination of psychodynamic conceptualization and the thinking of group as an entity of its own (once there is a mutually organizing goal among several or many people) can be seen as an example of the psychodynamic concept of the group-as-a-whole. The concept of Ubuntu is based on the notion that groups are at the core of human existence and survival; for thousands, perhaps millions, of years, groups have been valued as fundamental for healthy development and the containment of healing properties. Today, optimally, we may define *group psychotherapy* as a democratic, cost-effective, and inclusive form of psychosocial treatment. In fact, from the outset, the therapeutic value of groups has been strongly associated with survival, both physical and emotional.

Group-as-a-Whole

Whether for clinical, organizational, or political purposes, when individuals form a group, the resulting coalition becomes an entity, with developmental, structural, dynamic, and relational properties that both reflect and rise above the individuals who make it up (Ettin et al., 1995).

This statement captures the concept of group-as-a-whole as it was embraced by the staff of HUCS, under the initial leadership of Dr. Carolyn Payton. Through this description of group by European and North American clinical scholars, what is made clear is that the universality of cultural formations of groups transcends oceans and centuries. Understanding this concept to be one of the organizing principles in ancient African culture and philosophy explains the logic of how Howard University, an HBCU (historically Black college and university), could so naturally embrace a psychodynamic theory that conceptualizes the group as its own entity.

Application of Theory

The development of group therapy, which includes the concept of the group-as-a-whole, is most typically attributed to Bion and Foulkes. Influenced by two world wars and the ramifications imprinted on communities related to daily life, they continued developing their theories. However, Foulkes saw the individual as the primary focus of healing, while Bion saw the group or organization as the entity to be healed (Bion, 1961, 1969).

Other theories of psychodynamic group psychotherapy have also made valuable contributions to the field. Interpersonal, relational, and object relations theories emphasize important dynamics that can be integrated into the work. While HUCS fully embraced group-as-a-whole theory, the group therapist also paid attention to the interactions of members, how relational patterns in members may change and develop, listening and observing the way members reflect their early connections to parental objects, and so on. These observations are noted, but always through a lens of seeing the group itself as an entity, with attention given to what message the group is conveying.

The use of psychodynamic theory has been most helpful in the efforts of providing treatment to the African American population. While HUCS provided, and continues to provide, care for the student population, it has a chronologically diverse population consisting of young adults, 17–18 years of age to 20s and 30s (usually returning veterans). There is also a smaller segment in their 40s and older. This age variation in the population is primarily due to the extensive offerings of the university. So not only were we treating undergraduate students, but we have also provided treatment and additional services to graduate and professional students from a large variety of disciplines. HUCS staff is the usual source for crisis interventions, particularly when several students, as well as university staff, are involved. Immediate interventions centering on harmful experiences with campus police are also provided and typically followed up with short-term group interventions designed specifically to address the trauma. Given that the clinical staff are aware of the good fit between psychodynamic theory and the population, treatment addresses various levels of trauma. Because trauma is so frequently subject to repression and dissociation, as well as defenses, such as denial, attention to the unconscious is essential to enhance the understanding of who is being treated and what needs to be addressed. Groups can be effective in addressing and validating the feelings of isolation and the sense of being the only one who has experienced trauma. Through the information provided by the group process, the group therapist/facilitator can access information that provides greater insight into the behavior and the needs of group members/clients and a guide for determining theoretical interventions.

A large group experience is offered monthly to anyone, from students to board members, who wishes to attend. It provides meaningful learning for university administrators, faculty, staff, and students, catering student activity, staff, and all interested parties at the university. It is the attention to the large group process that serves to provide the therapeutic experience and knowledge that participants are typically unaware of which enhances the means for healing and recovery, education and self-awareness, and the opportunity to discover the ways in which we are all connected.

Discussion

Consideration of concepts related to diversity, equity, and inclusion (DEI) is of great value when treating diverse populations. The inception of utilizing these DEI concepts with the HUCS population was based on the previously stated principle. Howard University has been known as one of the institutions with the greatest international representation in the world. This degree of diversity was, and continues to be, reflected in the clientele served by HUCS as well as in its clinical trainees. The services and training were made available to any student in need of clinical services, as well as any trainee interested in learning about the provision of clinical services to a diverse population. The extent of the diversity covered areas such as age, race, gender, sexual orientation, sexual identity, nationality, ethnicity, disability, and religion. This high level of diversity is reflective of diversities within the African American communities historically. Large segments of its student bodies were at times native to African and Caribbean countries. Moreover, Dr. Carolyn Payton's prior Peace Corps experience in the Caribbean, and later as National Peace Corp director, added an aura of internationality to her presence as the dean and director of HUCS and the HU Career Development Center. HUCS students and administrators have included James Nabritt, former HU president and one of the architects of the 1954 *Brown v. Topeka* school desegregation lawsuit; Ewart Brown, prime minister of Bermuda (2006–2010) and 1968 HU student body president and alumnus, medical school graduate in 1972; and Kamala Harris, Jamaican, 1986 HU graduate, and first female vice president of the United States, elected in 2021. The same range of services was offered and available to every student client. Treatment recommendations were determined by diagnostic indicators, presenting request for services, and presenting concerns, diversity in culture, gender, race, age, style of communication, and a category frequently ignored, national and international social and socioeconomic status (SES). People of African descent, whether African, American, Caribbean, or European-born, were seen and welcomed at HUCS. Despite the common belief that Blacks were not open to participation in counseling and clinical services, this was not the case at HUCS. From early mornings to late evenings, including weekends, groups were filled with members reflecting the diversities represented at HU. As new clinicians and trainees joined the staff, expectations were shaped by the high levels of participation. Relationships between traumatized people of Color from across the globe, diversities among students at HU, and high levels of participation in groups at HUCS were actualized.

Future research is suggested to demonstrate the extent to which the experiences of HUCS might change the belief that Blacks are not candidates for group work. Empirical, evidence-based research focused on the training, supervision, and consultation, historically routine at HUCS, could shed light on the incorporation of a major focus of the impact of diversity into the treatment of those from diverse backgrounds. The importance of diversity in staff, mirroring the diversities in students, may also emerge from such research.

References

American Psychiatric Association. (2017). *Mental health disparities: Diverse populations*. https://www.psychiatry.org/getmedia/bac9c998-5b2d-4ffa-ace9- d35844b8475a/Mental-Health-

Battle, M. (1997). *Reconciliation: The Ubuntu theology of Desmond Tutu*. Pilgrim Press. https://thepilgrim-press.com/products/reconciliation-the-ubuntu-theology-of-desmond-tutu-revised-updated-battle

Bion, W. R. (1961). *Experiences in groups*. Tavistock. https://doi.org/10.4324/9780203359075

Bion, W. R. (1969). *Experiences in groups: And other papers*. Routledge. https://www.routledge.com/Experiences-in-Groups-and-Other-Papers/Bion/p/book/9780415040204

Bridge, J. A., Horowitz, L. M., Fontanella, C. A., Sheftall, A. H., Greenhouse, J., Kelleher, K. J., & Campo, J. V. (2018). Age-related racial disparity in suicide rates among US youths from 2001 through 2015. *JAMA Pediatrician, 172*(7), 697–699. https://doi.org/10.1001/jamapediatrics.2018.0399

Brown, I. (2005). *Azanubianism: The teaching of Ubuntu principles*. Self-Published Titles. https://www.amazon.com/Ubuntu-Principles-teachings-way-life/dp/1096740702

Coombs, N. C., Meriwether, W. E., Caringi, J., & Newcomer, S. R. (2021). Barriers to healthcare access among U.S. adults with mental health challenges: A population-based study. *SSM: Population Health, 15*, 100847. https://doi.org/10.1016/j.ssmph.2021.100847

Ehlers, C. L., Gizer, I. R., Gilder, D. A., Ellingson, J. M., & Yehuda, R. (2013). Measuring historical trauma in an American Indian community sample: Contributions of substance dependence, affective disorder, conduct disorder and PTSD. *Drug and Alcohol Dependence, 133*(1), 180–187. https://doi.org/10.1016/j.drugalcdep.2013.05.011

Ettin, M. F., Fidler, J. W., & Cohen, B. D. (Eds.). (1995). *Group process and political dynamics*. International Universities Press, Inc. https://psycnet.apa.org/record/1995-97146-000

Fenster, A. (1996). Group therapy as an effective treatment modality for people of color. *International Journal of Group Psychotherapy, 46*(3), 399–416. https://doi.org/10.1080/00207284.1996.11490787

Hankerson, S. H., Moise, N., Wilson, D., Waller, B. Y., Arnold, K. T., Duarte, C., Lugo-Candelas, C., Weissman, M. M., Wainberg, M., Yehuda, R., & Shim, R. (2022). The intergenerational impact of structural racism and cumulative trauma on depression. *The American Journal of Psychiatry, 179*(6), 434–440. https://doi.org/10.1176/appi.ajp.21101000

Mann, C. (2005). *1491: New revelations of the Americas before Columbus*. Knopf. https://indigenous-peoplesresources.com/products/1491-new-revelations-of-the-americas-before-columbus

McKenna, E., & Pratt, S. L. (2015). *American philosophy: From wounded knee to the present*. Bloomsbury. https://www.bloomsbury.com/us/american-philosophy-9781441183750/

Rogers, N. (2007). Race and the politics of polio: Warm Springs, Tuskegee, and the March of Dimes. *American Journal of Public Health, 97*(5), 784–795. https://doi.org/10.2105/AJPH.2006.095406

Savio, C. (2022). *Native American history 101*. Independently Published. https://www.powells.com/book/native-american-history-101-9798838173867

Sibrava, N. J., Bjornsson, A. S., Pérez Benítez, A. C. I., Moitra, E., Weisberg, R. B., & Keller, M. B. (2019). Posttraumatic stress disorder in African American and Latinx adults: Clinical course and the role of racial and ethnic discrimination. *The American Psychologist, 74*(1), 101–116. https://doi.org/10.1037/amp0000339

Sotero, M. (2006). A conceptual model of historical trauma: Implications for public health practice and research. *Journal of Health Disparities Research and Practice, 1*(1), 93–108. https://ssrn.com/abstract=1350062

Williams, Chancellor, 1893–1992. (1987). *The destruction of Black civilization: Great issues of a race from 4500 B.C. to 2000 A.D.* Third World Press. https://thirdworldpressfoundation.org/products/destruction-of-black-civilization

8 Attachment-Focused Therapy and Racial Inequalities – Who Speaks and Who Listens

Carlos Canales

Seven therapists were asked to volunteer for a demonstration group during an open session at a national conference. Six were White, and the last person to approach the center of the room was a BIPOC woman who, just before taking her seat, shouted, "I can't be here! I don't feel safe in an all-White space!" She then stormed out of the fishbowl group and faded into the surrounding audience. Almost 100 people in the workshop became silent for a lengthy minute. Everyone froze, unclear as to how to proceed. With apprehension and desire to work with the trainer, I stood up and took the available chair. The group leader confidently stated, "I know this man!" His words welcomed me to the group, and that made all the difference.

This demonstration group started with significant challenges for the group leader and members. A loss had occurred during the embryonic phase of the group, before anyone said hello or explicitly set the frame for the demonstration. Whom was the BIPOC member speaking to when she announced she lacked safety? Was she letting everyone know about a more dominant, implicit social understanding that pre-existed the invitation for volunteers?

Without dialogue, all we have is projection. *Dialogue* is a conversation between subjects where ideas and feelings are exchanged, at its best, where polarities are explored. Schlapobersky (2016) states that there are three forms of speech: a monologue (speaking alone, with or without an audience), a dialogue (a two-body exchange, potentially in search of closeness), and a discourse (a speech pattern between three or more people where witnessing and complexity are uncovered). In this case, the unsafe feeling of one member, spoken as a personal declaration, temporarily erased everyone's capacity to think and relate. It paralyzed the entire room with fear!

Indirect, subtle, unintentional, and/or direct statements about race that can be perceived as discriminatory against members of a marginalized group have profound ethical, personal, psychological, and systemic implications. Generally, people join psychotherapy and demonstration groups because they are interested in growing as individuals (Gray, 2007) and/or improving relationships. However, without basic trust, intersubjective relating is compromised, including one's capacity to think and behave. Thinking is primarily an emotional need, and it matures in the context of interpersonal communication (Billow, 2000; Bion, 1961).

Traditionally, it is thought that every group starts in the mind of the therapist (Schlapobersky, 2016). Ideally, at the present time, race should be in the forefront of the group therapist's mind when beginning a group.

DOI: 10.4324/9781003546252-13

Racialized Reactivity, Too Much Diversity, and Difference in Groups

The content of this chapter emanated from my reflections about challenging clinical moments, like the earlier vignette. When group members establish a satisfying sense of connection with each other, they feel safe enough to think, feel, and dialogue with one another. Members trust that the sharing of feelings and perceptions will be allowed, attended to, accepted, and affirmed. However, when significant racially related discrepancies in perception and expectation arise, there is a clear disruption in connectivity so that the quality of thinking and feeling among members is observably disrupted.

Altman (2000) suggests that the concept of race emerges from dichotomized thinking: those who are "me" or "like-me" and those who are "not-me" or "not-like-me." For minority groups in particular, the trauma of racialized socialization intensifies this mindset with an alarming, survival-like response (Riordan et al., 2019) – before one is able to consciously think. A profound distrust or refusal to relate to others occurs (Billow, 2006): "You don't get me" or "We are not close." Immediately, hypervigilance and separation-anxiety distress spread within the group.

I believe group leaders and members benefit from diversity in their groups because difference is stimulating. However, too much differentiation may be experienced as a threat. According to Nitsun (2015), too much difference between members "stimulates regressive projections and a fragmented sense of self and others" (p. 39). He proposed this can lead to the evocation of the anti-group – a destructive element that threatens the integrity of the group or its development. However, when diversity matters are adequately processed and contained, the energy of the anti-group is harnessed in the service of creativity, in this case enhancing the potential to enrich the group's development and solidify trust among members.

Race and Attunement to Race by the Leader

Race, assumed by one's skin color, is a visible variable that touches everything (Hardy, 2023). In the human species, race does not provide an accurate representation of biological diversity, since 99.9% of our DNA is found among all of us (Fuentes, 2022; Trent, 2023). Race does not exist in nature. It is a socially constructed human invention, a classification system that establishes hierarchy among people (Altman, 2000; McGhee, 2021). Every group member has been racially socialized or programmed to make assumptions about other group members. Thus, there are no securely attached individuals during the forming phases of a racially polyculture group (Hardy, 2023).

From the beginning, racially diverse group members are uncomfortable with each other because they do not share the same cultural background based on their skin color. According to Johnson (2018), every individual must work out some form of social justice in regard to their body type and skin tone. For instance, the social experience for lighter-skinned Latinos is more privileged than it is for those with darker complexions and can lead to discrimination and/or prejudices on the part of lighter-skinned Latinos toward darker-skinned Latinos. These implicit intracultural biases are different from the interracial discrimination for Blacks by Whites, generally speaking. Color matters worldwide! White is normative, and darker or black is seen as deviant, less, dangerous, or bad (DiAngelo, 2018, 2021).

Out of necessity, during our development, each of us acquires social identities, cultural habits, beliefs, and ways of sensing and experiencing based on our race. Before we can talk, parent–child coding of cultural dynamics takes place through affectively regulated, mostly nonverbal, relational patterns that are imprinted as procedural memory, which is the way our bodies know culture. This integral organic fabric of fundamental knowing, the "unknown thought" (Bollas, 1987, p. 280), is our most concrete attachment-based foundation of self-experience (Chefetz & Bromberg, 2004). Our parents encode us with a hierarchical social template about the world, a relational consciousness related to, among other parameters, race and skin color. And our unique racialization process, our ways of differentiating, provides a multiplicity of overlapping and conflicting values which inherently favors some and not others (Dalal, 2006).

My parents reiterated an old Spanish saying, "Dime con quien andas y te diré quién eres," metaphorically, "You are the company you keep." This phrase was first found in *Don Quixote*, a novel written by Cervantes in the early 1600s (López, 2020). Ever since I emigrated from Peru to the United States, I have been surrounded by White people and feel mostly at home in many environments. However, I will never be White, identify as White, or be identified as White. It is not something I can practice, will for myself, or acquire by sheer company. In my core, I see myself as containing vital Latin psychological organs that inhabit and organize me. I am, in essence, different from White, a self-awareness that provides an interoceptive homeostasis or a stable, sheltered, felt sense about me in relationship to my social environment (Damasio, 2021; Fotopoulou & Tsakiris, 2017). When around Latino groups, I feel my internal organs rest. When surrounded by Whites, I hold myself differently.

Racial identity is a pre-reflective knowing; it lives in our bodies and does not require deliberate thinking. It orients us to have a primordial bond toward those we feel safe with. The assumption is, those who look like me will understand me. It is emotionally cumbersome, almost painful, and somewhat ludicrous, to think about what I would need to give up or add to become White – like taking the roundedness or brightness out of the sun, since both characteristics define it. In my bones, through reflexive neuroception (Dana, 2018), I am never unaware of who I am in relationship to my social world, and I am always aware which environments allow my body to feel safe.

From this perspective, it is important for a modern, attachment-focused orientation to incorporate the notion that safety and security vary among BIPOC clients. Accepting and valuing this phenomenon within therapeutic groups is of utmost importance since it preemptively organizes the therapeutic alliance. This condition precedes the traditional clinical goals of making the unconscious conscious or understanding resistances.

Case Illustration 1

Shanti, a dark-skinned South Asian middle-aged woman, requested to join a long-term psychotherapy group in Des Moines, the heart of the Midwest. Shanti wanted to address her persistent and severe anxiety, which contributed to feeling unproductive at work, and her fears of being judged negatively by others. During the intake session, her anxiety was noticeable, as evidenced by quivering hands, apprehensive tone of voice, noticeably shallow breathing with brief sporadic gasps, and her posture (slumped shoulders, fingers, and legs tightly crossed).

She offhandedly revealed that her average resting heart rate was 105 beats per minute. She followed with, "Don't worry, that is not the problem. . . . It's been like this for a long time. I need to get my work done . . . like others." I suggested that it was possible that matters of race may be contributing to the issues she was describing, and invited her to examine the possibility that her heart was pounding rapidly because she had been chronically stressed, an embedded startle response, since her migration to the United States, which was an unfamiliar, unsafe environment. I argued that perhaps it was also likely that her great effort to fit in and be like everyone else was unreasonable, or even impossible! She had become an expert in observing the majority culture ("others"), but no one responded with satisfying attunement to her inner experience. Even though she immigrated with her nuclear family when she was 10, she had lived the trauma of non-recognition (Leiderman, 2020).

Immediately following my comment, her eyes lifted, as if seeing the moon for the first time, some light amidst a chronic darkness. She had never considered a systems explanation, that her body was unsettled in this ecosystem, that her race made her stand out among Whites while her organism was trained to fit in and be like everyone else. She mentioned that the mental health providers she worked with over the years never shared that hypothesis with her. In fact, her race was never mentioned, perhaps demonstrating cultural incompetence (Chang-Caffaro & Caffaro, 2018). In *The Myth of Normal*, Maté and Maté (2022) argue that clinicians are trained to overfocus on symptomatology and dismiss environmental matters like culture of origin and racial socialization. It is also possible that Shanti's previous providers thought about race but decided not to speak about race (Hardy, 2023).

Attachment Holding

Winnicott spoke of the *holding environment* as the literal and figurative psychological space provided by parents to encourage their infant's development (Akhtar, 2009). Its function is to enhance the child's orientation to its external environment through the unidirectional attunement of the parents to the child's emotional and physical needs, resulting in the cultivation of his or her subjectivity.

Holding space for each group member is a core feature of attachment practice (Marmarosh, 2018; Marmarosh et al., 2013). Only recently has the group psychotherapy literature focused on what the impact might be on BIPOC members when they are referred to predominantly White groups (Eason, 2009; White, 2006). When BIPOC members suffer from basic environmental distrust or racial hypervigilance before entering a group, the therapist's race and cultural manner are a guiding baseline for how much holding the group environment can provide (Chang-Caffaro & Caffaro, 2018). Just like Eastman's (1998) children's book *Are You My Mother?* group members often look for their metaphorical cultural mother when participating in groups (Scheidlinger, 1974). Unlike the book, they readily know who their mother is not, so that they assess the group as unlikely to be a safe, non-judgmental holding environment.

Attachment Containment

According to Bion (1961), the power of groups includes the group providing containment, that is, a psychological experience of feeling held, taken care of, protected both in the physical and emotional sense, which advances one's capacity to freely think and feel. All containment is felt in the body through sensations, gut feelings, or other markers of belonging facilitated by the vagus nerve, which is responsible for noticing whether we are safe to explore or compromised and threatened (Menakem, 2017).

The container (group leader) always impacts the contained (member) since their interplay is intimate and constant. Containment fails when the projected messages are rejected, which may be experienced as an absolute denial of the speaker. Thus, containment is a necessary function for the processing of racialized trauma (Menakem, 2017).

Holding and containing functions are fundamental to attachment work since they allow for "moments of meeting," which create new conceptualizations in the group member's implicit procedural knowledge, an internal working template (Stern et al., 1998; Tronick & Gold, 2020). These functions allow good-enough relational trust and safety, wherein group members can develop confidence that their presence and participation are not only accepted but also desirable, capable of interplay, resonance, verbalization, and dialogue.

Attachment-Focused Models, Culture, and Race

The attachment model incorporates somatic principles, polyvagal theory, psychodynamic concepts, and interpersonal theory in efforts to enhance the autonomy and capacity for belonging in a polyculture society. Optimal living involves regulated breathing, sensing one's own body, thinking, feeling, and acting in congruence with oneself, while making psychological space for others (Dana, 2018; Fonagy, 2001). This combination is the portrait of a securely attached person (Marmarosh, 2018; Marmarosh et al., 2013; Mikulincer & Shaver, 2016).

Secure attachment is a dynamic relational experience, not an independent, static, private phenomenon reliably applied to all situations. For example, a child may be securely attached to their mother but relate with apprehension toward their father. Similarly, they may feel more secure in the Midwest compared to Miami or New York. When humans share something with each other enough times, their relational habits become reinforced and solidified, allowing for culture to emerge. Culture is how our bodies and minds retain and re-enact history in an ongoing way (Eagle, 2013; Menakem, 2017). Culture provides the context for empathy, joining, mirroring, and the reinforcement of self-concepts (Gitterman, 2019). Thus, establishing relational security is related to interpersonal and environmental regulating functions (Riordan et al., 2019).

Curiously, attachment theory has been mostly silent about addressing matters of race and racialization (White, 2006). Even though Ainsworth expanded the application of attachment theory across the globe starting with her studies in Uganda, the theory has been mostly ethnocentric and Eurocentric (Eason, 2009; Schmidt, 2018).

It is possible that attachment-focused clinicians have not addressed racial dynamics in groups because they assume a universal biological need for closeness and overvalue the inherent safety- and security-seeking patterns we possess (Tronick & Gold, 2020). Bonding moments are prioritized over exploring the propensity for selfishness, competition, exclusion, and refusal to mentalize or imagine a reality different from our own (Billow, 2003, 2006).

Bowlby focused on the universal function of the attachment system in the context of evolution but failed to consider the role of cultural forces in attachment dynamics throughout a lifespan (Stern et al., 2021). Sociopolitical movements have reawakened the mental health field to a need to revisit the harm of marginalization and discrimination. The lack of attention in attachment theory to cultural diversity can lead one to ask the following three questions:

1. *What happens to attachment security when society favors some and discounts others?*
   Racial inequities, or the spectrum of social privilege, represent the inclusion or exclusion of membership in many realms of society. Those less favored, it would seem, have

increased vulnerabilities to insecure attachment. We can assume these dynamics will manifest in our therapy groups.

2. *How do we work with racial distrust when it materializes in one three-hundredth of a second?* Attachment-focused therapy has been criticized because it requires time and practice for interdependence, holding and containing, to develop (Eagle, 2013). Group leaders utilizing this approach can make use of the group container. The leader can identify effective containment when members pursue non-attachment goals, like play, humor, enhancement of social skills, sexuality, or the pursuit of wisdom (Flores, 2017; Mikulincer & Shaver, 2017). Leader reinforcement of these characteristics promotes dissolution of the racial mistrust.

3. *How, then, does a therapist establish a good-enough platform for exploration of racially loaded schemas?* The group therapist fosters an atmosphere that promotes containment and productive working through of racial trauma, social injustice, and the emotional pain related to racial wounds and harm for BIPOC and marginalized members (Hardy, 2023). Therapists being explicit from the beginning that matters of race and difference can be talked about with the potential for repair (Tronick & Gold, 2020) enhances working through. BIPOC members trust the group-as-a-whole with their pain when the group-as-mother creates a dynamic that is sensitive to their calls of distress and responds to them.

From the opening vignette, having the leader recognize me with the declaration "I know this man" potently conveys acceptance and affirmation arising through implicit relational knowing and desire from the authority in the group (Stern et al., 1998). As a person of Color, I realize those words created a contrast from "I can't be here!" before joining the group to an invitation and welcoming into the group. The welcoming statement erased my original apprehension. This is one example of how a group leader can introduce culture safely in the group (Rutan et al., 2014; Yalom & Leszcz, 2020). Consider the following case illustrations as examples of how race might be discussed in groups.

Case Illustrations 2

During the initial sessions of an online training group, a Black female clinician consistently conveyed empathy, care, and support toward a Latina group member, especially during moments of unambiguous suffering. The Latina therapist appeared unable to embrace her peer's compassion. As the group facilitator, I highlighted the resistance and reflectively stated, "Who wouldn't want a Black mother?" evoking the social unconscious idea of a nurturing and inclusive African American mother. Immediately, another BIPOC group member anxiously asked, "Are we talking about race? Is this happening?" The Latina therapist set her eyes on the Black therapist, as if recognizing the maternal provision available to her for the first time. Several members became still and vigilant. In a moment, a White clinician, worried that this statement might be microaggression (Schmidt, 2018), felt compelled to check in to determine if the Black therapist felt offended. After a few seconds of consideration, the Black clinician communicated feeling seen and valued for herself. "It is accurate," she said. Then, the group appreciated the spontaneity and personableness of the comment. The group's seal around race was broken, and conversations about the racial diversity of the group developed.

Case Illustration 3

In the second session of an online client process group, a White member started praising the colorful screen backgrounds of his peers. Enthusiastically he mentioned the wonderful reds, blues, yellow, and beige wall colors. "Such wonderful colors!" Conventional smiles were shared, but nothing meaningful followed. As the group facilitator, I appreciated the bonding investment in the comment and invited reflection about the silence. As an immigrant and a second-language speaker, I often feel like an invited consultant for cultural matters. This position frees me to behave with a certain amount of curiosity and naivety to racial encounters. I said, "Might we be talking about wall colors as a way of talking about skin colors in the group?" I invited the speaker to consider his interest and speak more directly and candidly about the diversity of skin colors around him if this was his interest. Several BIPOC members expressed relief and freedom to participate. They heard my invitation and pursued addressing race in the group. The White member paused but then joined the exploration with increased ease and fluidity.

Case Illustration 4

During the third session of an in-person process group with only White participants, a middle-aged group member shared a dream with naïve matter-of-factness and emotional detachment. In the dream, he and his family were visiting a run-down Mexican market. He clarified that he would never visit such a place in real life and felt disconcerted that this was his dream. The person in charge of the market was this scruffy, shady Latino – "Mean, quite unkept . . . a drug dealer for sure, a dangerous man." He really did not want to be there and, while "unafraid," kept scanning for the first exit available, trying not to be noticed by the menacing Latino. When the opportunity arose, he took a chance, ducked down, and bolted toward the closest gate. At that point, he commented that he did not even care about the whereabouts of his family. As he neared the exit, the Latino shot him in the rear. The group laughed anxiously, and silence followed.

I was immersed in the dream. Was I dangerous to him? A drug dealer? Can the stereotypes, discrimination, and racism conveyed in his dream be safely processed with me and the group? Is this group member speaking for other members who may have unaddressed racism toward me? Is the group seen as a market? Unable to ground, I invited the group into my considerations: "Was this dream an offering to an all-White group about its leader in the public market of emotions? Do you want to be here, in a place where someone from another race and culture is in charge? Am I threatening in some way?"

BIPOC members are often accustomed to adjusting themselves to fit into new settings that do not claim them as equal. In psychotherapy, they seek a presence that would accept them and respond to their emotional needs. BIPOC folx are never unaware of their minority, disempowered, or marginalized status. Racial inequities and being unrepresented in White forums are obvious to them. For example, when an African American potential group member asks if there are other Black members in the group they are hoping to join, they may be addressing issues of safety in terms of being the only Black member and/or member of Color. If they are psychologically minded, they might also ask how racial issues are addressed in the therapist's practice. Their reality is that joining any group is daunting, not only because being emotionally vulnerable is challenging, but also because their skin color signals difference, and their lived experiences are not readily acknowledged and affirmed in society. In contrast, a White person seldom, if ever, asks if there are other Whites in the group. While joining a group of strangers usually stirs anxiety for all new group members, persons of Color carry this additional layer of fear based on their racial status or past/present racial trauma.

Group, as a microcosm of society, provides the ideal arena for the exploration and renegotiation of relational patterns (Yalom & Leszcz, 2020), which include racial dynamics. In attachment-focused groups, the leader pays attention to how emotional bonds are negotiated. The group nurtures more inclusivity if the leader acknowledges racial, cultural, and marginalized identity background differences from the start. There are different markers of security and insecurity for those from different races and identities. Thus, inclusiveness involves an ongoing commitment to creatively develop holding and containment functions for all group participants.

Markers of Attachment-Focused Group Psychotherapy

The goal for the attachment-focused group is to establish itself as a haven and secure base for its members (Marmarosh et al., 2013) so that struggles within relationships can be freely examined and improved. This is accomplished by the leader's awareness of somatic attunement, emotional regulation, and opportunities to foster connection among and between members. The therapy is focused on moments of intimacy, clarifying emotional contact, and slowing down while processing ruptures in connection.

If the group leader is emotionally available, caring, and predictable, opportunities for the development of a secure attachment to the group are enhanced (Flores & Porges, 2017). Following is a list of theoretical constructs that support an attachment-focused frame for group facilitation when addressing racial dynamics and trauma:

1. Remember that everyone present is seeking connection and is interested in developing a felt sense of security and belonging (Rutan et al., 2014; Yalom & Leszcz, 2020).
2. Provide special attention to moments of connection and bonding. As mammals, we all seek care, contact, and comfort and send out signals when distressed (Billow, 2003; Panksepp, 2004). Work slowly, considering that trust and interdependence take time to develop.
3. Foster cohesion in the group by prioritizing group process and exploration of here-and-now dynamics over content-oriented communication (Billow, 2003; Schmidt, 2018).
4. Attend to physiological responses and reactions (Dana, 2018) as representative of movement toward, away, or against relationship. Racial trauma lives in the body.
5. Highlight and support emotionally rich communications. Vulnerability is therapeutically valuable; it builds trust and intimacy (Johnson, 2019; Marmarosh, 2018). However, vulnerability without resonance is painful. Use emotions to link people (Billow, 2002, 2003), and support dialogue that includes the exploration of multiple meanings.
6. Readily attend to moments of separation distress (panic), threats to belonging, isolation (Johnson, 2019), and rage (Davis, & Montag, 2019; Panksepp, 2010). These are powerful opportunities to witness, respond to, and heal racial trauma.

7. Support individual members and the group-as-a-whole in the metabolizing of emotional experiences and practicing containing functions (Bion, 1961).
8. Review and consolidate learning, emphasizing the added interpersonal markers of security.

Attachment therapy benefits from biological principles corresponding to all mammals, particularly in the negotiation of separation distress, fear, and rage responses, while evoking seeking behaviors and caring proclivities (Panksepp, 2004, 2010). But before expanding on attachment-focused interventions relevant to primal emotions, an elaboration of racial inequities is necessary.

On Racial Inequities

Menakem (2017) states that "race is a myth, but a myth with teeth and claws. Institutions, structures, beliefs, and narratives have been centered around it" (p. 88). Racism is not merely the result of individual bias or prejudice but is embedded in systems, societal habits, and policies involving subjugation and preferential treatment of one group over another (Stern et al., 2021). Like the air we breathe, these mainly non-conscious practices are infused in all ordinary living. While the Diagnostic and Statistical Manual for Mental Disorders (DSM-5) lists criteria for over 300 disorders, it does not reference the chronic and oppressive forces related to racial trauma and discrimination (Hardy, 2023); therefore, the psychotherapy community is behind when considering appropriate interventions to address its complicated presentations and impacts.

There is plenty of information and discourse published about the historical, capitalist, greedy, and oppressive trends in which racial discrimination has trained our unconscious minds (McGhee, 2021). The scarcity aspect of this mindset produces an added layer of aggressiveness about possessing power and controlling resources, elections, who is in and who is not, who receives and advances and who does not. Similarly, there is plenty of evidence and literature about the reality of White privilege across the world (DiAngelo, 2018, 2021). Awareness and change at the societal level are necessary.

Since attachment theory is informed by ethological investigations, particularly the study of mammals, it is relevant to comment that racial inequities are not just supported by cultural presentations, differences in upbringing, or nurture. Nature equipped humans with simple and rudimentary ways to orient and categorize (Damasio, 2021). Discrimination lives in nature (Peterson, 2018), or it is in our nature to organize the world hierarchically and to pull toward our own when it comes to survival.

One rationale of a biological setup for racial inequities is proposed by Peterson (2018) and involves serotonergic circuitries and the perception of hierarchies. Peterson argues that lobsters, who have been in existence for approximately 350 million years, are territorial creatures. They use their postural flexion to signal dominance over one another. Peterson (2018) argues that dominance hierarchies are an essentially permanent feature of the environment to which all complex life has adapted. Humans continuously size up one another, and this biological imperative process is culturally coded. Thus, discrimination on the bases of power differentials may be part of not just our implicit attachment-based legacy but also, by nature's design, the way humans survive in the world.

It is possible that this biological propensity for dominance has innately programmed humans to perceive the world racially. In fact, the affective neuroscientist Panksepp (2004) considered social dominance as a primary emotion but did not find sufficient evidence to support this hypothesis.

It may be helpful to hypothesize that being fully human includes a universal potential for oppression and that racism has biological, cultural, and psychological determinants. However, *Homo sapiens* also have the capacity to transcend that biological imperative and the original psychological setup because of higher values, like attachment, collaboration, social concern, and harmony. Clinically, it is useful to conceptualize that a regulated nervous system or the pursuit of physiological settling of heightened activation, which are central to secure attachment, is potentially the most important contributor to the human innate capacity for achieving connection and safety when facing racial inequity or racial trauma moments.

Attachment-Focused Interventions and Primal Emotions

Case Illustration 1 (Continued)

Shanti, the South Asian woman from the first case illustration, came to a group session agitated and unsettled. On her way to group, she witnessed a White middle-aged preschool teacher yelling loudly at a Black child who appeared to be completely shut down. Shanti also noticed that all the other children in the day care were White. The teacher shouted, "Why can't you be like the other kids?" Shanti, who had been working on recognizing marginalization and standing up for herself as a minority in a predominantly White society, began the group recounting this experience with rage, confusion, and panic. She said she felt guilty not intervening and looked directly at me for guidance. A White group member responded, "You don't know what the kid did. Maybe the teacher is right. Maybe he needs to learn how to behave!" Shanti's expression changed from bewildered to furious. Her hands started trembling, and her voice was quivering. Group members showed signs of apprehension and became silent. Partially aware of the mis-attunement, the White group member casually stated, "I am just saying . . ."

Given her history of feeling invisible, Shanti was overactivated when she came into the group, hoping her fellow group members would contain her emotions as she reported her narrative. She was trying to resolve an overwhelming moment that evoked unresolved relational trauma in her life. While sharing her story with the group, a White member was not empathically attuned to the vicarious racial trauma she witnessed and its impact. Consequently, Shanti's nonverbal response communicated that she felt injured.

The group's inability to think, feel, and act in the moment represented a freeze in the flow of communication. Connection was ruptured by the racially tinged contrast in perception and interpersonal mis-attunement. The group's cohesion and sense of belonging became threatened. Heightened emotions were present, but these negative feelings (fear, separation panic, and rage) could hardly be verbally accessed in the service of relational linking or bonding. The group's stillness and quietness symbolized the enactment of the rupture of two different attachment alliances.

Shanti's decisive look at me when bewildered was an attachment bid for recognition and support. Her nervous system was overwhelmed and in need of calming, which would happen if she were to receive understanding and validation over the lack of safety she was experiencing in that moment. When somatic psychotherapy is incorporated into attachment-focused therapy, the inclusion of orienting strategies, such as allowing one's eyes to look around to find kind and empathic facial expressions, is helpful (Canales, 2024). Our social engagement, soothing, and care-receiving systems turn on when we find ourselves in the eyes of a trusted other (Riordan et al.,

2019). Panksepp (2004) stipulates that eye contact is one of the most powerful sensory signals of care which, together with touch, activates endogenous and opioid systems that reinforce social bonding and physiological regulation.

Shanti's use of gaze was a relevant and useful resource to bring regulation to her distressed nervous system. Given that she sought me out with her eyes as she reported her experience, I invited her to find me again and to stay with me for a moment, noticing her body. My intention was to decrease her fight-and-flight survival reactivity, increase parasympathetic responses (i.e., noticing one's breath, rhythm, and internal sensations), and rekindle social engagement functions (appreciating the disposition of another) (Dana, 2018; Flores & Porges, 2017). Gradually, while engaged with me, she was able to track the tightness in her hands, the prickling sensation in her feet, and the nurturing quality of her breath. Gradually and slowly, Shanti became aware that many group members also shared a warm and concerned look in their faces.

Conclusion

Therapists from all orientations have been challenged with racial reconciliation and healing. The fostering of safety and security for those with racialized trauma is enhanced by the holding and containing applications provided in the therapeutic clinical setting. Attachment-focused group psychotherapy is an effective modality when the therapist uses inclusive approaches, including conversations about racial differences. The attachment model is particularly sensitive to separation distress, disconnection, fear, and rage when working with interpersonal ruptures. Taking into consideration that our bodies and minds are informed by our culture is vital when offering settling and soothing interventions. Regulated people offer contact with vulnerability and openness and dialogue with curiosity. Race and racial wounds are embodied; therefore, healing does not happen in our heads or through instruction. Through the application of the attachment model to conversations about race in our groups, healing can happen as we renegotiate a new living space.

References

Akhtar, S. (2009). *Turning points in dynamic psychotherapy: Initial assessment, boundaries, money, disruptions, and suicide.* Karnac Books. https://doi.org/10.4324/9780429484407

Altman, N. (2000). Black and white thinking, a psychoanalyst reconsiders race. *Psychoanalytic Dialogues, 10*(4), 589–605. https://doi.org/10.1080/10481881009348569

Billow, R. M. (2000). Relational levels of the "container-contained" in group therapy. *Group, 24*(4), 243–259. https://www.jstor.org/stable/41718947

Billow, R. M. (2002). Passion in group: Thinking about loving, hating, and knowing. *International Journal of Group Psychotherapy, 52*(3), 355–372. https://doi.org/10.1521/ijgp.52.3.355.45517

Billow, R. M. (2003). Bonding in group: The therapist's contribution. *International Journal of Group Psychotherapy, 53*(1), 83–110. https://doi.org/10.1521/ijgp.53.1.83.42805

Billow, R. M. (2006). On refusal. *International Journal of Group Psychotherapy, 57*(4), 419–449. https://doi.org/10.1521/ijgp.2007.57.4.419

Bion, W. R. (1961). *Experiences in groups.* Tavistock. https://doi.org/10.4324/9780203359075

Bollas, C. (1987). *The shadow of an object – Psychoanalysis of the unknown thought.* Columbia University Press. https://doi.org/10.4324/9781315437613

Canales, C. (2024). Somatic experiencing informed group psychotherapy online. In H. Weinberg, A. Leighon, & A. Rolnick (Eds.), *The virtual group therapy circle: Advances in online group theory and practice* (pp. 234–245). Routledge. https://doi.org/10.4324/9781003248606-22

Chang-Caffaro, S., & Caffaro, J. (2018). Differences that make a difference: Diversity and the process group leader. *International Journal of Group Psychotherapy, 68*(4), 483–497. https://doi.org/10.1080/00207284.2018.1469958

Chefetz, R. A., & Bromberg, P. M. (2004). Talking with "Me" and "Not-Me": A dialogue. *Contemporary Psychoanalysis, 40*(3), 409–464. https://doi.org/10.1080/00107530.2004.10745840

Dalal, F. (2006). Racism – Processes of detachment, dehumanization, and hatred. In K. White (Ed.), *Unmasking race, culture, and attachment in the psychoanalytic space*. Karnac. https://doi.org/10.4324/9780429484605

Damasio, A. (2021). *Feeling and knowing, making minds conscious*. Pantheon Books. https://www.penguinrandomhouse.com/books/572664/feeling-and-knowing-by-antonio-damasio/

Dana, D. (2018). *The polyvagal theory in therapy, engaging the rhythm of regulation*. W.W. Norton and Company. https://wwnorton.com/books/9780393712377

Davis, K., & Montag, C. (2019). Selected principles of Pankseppian affective neuroscience. *Frontiers in Neuroscience*. www.frontiersin.org/article/10.3389/fnins.2018.01025

DiAngelo, R. (2018). *White fragility: Why it's so hard for white people to talk about racism*. Beacon Press. https://www.beacon.org/White-Fragility-P1631.aspx

DiAngelo, R. (2021). *Nice Racism, how progressive white people perpetuate racial harm*. Beacon Press. https://www.beacon.org/Nice-Racism-P1678.aspx

Eagle, M. N. (2013). *Attachment and psychoanalysis – Theory, research, and clinical applications*. Guilford Press. https://www.guilford.com/books/Attachment-and-Psychoanalysis/Morris-Eagle/9781462508402

Eason, A. E. (2009). Diversity and group theory, practice, and research. *International Journal of Group Psychotherapy, 59*(4), 563–574. https://doi.org/10.1521/ijgp.2009.59.4.563

Eastman, P. D. (1998). *Are you my mother?* Random Book House for Young Readers. https://www.penguinrandomhouse.com/books/44562/are-you-my-mother-by-pd-eastman/

Flores, P. J. (2017). Attachment theory and group psychotherapy. *International Journal of Group Psychotherapy, 67*(1), 50–59. https://doi.org/10.1521/ijgp.2008.58.1.127

Flores, P. J., & Porges, S. W. (2017). Group psychotherapy as a neural exercise: Bridging polyvagal theory and attachment theory. *International Journal of Group Psychotherapy, 67*(2), 202–222. https://doi.org/10.1080/00207284.2016.1263544

Fonagy, P. (2001). *Attachment theory and psychoanalysis*. Other Press. https://doi.org/10.4324/9780429472060

Fotopoulou, A., & Tsakiris, M. (2017). Mentalizing homeostasis: The social origins of interoceptive inference. *Neuropsychoanalysis, 19*(1), 3–28. https://doi.org/10.1080/15294145.2017.1294031

Fuentes, A. (2022). *Race, monogamy, and other lies they told you – Busting myths about human nature* (2nd ed.). University of California Press. https://www.ucpress.edu/book/9780520379602/race-monogamy-and-other-lies-they-told-you-second-edition

Gitterman, P. (2019). Social identities, power, and privilege: The importance of difference in establishing early group cohesion. *International Journal of Group Psychotherapy, 69*(1), 99–125. https://doi.org/10.1080/00207284.2018.1484665

Gray, A. A. (2007). Psychoanalytic group psychotherapy: The leader, the individual, the process. In P. Buirski & A. Kotter (Eds.), *New developments in self psychology practice* (pp. 127–148). Jason Aronson. https://rowman.com/ISBN/9781461629733/New-Developments-in-Self-Psychology-Practice

Hardy, K. H. (2023). *Racial trauma – Clinical strategies and techniques for healing invisible wounds*. Norton Professional Books. https://wwnorton.com/books/9781324030430

Johnson, D. H. (2018). *Diverse bodies, diverse practices – Towards an inclusive somatics*. North Atlantic Books. https://www.northatlanticbooks.com/shop/diverse-bodies-diverse-practices/

Johnson, S. M. (2019). *Attachment theory in practice – Emotionally focused therapy with individuals, couples, and families*. The Guilford Press. https://www.guilford.com/books/Attachment-Theory-in-Practice/Susan-Johnson/9781462538249

Leiderman, L. M. (2020). Psychodynamic group therapy with Hispanic migrants: Interpersonal, relational constructs in treating complex trauma, dissociation, and enactment. *International Journal of Group Psychotherapy, 70*(2), 162–182. https://doi.org/10.1080/00207284.2019.1686704

López, A. (2020, January 8). *¿De dónde proviene el famoso refrán 'Dime con quién andas, y te diré quién eres'?* https://blogs.20minutos.es/yaestaellistoquetodolosabe/de-donde- proviene-el-famoso-refran-dime-con-quien-andas-y-te-dire-quien-eres/

Marmarosh, C. L. (Ed.). (2018). *Attachment in group psychotherapy*. Routledge Taylor & Francis Group. https://www.routledge.com/Attachment-in-Group-Psychotherapy/Marmarosh/p/book/9780367535841

Marmarosh, C. L., Markin, R. D., & Spiegel, E. B. (2013). *Attachment and group psychotherapy*. American Psychological Association. https://www.apa.org/pubs/books/4317309

Maté, G., & Maté, D. (2022). *The myth of normal: Trauma, illness, and healing in a toxic culture.* Avery. https://www.penguinrandomhouse.com/books/608273/the-myth-of-normal-by-gabor-mate-md-with-daniel-mate/

McGhee, H. (2021). *The sum of us, what racism costs everyone and how we can prosper together.* One World. https://www.penguinrandomhouse.com/books/564989/the-sum-of-us-by-heather-mcghee/

Menakem, R. (2017). *My grandmother's hands – Racialized trauma and the pathway to mending our hearts and bodies.* Central Recovery Press. https://centralrecoverypress.com/product/my-grandmothers-hands-racialized-trauma-and-the-pathway-to-mending-our-hearts-and-bodies-paperback

Mikulincer, M., & Shaver, P. (2016). *Attachment in adulthood – Structure, dynamics, and change.* The Guilford Press. https://www.guilford.com/books/Attachment-in-Adulthood/Mikulincer-Shaver/9781462533817

Mikulincer, M., & Shaver, P. (2017). Augmenting the sense of attachment security in group contexts: The effects of a responsive leader and a cohesive group. *International Journal of Group Psychotherapy, 67*(2), 161–175. https://doi.org/10.1080/00207284.2016.1260462

Nitsun, M. (2015). *The anti-group – Destructive forces in the group and their creative potential.* Routledge Taylor & Francis Group. https://www.routledge.com/The-Anti-Group-Destructive-Forces-in-the-Group-and-their-Creative-Potential/Nitsun/p/book/9780415813747

Panksepp, J. (2004). *Affective neuroscience, the foundations of human and animal emotions.* Oxford University Press. https://global.oup.com/academic/product/affective-neuroscience-9780195178050?cc=us&lang=en&

Panksepp, J. (2010). Affective neuroscience of the emotional BrainMind: Evolutionary perspectives and implications for understanding depression. *Dialogues in Clinical Neuroscience, 12*(4), 533–545. https://doi.org/10.31887/DCNS.2010.12.4/jpanksepp

Peterson, J. (2018). *12 Rules for life, an antidote to chaos.* Random House Canada. https://www.penguinrandomhouse.ca/books/258237/12-rules-for-life-by-jordan-b-peterson-foreword-by-norman-doige-md-illustrated-by-ethan-van-sciver/9780345816023

Riordan, J. P., Blakeslee, A., & Levine, P. (2019). Attachment focused-somatic experiencing, secure phylogenetic attachment, dyadic trauma, and completion across the life cycle. *International Journal of Neuropsychotherapy, 7*(3), 57–90. https://www.iaan.com.au/wp-content/uploads/2019/12/IJNPT-V7-3-Riordan.pdf

Rutan, S., Stone, W., & Shay, J. (2014). *Psychodynamic group psychotherapy* (5th ed.). The Guildford Press. https://www.guilford.com/books/Psychodynamic-Group-Psychotherapy/Rutan-Stone-Shay/9781462516506

Scheidlinger, S. (1974). On the concept of the "mother-group". *International Journal of Group Psychotherapy, 24*(4), 417–428. https://doi.org/10.1080/00207284.1974.11491849

Schlapobersky, J. R. (2016). *From the couch to the circle: Group-analytic psychotherapy in practice.* Taylor & Francis Group. https://doi.org/10.4324/9781315670096

Schmidt, C. (2018). Anatomy of racial micro-aggressions. *International Journal of Group Psychotherapy, 68*(4), 585–607. https://doi.org/10.1080/00207284.2017.1421469

Stern, D. N., Sander, L. W., Nahum, J. P., Harrison, A. M., Lyons-Ruth, K., Morgan, A. C., Bruschweiler-Stern, N., & Tronick, E. Z. (1998). Non-interpretative mechanisms in psychoanalytic therapy: The "something more" than interpretation. *International Journal of Psychoanalysis, 79*, 903–922. https://api.semanticscholar.org/CorpusID:6349418

Stern, J., Barbarin, O., & Cassidy, J. (2021). Working toward anti-racist perspectives in attachment theory, research, and practice. *Attachment and Human Development, 24*(3), 392–422. https://doi.org/10.1080/14616734.2021.1976933

Trent, S. (2023, October 16). Race isn't real, science says. Advocates want the census to reflect that. *The Washington Post.* https://www.washingtonpost.com/dc-md-va/2023/10/16/census-race-eliminate-race-box/

Tronick, E., & Gold, C. (2020). *The power of discord, why the ups and downs of relationship are the secret to building intimacy, resilience, and trust.* Little, Brown Spark. https://thepowerofdiscord.com

White, K. (Ed.). (2006). *Unmasking race, culture, and attachment in the psychoanalytic space.* Karnac. https://www.karnacbooks.com/product/unmasking-race-culture-and-attachment-in-the-psychoanalytic-space/22706/

Yalom, I. D., & Leszcz, M. (2020). *The theory and practice of group psychotherapy* (6th ed.). Basic Books. https://www.hachettebookgroup.com/titles/irvin-d-yalom/the-theory-and-practice-of-group-psychotherapy/9781541617568/?lens=basic-books

Specialized Models

The Large Group
Groups to Treat Sexual Abuse

9 Social Trauma and the Social Unconscious – Using the Large Group for Healing

Haim Weinberg

The impact of some trauma goes beyond the people who are directly affected, sometimes into boundless circles, like a bomb. Entire societies – in fact, the entire world – can feel its impact. In essence, this is the meaning of *social trauma*. From this perspective, trauma is never purely an individual matter. It does not belong solely to the individual, the family, or even the family ancestors. The cumulative effects of any trauma go beyond communities, geographies, or nations. The impact inevitably reaches the larger society, expanding its circles to those who seem to have little to do with the original traumatic event, except for sharing a common identity with the sufferer. In this chapter, I will address the unconscious impact of social trauma on populations and propose the utilization of the Large Group modality as a healing instrument.

My Frame of Reference

This chapter builds on the group analytic approach developed by Foulkes following WWII. Group analysis offers a relational perspective, since it perceives the individual as embedded in a social/cultural/large group context. Thus, social trauma can appropriately be explored through this theoretical lens. Foulkes believed that "each individual [is] itself an artificial, though plausible, abstraction" (Foulkes, 1948/1984, p. 10). Dalal (1998), paraphrasing Winnicott, emphasized that there is no such a thing as an individual outside the context of the group that is society, reflecting a deep understanding that people live in an intersubjective field that is common to and co-created by all of us, even if we feel separate and unrelated. This frame of reference has not been readily accepted in North America, where the culture emphasizes individuality. Social trauma cannot be explained or understood by focusing on individuals; it requires a social lens perspective.

What Is Trauma? When Is It Social Trauma?

According to the World Health Organization (2022), traumatic experiences have lasting adverse effects on both people's mental and physical well-being. Trauma can manifest in various ways, impacting individuals differently. It encompasses a wide range of responses, from temporary distress to life-changing symptoms.

Traumatic events can include the following:

- Personal experiences people have undergone
- Witnessing such events happening to others
- Learning about traumatic incidents involving close loved ones
- Exposure to extreme details of a traumatic event

DOI: 10.4324/9781003546252-15

This understanding of trauma is from an individual and intrapsychic perspective. If we look at it from an interpersonal or social perspective, we find that, in addition to the personal factors that determine whether people experience an event as traumatic, the relational, group, and social factors are also impactful. For example, attachment trauma theory incorporates an intersubjective lens emphasizing the impact of relating to others and the world around us (Erkoreka et al., 2022; Kuzminskaite et al., 2021).

From a group perspective, trauma is influenced by the degree of cohesion within the group, and posttraumatic stress disorder (PTSD) symptoms are reduced the more people feel a sense of belonging and safety within the group-as-a-whole (Baird & Alaggia, 2021; Marmarosh & Van Horn, 2011). In the social arena, traumatic experiences of loss, separation, and failed dependency with authority are predisposing factors to social trauma (Hopper, 2011). Unsafe and fear-provoking global conditions and events as conveyed via media and electronic sources can also lead to the mass trauma of populations, large and small groups.

Social trauma refers to the collective psychological impact experienced by a group of individuals due to significant, overwhelming, stressful events or conditions that impact the social fabric of their community or society. Key characteristics of social trauma include thus:

1. **Collective impact.** Social trauma collectively impacts groups, communities, or populations rather than individuals alone. The trauma is shared and can lead to shared experiences of grief, fear, and anxiety.
2. **Roots in social systems.** Social trauma is often linked to systemic issues, such as poverty, racism, sexism, and other forms of inequality or injustice, that impact people's lives collectively.
3. **Intergenerational transmission.** The effects of social trauma can be passed down through generations, affecting not only those who directly experienced the traumatic events but also their descendants, whose mental health, worldview, and social interactions are influenced.
4. **Community disruption.** Social trauma can disrupt social bonds and support systems within communities, leading to feelings of isolation, mistrust, and disconnection among individuals.

Intergenerational Transmission of Social Trauma

Social trauma is transmitted from one generation to another (Atlas, 2022; Dekel & Goldblatt, 2008). Recent findings emphasize epigenetics, providing a physiological explanation of how transgenerational trauma is transmitted (Krippner & Barrett, 2019). Unprocessed trauma that lived inside of our ancestors can be inherited and transmitted to future generations. For example, second- and third-generation Holocaust survivors can manifest symptoms related to the unprocessed traumatic experience of the parents and grandparents in the concentration camps and ghettos (Baumel-Schwartz & Amit, 2023; Danieli, 1998; Guralnik, 2014; Wardi, 1992). The transgenerational transmission of trauma not only impacts the family system but can also affect other systems, including the society at large. The social unconscious then becomes relevant in the understanding of these phenomena further.

What Is the Social Unconscious?

An important concept in group analysis is the *social unconscious*, a concept stemming from group analysis's primary idea that we cannot talk about the individual outside their social context. Hopper and Weinberg (2011, 2015, 2017) described the social unconscious as the co-constructed, shared unconscious of members of a certain social system, such as community, society, nation, or culture. It refers to the existence of social, cultural, and communicational "arrangements" of which people are "unaware." The *social unconscious* simply means that people are unconsciously affected by the society in which they grew up and by the historical events in the past of that society. Just as we are all unconsciously influenced by our individual history, our family of origin, and traumatic events in our past, we are also unconsciously impacted by the society in which we live, its history, and its past social traumas. Social traumas are one of the building bricks of the social unconscious. Massive social traumas are passed from one generation to another in many ways, including through the body.

Further explanation is needed to understand how social trauma creates disorders in individuals. The theoretical framework of Foulkes (1964) preceded the radical view of human, problematic, relational manifestations, focusing on intersubjective processes. He considered the "location" of pathology outside the individual – in society. He understood the location of the disturbance as not inside the individual but *between* individuals. This description can easily be expanded to include social dynamics, traumas, and subgroups. We can find similar perspectives in the relational approaches (Mitchell & Aron, 1999) that shifted from a "one-person" psychology to a "two-person" psychology, explaining people's behaviors as co-created through the intersubjective interaction. Pathology and problematic behavioral expressions are not considered solely a result of inner unconscious dynamics but as stemming from interactions or relationships, the impact of which people are unaware. The same idea applies to the group therapy arena, where we can see the difficult patient and their problematic behavior as co-created by the group, the conductor (group therapist), and the group members (see Gans & Alonso, 1998). Moving one step further from a two-person to multi-person psychology, we can see disturbances as stemming from social situations, social traumas, and unconscious social forces. As individual trauma affects people's behavior unconsciously, so does social trauma. Social trauma includes many people experiencing the same trauma. For example, trauma that is associated with shared experiences, such as violence, war, discrimination, or natural disasters, creates shared identifications, that is, when individuals within a shared identity group (an ethnic group, religious community, or social class) experience distressing events together, such as systemic oppression, or share a common historical suffering; both can influence the mental and emotional well-being of individuals within the affected society.

The following is a summary of how unconscious social processes and traumas are reflected in the American psychoanalytic relational literature. These articles and books explain the origin of problematic individual behavior as related to social traumas as well. Relational psychoanalysts give culture and history a more influential place in the meta-narrative of personhood than previous psychoanalytic thinkers. Relational literature situates the human subject within the social, historical, and cultural context and the correlations between sociocultural pressures, traumas, and the unconscious: Layton (2019) advocates what she calls social psychoanalysis. Dimen's (2011) attention is consistently attuned to the psychological, the political, and the social as forces that unfold in conscious and unconscious ways. Hartman (2010) assumes that the psyche is saturated by the social context and claims that it would be impossible to find a pristine moment before the psyche and the social were interwoven (a classical group analytic claim). Rozmarin (2009) suggests that social and historical forces play an unconscious yet decisive role in our lives.

Some people confuse the Jungian collective unconscious idea with the concept of the social unconscious. While the social unconscious differentiates between societies (showing how, in each society, there are different unconscious processes, stories, and narratives), the collective unconscious unites cultures (showing how societies are similar in the archetypes that create the same themes in the fairy tales).

Let me examine the traumatic impact of several societal events from recent years on our society and culture.

The COVID-19 Pandemic as a Case of Social Trauma

The COVID-19 pandemic death toll exceeds more than 7 million worldwide (January 2024, according to Wikipedia: https://en.wikipedia.org/wiki/COVID-19_pandemic_deaths) and has changed our lifestyles in ways that could not have been foreseen. The impact on the world economy has been enormous. During the peak of the pandemic, social behavior and interpersonal connections diminished, and people distanced from each other. Isolation and loneliness led to a rising number of anxiety and depressive symptoms, influencing public mental health significantly (Kira et al., 2021; Kupcova et al., 2023). The cumulative impact of the pandemic created a traumatic social experience among large populations – the peoples of the world.

As a social scientist and group therapist, I am curious how the pandemic influenced us unconsciously, how it might call up unconscious processes pre-existing in our minds, and how it is connected to the social unconscious. For example, the pandemic can be associated with a deep threat of death, an issue that people usually deny or try to avoid thinking about. The denial of death (Becker, 1973) is common in most societies, even though death is part of life and all lives end eventually.

Human beings are mortal, even though we do not want to think about it. Although the world feels more and more dangerous, we usually live our lives surrounded by a healthy narcissistic envelope, believing that "it will not happen to us." When this shield is pierced (for example, in PTSD), people are flooded with anxiety, worries, and even nightmares. The COVID-19 pandemic penetrated the forementioned envelope for almost everyone, as the "smell of death" was in the air – traumatic for many people. Some reacted with extreme isolation, avoiding any contact with other human beings, since they believed that danger was ubiquitous. Other people reacted with opposite extremely defensive behavior, ignoring the threat and believing that all communications about the dangers were fake news. Both extremes are reactions to the traumatic experience of the fear of death. Although the fear of death was more conscious during the pandemic, the specific reactions of other people and how they experienced fear remained out of awareness for many (which is consistent with Hopper's definition of the *social unconscious* that calls attention to the different degrees and layers of which people are unaware; see Hopper & Weinberg, 2011). Fear of death belongs to the collective unconscious, since it is part of our human nature, but manifests differently in different societies; thus, it is a feature of the social unconscious.

We can only speculate about the long-term impact of physical distancing on people, especially on children's development. Will it be internalized as a new form of object relations, that is, withdrawing from human touch and wearing masks in public? Physical distance both reflects and unconsciously influences people's relationships.

Polarization and the Rise of Populism – A Ubiquitous Unsafe Environment

Even before the pandemic, the world was changing dramatically, which created a deep sense of instability. The waves of migrants that flooded Europe and the fear of migrants in the USA created a new global situation. White nationalists fanned the flames of fear with prejudicial misinformation about the dangers posed by migrants. Research, however, overwhelmingly indicates that migrants are less likely than US natives to commit violent and property crimes (Orrenius & Zavodny, 2019).

Additional threats to finding safety in the world include recent mass traumas, such as the climate crisis and increases in the number of hate crimes against minority populations in the USA. According to the Center for the Study of Hate and Extremism at California State University, hate crimes surged in 2023 in several major cities across the United States (see USA Today, 2023). Deprived of a sense of safety, people legitimately feel alienated, distrustful, and isolated. Many Western countries nowadays face a difficult dilemma between the need to maintain security, in part by protecting their boundaries, and on the other hand caring for suffering refugees by welcoming them (Berlinger, 2019). Sociopolitically, this situation became fertile ground for the rise of populistic, autocratic movements internationally (Shehaj et al., 2021). Thus, in the systemic large group that is the world, polarization and splitting have become ubiquitous, resulting in an increase in feelings of being in danger everywhere by many populations.

In the social large group (Volkan, 2004), the fourth basic assumption, described by Hopper (2019) as a pendulum shift between massification and aggregation, has governed systems. These powerful dynamics result in people either feeling isolated, rigidly protecting their own boundaries, focusing on taking care of their own needs, and totally ignoring the interests of the group, or people massifying in a way that melts personal boundaries, facilitating the following of charismatic autocratic, narcissistic leaders by citizens and losing the capacity to think on the level of the individual. The traumatic conditions of the COVID-19 pandemic only increased the oscillations between these two poles.

In the USA, the emphasis on individualism, which is already deeply rooted in the foundational matrix of the American culture, only increased, contributing to many people ignoring giving consideration to the welfare of the majority in favor of their individual needs. When massification is present, it manifests in a letting go of critical thinking in favor of "group think" (Janis, 1972). Findings from a survey conducted by the American Psychological Association (APA, 2017) revealed a correlation between the impact of the sociopolitical factors related to the 2016 election and the stress which was at its highest levels in a decade.

A compelling question begging for understanding is the following: Why do people follow charismatic, narcissistic leaders and join Fascist groups, thus losing their individuality and sense of morality? A simple answer is that Bion's (1961) dependency basic assumption (BA) is strongly activated under these stressful, threatening conditions. In this BA, members of a group (small or large) act as if their primary task is to seek security and protection from authority, looking for a strong leader. Adorno et al. (1950) described the authoritarian personality to be split into two versions: subjugation to authority or becoming authoritarian. The deep need for human beings to belong to a group pushes people to succumb to those groups in which massification facilitates this deep need. Authoritarian impulses have far-reaching effects, impacting both individual well-being and societal harmony. According to Osborne et al. (2023), the resurgence of authoritarianism globally weakens democratic institutions and undermines citizens' political rights and civil liberties. It increases group hostility, anti-immigration sentiment, and a general intolerance of marginalized groups. It sows division, threatens personal freedoms, and erodes the democratic foundations upon which these rights are enshrined.

These two examples of social trauma (the pandemic surfacing the fear of dying; democracy vs. autocracy) illustrate how social traumas affect social dynamics (for example, the fourth basic assumption) and trigger people's behaviors in ways out of people's awareness (for example, leading to divisiveness).

Diversity, Multiculture, and the Large Group

Diversity and multicultural issues are present in any group. Social issues, such as structural and systemic racism and women's empowerment ("MeToo"), take over, not only the public discourse, but also small and large group discourses. These are very sensitive issues which can, at times, polarize groups, creating schisms while re-enacting social traumas, just as they do in the public sphere (Banaji et al., 2021; Wetts & Willer, 2018). Group therapists need special training in learning how to deal with Diversity, Equity, and Inclusion (DEI) issues; how to avoid splitting; how to work with trauma; and how to enhance a healthy dialogue on very controversial topics. Knowledge and skills about how to address DEI issues should be added to the training of trauma group therapists. Knowledge about the social unconscious and understanding how to apply this knowledge to clinical practice is crucial in leading groups in today's world. To heal social trauma, the group leader, and certainly those who facilitate large groups, should be aware of these unconscious social dynamics.

Large Groups: Healing Social Traumas

In the face of unstable sociopolitical conditions and the traumatic impact of feeling unsafe in the world conditions presented, such as in polarization and during the pandemic, group therapy addresses the human need to belong. In groups, especially in Large Groups, people can examine their attraction to charismatic leaders, understand the danger of blindly following, and feel a sense of connection derived from comradery and belonging. Large Groups (LG) may be the most effective therapeutic tool to address sociocultural trauma-based issues (Weinberg & Schneider, 2003). The LG focuses on sociotherapy more than psychotherapy; social issues are spontaneously brought into the discussion when utilizing this modality. In individual therapy, people can work through their intrapsychic and interpersonal issues. The LG focus is on transpersonal issues beyond the personal and the interpersonal, with consideration given to unconscious social processes. "As a social microcosm, the large group has the potential to illuminate conscious, preconscious, and unconscious dimensions of the broader sociocultural and political environment that influences our therapy groups, members, and ourselves as leaders" (Dluhy et al., 2019, p. 288). LGs reflect democratic values (Weinberg & Schneider, 2003) and enable members to work through differences, political conflicts, social traumas, and social mourning (Friedman, 2018). This setting can become the only place to reflect, elaborate, and discuss these issues. The danger of re-traumatization in LGs exists, but a skilled team of convenors can facilitate the group's successful transition from a fight-or-flight state back to a relationally safe and connected state.

> We can find corrective emotional experiences, collective action, protest, advocacy, as well as more just and inclusive social relationships amid very difficult and painful sociocultural environments. In large groups, the relative safety of a supportive, well-contained small group is completely absent. The task is to find enough co-regulation from the participants to make meaning of the experience and to find one's large group voice. This mirrors the task of being a global citizen.
>
> (DeSilva, 2024)

This is a forum for the healing of social traumas. Group therapists may facilitate an LG with hundreds of participants, thereby providing a context where "social psychotherapy" (Foulkes, 1975, p. 250) happens. Participants in this innovative setting report acquiring significant insights related to society, social traumatic events, and their own participation in systemic racism. The impact of the LG spreads beyond the individuals who participate in the specific LG event, and beyond healing them from their individual trauma triggered by sociopolitical stressors. If the LG process is successful, members learn a different way of communicating about divisive social issues, moving from a binary debate (in which each side brings the best arguments to convince the other that they hold the absolute truth) to a dialogue (in which each party is curious about the point of view of the other). The result is that circles of healing are spread in social spheres. The more LGs are conducted in a specific society, the more it impacts both individual, social, and mass trauma.

Leiderman and Klein (2022) reviewed the literature on psychological reactions to mass/sociopolitical trauma and proposed an integrative systems-oriented, interpersonal, relational trauma group model for LGs and small psychotherapy groups to address the cumulative and systemic impacts of mass trauma in response to the pandemic and heightened sociopolitical stressors. Herman (1997) recommended short-term trauma groups as only the first stage in the treatment of trauma, referring the patient afterward to a heterogeneous psychotherapy group so the work could proceed on to integrating their traumas into their relational world. Integrating traumatized individuals into society raises the dilemma of how to encourage a pluralistic social perspective, expressing solidarity with the traumatized individuals and social support for survivors. When relating to trauma, one of the social challenges is to create an inclusive society which takes care of the traumatized and injured people from an attitude of equality and an openness to dialogue. This can be done with the LG. As we will see later, it also enables mourning losses in the social arena.

Now that LGs can also be conducted online, they have become enormously popular, changing the meeting of a mass of bodies into a mass of faces (Friedman, 2023). The obvious technical advantage of an online large group of a hundred people is its low cost and easy participation from many locations. People can join online from anywhere on Earth to work on international conflicts and national traumas. The fact that people who are considered as "the enemy" or "the perpetrator" by one another participate in these groups offers hope. The LG becomes a powerful forum for the repair of trauma when those who are considered "the enemy" can acknowledge and empathize with the pain of those who "feel victimized."

LGs often begin with massive projections on "the other" (for example, BIPOC people relating to White people only as racists or privileged, Ukrainians perceiving all Russians as supporting the war against Ukraine, Palestinians perceiving all Israeli Jews as wanting to take their lands). *Splitting* is an unconscious process, resulting in attributing certain negative qualities onto the "other." These dynamics might continue for some time, but with the support of the LG conveners (leaders), interpreting the LG unconscious social processes that govern the scene in the here and now as parallel processes reflecting social dynamics, a *safe-enough space* is created to explore these projections and see the "other," thereby reducing binary concepts of others, represented by the overuse of ingrained stereotypes. Sometimes, people are shocked by what they learn during this process, including how mistaken they were, distorting, over-generalizing, and demonizing the other individuals. When such a process occurs, social traumas related to marginalization, discrimination, and international conflicts are reduced, starting in the specific LG and spreading its impact centrifugally in society.

Exploring relationships with authority is almost always part of the LG work. When this dynamic is examined, the disappointment and frustration with political and institutional leaders are transferred onto the LG conveners. Since failed dependency on leadership is one of the dynamics that leads to social traumas (even in cases of natural disasters, when help does not come), exploring this aspect of social trauma in the LG, and working it out, reveals its deep and unconscious impact on the citizens.

Inability to Mourn

The inability to mourn is a concept that Mitscherlich and Mitscherlich (1967) believed to be a defense against mass melancholia in postwar Germany. "The Federal Republic did not succumb to melancholia; instead, as a group, those who had lost their 'ideal leader,' the representative of a commonly shared ego-ideal, managed to avoid self-devaluation by breaking all affective bridges to the immediate past" (p. 26). In a way, this is a defense against the pain and devastation experienced in the loss of the "Fatherland." Ogimoto and Plaenkers (2023) applied this concept to Japan and claimed that Japanese people lost the God Emperor and the Empire-motherland after WWII, but instead of entering a "depressive position," they avoided grief. Like in Germany, the Japanese identified with the economic system and industrial achievements as a defense against the pain of the loss.

The mourning process encompasses the emotional, physical, and psychological reactions that individuals experience after the loss of a loved one. Mourning is important not only in response to personal losses but also in response to social traumas, including losses of social privileges. For privileged social subgroups (such as White people in the USA) to give up their privileges and allow for a social change to occur, a long and deep mourning process is necessary. Butler (2003) argues that nonviolence is the consequence of successful mourning, explicating a link between mourning and the formation of political communities based on equality. Moglen (2005) joins her in advocating social mourning, claiming that the damage and destruction done to libidinally invested ideals (such as social justice) must be made conscious and named for a different future to be envisioned. Rao (2022) uses their ideas to conclude that social justice practice is a consequence of successful group mourning. The inability to mourn includes what Hopper (2014) describes as a perverse form of inauthentic mourning, which exacerbates social trauma via continuing cycles of turning away from difficult truths.

The inability to mourn can help in understanding long-term national conflicts, such as the Israeli–Palestinian one. Jews longed for and dreamt about Zion/Israel for centuries from when they were exiled from their land. According to Falk (1993), "for many centuries the Jews lived in a kind of a-historic time bubble. They lived more in fantasy than in reality, more in the past than in the present" (p. 299).

> Zionism sought to turn back the wheel of history, to restore the losses rather than to mourn them, and to mend the damaged Jewish self. It denied the demographic Arab reality of Palestine, proclaiming "a land without a people for a people without a land."
>
> (p. 300)

The concept of mourning is part of Jewish culture and tradition, and there are many rituals that help bereaved Jews mourn, but they were not applied to mourning the loss of the land. The result is the fantasy of a "Greater Israel" held by many Israelis. They see themselves not as occupying the Palestinian territories but as liberating them. Most of the Israeli public finds it difficult to mourn the loss of this dream and to give up the longstanding fantasy of "returning to [their] homeland and [the] holy places of [their] forefathers." This fantasy affects not only religious Jews. To be able to compromise, Israeli Jews must go through a long and painful mourning process, which they still avoid or are unable to do.

The same process applies to the Palestinian side. The Nakba trauma is still fresh in the minds of the first and second generations, and they cannot give up the dream of returning to their homes and villages. (The Arabic word *Nakba* means "catastrophe." It is referenced with the Israeli–Palestinian conflict and refers to the Palestinians' having lost their homeland during and after the 1948 Arab–Israeli War.) Palestinians all over the world continue to hold the keys to the homes they have left behind. They present these keys at demonstrations and mass events as proof of their ownership of the homes and the lives they have left behind. In pragmatic terms, the vast majority of these houses have already been demolished or renovated in ways that completely obfuscate the memory of the life that existed in them before. It means that the way to a peace settlement might only happen through some compensation and by not returning home. However, most of Palestinian refugees, especially those still living in refugee camps in Gaza, the West Bank, or Arab countries, who are geographically detached from what happens in Israel, continue to express sentiments of their dream to return home. They want to return to the houses they had before the Nakba, and they continue to claim the right of return, a dream they hold even after more than 70 years have passed. Holding on to this dream, whatever its connection to reality and the likelihood that it will come true, signifies the need to protect the Palestinian people from total erasure, disintegration, and loss of hope. They are unable to mourn the loss of their villages and to accept the new reality. It endangers their identity and evokes their deep fears of being forgotten.

Case Illustration 1

Following is a vignette from a LG that occurred in a conference for mental health professionals in Israel shortly after the Israeli Defense Force (IDF) military operation following the Hamas missile attacks more than 12 years before October 7, 2023. The military operation occurred in the Gaza Strip, having highly controversial ramifications both in Israel and abroad.[1]

A Jewish Israeli woman in the LG who identified with the suffering of the Palestinians told the group that in the middle of the war, when she heard about the life-threatening danger to children in Gaza, she and her daughter created a project with its goal being to evacuate 500 children from the Gaza Strip. At first, they asked Israeli Jewish families from the southern parts of Israel to host these children and were answered positively. When they understood that the Palestinians would never agree to come to Israel, they approached Palestinian families in the West Bank. The project was delayed when the Palestinian families in Gaza responded that they were not ready to send their children away. The families were suspicious that this was an Israeli manipulation so that they, the Israelis, would not feel guilty, because following the children's evacuation, the Israelis could more freely consider bombing them. The Palestinians said that this was a trick to take their land: First, move the children, then move the adults, making them refugees again.

> The LG room was filled with emotions: The Israelis felt hurt that their good intentions were labeled "manipulative." The Palestinians felt misunderstood as well, and the participants from outside Israel felt excluded. The turbulent atmosphere changed when one Palestinian asked, "So do you mean that Palestinian mothers care less about their children than do Jewish mothers?" In addition, a British woman reported that research regarding the evacuation of children from London in WWII indicated that the children who were evacuated during war conditions suffered more posttraumatic stress disorder symptoms than those who had stayed with their families in London. These communications helped the group become less reactive and more communicative.

These LG meetings show the transformation of the social-political conflict to a dialogue in which the parties in conflict could start listening to the pain of the other side (in the presence of a third party). Instead of fighting with each other, the group started mourning together. Social mourning can be important in the case of social traumas that are not processed in public discourse. Social trauma can create highly regressed social groups and, if not addressed, can unconsciously impact the behaviors and attitudes of generations to come, becoming part of the social unconscious. One of the ways to facilitate social mourning is to "mourn together" in an LG setting. This process is different from re-experiencing trauma since it lacks the intrusive memories and flashbacks typical in re-traumatization. The emotional and physical reactions are still there as in traumatization since the process of mourning together in the LG involves pain and sadness; however, the result is abreaction and a sense of relief, rather than continuous distress.

Case Illustration 2

The author convened a series of annual LG conferences in China in which social traumas were brought up and mourned. For example, a participant described the period of the Great Famine and how his family in the village begged for a rice bowl for him. The disclosure led to others describing unbearable traumas that they or their family suffered during times of war and famine (i.e., people who sold their bodies for food). Almost everyone in the LG cried. Many of the participants recounted how their parents or their grandparents' generation suffered during the Cultural Revolution: Some were exiled to villages, others imprisoned for many years, and some were executed.

These are topics that are not discussed in the public discourse in China, so it was important that the participants could openly share their personal and family stories and cry together. There was a sense that the LG provided a space for a mourning process that was not allowed publicly in China. As stated previously, when discussing transgenerational transmission of trauma, unprocessed social traumatic events that occurred in the history of a nation continue to be embedded in the social unconscious of the people of that nation. As in the previous example, the "mourning together" allowed elaboration, the beginning of a healing process, and a sense of relief, rather than a re-traumatizing experience.

The LG, in addition to exploring unconscious social processes, relationships with authority and other common goals (Weinberg & Schneider, 2003) can serve as a vehicle to enhance therapeutic social mourning. Perhaps this is the "sociotherapy" part of the LG which de Mare (1991) points out.

I deliberately chose two examples that are taken from non-American, international cultures to demonstrate how the use of the LG can enhance a healing process in any culture and transform traumatic stress to posttraumatic growth. I believe that the difficult social dynamics that are traumatizing North American society nowadays, as described in this chapter, can also be healed using many Large Group meetings across the United States.

Conclusion

Trauma damages the human capacities for trust, connection, and belonging, which is why group therapy, where people connect on an emotionally deep level, is very effective in the treatment of trauma. Social trauma is experienced by members of the family, group, community, or nation; is passed down from one generation to another; and is the reason that the LG, which reflects society, is effective in diminishing it. However, as group therapists, to be able to address social and collective traumas, we must be aware of unconscious social processes that affect people's behavior. Learning about the social unconscious is crucial to leading trauma groups, especially LGs.

Note

1 This vignette is taken from Weinberg & Weishut (2012)

References

Adorno, T. W., Frenkel-Brunswik, E., Levinson, D. J., & Sanford, R. N. (1950). *The authoritarian personality*. Harpers.
American Psychological Association (APA). (2017). *Many Americans stressed about future of our nation, new APA Stress in America™ survey reveals*. https://www.apa.org/news/press/releases/2017/02/stressed-nation
Atlas, G. (2022). *Emotional inheritance: A therapist, her patients, and the legacy of trauma*. Hachette UK. https://www.hachette.co.uk/titles/galit-atlas/emotional-inheritance/9781780726083/
Baird, S. L., & Alaggia, R. (2021). Trauma-informed groups: Recommendations for group work practice. *Clinical Social Work Journal, 49*, 10–19. https://doi.org/10.1007/s10615-019-00739-7
Banaji, M. R., Fiske, S. T., & Massey, D. S. (2021). Systemic racism: Individuals and interactions, institutions and society. *Cognitive Research: Principles and Implications, 6*(1), 1–21. https://doi.org/10.1186/s41235-021-00349-3
Baumel-Schwartz, J. T., & Amit, S. (2023). *Routledge international handbook of multidisciplinary perspectives on descendants of holocaust survivors*. Taylor and Francis. https://www.routledge.com/Routledge-International-Handbook-of-Multidisciplinary-Perspectives-on-Descendants-of-Holocaust-Survivors/Baumel-Schwartz-Shrira/p/book/9781032254333
Becker, E. (1973). *The denial of death*. Free Press.
Berlinger, N. (2019). Is it ethical to bend the rules for undocumented and other immigrant patients? *AMA Journal of Ethics, 21*(1), E100–E105. https://doi.org/10.1001/amajethics.2019.100
Bion, W. R. (1961). *Experiences in groups and other papers*. Tavistock Publications.
Butler, J. (2003). Violence, mourning, politics. *Studies in Gender and Sexuality, 4*(1), 9–37. https://doi.org/10.1080/15240650409349213
Dalal, F. (1998). *Taking the group seriously: Towards a post-Foulkesian group analytic theory*. Jessica Kingsley. https://us.jkp.com/products/taking-the-group-seriously
Danieli, Y. (Ed.). (1998). *International handbook of multigenerational legacies of trauma*. Springer Science & Business Media. https://link.springer.com/book/10.1007/978-1-4757-5567-1
De Mare, P. (1991). *Koinonia: From hate through dialogue to culture in the larger group*. Karnac Books. https://www.karnacbooks.com/product/koinonia-p/3793/
Dekel, R., & Goldblatt, H. (2008). Is there intergenerational transmission of trauma? The case of combat veterans' children. *The American Journal of Orthopsychiatry, 78*(3), 281–289. https://doi.org/10.1037/a0013955

DeSilva, J. (2024, Summer). Large group work at AGPA and beyond: Finding ourselves in a global context. *The Group Circle: Newsletter of the American Group Psychotherapy Association* (p. 1).

Dimen, M. (Ed.). (2011). *With culture in mind: Psychoanalytic stories*. Routledge. https://www.routledge.com/With-Culture-in-Mind-Psychoanalytic-Stories/Dimen/p/book/9780415884877

Dluhy, M., Watkins-Northern, A., Segalla, R., Paparella, L., Schulte, R., Avula, K., Lovett, H., & Nettles, R. (2019). The large group experience: Affiliation in a learning community. *International Journal of Group Psychotherapy, 69*(3), 287–307. https://doi.org/10.1080/00207284.2019.1570212287

Erkoreka, L., Zamalloa, I., Rodriguez, S., Muñoz, P., Mendizabal, I., Zamalloa, M. I., Arrue, A., Zumarraga, M., & Gonzalez-Torres, M. A. (2022). Attachment anxiety as mediator of the relationship between childhood trauma and personality dysfunction in borderline personality disorder. *Clinical Psychology & Psychotherapy, 29*(2), 501–511. https://doi.org/10.1002/cpp.2640.

Falk, A. (1993). The problem of mourning in Jewish history. In L. B. Boyer, R. M. Boyer, & S. M. Sonnenberg (Eds.), *The psychoanalytic study of society* (pp. 299–316). Routledge. https://doi.org/10.4324/9780203727744

Foulkes, S. H. (1964). *Therapeutic group analysis*. George Allen and Unwin.

Foulkes, S. H. (1975). *Group analytic psychotherapy: Method and principles*. Gordon and Breach, reissued Karnac 1986 and 1991.

Foulkes, S. H. (1984). *Introduction to group-analytic psychotherapy: Studies in the social interaction of individuals and groups*. Karnac (Original work published 1948).

Friedman, R. (2018). Beyond rejection, glory and the Soldier's Matrix: The heart of my group analysis. *Group Analysis, 51*(4), 1–17. https://doi.org/10.1177/0533316418792487

Friedman, R. (2023). Group analytic therapy and the online groups: Some principles of the group analytic approach to online group therapy. In H. Weinberg, A. Rolnick, & A. Leighton (Eds.), *The virtual group therapy circle: Advances in online group theory and practice* (1st ed., pp. 101–111). Routledge. https://doi.org/10.4324/9781003248606

Gans, J. S., & Alonso, A. (1998). Difficult patients: Their construction in group therapy. *International Journal of Group Psychotherapy, 48*(3), 311–326. https://doi.org/10.1080/00207284.1998.11491545

Guralnik, O. (2014). The dead baby. *Psychoanalytic Dialogues, 24*(2), 129–145. https://doi.org/10.1080/10481885.2014.893754

Hartman, S. (2010). L'état c'est moi – Except when i am not: Commentary on paper by Orna Guranlik and Daphne Simeon. *Psychoanalytic Dialogues, 20*(4), 428–436. https://doi.org/10.1080/10481885.2010.502502

Herman, J. L. (1997). *Trauma and recovery* (revised ed.). Basic Books. https://www.hachettebookgroup.com/titles/judith-lewis-herman-md/trauma-and-recovery/9781541602953/?lens=basic-books

Hopper, E. (Ed.). (2011). The theory of the basic assumption of Incohesion: Aggregation/massification or (ba) I:A/M'. Appendix to *Trauma and Organisations*. Karnac Books. https://www.karnacbooks.com/product/trauma-and-organizations/28847/

Hopper, E. (2014). The theory of incohesion: Aggregation/massification. In L. Auestad (Ed.), *Nationalism and the body politic: Psychoanalysis and the rise of ethnocentrism and xenophobia* (pp. 87–106). Karnac. https://doi.org/10.4324/9780429477522

Hopper, E. (2019). "Notes" on the theory of the fourth basic assumption in the unconscious life of groups and group-like social systems – Incohesion: Aggregation/massification or (ba) I:A/M. *Group, 43*(1), 9–27. https://doi.org/10.13186/group.43.1.0009

Hopper, E., & Weinberg, H. (Eds.). (2011). *The social unconscious in persons, groups, and societies–Volume I:Mainly theory*. Karnac. https://www.routledge.com/The-Social-Unconscious-in-Persons-Groups-and-Societies-Mainly-Theory/Hopper-Weinberg/p/book/9781855757684

Hopper, E., & Weinberg, H. (Eds.). (2015). *The social unconscious in persons, groups and societies: Volume 2: Mainly foundation matrices*. Karnac. https://www.routledge.com/The-Social-Unconscious-in-Persons-Groups-and-Societies-Volume-2-Mainly-Foundation-Matrices/Hopper-Weinberg/p/book/9781782201854

Hopper, E., & Weinberg, H. (Eds.). (2017). *The social unconscious in persons, groups and societies: Volume 3: The foundation matrix extended and reconfigured*. Karnac. https://doi.org/10.4324/9780429483257

Janis, I. L. (1972). *Victims of groupthink*. Houghton Mifflin.

Kira, I. A., Shuwiekh, A. M., Rice, K. G., Ashby, J. S., Elwakeel, S. A., Sous, M. S. F., Alhuwailah, A., Baali, A., Azdaou, C., Oliemat, E. M., & Jamil, H. J. (2021). Measuring COVID-19 as traumatic stress: Initial psychometrics and validation. *Journal of Loss & Trauma, 26*(3), 220–237. https://doi.org/10.1080/15325024.2020.1790160

Krippner, S., & Barrett, D. (2019). Transgenerational trauma: The role of epigenetics. *The Journal of Mind and Behavior*, *40*(1), 53–62. https://www.jstor.org/stable/26740747

Kupcova, I., Danisovic, L., Klein, M., & Harsanyi, S. (2023). Effects of the COVID-19 pandemic on mental health, anxiety, and depression. *BMC Psychology*, *11*, 108. https://doi.org/10.1186/s40359-023-01130-5

Kuzminskaite, E., Penninx, B. W. J. H, van Harmelen, A. L., Elzinga, B. M., Hovens, J. G. F. M., & Vinkers, C. H. (2021). Childhood trauma in adult depressive and anxiety disorders: An integrated review on psychological and biological mechanisms in NESDA cohort. *Journal of Affective Disorders*, *283*, 179–191. https://doi.org/10.1016/j.jad.2021.01.054

Layton, L. (2019). Transgenerational hauntings: Toward a social psychoanalysis and an ethic of dis-illusionment. *Psychoanalytic Dialogues*, *29*, 105–121. https://doi.org/10.1080/10481885.2019.1587992

Leiderman, L. M., & Klein, R. H. (2022). An integrative systems-oriented interpersonal/relational group approach to understanding and treating mass trauma, dissociation and enactments during the COVID-19 pandemic. *International Journal of Group Psychotherapy*, *72*(1), 34–63. https://doi.org/10.1080/00207284.2021.1991234

Marmarosh, C. L., & Van Horn, S. M. (2011). Cohesion in counseling and psychotherapy groups. In R. K. Conyne (Ed.), *The Oxford handbook of group counseling* (pp. 138–163). Oxford Library of Psychology. https://doi.org/10.1093/oxfordhb/9780195394450.013.0009

Mitchell, S. A., & Aron, L. (1999). *Relational psychoanalysis, volume 1: The emergence of a tradition*. Routledge. https://www.routledge.com/Relational-Psychoanalysis-Volume-1-The-Emergence-of-a-Tradition/Mitchell-Aron/p/book/9780881632705

Mitscherlich, A., & Mitscherlich, M. (1967). *The inability to mourn: Principles of collective behavior*. Random House.

Moglen, S. (2005). On mourning social injury. *Psychoanalysis, Culture & Society*, *10*(2), 151–167. https://doi.org/10.1057/palgrave.pcs.2100032

Ogimoto, K., & Plaenkers, T. (2023). The manic defense of reconstruction and the inability to mourn in post-war Japan. In E. Hopper (Ed.), *The tripartite matrix in the developing theory and expanding practice of group analysis* (pp. 222–230). Routledge. https://doi.org/10.4324/9781003425915

Orrenius, P., & Zavodny, M. (2019). Do immigrants threaten US public safety? *Journal on Migration and Human Security*, *7*(3), 52–61. https://doi.org/10.24149/wp1905

Osborne, D., Costello, T. H., Duckitt, J., & Sibley, C. G. (2023). The psychological causes and societal consequences of authoritarianism. *Nature Reviews Psychology*, *2*, 220–232. https://doi.org/10.1038/s44159-023-00161-4

Rao, J. M. (2022). The insistence on exclusion: The anti-integrative impulse and thwarted mourning in large groups. *International Journal of Applied Psychoanalytic Studies*, 1–13. https://doi.org/10.1002/aps.1747

Rozmarin, E. (2009). I am yourself: Subjectivity and the collective. *Psychoanalytic Dialogues*, *19*(5), 604–616. https://doi.org/10.1080/10481880903337469

Shehaj, A., Shin, A. J., & Inglehart, R. (2021). Immigration and right-wing populism: An origin story. *Party Politics*, *27*(2), 282–293. https://doi.org/10.1177/1354068819849888

USA Today. (2023). *Hate crimes hit record levels in 2023: Why 2024 could be even worse*. www.usatoday.com/story/news/nation/2024/01/05/hate-crimes-hit-record-levels-in-2023-why-2024-could-be-even-worse/72118808007

Volkan, V. D. (2004). *Blind trust: Large groups and their leaders in times of crisis and terror*. Pitchstone Publishing. https://archive.org/details/blindtrustlargeg0000volk/page/n5/mode/2up

Wardi, D. (1992). *Memorial candles: Children of the holocaust*. Routledge. https://doi.org/10.4324/9781315812779

Weinberg, H., & Schneider, S. (2003). Introduction: Background, structure and dynamics of the large group. In S. Schneider & H. Weinberg (Eds.), *The large group revisited: The Herd, primal Horde, crowds and masses*. Jessica Kingsley Pub. https://books.google.com/books/about/The_Large_Group_Re_Visited.html?id=VfsSA0zqueoC

Weinberg, H., & Weishut, D. J. N. (2012). Chapter 23: The large group: Dynamics, social implications and therapeutic value. In J. L. Kleinberg (Ed.), *The Wiley-Blackwell handbook of group psychotherapy* (pp. 457–479). Wiley-Blackwell. https://doi.org/10.1002/9781119950882.ch23

Wetts, R., & Willer, R. (2018). Privilege on the precipice: Perceived racial status threats lead white Americans to oppose welfare programs. *Social Forces*, *97*(2), 793–822. https://doi.org/10.1093/sf/soy046

World Health Organization. (2022). *ICD-11: International classification of diseases* (11th revision). https://icd.who.int/

10 An Integrative Experiential Group Therapy Approach to Treat the Trauma of Sexual Abuse

Bojun Hu and J. Joana Kyei

Sexual abuse involves any sexual activity that occurs without an individual's consent and is a pervasive public health concern that disproportionately affects females (Abeid et al., 2015; Al-Zayed et al., 2020; Stoltenborgh et al., 2011). According to the Centers for Disease Control (CDC, 2022), over half of women in the United States have experienced a sexually violent act during their lifetimes, while the World Health Organization (2021) estimates that nearly one in three women, worldwide, has been subjected to sexual violence. The literature reveals that sexual abuse begins early, with more than four in five female rape survivors having experienced rape for the first time before the age of 25; almost half of survivors are first raped prior to the age of 18 (Barth et al., 2013; CDC, 2022). Nearly eight in ten male survivors are raped before the age of 25 (CDC, 2022).

The consequences of childhood sexual abuse (CSA) are long-lasting and include a spectrum of medical conditions ranging from chronic headaches, unremitting pelvic pain, and obesity. The psychological aftermath can include anxiety disorders, sexual dysfunction in adulthood, substance use disorders, dissociative identity disorder, and refractory psychosis (Hailes et al., 2019; Irish et al., 2010; Isely, 2008; Molnar et al., 2001; Pan et al., 2021). CSA involving penetration and/or the threat of force by a parental figure has been correlated with some of the more severe medical and/or psychiatric conditions (Alexander & Lupfer, 1987; Beitchman et al., 1992; Molnar et al., 2001).

Briere and Elliott (1994) classified the long-term psychological sequalae of childhood sexual abuse into five categories: posttraumatic stress, cognitive distortions, emotional pain, avoidance, an impaired sense of self, and poor interpersonal relatedness. These five categories are commensurate with the symptomatology of complex posttraumatic stress disorder (complex PTSD), a chronic mental health condition (Herman, 1992; Kliethermes et al., 2014; Maercker et al., 2022; Molnar et al., 2001).

Given that CSA involves a violation of an intimate nature, CSA survivors are more likely to exhibit maladaptive sexual behaviors, such as engaging in promiscuous sex or having difficulty establishing long-term, healthy intimate and interpersonal relationships (Briere & Runtz, 1990; Davis & Petretic-Jackson, 2000). In nonromantic relationships, CSA has been associated with adult attachment issues, mistrust of others, difficulty in the parental role, conflict resolution difficulties, and interpersonal sensitivity (Duncan, 2005; Huh et al., 2014).

Negative physical consequences, including reproductive health problems and the psychological sequalae of substance abuse, eating disorders, anxiety, depression, self-harm and suicidality, posttraumatic stress disorder, and self-blame, have been correlated with those who experience sexual abuse for the first time in adulthood (Brown et al., 2019; Regehr et al., 2013; WHO, 2013). Irrespective of whether sexual abuse is experienced in childhood or in adulthood, the negative consequences of sexual abuse can be long-lasting.

DOI: 10.4324/9781003546252-16

Group Therapy for the Treatment of Sexual Abuse

The treatment of persons with a history of sexual abuse involves addressing issues such as traumatic grief and loss, inability to trust others, affect dysregulation, impaired self-esteem, stigmatization, and shame (Armitage et al., 2023; Bordere, 2017). Group therapy is an efficient treatment modality that provides (1) an intersubjective forum for members to develop trust, increase resilience, and improve coping skills, which lead to more adaptive ways of relating (Hegeman & Wohl, 2000), and (2) a shared safe space where survivors can work through internalized shame and stigmatization (Buchele, 2000; Wyles et al., 2023), a salient aspect of sexual abuse when compared with most other types of traumas. The group bears witness to each member's personal and traumatic experiences, thereby breaking the shame-filled silence most survivors were forced to keep.

An Integrative, Experiential Group Approach

Treating sexual abuse survivors is challenging and complex. Research suggests that clinicians integrate a broader range of modalities and techniques into the treatment since existing evidence-based models are too narrowly focused (Gaskill & Perry, 2014; Lanktree & Briere, 2013).

In recent years, integrative practices have included combining trauma-focused approaches with psychoeducation, a feminist orientation, a mindfulness approach, culturally specific interventions, and social advocacy, as well as activism aimed at enhancing the group members' senses of self (Bryant-Davis et al., 2021; Driscoll, 2016; Fouché & Walker-Williams, 2016; Fraenkel, 2019; Luna, 2016). The various integrative models are designed especially to address shame, other painful emotions, and negative cognitions and to target impaired self-concepts in culturally informed ways.

Integrative group therapy approaches emphasize the primary needs of a population and tailor the treatment to address these needs (Gilbert & Orlans, 2011). An integrative approach values constant re-evaluation and therapist self-scrutiny, including examining countertransferences (Norcross & Beutler, 2014). Integrative trauma group approaches address intrusive, dissociative, and avoidance symptoms, as well as emotional dysregulation; this model facilitates the working through of relational obstacles, such as traumatized sexualization, fear of betrayal, shame, difficulties trusting others, and addressing distortions in the views of self and others (Charak et al., 2018; Easton et al., 2019; Finkelhor & Browne, 1985; Maercker et al., 2022).

Psychodynamic Group Therapy Approaches

Psychodynamic practitioners and theorists have emphasized the role of the therapist's countertransference and the importance of the intersubjective relationships among group members (Erskine, 2010). Central to this approach is the intersectionality of the intrasubjective and intersubjective fields. *Intrasubjectivity* refers to the multiple self-parts and self-states within each person (Benjamin, 2010). *Intersubjectivity* refers to the dynamic interactions between and among all members, including the group therapist; this view is not based on a therapist-looking-in-upon-the-group, an observer–subject relationship. The group is conceptualized as a developing organism (Grossmark & Wright, 2014), and the therapist, as a part of the system, utilizes her awareness of multiple self-states to help the group become more aware of itself (Billow, 2003). In particular, the therapist is alert to when she is pulled into action, giving into demands, dissociating, fighting, or fleeing.

A therapist facilitating sexual trauma groups may experience a range of countertransferential reactions (Ganzarain & Buchele, 1988). Her task is to feel and think about these emotional reactions and share these with the group whenever they serve the goal of promoting therapeutic action. Thus, in the psychodynamic sexual trauma group, the therapist does not hold the traditional analytic role of being a neutral observer, analyzing group dynamics from outside the group. She is integral to the group's relational field and is present in the group with the multiplicity of relational constellations within her (Grossmark & Wright, 2014).

As Herman (2015) pointed out, the therapist can be pulled and compelled into different roles in the therapeutic process; those roles include that of the perpetrator, who is harming or neglecting; the bystander, who observes but feels helpless; and the victim, who is violated, intruded upon, or disregarded. Herman labeled the combination of these roles the *trauma triad*. These internalized roles exemplify the multiplicity of self-experiences both within the therapist and within the group members. The therapist's awareness and embodiment of these different self-states, however primitive, embolden group members to accept their self-states and those of others (Billow, 2003).

Case Illustration 1

The following case example illustrates how the principal author incorporated her countertransference and understanding of her personal multiple self-states into a trauma group for survivors of sexual abuse. In one session, Pete wanted Shui, a new member, who came into the group with a history of childhood sexual abuse, emotional neglect, and adult sexual violations by colleagues and strangers, to express her feelings more directly. Shui reacted defensively to his comments. Pete then stated that he was not allowed to express emotions as a child, that his parents had abused him physically and sexually, and that he was enraged about it. The group therapist (GT) felt overwhelmed by the graphic descriptions of the abuse he had endured. GT also noticed that group members were withdrawing and dissociating. In the past, GT had interrupted Pete, attempting to affirm his feelings and inviting others to share their reactions, which had led him to experience the GT as shutting him down, that is, dismissing him, like how his mother had treated him. During the aforementioned interaction, GT chose to wait for him to finish. Countertransferentially, the GT felt a range of feelings, including feeling victimized by being forced to listen to his diatribe about the abusive acts, as well as feeling torn between either re-enacting his mother's neglect/intrusiveness or losing the rest of the group to dissociation. GT realized she was embodying both the perpetrator and the helpless child, experiencing internally this conflict that was also being felt within the group. Another member, Jo, who was feeling the roles of witnessing the vulnerable child, both in session and in her daily life, suggested to Pete that instead of feeling like a victim, shut down by the new member and previously by his parents, he could speak up for his needs. In the following session, Pete was empathic and attuned to a member. Another member shared her appreciation of him, saying how he seemed to embody the role of a caring parent, not only to other members, but also to himself. He responded with sadness, stating that this was the type of parental relationship he had longed for and never experienced as a child. Different self-states embodied by members and the therapist of the group alerted Pete to different potentials within himself so that his sense of powerlessness was no longer entrenched but a self-state for which there were now behavioral alternatives.

Another foundational element of a psychodynamic orientation is the role of disso-ciation, which can show up ranging from "spacing out" to derealization (Zerubavel & Messman-Moore, 2015). In groups, these dissociated parts of the self are experienced as "not me" and can be re-enacted and therapeutically addressed in the group process. For example, shame may be too emotionally painful for some sexual abuse survivors so that it is dissociated and disconnected from their conscious experience. When the group bears witness to a member's emotional pain, the group provides the opportunity for that member to feel validated by recognizing the continued emotional suffering of that member. This "enactive witnessing" in the group process can foster entry of the traumatized, shamed, dis-sociated parts into awareness and out of isolation, thereby mending the traumatic wound ensconced in isolation and non-recognition (Grossmark, 2017).

Sexual trauma survivors, through transferential reactions, may find the group-as-a-whole, the therapist, and/or members as behaving in abusive, intrusive, unresponsive, or punishing ways, replicating/enacting the neglect and abuse and/or the terror and helplessness of their sexual abuse experienced in the family, but now within the context of the group (Tyson & Goodman, 1996).

Another element of the psychodynamic approach is to work through projections and identifications so that all members can be more emotionally available and relate more intimately with one another (Benjamin, 2007). For example, incest survivors can have an unconscious desire be the favorite, the most valued, as it replicates the family environment where special privileges accompanied the sexual abuse (Ganzarain & Buchele, 1988). By re-experiencing, identifying, and becoming aware of traumatic familial roles that are re-enacted in the group dynamics, members have an opportunity to foster new, more adaptive ways of relating to others.

Psychodramatic Techniques

It is relatively easy to integrate psychodramatic techniques into a psychodynamic model which then fosters awareness and embodied expressions of enactments to ac-tivate internal and interpersonal resources. Psychodramatic techniques can be utilized to externalize inner experiences via speech, expressions, movements, and actions. In psychodrama, what is talked *about* becomes enacted. Constellations of experiences marked by thoughts and feelings, previously invisible and unexpressed, are given form and become alive in real time, to be repaired and reintegrated (Hudgins & Toscani, 2013; Ringel & Brandell, 2011; Treadwell & Abeditehrani, 2025). Through embodiment and the conscious taking on of a "role," implicit, traumatic memories are accessed and reprocessed (Arden, 2019; Tinnin & Gantt, 2013). To address the terror and helplessness of members' sexual abuse, psychodrama can be utilized in two broad ways: bringing unconscious elements contained with the enactment into conscious awareness and fos-tering emotional regulation.

Inspired by Gestalt Therapy and Emotional Focused Therapy, the utilization of chair work provides opportunities for emotions to be accessed, felt, and thus more easily differenti-ated, explored, and meaning-derived. The presence of an empty chair, representing a part of the inner experience, helps stimulate emotional schematic memories associated with specific roles, as well as the expression of the accompanying needs and emotions (Green-berg, 2021). The "interactions of the prescriptive roles are what creates intrapsychic change" (Giacomucci, 2021, p. 137). For survivors who can be trapped in helpless self-states, the practice of conversing among differing internalized roles is a form of self-responsiveness and empowerment (DePrince & Gagnon, 2018).

"Doubling," a primary psychodrama technique, is used for emotional containment and regulation. The double attempts to give voice to the inner world of the protagonist (the group member who is being addressed) as well as doubling the body. This is typically done by standing next to the protagonist, mirroring the physical stance of the body, and speaking in the first person as if the double is the protagonist. If the doubling is correct, the protagonist repeats it. Doubling serves implicitly to offer the protagonist empathy in the form of inter-personal identification and connection (Giacomucci, 2021). This technique, along with the two other basic psychodrama techniques of mirroring and role reversal, can be beneficial for sexual abuse survivors so that they can become more aware of their feelings and sensations, label experiences, integrate new perspectives, and connect with an embodied sense of themselves and others (Dayton, 2005, 2014).

Mindfulness and Bodily- Focused Practices

Mindfulness, including intentional awareness of bodily somatic processes and the assuming of a compassionate attitude, can address emotional dysregulation, increase emotional tolerance, and facilitate integration of internal stimuli into conscious experience (Keng et al., 2011; Shapiro et al., 2006). For sexual trauma survivors, the site of trauma is the body. The body holds the muscular and neurological imprints of trauma (van der Kolk, 2015). Mindfulness interventions are incorporated in two ways, first as affect regulation, grounding, and increasing emotional tolerance, and second as exposure and experiential deepening.

Integration of mindfulness techniques can include: Sessions begin with a mindfulness practice with five to ten minutes of breathing exercises, meta loving-kindness meditation, guided imagery, naming three things group members can hear/touch with their skin, self–facial massage, and investigation of Laban's five contrasting qualities of thoughts and emotions (Payne, 2017). Mindfulness invites participants to become aware of bodily sensations, senses, voluntary and involuntary movements, felt experiences, emotional tones, and associated thoughts (Khoury et al., 2017). Mindful practices deepen group process through encouraging group members to notice the interplay among these experiences: the constellation of thought/feeling/sensation/movement that accompanies the experiences and roles. Group mindfulness invites the members to be aware of the group's level of tension/relaxation, emotional tone, sense of closeness/distance, fantasies, and group imaginings. Beginning a session with a mindfulness practice helps regulate emotions (e.g., for people who are coming in late, arriving with expectations of the group, arriving with emotional valences) and provides grounding. Group members' observing and naming their feelings, for example, noticing that what one is feeling is shame, are important parts of symptom stabilization and regulation.

Therapists can also intentionally engage the group in mindful practices when participants are visibly dissociating and/or stressed. In contrast to dissociation that is characterized by separation and putting out of awareness, in mindfulness, one is aware of the connection to self, others, and the world. Mindfulness also addresses members' fearful and avoidant tendencies, by emphasizing what is happening in the here and now, sensationally, emotionally, cognitively. It prevents disconnection and dissociation while facilitating a reconnection of the body and emotional experiences.

Case Illustration 2

Two members simultaneously dissociated as they engaged in a conflict with one another. Before dissociating, one of them, Jared, heard an internalized parental voice saying, "You cannot express your feelings, especially angry feelings." The second group member, Emma, experienced Jared's anger as replicating episodes in her childhood home, where anger was often associated with physical and sexual abuse. Their voices rose in anger with one another; other group members looked down or away. The therapist invited the group to pause and be aware of what they were experiencing in their bodies, emotions, and minds in that moment, as well as what they were aware of in the group-as-a-whole. Members were all invited to rate their level of being present, then to orient their bodies and minds, by walking in the room and noticing something in the space that drew their attention and brought them comfort. As Emma's anxiety lessened, she was able to feel more grounded and to access the agency to talk more explicitly about her unresolved childhood traumas and what was being re-enacted as Jared raged. Jared, with the support of the group, realized that his rage was directed at his perpetrator and displaced onto the people around him.

When mindfulness is directed toward members' internal experiences, observation serves as a tool to increase emotional awareness and tolerance (Linehan, 1993; Shapiro et al., 2006).

Mindfulness cultivates the phenomenological attitudes of curiosity, compassion, and non-judgment. The practice of mindfulness is incorporated into group sessions via questions and Gestalt experiments, such as "What is the group aware of in the moment?" (Gold & Zahm, 2018). Specifically, there are three ways of deepening awareness using mindfulness. First, members are encouraged to become aware of how the different modalities of perception are interrelated and inform one another: movements, sensations, interoception (like tension creating ruminations and/or tension in a particular part of the body), behaviors, and cognitive patterns (McConnell, 2020). Explicit questions can increase group member awareness, questions such as "What are the sensations, feelings, thoughts, and impulses people are aware of in the room right now?" Experiments can also be useful, that is, "Notice what it is like to sit with both the love and the hate for the abuser in the family." The very acts of observing and naming feelings or painful bodily sensations help regulate emotions and contain affective intensity (Linehan, 1993). Second, group members become aware of insights as well as emotional/cognitive patterns associated with frequently enacted roles and trauma scripts. For example, a member may become aware of the self-defeating pattern related to "It is no use fighting, because they will never understand." A third way to enhance awareness includes members becoming aware of their ego strengths, loving capacities, abilities, hopes, resources, and resilience, particularly in the context of relationships. Mindfulness strategies can be implemented to reinforce agentic self-states. This is formally known as "resourcing" (Ogden, 2003), that is, when the Gestalt of self-in-relation is brought into awareness and linked with a sensation, memory, image, or phrase that crystallizes the self-state. Bookmarking awareness makes it more accessible in the future as an integrated role or an internal resource of strength in the face of emotional triggers and challenging stressors.

Specific Considerations When Forming and Facilitating Sexual Trauma Groups

Heterogeneous vs. Homogenous Groups

Candidates for group therapy can receive treatment in a homogenous group of members with a shared history of sexual abuse, or in a heterogeneous group consisting of members with sexual abuse and/or other relational trauma histories, as well as those with no identified trauma in their backgrounds. Homogeneous groups promote cohesion initially but limit depth; heterogeneous groups are slower to coalesce but have a stronger potential to facilitate in-depth work (Yalom & Leszcz, 2020).

The homogeneous group maximizes similarities in experience, thus promoting cohesion. Differences among members are minimized, and breaking the seals of secrecy initially is very important. However, with a relative absence of difference, the experience of the trauma is emphasized and can become a ticket to admission to the group, thus serving as a defense against the deepening of the group process which is fostered by the presence of differences. Then, growing beyond the trauma, due to an insufficient working through, which can be stimulated by an awareness of differences, is limited.

Homogenous groups can be gender-based, such as an all-men's group, or identity-based, such as an all-female group within a particular religion, where it is a taboo to talk about their experiences with the opposite gender present. The sense of group cohesion can be established quickly in homogenous groups, particularly in collectivistic cultures, where there is the taboo of sharing personal histories with outsiders (Fleming et al., 2021). Members quickly learn to experience one another, not as outsiders, but as part of a group with a shared history. However, the disadvantages of this similarity in background can limit in-depth work and foster solidifying an identity as a victim.

There are various types of heterogeneous groups, including survivors at different stages of recovery; survivors of different genders, including those on the LGBTQ+ spectrum; and members with different types of sexual trauma, such as sex trafficking, incest, domestic violence, drug-assisted assault, religion-based assaults, and other general psychiatric conditions not specific to trauma. Groups can be composed of those who have experienced sexual trauma combined with nonsexual traumas, such as health-related and war traumas, parental neglect and/or abuse, just to name a few. From the review of 92 US agencies providing sexual trauma group therapy in thematic groups, such as LGBTQ+, incest survivors' group, or eating disorder and sexual trauma groups, most program directors have found gender-inclusive, combined sexual abuse and trauma-inclusive groups to be similarly helpful and effective with members (Macy et al., 2013).

Impact of Culture on Treatment and Recovery

Sexual abuse is addressed differently internationally. For example, research supports better outcomes in addressing the shame of a sexual abuse survivor who resides in a democratic country versus one who resides in a country with a collectivistic culture (Sawrikar & Katz, 2017; Yamawaki et al., 2015). In a collectivistic culture like China, shame is experienced collectively by both the individual and the family. The family system may feel familial shame in response to having a family member who is sexually abused. Shame in collectivistic cultures dictates what can be talked about and what cannot be talked about. This shame can also lead to, at times, victims being shamed by the family because they are viewed as having brought shame upon the family's reputation.

Different cultures and subcultures have differing socially accepted and circulated narratives regarding sexual violence, further influencing the experience of shame and one's capacity to access resources. For example, in the Chinese culture, women in both public and private company cultures are often pressured into accompanying men in power to restaurants and interacting as drinking partners. The sexual harassment and assaults that can arise from these conditions are often seen as part of "the job" and not named as abuse.

When males are raped, or generally when assaults occur by member of the same gender, societal messages such as "Men cannot be raped" or "Rape cannot happen between people of the same gender" prevent traumatized people from recognizing experiences as non-consensual acts of sexual abuse. Survivors in these circumstances are likely to normalize what happened and label their emotions and reactions as shameful and themselves as "overreacting" to what had happened.

Environmental support is a crucial component in recovery from sexual assault, but depending on the culture, that support can be variable and can possess characteristics that compromise its helpfulness. In autocratic cultures and countries like Saudi Arabia, Russia, and China, as well as in hierarchical institutions, such as the church and some businesses, there is higher potential for abuse (Haboush & Alyan, 2013; Kyei, 2022; Sawrikar & Katz, 2017). In these countries and institutions, gender roles may be more traditional, demarcated, and inflexible, equating the male gender with authority and power. Societal blaming of the victim can occur more readily in these cultures.

Future Application and Research

The cognitive, emotional, somatic, and relational imprints of sexual trauma necessitate an integrative group therapy approach. There is creative potential for increasing the number of integrative approaches to address trauma symptoms, powerlessness, betrayal of trust, grief, shame, victimhood, and other correlates of sexual trauma. Future group psychotherapy research for sexual trauma needs to include investigating which interventions foster posttraumatic growth, specifically utilizing the resilience potential of individuals to metabolize and transform their trauma experiences into growth experiences (Guggisberg et al., 2021), but taking cultural contexts into account.

References

Abeid, M., Muganyizi, P., Massawe, S., Mpembeni, R., Darj, E., & Axemo, P. (2015). Knowledge and attitude towards rape and child sexual abuse – A community-based cross-sectional study in Rural Tanzania. *BMC Public Health, 15,* 1–12. https://doi.org/10.1186/s12889-015-1757-7

Alexander, P. C., & Lupfer, S. L. (1987). Family characteristics and long-term consequences associated with sexual abuse. *Archives of Sexual Behavior, 16,* 235–245. https://doi.org/10.1007/BF01541611

Al-Zayed, B., Alshehri, A. A. A., Alshanawani, H., Alresheedi, Z. O., Alshammari, R. D. A., Alrashed, N., & Ibrahim, S. F. (2020). Reported child maltreatment in the Riyadh region of Saudi Arabia: A retrospective study. *Forensic Science International: Reports, 2,* 100125. https://doi.org/10.1016/j.fsir.2020.100125

Arden, J. B. (2019). *Mind-brain-gene: Toward psychotherapy integration.* Norton. https://wwnorton.com/books/9780393711844

Armitage, R., Wager, N., Wibberley, D., Hudspith, L. F., & Gall, V. (2023). "We're not allowed to have experienced trauma. We're not allowed to go through the grieving process" – Exploring the indirect harms associated with Child Sexual Abuse Material (CSAM) offending and its impacts on non-offending family members. *Victims & Offenders,* 1–27. https://doi.org/10.1080/15564886.2023.2172504

Barth, J., Bermetz, L., Heim, E., Trelle, S., & Tonia, T. (2013). The current prevalence of child sexual abuse worldwide: A systematic review and meta-analysis. *International Journal of Public Health, 58,* 469–483. https://doi.org/10.1007/s00038-012-0426-1

Beitchman, J. H., Zucker, K. J., Hood, J. E., DaCosta, G. A., Akman, D., & Cassavia, E. (1992). A review of the long-term effects of child sexual abuse. *Child Abuse & Neglect, 16*(1), 101–118. https://doi.org/10.1016/0145-2134(92)90011-F

Benjamin, J. (2007). *Intersubjectivity, thirdness, and mutual recognition.* [Speech transcription]. Terapia. https://terapia.co.uk/wp-content/uploads/2020/05/Reading-14-Jessica-Benjamin-Intersubjectivity.pdf

Benjamin, J. (2010). Where's the gap and what's the difference? The relational view of intersubjectivity, multiple selves, and enactments. *Contemporary Psychoanalysis, 46*(1), 112–119. https://doi.org/10.1080/00107530.2010.10746042

Billow, R. M. (2003). *Relational group psychotherapy: From basic assumptions to passion.* J. Kingsley Publishers. https://www.powells.com/book/relational-group-psychotherapy-9781843107392

Bordere, T. (2017). Disenfranchisement and ambiguity in the face of loss: The suffocated grief of sexual assault survivors. *Family Relations, 66*(1), 29–45. https://doi.org/10.1111/fare.12231

Briere, J., & Runtz, M. (1990). Differential adult symptomatology associated with three types of child abuse histories. *Child Abuse & Neglect, 14*(3), 357–364. https://doi.org/10.1016/0145-2134(90)90007-G

Briere, J. N., & Elliott, D. M. (1994). Immediate and long-term impacts of child sexual abuse. *The Future of Children, 4*(2), 54–69. http://www.jstor.com/stable/1602523

Brown, S. J., Khasteganan, N., Brown, K., Hegarty, K., Carter, G. J., Tarzia, L., Feder, G., & O'Doherty, L. (2019). Psychosocial interventions for survivors of rape and sexual assault experienced during adulthood. *The Cochrane Database of Systematic Reviews, 2019*(11). https://doi.org/10.1002/14651858.CD013456

Bryant-Davis, T., Fasalojo, B., Arounian, A., Jackson, K. L., & Leithman, E. (2021). Resist and rise: A trauma-informed womanist model for group therapy. *Women & Therapy, 47*(1), 34–57. https://doi.org/10.1080/02703149.2021.1943114

Buchele, B. J. (2000). Group psychotherapy for survivors of sexual and physical abuse. In R. H. Klein & V. L. Schermer (Eds.), *Group psychotherapy for psychological trauma* (pp. 170–187). The Guilford Press. https://www.betterworldbooks.com/product/detail/group-psychotherapy-for-psychological-trauma-1572305576

Centers for Disease Control. (2022). *Fast facts: Preventing sexual violence.* https://www.cdc.gov/violenceprevention/sexualviolence/fastfact.html

Charak, R., DiLillo, D., Messman-Moore, T. L., & Gratz, K. L. (2018). Latent classes of lifetime sexual victimization characteristics in women in emerging adulthood: Differential relations with emotion dysregulation. *Psychology of Violence, 8*(5), 570. https://doi.org/10.1037/vio0000154

Davis, J. L., & Petretic-Jackson, P. A. (2000). The impact of child sexual abuse on adult interpersonal functioning: A review and synthesis of the empirical literature. *Aggression and Violent Behavior, 5*(3), 291–328. https://doi.org/10.1016/S1359-1789(99)00010-5

Dayton, T. (2005). *The living stage: A step-by-step guide to psychodrama, sociometry, and experiential group therapy.* Health Communications Inc.

Dayton, T. (2014). *Relational trauma repair (RTR) therapist's guide (Revised).* Innerlook Inc. https://archive.org/details/relationaltrauma0000drti

DePrince, A. P., & Gagnon, K. L. (2018). Understanding the consequences of sexual assault: What does it mean for prevention to be trauma-informed? In L. M. Orchowski & C. A. Gidycz (Eds.), *Sexual assault risk reduction and resistance: Theory, research, and practice* (pp. 15–35). Academic Press. https://www.sciencedirect.com/book/9780128053898/sexual-assault-risk-reduction-and-resistance

Driscoll, L. E. (2016). *Reclaiming relationships: An integrative psychotherapy group for adolescents who have experienced sexual violence* [Doctoral Dissertation, James Williams College]. https://search.proquest.com/openview/321eea0d8fb227cdf94b2560aeb90f42/1?pq-origsite=gscholar&cbl=18750

Duncan, K. A. (2005). The impact of child sexual abuse on parenting: A female perspective. In G. R. Walz & R. K. Yep (Eds.), *VISTAS: Compelling perspectives on counseling, 2005* (pp. 267–270). American Counseling Association. https://www.thefreelibrary.com/VISTAS%3B+compelling+perspectives+on+counseling+2005.-a0138410684

Easton, S. D., Leone-Sheehan, D. M., & O'Leary, P. J. (2019). "I will never know the person who I could have become": Perceived changes in self-identity among adult survivors of clergy-perpetrated sexual abuse. *Journal of Interpersonal Violence, 34*(6), 1139–1162. https://doi.org/10.1177/0886260516650966

Erskine, R. G. (2010). Relational group psychotherapy: The healing of stress, neglect, and trauma. *International Journal of Integrative Psychotherapy, 1*(1), 1–10. https://www.integrative-journal.com/index.php/ijip/article/view/2

Finkelhor, D., & Browne, A. (1985). The traumatic impact of child sexual abuse: A conceptualization. *American Journal of Orthopsychiatry, 55*(4), 530–541. https://doi.org/10.1111/j.1939-0025.1985.tb02703.x

Fleming, P., Bayliss, A. P., Edwards, S. G., & Seger, C. R. (2021). The role of personal data value, culture and self-construal in online privacy behaviour. *PLoS One, 16*(7), e0253568. https://journals.plos.org/plosone/article?id=10.1371/journal.pone.0253568

Fouché, A., & Walker-Williams, H. J. (2016). A group intervention programme for adult survivors of childhood sexual abuse. *Social Work, 52*(4), 525–545. https://doi.org/10.15270/52-2-529

Fraenkel, P. (2019). Incest and relational trauma: The systemic narrative feminist model. In P. J. Pitta & C. C. Datchi (Eds.), *Integrative couple and family therapies: Treatment models for complex clinical issues* (pp. 47–70). American Psychological Association. https://doi.org/10.1037/0000151-003

Ganzarain, R. C., & Buchele, B. J. C. (1988). *Fugitives of incest: A perspective from psychoanalysis and groups.* International Universities Press. https://doi.org/10.1176/ajp.146.11.1506-a

Gaskill, R. L., & Perry, B. D. (2014). The neurobiological power of play: Using the neurosequential model of therapeutics to guide play in the healing process. In C. A. Malchiodi & D. A. Crenshaw (Eds.), *Creative arts and play therapy for attachment problems* (pp. 178–194). Guilford Press. https://www.guilford.com/books/Creative-Arts-and-Play-Therapy-for-Attachment-Problems/Malchiodi-Crenshaw/9781462523702

Giacomucci, S. (2021). *Social work, sociometry, and psychodrama.* Springer. https://library.oapen.org//handle/20.500.12657/47303

Gilbert, M., & Orlans, V. (2011). *Integrative therapy: 100 key points and techniques.* Routledge/Taylor & Francis Group. https://www.routledge.com/Integrative-Therapy-100-Key-Points-and-Techniques/Gilbert-Orlans/p/book/9780415413770

Gold, E. K., & Zahm, S. G. (2018). *Buddhist psychology & gestalt therapy integrated: Psychotherapy for the 21st century.* Metta Press. https://www.gttcnw.org/our-book

Greenberg, L. S. (2021). *Changing emotion with emotion: A practitioner's guide.* American Psychological Association. https://doi.org/10.1037/0000248-000

Grossmark, R. (2017). Narrating the unsayable: Enactment, repair, and creative multiplicity in group psychotherapy. *International Journal of Group Psychotherapy, 67*(1), 27–46. https://doi.org/10.1080/00207284.2016.1202680

Grossmark, R., & Wright, F. (2014). *The one and the many: Relational approaches to group psychotherapy.* Taylor & Francis. https://www.routledge.com/The-One-and-the-Many-Relational-Approaches-to-Group-Psychotherapy/Grossmark-Wright/p/book/9780415621816

Guggisberg, M., Bottino, S., & Doran, C. (2021). Women's contexts and circumstances of posttraumatic growth after sexual victimization: A systematic review. *Frontiers in Psychology, 12.* https://doi.org/10.3389/fpsyg.2021.699288

Haboush, K. L., & Alyan, H. (2013). "Who can you tell?" Features of Arab culture that influence conceptualization and treatment of childhood sexual abuse. *Journal of Child Sexual Abuse, 22*(5), 499–518. https://doi.org/10.1080/10538712.2013.800935

Hailes, H. P., Yu, R., Danese, A., & Fazel, S. (2019). Long-term outcomes of childhood sexual abuse: An umbrella review. *The Lancet Psychiatry, 6*(10), 830–839. https://doi.org/10.1016/S2215-0366(19)30286-X

Hegeman, E., & Wohl, A. (2000). Management of trauma-related affect defenses and dissociation. In R. Klein & V. Schermer (Eds.), *Group psychotherapy for psychological trauma* (pp. 47–63). Guilford Press.

Herman, J. (2015). *Trauma and recovery: The aftermath of violence – From domestic abuse to political terror.* Basic Books. https://doi.org/10.1176/appi.psychotherapy.2015.69.4.455

Herman, J. L. (1992). Complex PTSD: A syndrome in survivors of prolonged and repeated trauma. *Journal of Traumatic Stress, 5*(3), 377–391. https://doi.org/10.1002/jts.2490050305

Hudgins, M. K., & Toscani, F. (2013). *Healing world trauma with the therapeutic spiral model: Stories from the frontlines.* Jessica Kingsley Publishers. https://us.jkp.com/products/healing-world-trauma-with-the-therapeutic-spiral-model

Huh, H. J., Kim, S. Y., Yu, J. J., & Chae, J. H. (2014). Childhood trauma and adult interpersonal relationship problems in patients with depression and anxiety disorders. *Annals of General Psychiatry, 13,* 1–13. https://doi.org/10.1186/s12991-014-0026-y

Irish, L., Kobayashi, I., & Delahanty, D. L. (2010). Long-term physical health consequences of childhood sexual abuse: A meta-analytic review. *Journal of Pediatric Psychology, 35*(5), 450–461. https://doi.org/10.1093/jpepsy/jsp118

Isely, P. J., Isely, P., Freiburger, J., & McMackin, R. (2008). In their own voices: A qualitative study of men abused as children by Catholic clergy. *Journal of Child Sexual Abuse, 17*(3–4), 201–215. https://doi.org/10.1080/10538710802329668

Keng, S. L., Smoski, M. J., & Robins, C. J. (2011). Effects of mindfulness on psychological health: A review of empirical studies. *Clinical Psychology Review, 31,* 1041–1056. https://www.ncbi.nlm.nih.gov/pmc/articles/PMC3679190/?utm_medium=organic&utm_source=blog&utm_campaign=mindful-eating-guide

Khoury, B., Knäuper, B., Pagnini, F., Trent, N., Chiesa, A., & Carrière, K. (2017). Embodied mindfulness. *Mindfulness, 8,* 1160–1171. https://doi.org/10.1007/s12671-017-0700-7

Kliethermes, M., Schacht, M., & Drewry, K. (2014). Complex trauma. *Child and Adolescent Psychiatric Clinics, 23*(2), 339–361. https://doi.org/10.1016/j.chc.2013.12.009

Kyei, J. J. (2022). Unravelling the Ghanaian "pull him/her down (PhD) syndrome" of malicious envy. *International Journal of Applied Psychoanalytic Studies, 19*(4), 483–498. https://doi.org/10.1002/aps.1740

Lanktree, C., & Briere, J. (2013). Integrative treatment of complex trauma. In J. D. Ford & C. A. Courtois (Eds.), *Treating complex traumatic stress disorders in children and adolescents: Scientific foundations and therapeutic models* (pp. 143–161). Guilford Press. https://www.guilford.com/books/Treating-Complex-Traumatic-Stress-Disorders-Children-Adolescents/Ford-Courtois/9781462524617

Linehan, M. M. (1993). *Cognitive-behavioral treatment of borderline personality disorder.* Guilford. https://www.guilford.com/books/Cognitive-Behavioral-Treatment-of-Borderline-Personality-Disorder/Marsha-Linehan/9780898621839

Luna, E. C. (2016). *Loving-kindness and compassion: Group psychotherapy for survivors of campus sexual assault* [Doctoral Dissertation, Alliant International University].

Macy, R. J., Rizo, C. F., Johns, N. B., & Ermentrout, D. M. (2013). Directors' opinions about domestic violence and sexual assault service strategies that help survivors. *Journal of Interpersonal Violence, 28*(5), 1040–1066. https://doi.org/10.1177/0886260512459375

Maercker, A., Cloitre, M., Bachem, R., Schlumpf, Y. R., Khoury, B., Hitchcock, C., & Bohus, M. (2022). Complex post-traumatic stress disorder. *The Lancet, 400*(10345), 60–72. https://doi.org/10.1016/S0140-6736(22)00821-2macy

McConnell, S. (2020). *Somatic internal family systems therapy: Awareness, breath, resonance, movement and touch in practice.* North Atlantic Books. https://www.northatlanticbooks.com/shop/somatic-internal-family-systems-therapy/

Molnar, B. E., Buka, S. L., & Kessler, R. C. (2001). Child sexual abuse and subsequent psychopathology: Results from the National Comorbidity Survey. *American Journal of Public Health, 91*(5), 753. https://doi.org/10.2105/ajph.91.5.753

Norcross, J. C., & Beutler, L. E. (2014). Integrative psychotherapies. In D. Wedding & R. Corsini (Eds.), *Current psychotherapies* (pp. 499–532). Cengage. https://www.cengage.uk/c/current-psychotherapies-11e-wedding-corsini/9781305865754/?searchIsbn=9781305865754

Ogden, P. (2003). *Building somatic resources: The theory and practice of sensorimotor psychotherapy in the treatment of trauma* [Doctoral Dissertation, Union Institute & University]. https://search.proquest.com/openview/4db4e391e200abf48043801e706b25b4/1?pq-origsite=gscholar&cbl=18750&diss=y

Pan, Y., Lin, X., Liu, J., Zhang, S., Zeng, X., Chen, F., & Wu, J. (2021). Prevalence of childhood sexual abuse among women using the childhood trauma questionnaire: A worldwide meta-analysis. *Trauma, Violence, & Abuse, 22*(5), 1181–1191. https://doi.org/10.1177/1524838020912867

Payne, H. (2017). The psycho-neurology of embodiment with examples from authentic movement and laban movement analysis. *American Journal of Dance Therapy, 39*, 163–178. https://doi.org/10.1007/s10465-017-9256-2

Regehr, C., Alaggia, R., Dennis, J., Pitts, A., & Saini, M. (2013). Interventions to reduce distress in adult victims of sexual violence and rape: A systematic review. *Campbell Systematic Reviews, 9*(1), 1–133. https://doi.org/10.4073/csr.2013.3

Ringel, S., & Brandell, J. R. (Eds.). (2011). *Trauma: Contemporary directions in theory, practice, and research.* Sage. https://sk.sagepub.com/books/trauma-contemporary

Sawrikar, P., & Katz, I. (2017). Barriers to disclosing child sexual abuse (CSA) in ethnic minority communities: A review of the literature and implications for practice in Australia. *Children and Youth Services Review, 83*, 302–315. https://doi.org/10.1016/j.childyouth.2017.11.011

Shapiro, S. L., Carlson, L. E., Astin, J. A., & Freedman, B. (2006). Mechanisms of mindfulness. *Journal of Clinical Psychology, 62*, 373–386. https://doi.org/10.1002/jclp.20237

Stoltenborgh, M., Van Ijzendoorn, M. H., Euser, E. M., & Bakermans-Kranenburg, M. J. (2011). A global perspective on child sexual abuse: Meta-analysis of prevalence around the world. *Child Maltreatment, 16*(2), 79–101. https://doi.org/10.1177/107755951140392

Tinnin, L., & Gantt, L. (2013). *The instinctual trauma response and dual-brain dynamics: A guide for trauma therapy.* Gargoyle Press. https://www.wob.com/en-us/books/linda-gantt-ph-d/the-instinctual-trauma-response-and-dual-brain-dynamics-a-guide-for-trauma-thera/9780985016227

Treadwell, T., & Abeditehrani, H. (2025). Integrating cognitive behavioral therapy with psychodrama theory and practice: A blended group model for trauma. In L. M. Leiderman & B. J. Buchele (Eds.), *Advances in group therapy trauma treatment* (1st ed.) (pp. 85–100). Taylor & Francis/Routledge. ISBN 9781032890784 https://www.routledge.com/Advances-in-Group-Therapy-Trauma-Treatment/

Leiderman-Buchele/p/book/9781032890784?srsltid=AfmBOoqw7hRcyUV7m3O5tRlxA2T4ocWg0
g9UaAplLqbTm5Bkiqc9wiVJ

Tyson, A. A., & Goodman, M. (1996). Group therapy for adult women who experienced childhood
sexual trauma: Is telling the story enough? *International Journal of Group Psychotherapy, 46,*
535–542. https://doi.org/10.1080/00207284.1996.11491509

Van der Kolk, B. A. (2015). *The body keeps the score: Brain, mind, and body in the healing of
trauma.* Penguin Publishing Group. https://www.penguinrandomhouse.com/books/313183/
the-body-keeps-the-score-by-bessel-van-der-kolk-md/

World Health Organization. (2013). *Global and regional estimates of violence against women: Prevalence and health effects of intimate partner violence and non-partner sexual violence.* Author. https://
www.who.int/publications/i/item/9789241564625

World Health Organization. (2021). *Violence against women.* https://www.who.int/news-room/
fact-sheets/detail/violence-against-women

Wyles, P., O'Leary, P., & Tsantefski, M. (2023). Bearing witness as a process for responding to trauma
survivors: A review. *Trauma, Violence, & Abuse, 24*(5), 3078–3093. https://doi.org/10.1177/
15248380221124262

Yalom, I. D., & Leszcz, M. (2020). *The theory and practice of group psychotherapy.* Basic Books.
https://www.hachettebookgroup.com/titles/irvin-d-yalom/the-theory-and-practice-of-group-
psychotherapy/9781541617568/?lens=basic-books

Yamawaki, N., Spackman, M. P., & Parrott, W. G. (2015). A cross-cultural comparison of American and
Japanese experiences of personal and vicarious shame. *Journal of Cognition and Culture, 15*(1–2),
64–86. https://doi.org/10.1163/15685373-12342141

Zerubavel, N., & Messman-Moore, T. L. (2015). Staying present: Incorporating mindfulness into therapy for dissociation. *Mindfulness, 6,* 303–314. https://link.springer.com/article/10.1007/s12671-
013-0261-3

11 Discussion

Why Group in the Treatment of Trauma

Leonardo M. Leiderman and Bonnie J. Buchele

The body of knowledge regarding the treatment of trauma in groups has undergone tremendous growth since the publication of *Group Interventions for Treatment of Psychological Trauma* (Buchele & Spitz, 2005). In this updated volume, the authors review many of the subsequent advancements. However, despite the wide dissemination of the new knowledge as well as the prevalence of posttraumatic stress disorder (PTSD) and complex PTSD (CPTSD) (Cloitre et al., 2020), group therapists often continue to overlook the impact of dissociation, PTSD, and CPTSD on their patients and within themselves, for several reasons. Group members may contribute to difficulties recognizing or conceptualizing unresolved trauma because they have little or no verbal recall of traumatic events. These experiences can be encoded nonverbally or are preverbal, meaning, that they are disconnected from the accompanying emotions, are never shared in words, and can be missed during initial psychiatric assessments/consultations. The result is a minimization of the impact of a traumatic event, multiple traumatic occurrences, or premorbid vulnerability so that the relevance of PTSD and CPTSD in psychological treatment is undetected or underestimated.

Trauma, by its very nature, is complex. As Grossmark (2025) eloquently points out in this volume, *trauma's signature is what is not known and not experienced*. These complexities involved in treating group members with unresolved trauma, especially CPTSD, cannot be overstated. We now know that the treatment is complicated by the multiple aspects of the *neuro-emotional-physiological* impact on trauma survivors. Leiderman (this volume, 2025) describes the brain–body disconnection that contributes to chronic problems with neurophysiological arousal modulation, affect regulation, somatosensory processing, intersubjective relating, and higher-order capacities. Lifelong problems with multisensory and emotional integration leading to difficulties in daily functioning, coping, and relating (all of which result from trauma's assault on the senses, as reported by Kearney and Lanius, 2022) are often not conceptualized as related to trauma because the actual traumatic events are first revealed via enactments.

Trauma is also associated with the loss of the psychological sense of self, coupled with a disembodied sense of self (Bluhm et al., 2009; Foa et al., 1999; Lanius et al., 2011, 2020). Group members with CPTSD report feeling ungrounded, broken, unsafe in the body, and an absence of bodily control. Emotionally, they may not know who they are, what they feel, and how to express their wants and needs to others. We have learned that overwhelming, unconscious, brain-based fear (Leiderman, 2025) leads to an unmoored psychological and physiological sense of self, persistent trauma symptoms, and entrenched avoidant behaviors. All these factors may contribute to the difficulties clinicians encounter in providing effective psychiatric treatment for this population. The difficulties are so noteworthy that, in fact, approximately 40% of patients with PTSD fail to respond to psychotherapy and

DOI: 10.4324/9781003546252-17

pharmacotherapy (Krystal et al., 2017; Shaw et al., 2023). Authors believe that these treatment failures are lacking in intensity and the addition of group therapy, so that progress is compromised. In fact, the great majority of psychotherapies provided in private practice are overwhelmingly individual versus group psychotherapy (Whittingham et al., 2023).

Group therapy, in several forms, is an effective modality for the treatment of unresolved PTSD and CPTSD (Schwartze et al., 2019; Sloan et al., 2013). Cognitive behavioral group therapy is considered a first line of treatment for traumatized individuals (Malejko et al., 2017; Yang et al., 2018) having acute and/or transient PTSD symptomatology, such as panic symptoms and cognitive distortions, contributing to fearful, avoidant behaviors. However, the characterological changes emanating from trauma are ideally addressed in long-term psychodynamically oriented trauma groups. Treatment goals include fostering *neuro-emotional-physiological* regulation; the restoration of sense of self; advancing intersubjective relating, including improved abilities to empathize; improving emotional resilience and coping; working through traumatic loss and grief; and managing self-hating tendencies with self-compassion. Interestingly, due to the difficulties, complexities, and poor efficacy of briefer treatments with foci limited to specific symptoms (lower than 50% in PTSD CBT group treatment models), contemporary research emphasizes that the appropriate group therapy treatment of trauma incorporates CBT models with other integrative group models (Yalch et al., 2022). One chapter in this volume describes an integrative short-term CBT and psychodrama group model to treat trauma (Treadwell & Abeditehrani, 2025). This final chapter addresses five core areas: (1) the question of why utilize group psychotherapy in the treatment of trauma; (2) contemporary trauma group models; (3) suggestions for group therapists working with the complexities in facilitating trauma groups; (4) self-care strategies for trauma group therapists; and (5) foci for future research and application.

The Question of Why Group Psychotherapy in the Treatment of Trauma

Groups are uniquely suited to trauma treatment because trauma originates in the context of social systems, such as the family, workplace, societies, and ethnic and cultural populations, whether man-made or happening naturally, and recovery occurs in system contexts as well. We know that an adequate social support network facilitates healing. The group is a system and can provide a mini society that counteracts larger societal biases which worsen the impact of many types of traumata (Canales, 2025; Schermer, 2025; Watkins-Northern & Nettles, 2025; Weinberg, 2025). The mass trauma and sociopolitical issues that are affecting group members on global or national scales will be transported into, mirrored, and in certain instances, repeated in small psychotherapy groups. Hopefully, these groups will systemically reawaken familial and sociopolitical trauma dynamics while providing an alternative, safe context to process, understand, contain, and validate the emotional impact and harm.

Trauma often happens in isolation. One of the core therapeutic benefits of group treatment is that the member's trauma now can be witnessed and compassionately addressed in multiple fields. The group member no longer has to bear the burden alone and in isolation.

As Yalom and Leszcz (2020) have conveyed, group therapy is a *triple E treatment*, meaning, that it is **e**ffective when compared to nonactive treatments; **e**quivalent to other active treatments, like individual therapy; and **e**fficient in terms of time and cost. However, compared to other psychotherapeutic treatment modalities, according to Burlingame (Leiderman, 2024), groups are comparatively an underutilized, underrecognized, and underappreciated treatment; this is noteworthy, considering the research strongly emphasizes how group is as effective when compared to other psychotherapeutic approaches, such as individual psychotherapy (Burlingame & Strauss, 2021). The results from two studies, the first a meta-analysis with results over the last 30 years from Rosendahl et al. (2021), and the second a meta-analysis examining 20 randomized controlled trials of 2,244 individuals by Schwartze et al. (2019), reveal that small group psychotherapy is effective when compared to nonactive treatment and is equivalent to other treatment approaches and that group treatments are associated with improvements in symptoms of PTSD. (Reader should note that in terms of the efficacy in treating trauma, the great majority of this meta-analytic research was conducted on short-term CBT groups [few psychodynamic groups] for PTSD; no research is reported on the efficacy of group treatment with those who have a CPTSD diagnosis.)

How Do Trauma Groups Work in Treating PTSD and CPTSD, and What Are We Treating?

Inoculation Constructs and the Fostering of Resilience in Trauma Psychotherapy Groups

Another indication that groups are an optimal setting for treatment of trauma concerns inoculation and resilience. Some trauma group models incorporate elements such as immediacy, inoculation theory, and emotional communication. Group psychotherapy has a long tradition of addressing unresolved trauma-based fearful patterns with immunization (Ormont, 1989) and insulation (Ormont, 1994) via measured and prolonged exposure therapy (Rauch et al., 2012). The guiding principle is that with repeated, titrated exposure, or going toward the feelings or situation that are most feared, the individual will ultimately acquire more adaptive skills, defenses, resilience, and ways of coping. It can be easily argued that *it is not the feelings* that ultimately harm trauma survivors but the *avoidance of the feeling(s)*, which ultimately harms. Groups provide unique opportunities to safely contain the fears of member(s) or the group-as-a-whole. In accordance with these concepts, group members are exposed to the very same fearful feelings, dynamics, and behaviors within the group that they have habitually avoided outside the group via immediacy (Yalom, 1985).

Ormont (1989) also emphasized the group leader's role in facilitating a group norm that emphasized three core emotional foci: what group members are *feeling in the moment* (to enhance a sense of self), verbalizing what *others are feeling* (to advance empathy capabilities), and verbalizing what one is *feeling toward others* (to foster intimacy and trust with others). Ormont's constructs address the preoedipal features (primitive personality characteristics before the development of language) in traumatized group members while optimally establishing a group norm of emotional communication during the group process. These constructs are also relevant in trauma groups because these capacities are often lacking or impaired.

Mucci (2022) proposes that embodied witnessing is crucial to recovery and developing resilience. Embodied witnessing, which is dialoguing about trauma in the presence of an attuned, trusted other (communication implicitly via right-brain-to-right-brain relating), facilitates repair, which then, in turn, paves the way for mourning. Although her model is conceptualized in the context of the dyad, it is reasonable to postulate that a group can provide an even more effective container for embodied witnessing. The group involves complex, multifaceted relating as a central component, incorporating the opportunity of witnessing and validation afforded by multiple others in the room in tune with multiple aspects of the experience so that multiple self-experiences for mirroring are simultaneously available, thus increasing healing possibilities of integration. Embodied witnessing involves the other group members in holding and containing the traumatized experience.

Dissociative Enactments

Groups are particularly suited to the emergence of dissociative enactments so characteristic of trauma treatment. In this volume, three chapters focus on the central importance of ther-apeutically addressing dissociative enactments, defined as unformulated, unsymbolized, regressed, preverbal experiences that are expressed in trauma groups (Grossmark, 2025; Leiderman, 2025; Schermer, 2025). Schermer (2025) defines the construct of the *dissociative matrix* to be the mutual containment of dissociative reactions in trauma groups by the group members:

> Over time, the members projectively identify the dissociated images, memories, and repetition enactments into other members, the therapist, and the group-as-a-whole. The recipients become "containers" of the projective identifications, and eventually can be helped to "return" them in an empathic way which facilitates re-integration of the self.
>
> (p. 74)

Dissociative enactments involving both group members and leaders are unconscious (origi-nating in the right hemisphere) and occur along spectrums of intensity that can include overreactive and underactive traumatic features. These authors propose that since trauma often manifests in psychotherapy groups via dissociation, examination, and resolution, of enactments is one of the most potent change agents for promoting growth.

The importance of the group-as-a-whole as a container, which includes therapeutic space, is crucial because enactments can be investigated by collectively accomplishing the follow-ing: (1) translating member(s) traumatic experiences, which are encoded preverbally into words with symbolic meaning; (2) bearing witness and offering validation; (3) detoxifying, holding, and containing internalized, fragmented, traumatic representations simultaneously; (4) restoring dissociated connections, coupling synchrony with others (i.e., being emotion-ally seen while emotionally seeing others), which in turn increases the group-as-a-whole cohesiveness; (5) re-establishing emotional equilibrium and co-regulation among and between group members; (6) co-creating alternative, meaningful, symbolic understandings of enactments; (7) helping members learn more adaptive ways of responding and coping; and (8) restoring hope and trust in others.

Psychological Wellness

Psychological wellness can be maximized via the integration of differing treatment models. Integrative models can be conceptualized in two distinct ways; a specific model may incor-porate several theories and/or strategies that address traumatic symptomatology simultane-ously, but the treatment of trauma can also be integrated by thinking about it sequentially, that is, emphasizing treatment of acute symptoms in the immediate aftermath of the trauma and subsequently addressing the characterological manifestations as sufficient distance from the actual event has occurred (Yalch et al., 2022). Sequential integration occurs when acute symptoms are first addressed via structured approaches, such as CBT, followed by long-term group therapy focused on characterological manifestations.

Acute Symptoms

Short-term trauma groups utilizing CBT, DBT, mindfulness, psychoeducation, and bodily focused interventions can be the first line of intervention, as meaningfully explained in this volume by Treadwell and Abeditehrani (2025). This approach can be useful in addressing acute and disparate emotional and physiological trauma symptoms, cognitive distortions, and fearful/avoidant behaviors, by teaching conscious techniques to reduce acute trauma symptoms, thereby improving levels of coping (Ruzek et al., 2023).

Long-Term Symptoms

The characterological aspect of trauma's impact can be viewed as helping to restore a psychological sense of self and embodied self as well as increasing self-compassion to neutralize self-hatred with the use of psychodynamic trauma group models. (Please note authors define *psychological sense of self* as having continuity and coherence over time and space, a basic sense of integrity and consolidation of various identities that are synthesized into a familiar sense of oneself. An *embodied sense of self* is the coherence between the psyche and the soma – an ability over time and space to identify what one physiologically feels in one's body. In the case of trauma, there is often a disconnection between one's body sense of self and the psychological sense of self, resulting in a state of being *disembodied*).

Long-term psychodynamic trauma psychotherapy groups may be more appropriate for those with long-term trauma symptoms because the chronicity and severity of psychopathology impact characterological functioning and interpersonal relations. For instance, a core area of psychological wellness that psychodynamic trauma groups can effectively address is the restoration of the psychological sense of self, as well as the disembodied self. Those who are subjected to familial trauma, characterized by neglect and abuse, growing up often survive without developing a formulated and integrated sense of self (Ulman & Brothers, 1988). As Klein emphasized, "[t]he most devastating impact of psychological trauma is on the sense of self and self-coherence, evidenced by fragmenting, destabilizing, and self-injurious behaviors. The overall goals of trauma treatment are the restoration of sense of self and self-coherence" (Leiderman, 2023, p. 21).

The restoration process can be complicated by unforeseen and frequent unconscious *rebound effect* patterns in treatment; these are triggered when group members suddenly regress into experiencing an unmoored sense of self as they are provided constructive criticism and praise and/or when they assert themselves in expressing their feelings, especially negative ones. This can happen instantly, without observable provocation, leading to withdrawal into a preverbal, disconnected state consumed with guilt, doubt, heightened ambivalence, self-deprecation, sadness, and the feeling of being physiologically ungrounded; the experience is complicated by its lack of words and emotional tools that ordinarily could be used to describe what is being endured.

The restoration of the sense of self in group members is a long-term goal. The group leader can be instrumental in this process by facilitating the maintenance of a safe container for the group process and establishing group norms that promote a number of factors: (1) attaching words, feelings, and symbolic meaning to unmetabolized current and past traumata stored in the body and unconscious; (2) encouraging emotional vulnerability in the expression of painful feelings (i.e., shame, grief, hurt, humiliation, etc.) and the disconnected, unintegrated feelings of emptiness (commonly experienced as a void), loneliness, dystonic neediness of unconditional love associated with trauma and neglect; (3) supporting the expression of negative feelings (i.e., disapproval, anger, rage, hatred, etc.) without retaliation, repercussions, or abandonment (especially by group leader); (4) exploring the identification with the aggressor (Mucci, 2022), an aspect of long-term psychodynamic treatment and integration of that particular self-experience into each member's identity; (5) co-creating opportunities for the intersubjective expression of feelings, perceptions, and constructive criticisms involving members' experiences of each other and the group leader in the moment; and (6) fostering an atmosphere in which emotional mis-attunements, conflicts, disappointments, regressions, mistakes, differences, diversity, and enactments can be contained, understood compassionately, and repaired.

The trauma group leader plays a critical role in promoting the development of a coherent sense of self in members. We now know that disorganized and insecure styles of attachment lay a foundation for vulnerability to subsequent trauma. Recovery is promoted within the context of a secure attachment (Marmarosh et al., 2025). Therefore, one task of the leader is to establish earned, secure attachments with group members. By being a trusted, protective, reliable, measured, compassionate, accepting, non-judgmental, authentic, consistent, and safe figure, the leader enhances the restoration of sense of self in members. Important to note here is that persons suffering from attachment trauma were often raised by parents with narcissistic traits (Shaw, 2021). These parents are likely transmitting their own unresolved trauma to their children. Traumatized and traumatizing parents can refuse to assume responsibility (thereby escaping culpability); rationalize their maltreatment/abuse of others without remorse, empathy, or apology as justified; and demand unconditional loyalty by resorting to threats or abandonment if they perceive others to be disloyal to them. Additionally, the repeated use of fearmongering (which activates the amygdala) can frighten, paralyze, foster dependence, and undermine independent thinking or taking action in the children; this lies at the core of the loss of a coherent sense of self. Group leaders are thereby encouraged to be aware of and accountable for their own dissociative regressions, mistakes, personality imperfections, misunderstandings, and mis-attunements. In addition, group leaders can foster a group process in which members assert their emotional wants and needs so that they confront others, especially the group leader, when they are feeling disappointed. (For more on the roles and responsibilities of the experience-near trauma group leader, refer to Leiderman & Klein, 2021.)

At times group leaders and members focus primarily on the abusive and negative aspects of parents. We encourage group leaders to heighten their awareness of the likelihood that traumatizing parents were frequently traumatized themselves. The eventual integration of the loving and hating aspects of one's parents not only aids in the acceptance and the working through of one's familial trauma and acceptance of their parent's negative and positive parenting qualities but also fosters integration of the sense of self.

Conquering Self-Hating Tendencies With Compassion for the Self

One of the more challenging aspects in facilitating trauma groups for survivors of trauma is softening self-hating tendencies (often found in those with CPTSD) by growing the capacity for self-compassion. As outlined in the introduction chapter of this volume, "[t]he neglect, symbolized by a lack of parental love, protection, and compassion, can reinforce the individual's self-hate and self-destructive behaviors accompanied by self-hating constructs" (Leiderman et al., 2025, p.36).

Long-term psychodynamic groups can address these issues using a multifaced approach. This includes creating the therapeutic space for members to emotionally elaborate on both self-hating and self-destructive tendencies as often as needed; this is crucial since the self-denigration is a result of traumatic neglect that arises in isolation (without the needed for emotional support of others). Self-compassion is fostered when members can repeatedly reveal their most dreadful and appalling features (or witness others doing the same) in the group and still be liked, accepted, supported, and understood.

Psychodynamic theory also suggests that unresolved feelings of shame, guilt, and self-hatred in many trauma survivors are related to the parental denial of the abuse, the parent(s)' own entitlement, and the role played by their projections in the traumatization (Fairbairn, 1952). These split-off projections are internalized and can lead to unformulated identifications that include a felt sense of badness or being damaged and/or broken. Psycho-dynamic trauma group leaders must contain the negative and at times hateful, cruel, sadistic feelings that are verbally externalized onto them as these negative identifications are worked through and abandoned.

In this volume, Hu and Kyei (2025) address a pattern employed by sexually abusive fathers wherein they, in effect, groom the child by favoring them. This development can lead to feelings of expansiveness coupled with self-hatred in survivors. Integration of grandiose, omnipotent feelings and experiences after being favored or given a special status (which can be a form of neglect) with anger in a self-compassionate manner is also a goal in some trauma treatments.

Incorporation of Contemporary Findings

There have been advances in neuroscience, diagnosis, group modalities, and the application of those modalities to understanding and treating traumatized individuals with PTSD, CPTSD, and sexual abuse since the publication of the American Group Psychotherapy Association's first edition of *Group Interventions for Treatment of Psychological Trauma*, in the aftermath of the 9/11 terror attacks (Buchele & Spitz, 2005). Since that edition, there has also been significant progress in understanding the relationship between trauma and systemic racism, microaggressions, macroaggressions, and other forms of societal hate and bigotry. This section addresses these issues and discusses the implications for contemporary topics and clinical approaches within the trauma group field.

Neurophysiological Advances

Models based on neuroscience, such as the integrated, interpersonal/relational, neuro-physiological approach in this volume, can be useful in affording more understanding and evidence-based support for group therapy techniques that foster co-regulation, coupling synchrony, and intersubjective relating when addressing fear-based trauma symptoms, especially during dissociative enactments (Leiderman, 2025).

Fear can be the dominant force behind the *neuro-emotional-physiological* symptoms, perceptions, behaviors, and ways of relating that are activated within trauma group members. Fear is also the cause of the discomfort members have experiencing positive feelings like praise and affection. Group leaders would do well to formulate interventions that include bypassing members' cortically impacted FEAR network (described in Chapter 2) because it can unconsciously reject positive feelings related to unconscious, brain-based fears of rejection, hurt, withdrawal, and anticipated loss of positive feelings. Exposure to small doses, that is, titration, of care, support, affection, protection, and love, by other group members is likely to be more tolerable (emotionally digestible) than overbearing, as can be the case in interactions outside the group or within a dyad.

Therapeutic effectiveness is enhanced as the group therapist's understanding of the impact of PTSD and CPTSD on cortical–subcortical networks and structures, as well as the complementary functions of the conscious left and unconscious right hemispheres, is incorporated into the work by doing the following: (1) tracking and minimizing the intellectualized, rational, detail- and defensive-oriented properties of the left hemisphere, as members may unintentionally avoid emotionally uncomfortable situations and/or topics that increase feelings of vulnerability; (2) utilizing advances in interpersonal neuroscience that emphasize the intersubjective "relational unconscious" by attending to indications of it, thereby affecting regulating properties of the right hemisphere among and between group members and leader to safely process unconscious, regressed, disconnected, dissociated traumatic, emotionally painful feelings; (3) restoring a sense of safety and intersubjective connection for group member(s) in order for hyper- and hypoaroused fear-driven trauma responses as well as the fragmented and the disembodied sense of self to emerge within the group; and (4) conceptualizing interventions that enhance right hemisphere, Temporo-Parietal-Occipital (rTPO) coupling synchrony among and between group members and leader, thereby fostering co-regulation, empathy, and emotional connection with others following *neuro-emotional-physiological* regressive dissociative enactments. Such interventions also involve the incorporation of nonverbal, attuned, and compassionate facial expressions and the utilization of the therapist's body, especially posture.

Attachment Models

Two chapters in this volume, Marmarosh et al. (2025) and Canales (2025), highlight the association between trauma and attachment. These authors elaborate on the long-term impact of trauma when growing up within the context of attachments having disorganized, insecure, chaotic, and neglectful features; in fact, we now know that these attachment disturbances can be precursors to a more severe impact from the trauma. The authors also explicate meaningful therapeutic interventions designed to improve attachment, security, and safety with group members.

Expanding on their theoretical approaches, we also suggest that group leaders incorporate two correlated constructs when addressing disorganized attachment: lack of intersubjective relatedness (limited capacities to demonstrate empathy and compassion for others) and lack of object permanence (failure to internalize others who are safe, secure, available, and loving).

It is important to emphasize (especially for early career group therapists) that trauma groups are not exclusively focused on a member's unresolved trauma and the symbolic resolution of dissociative enactments. Members often have underdeveloped attachment styles and interpersonal skills, thereby highlighting the need for the intersubjective group-as-a-whole process and interpersonal learning (Yalom & Leszcz, 2020). Trauma group members can have insufficient exposure to and experience calmly talking through differences, repairing ruptures, moments of intimacy, playfulness, laughing, and joking, with one another.

In terms of secure attachment, we also believe a long-term goal in trauma group treatment involves the internalization of the members, leader(s), and/or group-as-a-whole so that these internalizations can be accessed outside of therapy sessions, especially during moments of friction and loneliness. In other words, the creation of the capacity for an earned, secure attachment is a goal. Group leaders can maximize the internalization process by supporting deep emotional and loving connections within the group process, discussing alternative ways to increase internalization by members, and exploring resistances to internalization. For example, when group members have established sufficient trust, co-regulation naturally takes place, thus fostering an internalization of the other.

Diversity, Equity, and Inclusion Considerations

This volume offers an important contribution to the understanding of trauma and its relationship to matters concerning diversity, equality, and inclusion (DEI). Synthesizing the work of Canales (2025), Grossmark (2025), Schermer (2025), and Watkins-Northern and Nettles (2025) results in a significant increase in knowledge regarding the unconscious aspects of societal biases, such as racism, antisemitism, Islamophobia, misogyny, the harm they do in inflicting trauma, the origins of these "isms" as they exist within individuals living in groups, and potential interventions at the unconscious level within the dynamics of the group. For instance, Schermer (2025) suggests that racism can be understood as a "chosen" trauma in the United States à la Volkan, that is, transmitted on the national level from generation to generation unconsciously and emanating out of slavery at the country's origins. Gutmann and Toral might characterize this as a "founding trauma" of the United States, that is, a trauma early in the country's history that continues to be replayed in subsequent national groups and settings due to insufficient resolution of the conflicts that led to the US Civil War (Gutmann & Toral, 2018). As such, it manifests via enactments in the group setting, a concept at the core of Grossmark's (2025) conceptualization of the primary healing factor of group psychotherapy. Canales (2025) details how the traumatic experience associated with being a member of a minority, especially one with a darker skin color, is transmitted through generations via attachments with the neurological responses attendant to activation of fear responses, especially at unconscious and physiological levels.

Furthermore, these biases and hatreds are particularly suited to inclusion in treatment within the group setting because they originate and are enacted in groups; therefore, they flow into the content of the group interactions and can be addressed in ways that simply are not possible in individual treatment settings.

Group therapists would do well to notice, acknowledge, and address the potentially pernicious effects of power differentials that result from identity/cultural differences between group members and leader, leading to distress and harmful expressions of aggression. Effectively incorporating DEI concepts into the clinical practice of psychotherapy groups must be informed by an understanding of the origins and impact of bias as well as microaggressions and macroaggressions toward those having diverse cultural, racial, and ethnic backgrounds; varied identities; sexual orientations; housing and economic status; and ages (Watkins-Northern & Nettles, 2025) at both conscious and unconscious levels.

Group leaders can also consider issues of social justice, social inequalities, privilege, inclusion, and marginalization as they show up in the complexity of the group relationships. Appropriate utilization of these concepts can empower the group to examine ways of responding to one another based on frameworks sensitive to diversity and cultural differences that may, in turn, prevent harm while enhancing inclusion.

It is the leader's task to be sensitive to and responsible for repair of ruptures during this process and to monitor and preserve the safety and positive experience of all group attendees. Miles et al. (2021) propose the leader utilize their multicultural orientation (MCO) and cultural humility (i.e., a willingness and comfort in discussing culture) when addressing ruptures caused by microaggressions. In addition, the racial, cultural identity and privileged status of leaders who do not identify as Black, Hispanic, Brown, Indigenous, or any other marginalized group can also be examined in terms of the impact on safety and trust.

Using the Large Group for Healing Social Trauma

Related to the diversity, equity, and inclusion foci discussed earlier, Weinberg (2025) describes large-scale *social trauma* which occurs in the context of entire societies and populations when they are overwhelmed by worldwide sociopolitical events or disasters, natural or man-made. Today, large numbers of people are experiencing overwhelming stress vicariously by witnessing world events perceived as dangerous, uncontrollable, and unpredictable. As Weinberg emphasizes, "[t]he most effective therapeutic tool to address sociocultural trauma-based issues is the Large Group (LG)" (Weinberg & Schneider, 2003). LG focuses on sociotherapy more than psychotherapy, and social issues are spontaneously brought to discussion in this modality. This is the forum to resolve social traumas (Weinberg, 2025, pp. 302–303).

Incorporating a systems perspective (Agazarian, 2004; Hopper & Weinberg, 2017; Nitzgen & Hopper, 2017; Volkan, 2016) enables group leaders to understand how LGs constitute social microcosms that mirror societal mass trauma. The LG conveners (leaders) aim to create a safe, large container for exploring sociopolitical stressors and projections, ingrained stereotypes, and unresolved social traumas related to marginalization, discrimination, oppression, prejudice, and racism. The LG is a forum wherein binary ways of thinking and relating can be expressed and processed so that participants adopt a more nuanced perspective, thus affording an opportunity for stress reduction.

Sexual Abuse

Hu and Kyei (2025) are yet another set of authors advocating the use of an integrated approach for the treatment of trauma, in this case for survivors of sexual abuse. They tell us that, generally, people who undergo sexual abuse, especially within the family of origin, have symptomatology that is more severe than that resulting from other types of traumata. Because these individuals must adapt to their environments as children, the attendant compromises in conscious and unconscious functioning are woven into the character at considerable cost to the survivor. It may be that the experiential component of the group treatment provides a maximally favorable setting for addressing these longstanding and expensive functional compromises. The importance of addressing this characterological component in the total treatment plan for persons in this population is related to several factors: When sexual abuse occurs within the context of the family, the presence of insecure or disorganized attachment is inevitable, and a precursor to the trauma, because the comforter and the abuser can, at worst, be the same person or, at least, come from within the same system, subject to the same family dynamics that contribute to the abuse. Also, in the case of sexual abuse, the body is the site of the abuse, which may have implications regarding the dysregulation that accompanies trauma. Mindfulness promotes body awareness and may uniquely foster improved regulatory functioning, while psychodrama, which involves actual use of the body, may be more effective as well (Hu & Kyei, 2025). The authors also note that the cultural context of sexual victimization is very important, especially when survivors come from more authoritarian, male-dominated societies with traditional sex roles. These cultures tend to blame the victim and, in some cases, shame the victims' families. This has special implications for treatment for at least two reasons: (1) The culture/family will be less available to provide embodied witnessing for survivors, so the group's importance in this regard is heightened, and (2) the survivor is likely to need and/or want to return to the culture of origin, adding a particular wrinkle to recovery.

Complexities in Facilitating Trauma Groups

Group members with trauma histories can be challenging to treat. Trauma-associated painful feelings are often preoedipal, preverbal, unsymbolized, and dissociated, so that accessing and understanding them can be difficult for members. In addition, traumatic memories are, by definition, suppressed, unconscious, fragmented, and disconnected from conscious-ness, totally or partially. Members frequently utilize entrenched primitive defenses, such as splitting, projection, and denial. As they identify with the aggressor, they can take on charac-teristics of their traumatizer, such as limited intersubjective relating, feelings of entitlement, projection of blame, binary thinking and ways of relating, and engagement in bullying while experiencing themselves as victimized.

In long-term psychodynamically oriented trauma groups, group treatment can be especially difficult to navigate, even for seasoned group therapists. The group process can activate powerful dissociative enactments in group members and leaders, as well as regressive and primitive ways of relating that mirror the chaotic trauma a member experienced in the family of origin. Psychodynamic groups can be highly interpersonal and interactive because they parallel early familial dynamics, thereby periodically becoming a dysregulating and stimulating a process wherein the group leader and/or another member may be perceived as the traumatizer. The enactment of these dissociative phenomena can be overwhelming and disrupt the group process. One example of such enactments is an episode of encapsulated dissociative raging. This situation, often characterized by hair-trigger, intense responses, is challenging for the group-as-a-whole and leader to contain, deconstruct, detoxify, and metabolize so that meaning can be made collectively. When the former occurs, it is often related to a group member perceiving themselves as being shamed, humiliated, victimized, misunderstood, blamed or neglected by others in the group or the group leader.

The facilitation of psychodynamic trauma groups can elicit, within the practitioner, nega-tive countertransference and secondary/vicarious trauma that includes dissociative experi-ences as well as regressions, burnout, compassion fatigue, and depressive symptoms. As Herman recommended, "[t]herapists who work with traumatized people require an ongo-ing support system to deal with these intense reactions" (Herman, 1997/2015, p. 141). The following section provides suggestions for personal and professional care that help sustain effective leadership for trauma group therapists.

Self-Care for Therapists Facilitating Trauma Groups

Group therapists working with trauma survivors can be considered first responders since they are treating the traumata of their group members. Consequently, leaders are prone, over time, to having vicarious trauma reactions (Herman, 1997/2015). Additionally, as Schermer emphasizes,

> Group therapists are not detached observers; they are vulnerable and sometimes trau-matized human beings assigned a specific role as leaders. They have their own training, responsibilities, and boundary conditions, but like the group members, they have their own trauma, vulnerabilities, and defenses which must be addressed.
>
> (Schermer, 2025, p. 70)

Self-care strategies are essential to reduce burnout, fatigue, and co-morbid symptoms. It is useful to consider following the ABCs of self-care outlined by Saakvitne et al. (1996): (A) **a**wareness, by being attuned to one's emotional needs, limits, emotions, and resources; (B) **b**alance among all activities, especially work, play, and rest, which also includes culti-vating psychological resilience; and (C) **c**onnections to oneself, to others, and to something larger. Other self-care strategies include supervision, psychotherapy, peer group support, enhanced intimacy with emotionally rewarding relationships while avoiding toxic rela-tions, and practical strategies such as daily exercise, meditation, healthy eating and sleeping habits, and inclusion of liberal dose of fun, laughter, and humor (Irving, 2019) in the therapist's life. (The reader can refer to further suggestions made by Stockton et al. (2014) for beginning group therapists).

Setting and maintaining boundaries with group members is also an essential part of self-care. Establishing boundaries begins with conducting careful diagnostic evaluations as the leader considers adding a member to a trauma group; it is especially important that a potential member who might be harmful or destructive to the practitioner or the group process be ruled out beforehand (refer to the section on ethics in the introduction chapter). It may take several sessions to complete thorough assessment of the trauma, neglect, and neurophysiological symptoms, such as dissociation and raging. When new members are being considered for more developmentally mature trauma groups, a group leader can disclose an overview of their trauma group practice with information such as how the group might help the candidate, how the group contract safeguards the members, how that member might handle anticipated constructive feedback, and the intense nature of the intersubjective relating and process. It is not uncommon for members of a trauma group to challenge the parameters of one's group practice or the parameters of the group contract. They may demand special treatment, thus highlighting the need for the leader to maintain ongoing boundaries.

Co-leadership can be helpful when facilitating trauma groups (Mendelsohn et al., 2011; Wise & Nash, 2019). A variety of advantages has been associated with group co-leadership (Luke & Hackney, 2007). Benefits include supporting one another, not working in isolation, and utilizing the inherent opportunity for consultation in the presence of negative and positive countertransference or dissociative enactments. It must be noted, however, that nurturance of the relationship between the two leaders is essential, requiring additional time and effort. Inevitable differences, competition, disagreements, and conflicts necessitate processing both within and outside of the group.

Individual Supervision and/or Individual Therapy

Personal therapy or supervision for the leader that includes exploring and understanding one's personal trauma-driven dynamics is strongly recommended as part of ongoing self-care. Supervision and therapy can be useful in processing the negative feelings group members have toward the leader, including hate, the therapist's negative countertransference, discerning how to repair ruptures, and processing, understanding, and clinically addressing the therapist's regressions and dissociative experiences.

Supervision can be helpful when leaders receive or witness projective identifications that include feelings of shame, anger, guilt, sadness, grief, hopelessness/impotence, and splitting; these primitive defenses can arise prior to anger being addressed directly by member(s) or by the group-as-a-whole. Similarly, supervision can be useful in working through idealizing defenses and eventual devaluation, hatred, and sadistic feelings directed at the group leader. Leaders may be especially vulnerable to experiencing concordant countertransference stemming from overidentification with similar experiences, including their own unresolved traumata and feelings of traumatic loss and grief.

Participation in a Professional Supervision or Process Group

As mentioned previously, group psychotherapy is systems-oriented treatment. Membership in either a supervision or process group improves the group practitioner's clinical and personal experience by promoting experientially the understanding of the group modality's systems-oriented lens and, to some extent, replicating the experience undergone by group members. The recommended process group can also provide opportunities to witness how the unresolved trauma of others is addressed in a process group (Billow, 2020) and how other group leaders handle similar clinical challenges (Wepman, 2020); the process or supervision group can be a forum for understanding and receiving validation of the leader's negative feelings, especially anger. As Kirman (1995) noted, psychologists and group therapists are least prepared for the anger in their patients and in themselves (Kirman, 1995).

Areas of Focus for Future Research and Application

Where Are We Now With Evidence-Based Trauma Group Research, and Where Do We Need to Focus Our Attention in the Future?

A major development occurred in October 2023 with the launch of the *evidence-based group treatment website* (EBGT website) (Burlingame et al., in press) that includes the training and group research–supported treatment protocols for psychiatric and medical indications. The EBGT website provides resources on (1) how group treatments are effective for disorders commonly treated in clinical practice, such as trauma; (2) the therapeutic relationship links that empirically support how the therapeutic relationship is an evidence-based intervention to improve cohesion, alliance, and group climate measures; and (3) outcome monitoring and measures-based care instruments (empirically tested in randomized clinical trials) that can track member outcome in tandem with other measures that predict group member improvement, such as selection and process measures. The interested reader is encouraged to consult this high-level resource: https://evidencebasedgrouptherapy.org/.

Despite the enormous growth and increased interest in the trauma field, research investigating the efficiency and effectiveness of trauma groups is still in its infancy (Beck et al., 2024). There is a need for more empirical, evidence-based research as well as metaanalyses on short-term, long-term psychodynamic and integrative trauma group models (Burlingame, 2022; Burlingame & Strauss, 2021). According to Burlingame (Leiderman, 2024), non-CBT-focused group therapy research comprises about 20% of all research, and most group research is focused on short-term models (under 20 sessions). More research is needed on long-term psychotherapy groups utilizing models other than CBT.

Research incorporating Measurement-Based Care (MBC) (refer to Chapter 1 and Resnick & Hoff, 2020) could advance the understanding of which self-report trauma symptoms are best addressed in group treatment and which modalities are effective as reported by patient progress scores over time (Resnick & Hoff, 2020).

There is a need to publish non-Eurocentric approaches to trauma, especially by authors who identify as Black, Hispanic, Brown, Indigenous, and/or members of marginalized groups. Because recovery and re-entry into the original culture is central for all traumatized persons, research performed with subjects and trauma therapists from non-Eurocentric cultures is critical to maximize therapeutic benefit. More research is also needed regarding the intersection of sociopolitical stressors; this includes focusing on how to incorporate DEI concepts into the clinical practice of large and small psychotherapy groups utilizing interventions that address unconscious bias, microaggressions, and macroaggressions toward those having diverse cultural, racial, and ethnic backgrounds; varied identities; sexual orientations; housing and economic status; and ages.

The existing research has mainly been completed within the context of in-person settings. But with the increasing use of technology-assisted therapy, research on treatments that include the use of phone or online tools is urgently needed. Specific components that might be measured include witnessing embodiment, dissociative enactments, and the impact of right-hemisphere-to-right-hemisphere communications and interventions when occurring online.

An additional research question is whether the trauma that includes actual physical abuse, that is, beating or rape, impacts the brain development differently than when the trauma is solely emotional.

Lastly, authors could not find research regarding the long-term impact and harm of parental rage and the accompanying sensorial overload, which needs further investigation. We believe, in general, the impact of parental and/or spousal rage has been overlooked in the field, especially since encapsulated rage is a symptom of those who have a trauma history and most likely causes trauma. Raging is overwhelming and overstimulating by definition and leads to dysregulation when occurring by a parent toward a child with frequency. Future attention on this topic might enhance understanding how to more effectively help those with a history of parental raging in trauma group treatment.

Finally, advancing evidence-based group practices that reduce the presence and severity of psychiatric conditions, such as trauma, may be the gateway to bringing the modality of group therapy into the forefront of the mental health field.

References

Agazarian, Y. M. (2004). *Systems-centered therapy for groups*. Karnac Books. Original work published 1997. https://www.karnacbooks.com/product/systems-centered-therapy-for-groups/18440/

Beck, J. G., Free, B. L., Bowen, M. E., Majeed, R., Garrett, A. B., & Lewin, R. K. (2024). Conducting research on group treatments for traumatic stress disorders: Is science chasing practice? In J. I. Ruzek, M. M. Yalch, & K. M. Burkman (Eds.), *Group approaches to treating traumatic stress: A clinical handbook* (pp. 61–73). The Guilford Press. https://www.guilford.com/books/Group-Approaches-to-Treating-Traumatic-Stress/Ruzek-Yalch-Burkman/9781462553297

Billow, R. (2020). Working with group therapists in group. *The Group Circle*.

Bluhm, R. L., Williamson, P. C., Osuch, E. A., Frewen, P. A., Stevens, T. K., Boksman, K., Neufeld, R. W., Théberge, J., & Lanius, R. A. (2009). Alterations in default network connectivity in posttraumatic stress disorder related to early-life trauma. *Journal of Psychiatry Neuroscience, 34*, 187–194. PMCID: PMC2674971.

Buchele, B., & Spitz, H. (Eds.). (2005). *Group interventions for psychological treatment of trauma*. American Group Psychotherapy Association.

Burlingame, G., & Strauss, B. (2021). Efficacy of small group treatments: Foundation for evidence-based practice. In M. Barkham, W. Lutz, & L. G. Castonguay (Eds.), *Bergin and Garfield's handbook of psychotherapy and behavior change: 50th anniversary edition* (pp. 583–624). John Wiley & Sons, Inc. https://www.wiley.com/en-us/Bergin+and+Garfield's+Handbook+of+Psychotherapy+and+Behavior+Change%2C+7th+Edition-p-9781119536581

Burlingame, G. M. (2022). The future of group therapy is bright! *International Journal of Group Psychotherapy*, 1–19. https://doi.org/10.1080/00207284.2022.2133717

Burlingame, G. M., Bernhard, M., Strauss, B. M., & Clayton, D. (In Press). The complexity of becoming an evidence-based group clinician: Introducing an evidence-based group treatment website. *Group Dynamics*.

Canales, C. (2025). Attachment-focused therapy and racial inequalities, who speaks and who listens. In L. M. Leiderman & B. J. Buchele (Eds.), *Advances in group therapy trauma treatment* (1st ed.) (pp. 129–141). Taylor & Francis/Routledge. https://www.routledge.com/Advances-in-Group-Therapy-Trauma-Treatment/Leiderman-Buchele/p/book/9781032890784?srsltid=AfmBOoobDwivSES4RksUdtPC5XoSBQCol87art52OAKapyarNdb_W5lf

Cloitre, M., Brewin, C. R., Bisson, J. I., Hyland, P., Karatzias, T., LuegerSchuster, B., Maercker, A., Roberts, N. P., & Shevlin, M. (2020). Evidence for the coherence and integrity of the complex PTSD (CPTSD) diagnosis: Response to Achterhof et al., (2019) and Ford (2020). *European Journal of Psychotraumatology, 11*(1), 1739873. https://doi.org/10.1080/20008198.2020.1739873

Fairbairn, W. R. D. (1952). *Psychoanalytic studies of the personality*. Routledge & Kegan Paul. ISBN 0-7100-1361-2.

Foa, E. B., Ehlers, A., Clark, D. M., Tolin, D. F., & Orsillo, S. M. (1999). The posttraumatic cognitions inventory (PTCI): Development and validation. *Psychological Assessment, 11*, 303–314. https://doi.org/10.1037/1040-3590.11.3.303

Grossmark, R. (2025). Trauma and enactments in group psychotherapy. In L. M. Leiderman & B. J. Buchele (Eds.), *Advances in group therapy trauma treatment* (1st ed.) (pp. 103–116). Taylor & Francis/Routledge. ISBN 9781032890784 https://www.routledge.com/Advances-in-Group-Therapy-Trauma-Treatment/Leiderman-Buchele/p/book/9781032890784?srsltid=AfmBOoobDwivSES4RksUdtPC5XoSBQCol87art52OAKapyarNdb_W5lf

Gutmann, D., & Toral, S. (2018). Psychoanalytic organizational consulting: The role of the founding trauma. *Psychoanalytic Inquiry, 38*(4), 312–327. https://www.tandfonline.com/toc/hpsi20/38/4

Herman, J. L. (1997/2015). *Trauma and recovery: The aftermath of violence – From domestic abuse to political terror*. Basic Books. https://www.hachettebookgroup.com/titles/judith-lewis-herman-md/trauma-and-recovery/9780465098736/?lens=basic-books

Hopper, E., & Weinberg, H. (Eds.). (2017). *The social unconscious in persons, groups, and societies*. Routledge. https://www.routledge.com/The-Social-Unconscious-in-Persons-Groups-and-Societies-Mainly-Theory/Hopper-Weinberg/p/book/9781855757684

Hu, B., & Kyei, J. J. (2025). An integrative experiential group therapy approach to treat the trauma of sexual abuse. In L. M. Leiderman & B. J. Buchele (Eds.), *Advances in group therapy trauma treatment* (1st ed.) (pp. 158–169). Taylor & Francis/Routledge. ISBN 9781032890784 https://www.routledge.com/Advances-in-Group-Therapy-Trauma-Treatment/Leiderman-Buchele/p/book/9781032890784?srsltid=AfmBOoobDwivSES4RksUdtPC5XoSBQCol87art52OAKapyarNdb_W5lf

Irving, K. (2019). The role of humor in priming intersubjectivity. *Psychoanalytic Psychology, 36*(3), 207–215. https://doi.org/10.1037/pap0000221

Kearney, B. E., & Lanius, R. A. (2022). The brain-body disconnect: A somatic sensory basis for trauma-related disorders. *Frontiers in Neuroscience, 16*, 1015749. https://doi.org/10.3389/fnins.2022.1015749

Kirman, J. H. (1995). Working with anger in groups: A modern analytic approach. *International Journal of Group Psychotherapy, 45*(3), 303–329. https://doi.org/10.1080/00207284.1995.11491282

Krystal, J. H., Davis, L. L., Neylan, T. C., Raskind, M., Schnurr, P. P., Stein, M. B., Vessicchio, J., Shiner, B., Gleason, T. D., & Huang, G. D. (2017). It is time to address the crisis in the pharmacotherapy of posttraumatic stress disorder: A consensus statement of the PTSD Psychopharmacology Working Group. *Biological Psychiatry, 82*(1). https://doi.org/10.1016/j.biopsych.2017.03.007

Lanius, R. A., Bluhm, R. L., & Frewen, P. A. (2011). How understanding the neurobiology of complex post-traumatic stress disorder can inform clinical practice: A social cognitive and affective neuroscience approach. *Acta Psychiatrica Scandinavica, 124*, 331–348. https://doi.org/10.1111/j.1600-0447.2011.01755.x

Lanius, R. A., Terpou, B. A., & McKinnon, M. C. (2020). The sense of self in the aftermath of trauma: Lessons from the default mode network in posttraumatic stress disorder. *The European Journal of Psychotraumatology, 11*, 1807703. https://doi.org/10.1080/20008198.2020.1807703

Leiderman, L.M., & Klein, R.H. (2021). An integrative systems-oriented interpersonal/relational group approach to understanding and treating mass trauma, dissociation and enactments during the COVID-19 pandemic. *International Journal of Group Psychotherapy*, 1–30. https://doi.org/10.1080/00207284.2021.1991234

Leiderman, L. M. (2023). In memoriam and unedited email from Robert Klein. *International Journal of Group Psychotherapy, 73*(4), 350–374. https://doi.org/10.1080/00207284.2023.2268681

Leiderman, L. M. (2024). The evidence-based group treatment website (EBGT website): A major development in the training and group research-supported treatment protocols for psychiatric and medical indications. *The Group Circle*, Summer Edition.

Leiderman, L. M. (2025). The fear-driven brain: An integrated interpersonal/relational neurophysiological model to foster co-regulation and synchrony in trauma psychotherapy groups. In L. M. Leiderman & B. J. Buchele (Eds.), *Advances in group therapy trauma treatment* (1st ed.) (pp. 31–51). Taylor & Francis/Routledge. ISBN 9781032890784 https://www.routledge.com/Advances-in-Group-Therapy-Trauma-Treatment/Leiderman-Buchele/p/book/9781032890784?srsltid=AfmBOoobDwivSES4RksUdtPC5XoSBQCol87art52OAKapyarNdb_W5lf

Leiderman, L. M., Buchele, B.J., & Klein, R.H. (2025). Introduction and overview: Creating a container for healing trauma. In L. M. Leiderman & B.J. Buchele (Eds.), *Advances in group therapy trauma treatment* (1st ed.) (pp. 1-28). Taylor & Francis/Routledge. ISBN 9781032890784 DOI: 10.

4324/9781003546252-1 https://www.routledge.com/Advances-in-Group-Therapy-Trauma-Treatment/Leiderman-Buchele/p/book/9781032890784?srsltid=AfmBOoobDwivSES4RksUdtPC5XoSBQCol87art52OAKapyarNdb_W5lf

Luke, M., & Hackney, H. (2007), Group coleadership: A critical review. *Counselor Education and Supervision, 46,* 280–293. https://doi.org/10.1002/j.1556-6978.2007.tb00032.x

Malejko, K., Abler, B., Plener, P. L., & Straub, J. (2017). Neural correlates of psychotherapeutic treatment of post-traumatic stress disorder: A systematic literature review. *Frontiers in Psychiatry, 8,* 85. https://doi.org/10.3389/fpsyt.2017.00085

Marmarosh, C. L., Liu, Y., & Yifei Du, Y. (2025). Attachment and trauma in group psychotherapy: Theory, intervention, and fostering change. In L. M. Leiderman & B. J. Buchele (Eds.), *Advances in group therapy trauma treatment* (1st ed.) (pp. 55–67). Taylor & Francis/Routledge. ISBN 9781032890784 https://www.routledge.com/Advances-in-Group-Therapy-Trauma-Treatment/Leiderman-Buchele/p/book/9781032890784?srsltid=AfmBOoobDwivSES4RksUdtPC5XoSBQCol87art52OAKapyarNdb_W5lf

Mendelsohn, M., Herman, J. L., Schatzow, E., Coco, M., Kallivayalil, D., & Levitan, J. (2011). *The trauma recovery group: A guide for practitioners.* Guilford Press. https://www.guilford.com/books/The-Trauma-Recovery-Group/Mendelsohn-Herman-Schatzow-Coco/9781609180577

Miles, J. R., Anders, C., Kivlighan, D. M., III, & Belcher Platt, A. A. (2021). Cultural ruptures: Addressing microaggressions in group therapy. *Group Dynamics: Theory, Research, and Practice, 25*(1), 74–88. https://doi.org/10.1037/gdn0000149

Mucci, C. (2022). *Resilience and survival: Understanding and healing intergenerational trauma.* Confer Ltd. https://aisberg.unibg.it/handle/10446/228813

Nitzgen, D., & Hopper, E. (2017). The concepts of the social unconscious and of the matrix in the work of S. H. Foul kes. In S. H. Foulkes, E. Hopper, & H. Weinberg (Eds.), *The social unconscious in persons, groups, and societies: Volume 3: The foundation matrix extended and re-configured* (pp. 3–26). Karnac. https://www.routledge.com/The-Social-Unconscious-in-Persons-Groups-and-Societies-Volume-3-The-Foundation-Matrix-Extended-and-Re-configured/Hopper-Weinberg/p/book/9781782203551

Ormont, L. R. (1989). The role of the leader in managing the preoedipal patient in the group setting. *International Journal of Group Psychotherapy, 39*(2), 147–171. https://doi.org/10.1080/00207284.1989.11491157

Ormont, L. R. (1994). Developing emotional insulation. *International Journal of Group Psychotherapy, 44*(3), 361–375. https://doi.org/10.1080/00207284.1994.11490759

Rauch, S. A., Eftekhari, A., & Ruzek, J. I. (2012). Review of exposure therapy: A gold standard for PTSD treatment. *The Journal of Rehabilitation Research and Development, 49*(5), 679–687. https://doi.org/10.1682/jrrd.2011.08.0152

Resnick, S. G., & Hoff, R. A. (2020). Observations from the national implementation of Measurement Based Care in Mental Health in the Department of Veterans Affairs. *Psychological Services, 17*(3), 238–246. https://doi.org/10.1037/ser0000351

Rosendahl, J., Alldredge, C. T., Burlingame, G. M., & Strauss, B. (2021). Recent developments in group psychotherapy research. *American Journal of Psychotherapy, 74*(2), 52–59. https://doi.org/10.1176/appi.psychotherapy.20200031

Ruzek, J. I., Yalch, M. M., & Burkman, K. M. (2023). *Group approaches to treating traumatic stress: A clinical handbook.* Guilford Press. https://www.guilford.com/books/Group-Approaches-to-Treating-Traumatic-Stress/Ruzek-Yalch-Burkman/9781462553297

Saakvitne, K. W., Pearlman, L. A., & Traumatic Stress Inst, Ctr for Adult & Adolescent Psychotherapy, LLC. (1996). *Transforming the pain: A workbook on vicarious traumatization.* Norton & Co. https://psycnet.apa.org/record/1996-98464-000

Schermer, V. L. (2025). Deconstructing the wall of dissociation, regression, and primitive defenses in both group members and therapists: A holistic, systems perspective. In L. M. Leiderman & B. J. Buchele (Eds.), *Advances in group therapy trauma treatment* (1st ed.) (pp. 68–82). Taylor & Francis/Routledge. ISBN 9781032890784 https://www.routledge.com/Advances-in-Group-Therapy-Trauma-Treatment/Leiderman-Buchele/p/book/9781032890784?srsltid=AfmBOoobDwivSES4RksUdtPC5XoSBQCol87art52OAKapyarNdb_W5lf

Schwartze, D., Barkowski, S., Strauss, B., Knaevelsrud, C., & Rosendahl, J. (2019). Efficacy of group psychotherapy for posttraumatic stress disorder: Systematic review and meta-analysis of randomized controlled trials. *Psychotherapy Research, 29*(4), 415–431. https://doi.org/10.1080/10503307.2017.1405168

Shaw, D. (2021). *Traumatic narcissism and recovery: Leaving the prison of shame and fear* (1st ed.). Routledge. https://doi.org/10.4324/9781003182849

Shaw, S. B., Terpou, B. A., Densmore, M., Théberge, J., Frewen, P., McKinnon, M. C., & Lanius, R. A. (2023). Large-scale functional hyperconnectivity patterns in trauma-related dissociation: An rs-fMRI study of PTSD and its dissociative subtype. *Nature Mental Health, 1*(10), 711–721. https://doi.org/10.1038/s44220-023-00115-y

Sloan, D. M., Feinstein, B. A., Gallagher, M. W., Beck, J. G., & Keane, T. M. (2013). Efficacy of group treatment for posttraumatic stress disorder symptoms: A meta-analysis. *Psychological Trauma: Theory, Research, Practice, and Policy, 5*(2), 176–183. https://doi.org/10.1037/a0026291

Stockton, R., Morran, K., & Chang, S.-H. (2014). An overview of current research and best practices for training beginning group leaders. In J. L. DeLucia-Waack, C. R. Kalodner, & M. T. Riva (Eds.), *Handbook of group counseling and psychotherapy* (2nd ed., pp. 133–145). Sage Publications, Inc. https://doi.org/10.4135/9781544308555.n11

Treadwell, T., & Abeditehrani, H. (2025). Integrating cognitive behavioral therapy with psychodrama theory and practice: A blended group model for trauma. In L. M. Leiderman & B. J. Buchele (Eds.), *Advances in group therapy trauma treatment* (1st ed.) (pp. 85–100). Taylor & Francis/Routledge. ISBN 9781032890784 https://www.routledge.com/Advances-in-Group-Therapy-Trauma-Treatment/Leiderman-Buchele/p/book/9781032890784?srsltid=AfmBOoqw7hRcyUV7m3O5tRlxA2T4ocWg0g9UaApILqbTm5Bkiqc9wiVJ

Ulman, R. B., & Brothers, D. (1988). *The shattered self: A psychoanalytic study of trauma.* Analytic Press, Inc. https://www.routledge.com/The-Shattered-Self-A-Psychoanalytic-Study-of-Trauma/Ulman-Brothers/p/book/9780881631746

Volkan, V. (2016). *Immigrants and refugees: Trauma, perennial mourning, prejudice, and border psychology.* Routledge. https://www.routledge.com/Immigrants-and-Refugees-Trauma-Perennial-Mourning-Prejudice-and-Border-Psychology/Volkan/p/book/9781782204725

Watkins-Northern, A., & Nettles, R. (2025). Group-as-a-whole and psychodynamic group psychotherapy in treating trauma with the African American population at Howard University Counseling Service. In L. M. Leiderman & B. J. Buchele (Eds.), *Advances in group therapy trauma treatment* (1st ed.) (pp. 119–128). Taylor & Francis/Routledge. ISBN 9781032890784 https://www.routledge.com/Advances-in-Group-Therapy-Trauma-Treatment/Leiderman-Buchele/p/book/9781032890784?srsltid=AfmBOoobDwivSES4RksUdtPC5XoSBQCol87art52OAKapyarNdb_W5lf

Weinberg, H. (2025). Social trauma and the social unconscious – using the large group for healing. In L. M. Leiderman & B. J. Buchele (Eds.), *Advances in group therapy trauma treatment* (1st ed.) (pp. 145–157). Taylor & Francis/Routledge. ISBN 9781032890784 https://www.routledge.com/Advances-in-Group-Therapy-Trauma-Treatment/Leiderman-Buchele/p/book/9781032890784?srsltid=AfmBOoobDwivSES4RksUdtPC5XoSBQCol87art52OAKapyarNdb_W5lf

Weinberg, H., & Schneider, S. (2003). Introduction: Background, structure and dynamics of the large group. In S. Schneider & H. Weinberg (Eds.), *The large group revisited: The Herd, primal Horde, crowds and masses.* Jessica Kingsley Pub. https://books.google.com/books/about/The_Large_Group_Re_Visited.html?id=VfsSA0zqueoC

Wepman, B. (2020). Group supervision: A crucible for therapist development. *The Group Circle.*

Whittingham, M., Marmarosh, C. L., Mallow, P., & Scherer, M. (2023). Mental health care equity and access: A group therapy solution. *American Psychologist, 78*(2), 119–133. https://doi.org/10.1037/amp0001078

Wise, S., & Nash, E. (2019). *Healing trauma in group settings: The art of co-leader attunement.* Routledge. https://www.routledge.com/Healing-Trauma-in-Group-Settings-The-Art-of-Co-Leader-Attunement/Wise-Nash/p/book/9781138044920

Yalch, M. M., Moreland, M. L., & Burkman, K. M. (2022). Integrating process and structure in group therapy for survivors of trauma. *European Journal of Trauma & Dissociation, 6.* https://doi.org/10.1016/j.ejtd.2022.100272

Yalom, I. D. (1985). *The theory and practice of group psychotherapy* (3rd ed.). Basic Books. https://psycnet.apa.org/record/1985-97941-000

Yalom, I. D., & Leszcz, M. (2020). *The theory and practice of group psychotherapy.* Hachette UK. https://www.hachettebookgroup.com/titles/irvin-d-yalom/the-theory-and-practice-of-group-psychotherapy/9781541617568/?lens=basic-books

Yang, Z., Oathes, D. J., Linn, K. A., Bruce, S. E., Satterthwaite, T. D., Cook, P. A., Satchell, E. K., Shou, H., & Sheline, Y. I. (2018). Cognitive behavioral therapy is associated with enhanced cognitive control network activity in major depression and posttraumatic stress disorder. *Biological Psychiatry, 3,* 311–319. https://doi.org/10.1016/j.bpsc.2017.12.006

Index

For Product Safety Concerns and Information please contact our
EU representative GPSR@taylorandfrancis.com Taylor & Francis
Verlag GmbH, Kaufingerstraße 24, 80331 München, Germany